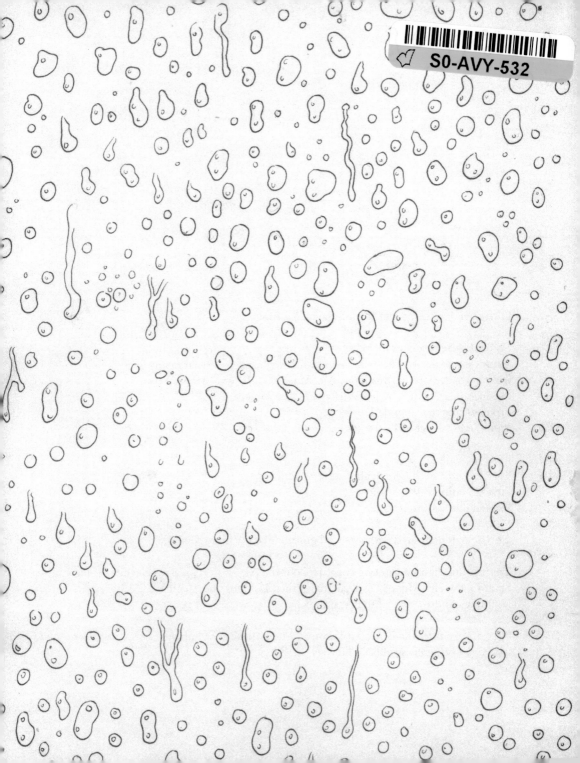

Production assistance by Jeff Wilson and Ted May.
Proofreading by Amanda Doyle
Published by Revival House Press.

www.revivalhousepress.com
Enquiries: davenuss@revivalhousepress.com
First US edition, May 2019
Printed in the United States

This book is dedicated with love and gratitude to my mum, Jeannie.

Thanks and shout-outs: Dave Nuss, Jeff Wilson, Alyssa Berg, Katie Haegele, Frank Santoro, the Her-Moans, Nick Abadzis, Ellen Lindner and Stephen Betts, John Dunning, Andrew Cruickshank, Bob Pelley.

Special thanks to Ted May and Veronica May, whose continuing love and awesomeness make all things possible.

MARDOU

SKY IN STEREO

Book 2

REVIVAL
HOUSE
PRESS

The story so far...

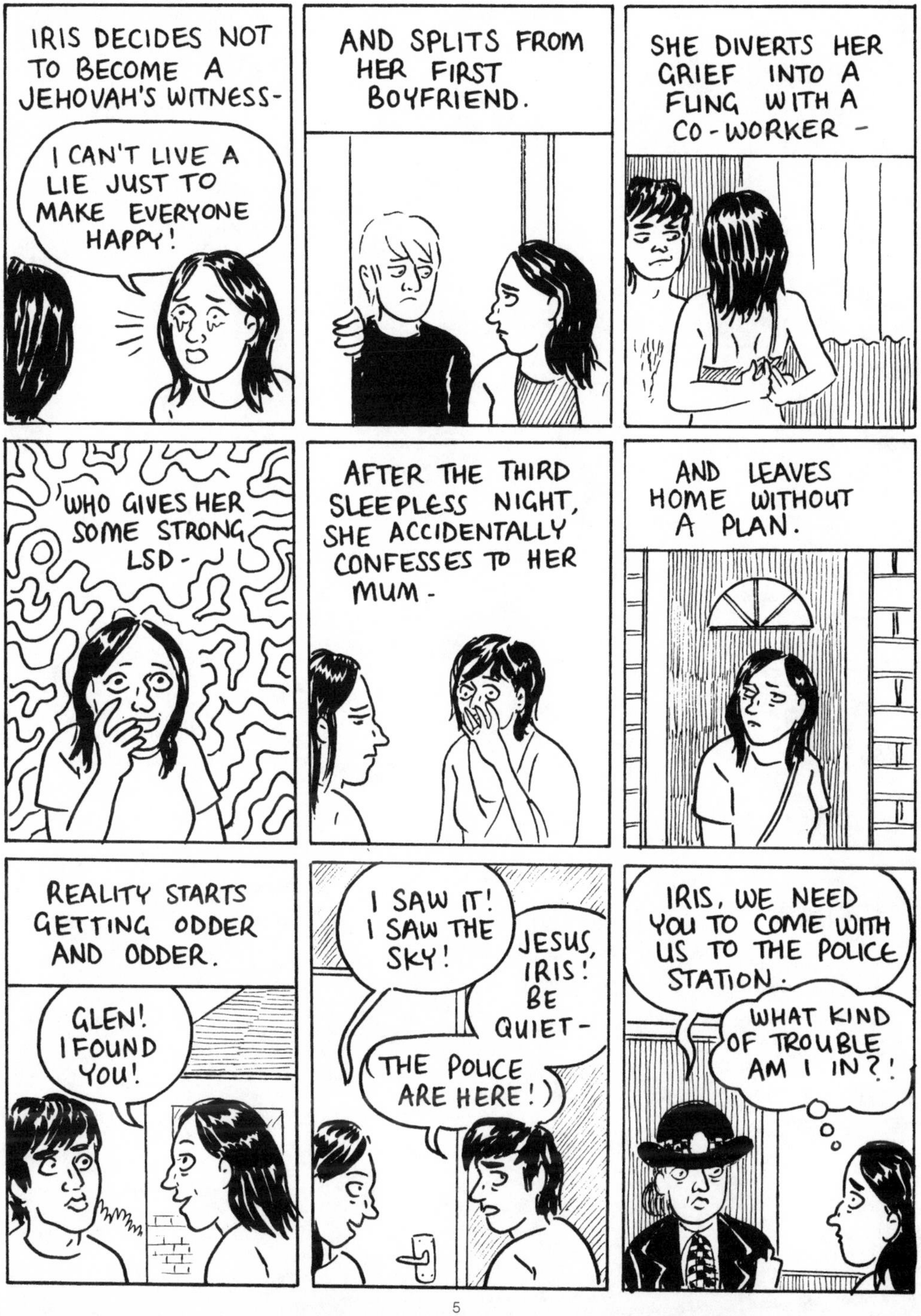
IRIS DECIDES NOT TO BECOME A JEHOVAH'S WITNESS-
I CAN'T LIVE A LIE JUST TO MAKE EVERYONE HAPPY!
AND SPLITS FROM HER FIRST BOYFRIEND.
SHE DIVERTS HER GRIEF INTO A FLING WITH A CO-WORKER -
WHO GIVES HER SOME STRONG LSD -
AFTER THE THIRD SLEEPLESS NIGHT, SHE ACCIDENTALLY CONFESSES TO HER MUM -
AND LEAVES HOME WITHOUT A PLAN.
REALITY STARTS GETTING ODDER AND ODDER.
GLEN! I FOUND YOU!
I SAW IT! I SAW THE SKY!
JESUS, IRIS! BE QUIET-
THE POLICE ARE HERE!
IRIS, WE NEED YOU TO COME WITH US TO THE POLICE STATION.
WHAT KIND OF TROUBLE AM I IN?!

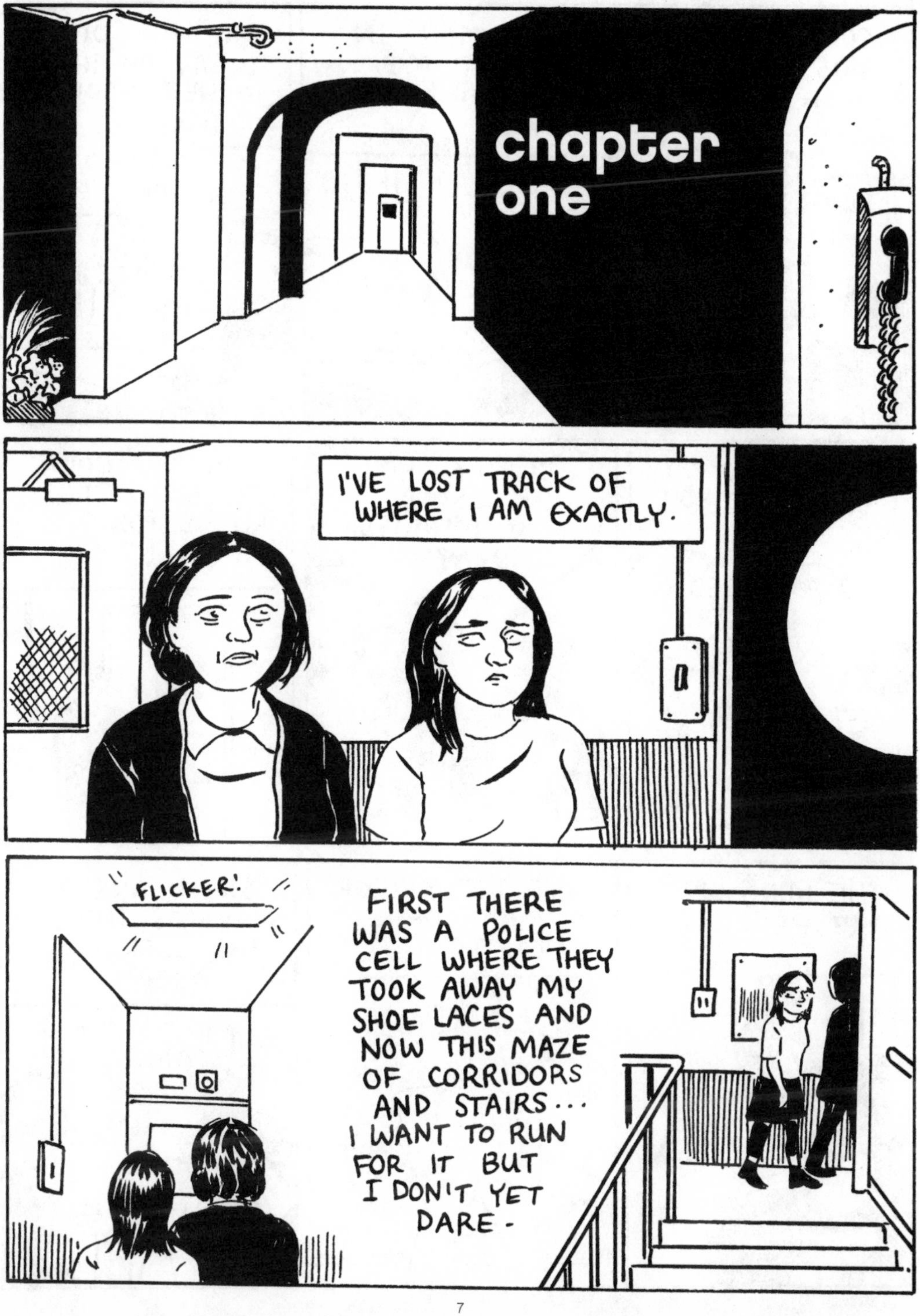
chapter one
I'VE LOST TRACK OF WHERE I AM EXACTLY.
FLICKER!
FIRST THERE WAS A POLICE CELL WHERE THEY TOOK AWAY MY SHOE LACES AND NOW THIS MAZE OF CORRIDORS AND STAIRS... I WANT TO RUN FOR IT BUT I DON'T YET DARE -

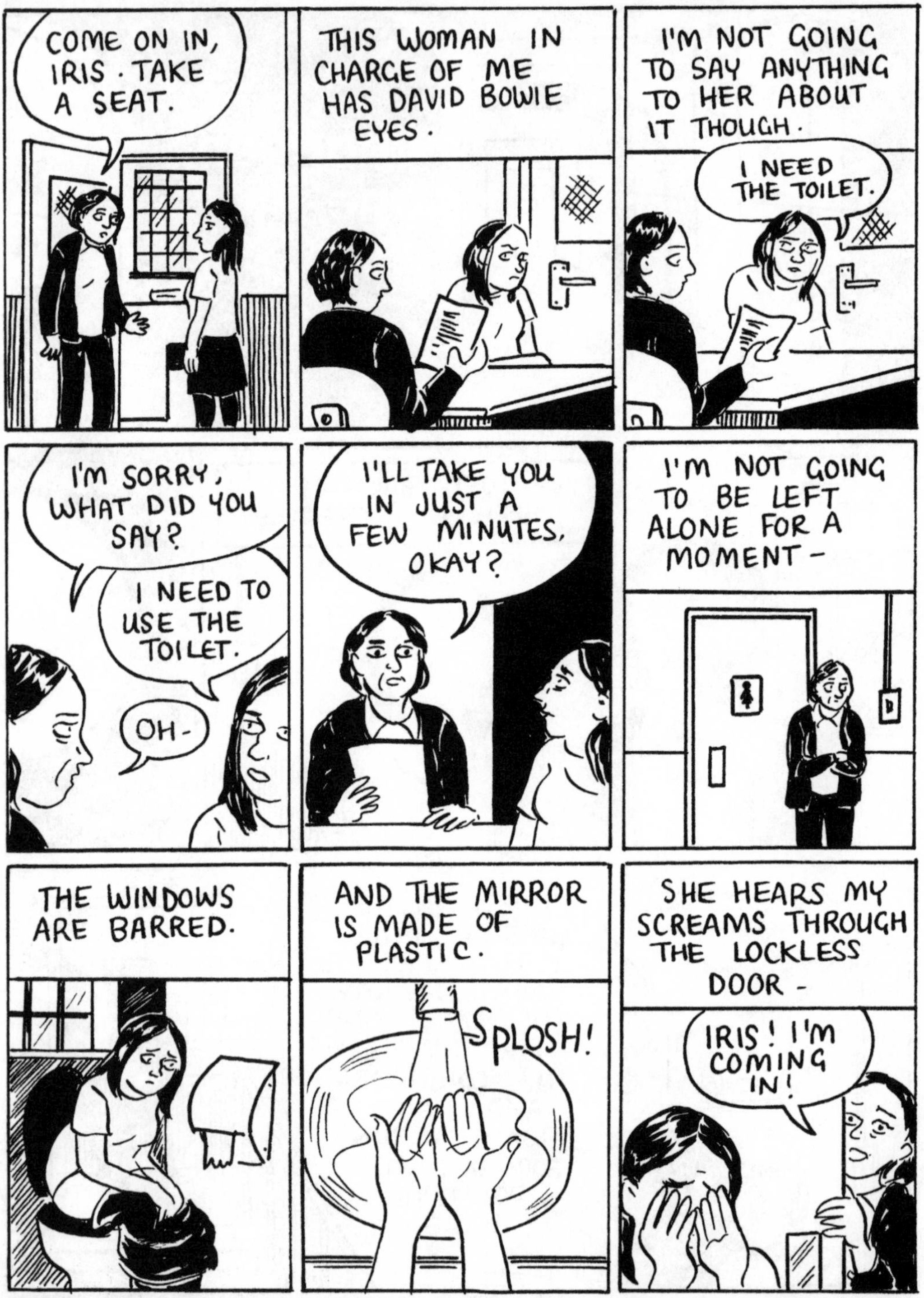
COME ON IN, IRIS. TAKE A SEAT.
THIS WOMAN IN CHARGE OF ME HAS DAVID BOWIE EYES.
I'M NOT GOING TO SAY ANYTHING TO HER ABOUT IT THOUGH.
I NEED THE TOILET.
I'M SORRY, WHAT DID YOU SAY?
I NEED TO USE THE TOILET.
OH-
I'LL TAKE YOU IN JUST A FEW MINUTES, OKAY?
I'M NOT GOING TO BE LEFT ALONE FOR A MOMENT-
THE WINDOWS ARE BARRED.
AND THE MIRROR IS MADE OF PLASTIC.
SPLOSH!
SHE HEARS MY SCREAMS THROUGH THE LOCKLESS DOOR-
IRIS! I'M COMING IN!

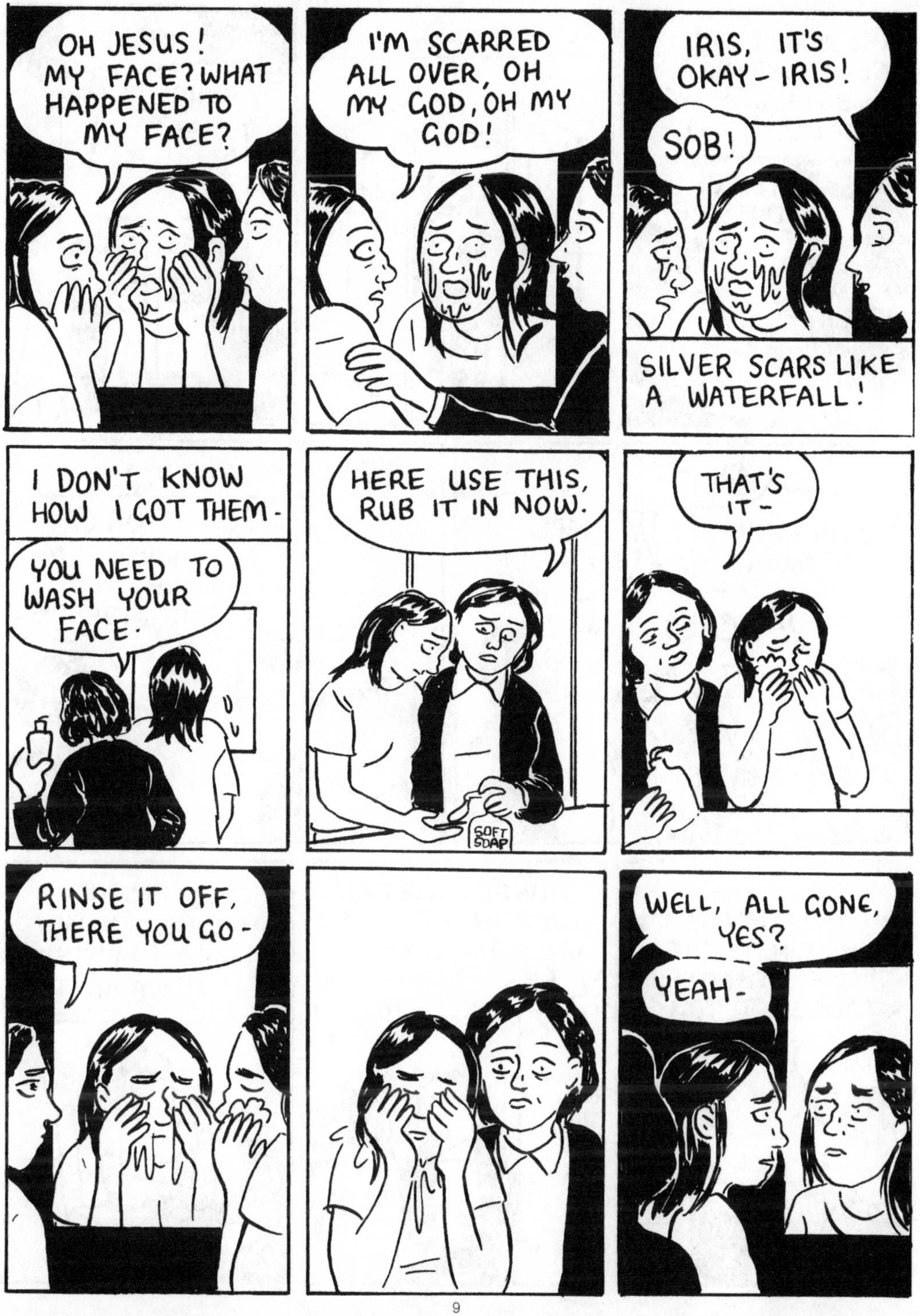
OH JESUS! MY FACE? WHAT HAPPENED TO MY FACE?
I'M SCARRED ALL OVER, OH MY GOD, OH MY GOD!
IRIS, IT'S OKAY - IRIS!
SOB!
SILVER SCARS LIKE A WATERFALL!
I DON'T KNOW HOW I GOT THEM -
YOU NEED TO WASH YOUR FACE.
HERE USE THIS, RUB IT IN NOW.
SOFT SOAP
THAT'S IT -
RINSE IT OFF, THERE YOU GO -
WELL, ALL GONE, YES?
YEAH -

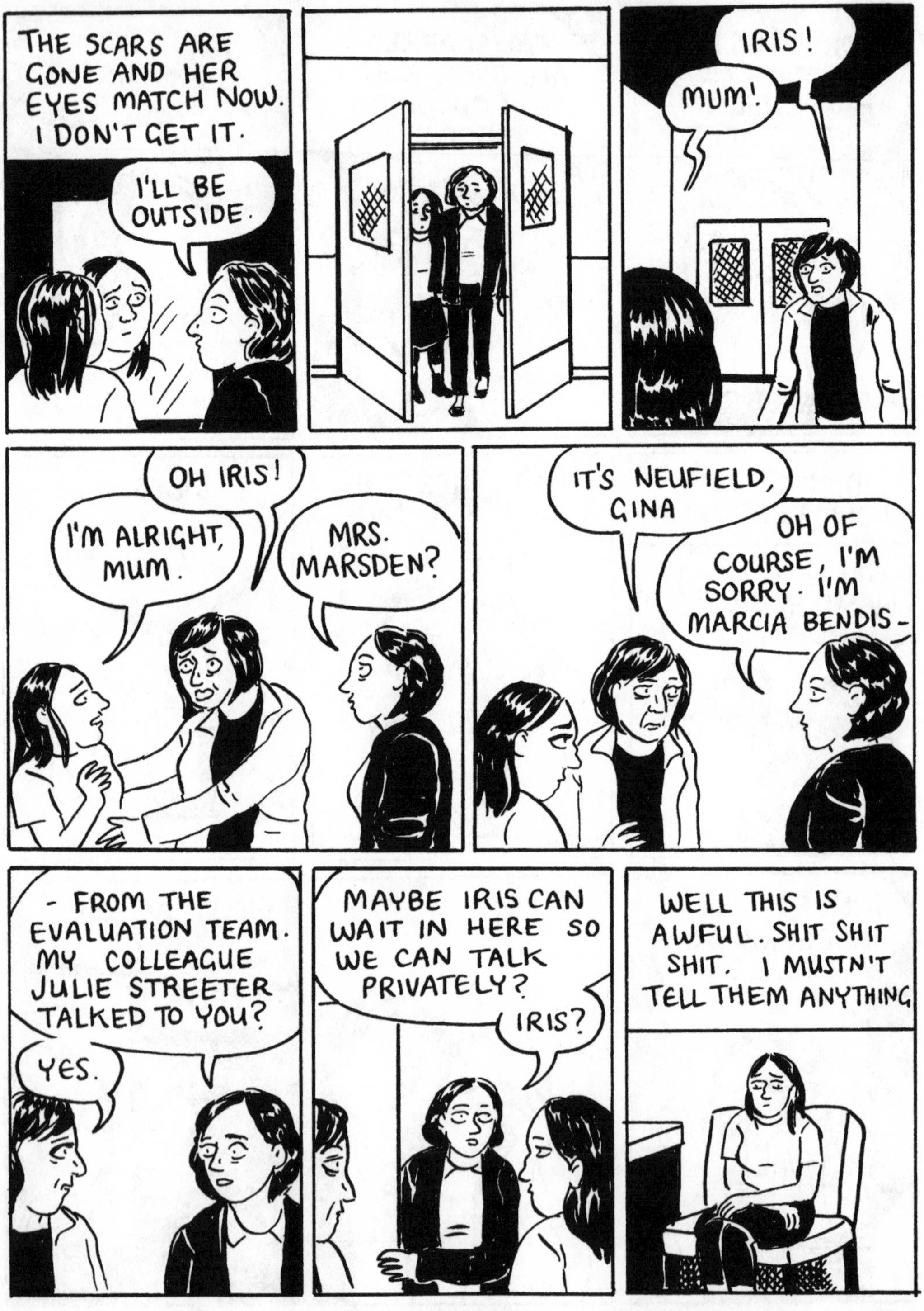
THE SCARS ARE GONE AND HER EYES MATCH NOW. I DON'T GET IT.
I'LL BE OUTSIDE.
IRIS!
MUM!
OH IRIS!
I'M ALRIGHT, MUM.
MRS. MARSDEN?
IT'S NEUFIELD, GINA
OH OF COURSE, I'M SORRY. I'M MARCIA BENDIS -
- FROM THE EVALUATION TEAM. MY COLLEAGUE JULIE STREETER TALKED TO YOU?
YES.
MAYBE IRIS CAN WAIT IN HERE SO WE CAN TALK PRIVATELY?
IRIS?
WELL THIS IS AWFUL. SHIT SHIT SHIT. I MUSTN'T TELL THEM ANYTHING

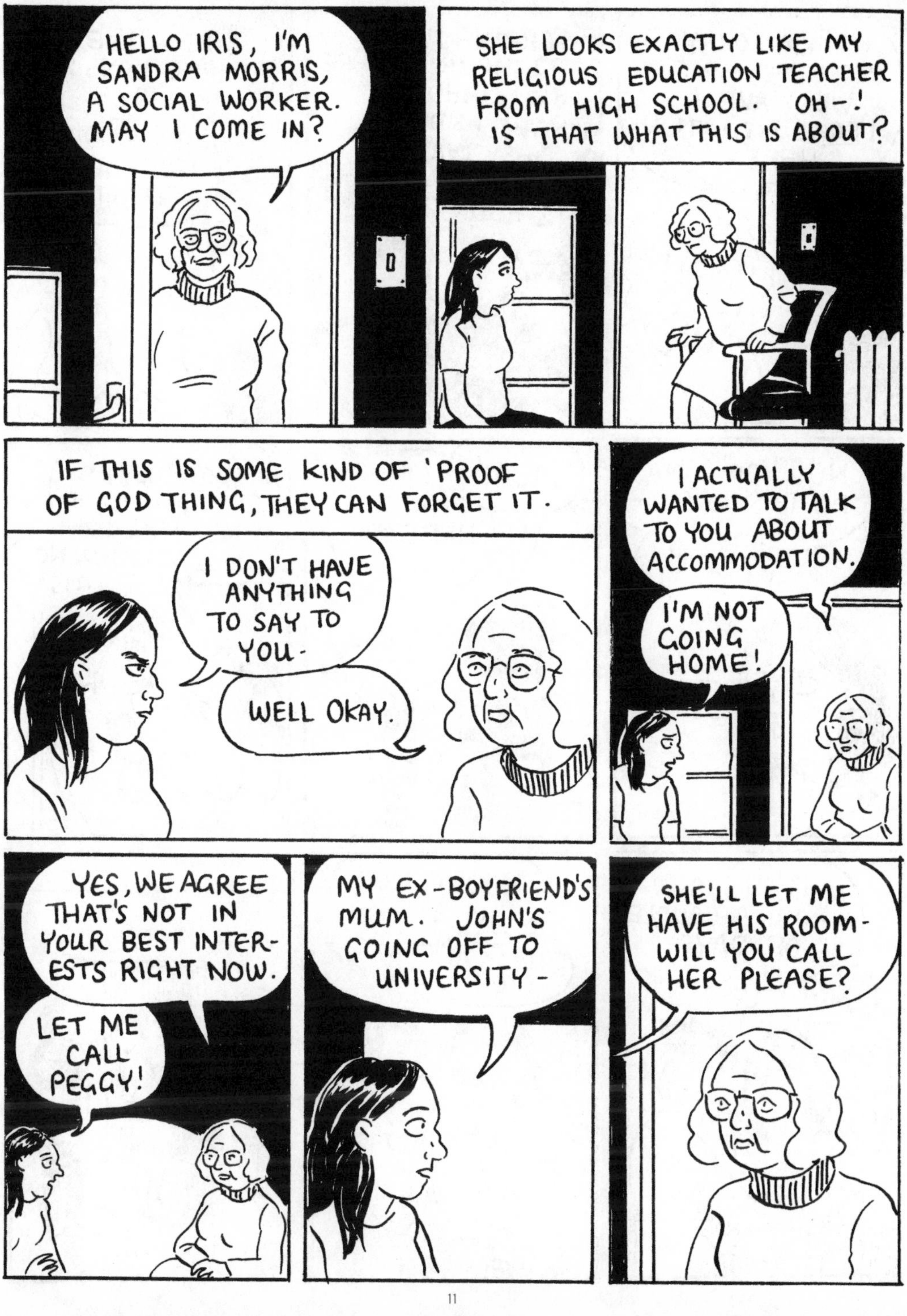
HELLO IRIS, I'M SANDRA MORRIS, A SOCIAL WORKER. MAY I COME IN?
SHE LOOKS EXACTLY LIKE MY RELIGIOUS EDUCATION TEACHER FROM HIGH SCHOOL. OH-! IS THAT WHAT THIS IS ABOUT?
IF THIS IS SOME KIND OF 'PROOF OF GOD THING, THEY CAN FORGET IT.
I DON'T HAVE ANYTHING TO SAY TO YOU-
WELL OKAY.
I ACTUALLY WANTED TO TALK TO YOU ABOUT ACCOMMODATION.
I'M NOT GOING HOME!
YES, WE AGREE THAT'S NOT IN YOUR BEST INTER-ESTS RIGHT NOW.
LET ME CALL PEGGY!
MY EX-BOYFRIEND'S MUM. JOHN'S GOING OFF TO UNIVERSITY-
SHE'LL LET ME HAVE HIS ROOM-WILL YOU CALL HER PLEASE?

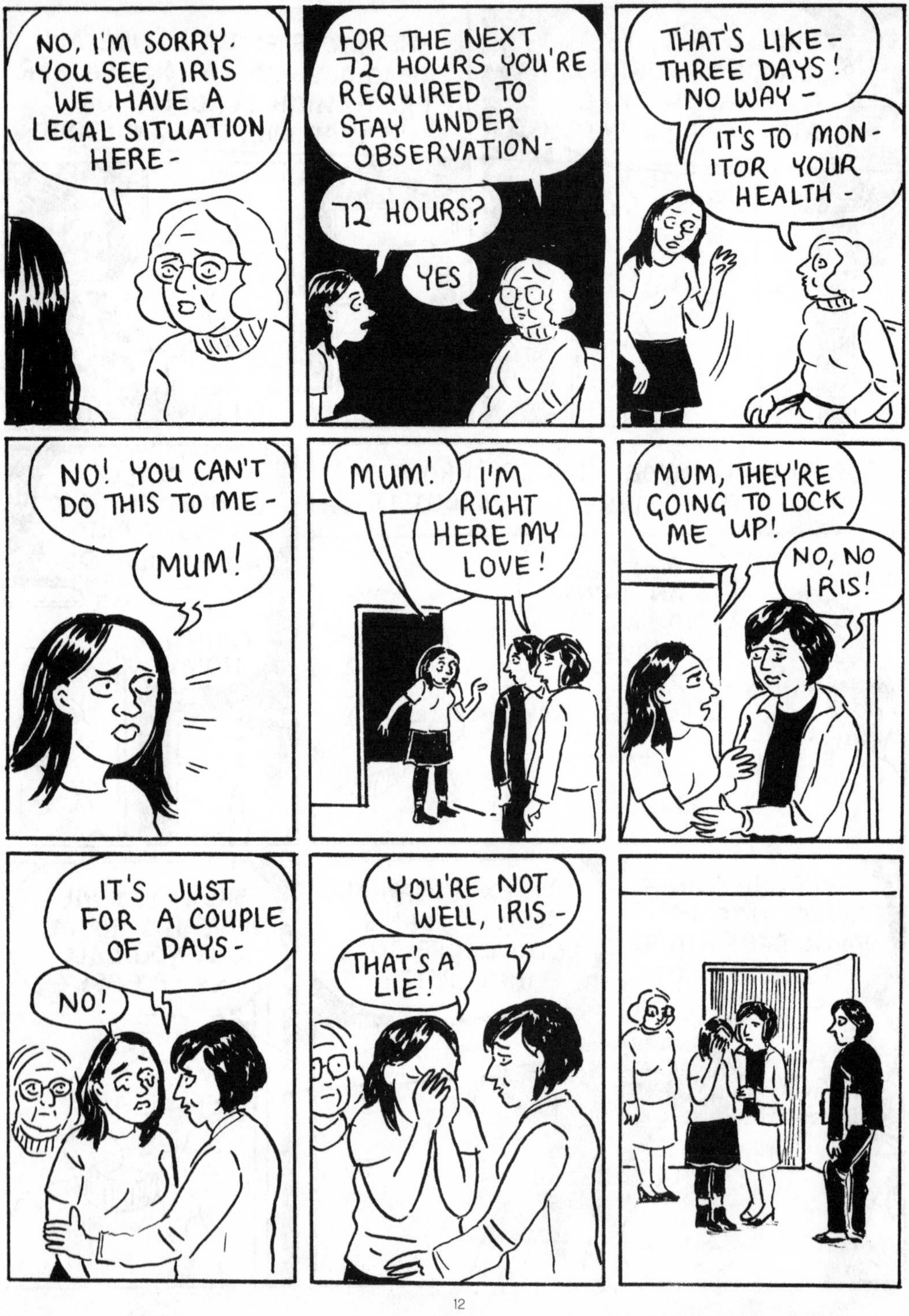
NO, I'M SORRY. YOU SEE, IRIS WE HAVE A LEGAL SITUATION HERE-
FOR THE NEXT 72 HOURS YOU'RE REQUIRED TO STAY UNDER OBSERVATION-
72 HOURS?
YES
THAT'S LIKE- THREE DAYS! NO WAY-
IT'S TO MONITOR YOUR HEALTH-
NO! YOU CAN'T DO THIS TO ME-
MUM!
MUM!
I'M RIGHT HERE MY LOVE!
MUM, THEY'RE GOING TO LOCK ME UP!
NO, NO IRIS!
IT'S JUST FOR A COUPLE OF DAYS-
NO!
YOU'RE NOT WELL, IRIS-
THAT'S A LIE!

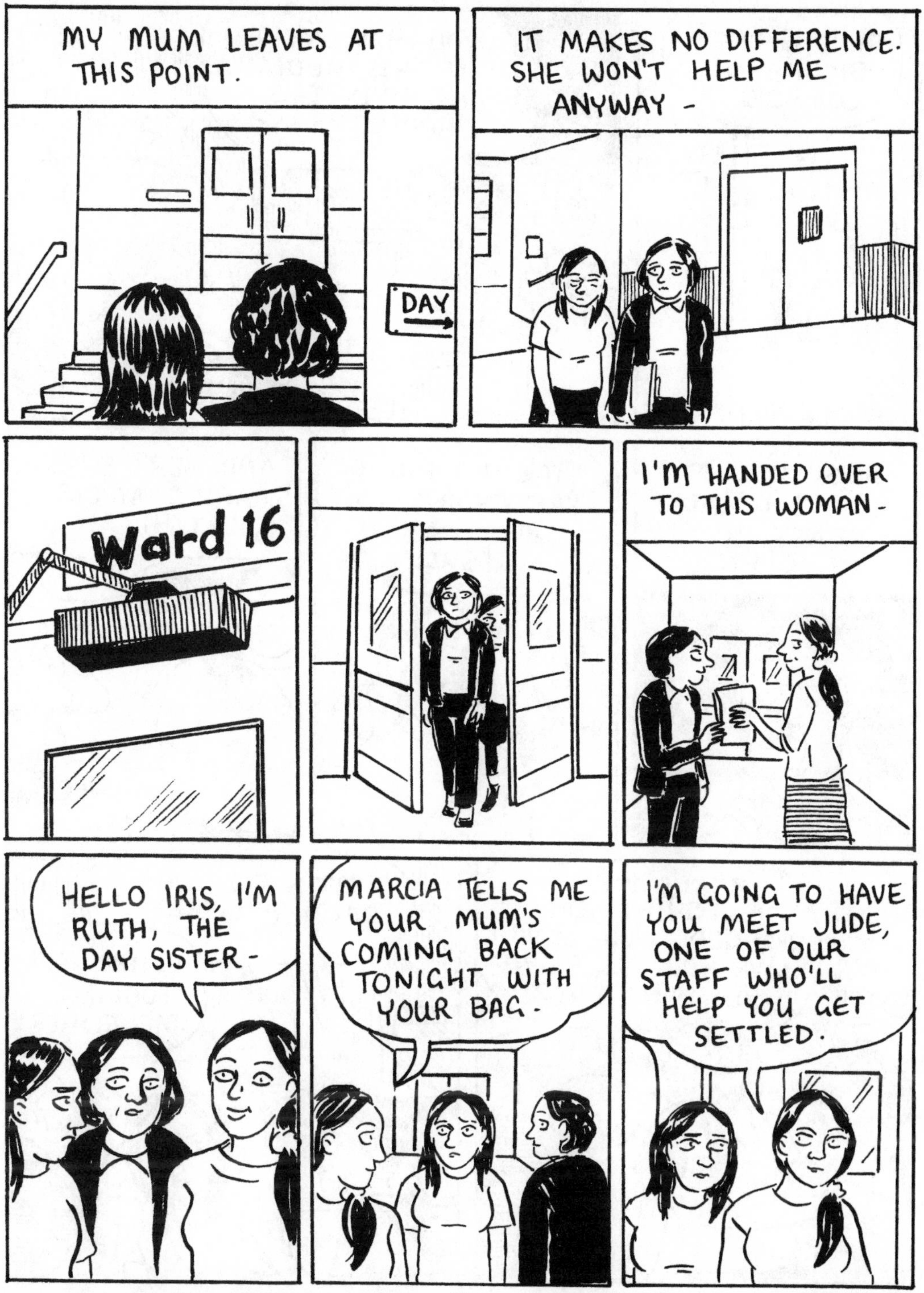
MY MUM LEAVES AT THIS POINT.
DAY
IT MAKES NO DIFFERENCE. SHE WON'T HELP ME ANYWAY -
Ward 16
I'M HANDED OVER TO THIS WOMAN -
HELLO IRIS, I'M RUTH, THE DAY SISTER -
MARCIA TELLS ME YOUR MUM'S COMING BACK TONIGHT WITH YOUR BAG.
I'M GOING TO HAVE YOU MEET JUDE, ONE OF OUR STAFF WHO'LL HELP YOU GET SETTLED.

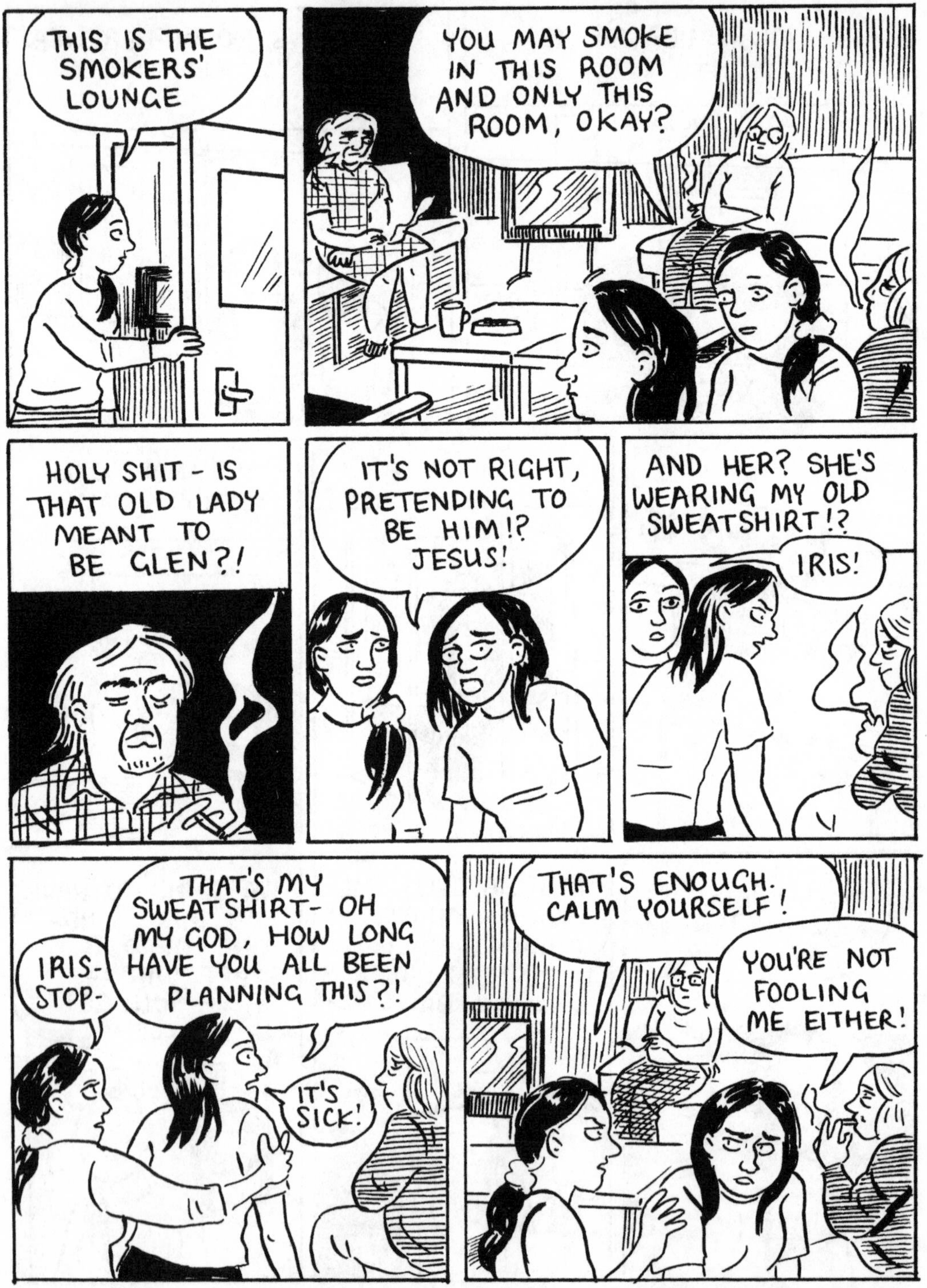
THIS IS THE SMOKERS' LOUNGE
YOU MAY SMOKE IN THIS ROOM AND ONLY THIS ROOM, OKAY?
HOLY SHIT - IS THAT OLD LADY MEANT TO BE GLEN?!
IT'S NOT RIGHT, PRETENDING TO BE HIM!? JESUS!
AND HER? SHE'S WEARING MY OLD SWEATSHIRT!?
IRIS!
IRIS- STOP-
THAT'S MY SWEATSHIRT- OH MY GOD, HOW LONG HAVE YOU ALL BEEN PLANNING THIS?!
IT'S SICK!
THAT'S ENOUGH. CALM YOURSELF!
YOU'RE NOT FOOLING ME EITHER!

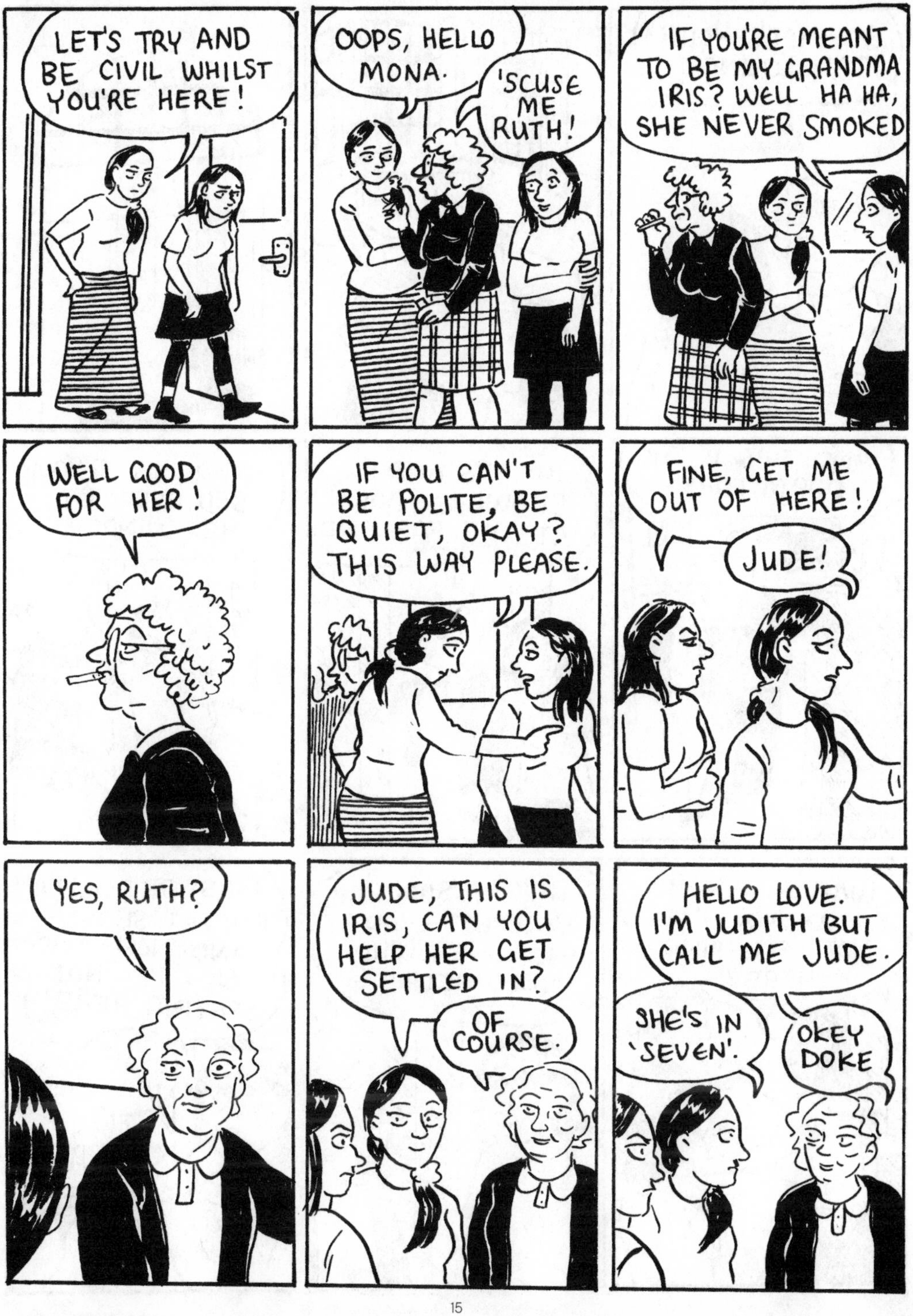
LET'S TRY AND BE CIVIL WHILST YOU'RE HERE!
OOPS, HELLO MONA.
'SCUSE ME RUTH!
IF YOU'RE MEANT TO BE MY GRANDMA IRIS? WELL HA HA, SHE NEVER SMOKED
WELL GOOD FOR HER!
IF YOU CAN'T BE POLITE, BE QUIET, OKAY? THIS WAY PLEASE.
FINE, GET ME OUT OF HERE!
JUDE!
YES, RUTH?
JUDE, THIS IS IRIS, CAN YOU HELP HER GET SETTLED IN?
OF COURSE.
HELLO LOVE. I'M JUDITH BUT CALL ME JUDE.
SHE'S IN 'SEVEN'.
OKEY DOKE

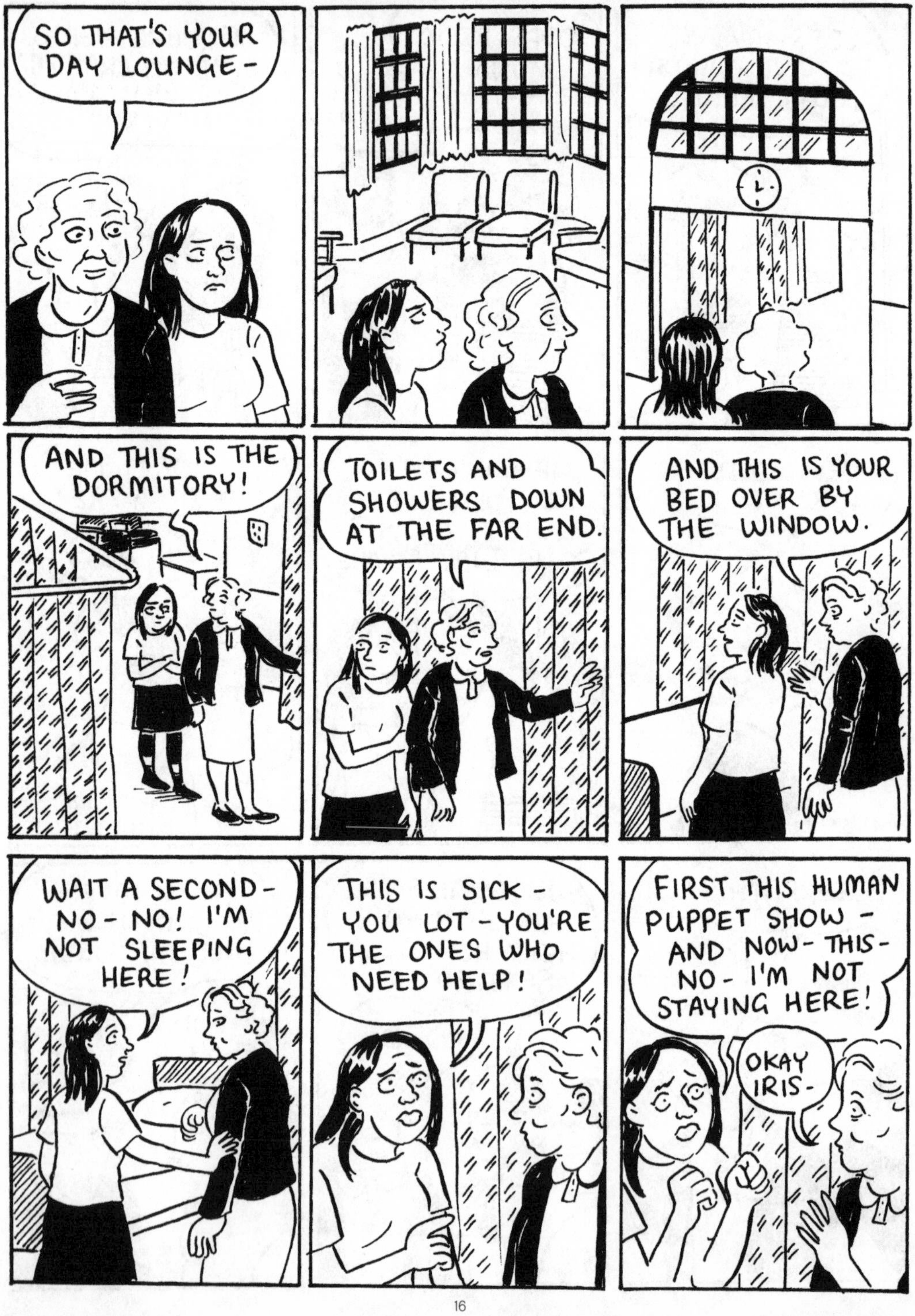

SO THAT'S YOUR DAY LOUNGE-
AND THIS IS THE DORMITORY!
TOILETS AND SHOWERS DOWN AT THE FAR END.
AND THIS IS YOUR BED OVER BY THE WINDOW.
WAIT A SECOND- NO- NO! I'M NOT SLEEPING HERE!
THIS IS SICK - YOU LOT - YOU'RE THE ONES WHO NEED HELP!
FIRST THIS HUMAN PUPPET SHOW - AND NOW- THIS- NO- I'M NOT STAYING HERE!
OKAY IRIS-

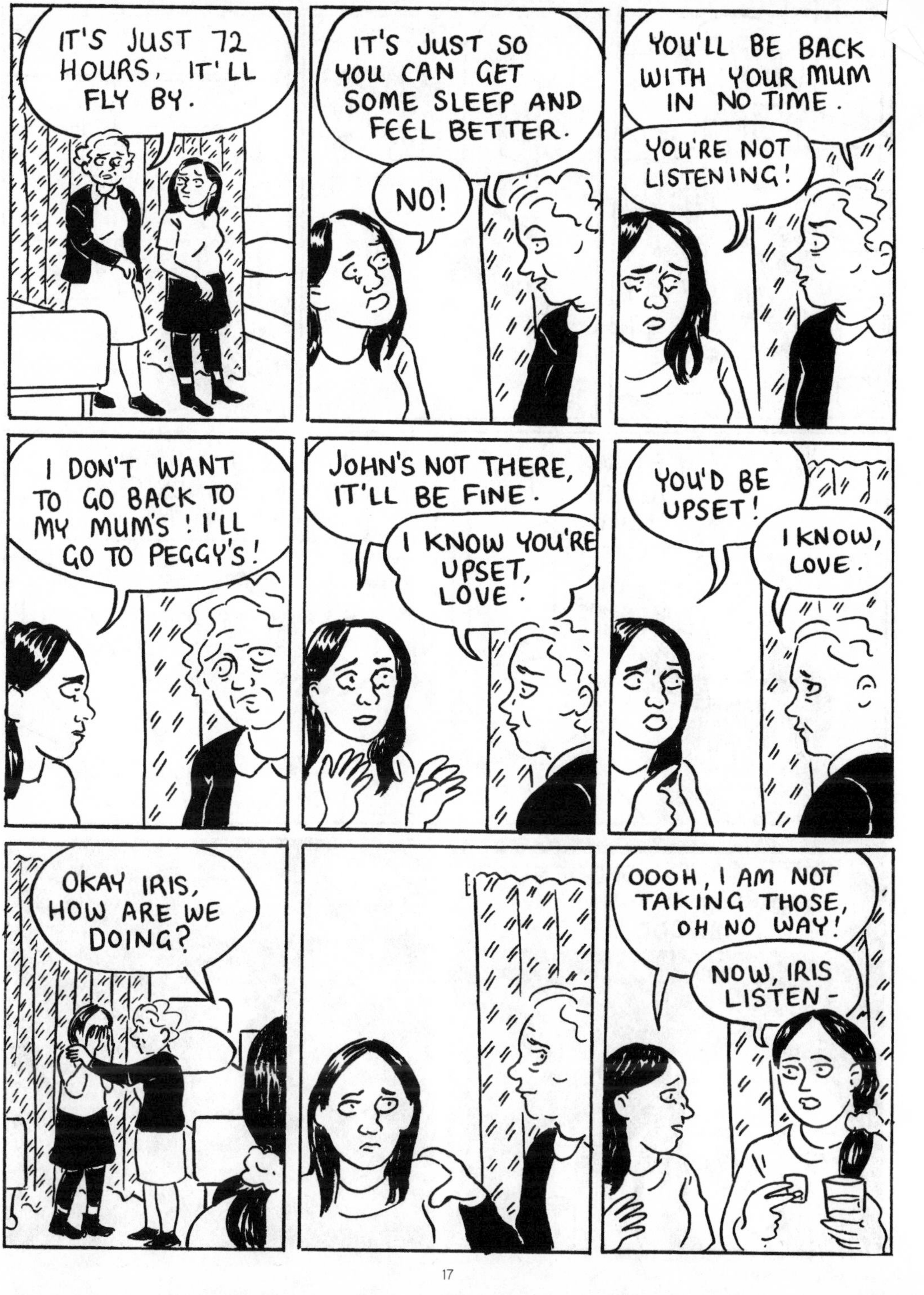
IT'S JUST 72 HOURS, IT'LL FLY BY.
IT'S JUST SO YOU CAN GET SOME SLEEP AND FEEL BETTER.
NO!
YOU'LL BE BACK WITH YOUR MUM IN NO TIME.
YOU'RE NOT LISTENING!
I DON'T WANT TO GO BACK TO MY MUM'S! I'LL GO TO PEGGY'S!
JOHN'S NOT THERE, IT'LL BE FINE.
I KNOW YOU'RE UPSET, LOVE.
YOU'D BE UPSET!
I KNOW, LOVE.
OKAY IRIS, HOW ARE WE DOING?
OOOH, I AM NOT TAKING THOSE, OH NO WAY!
NOW, IRIS LISTEN -

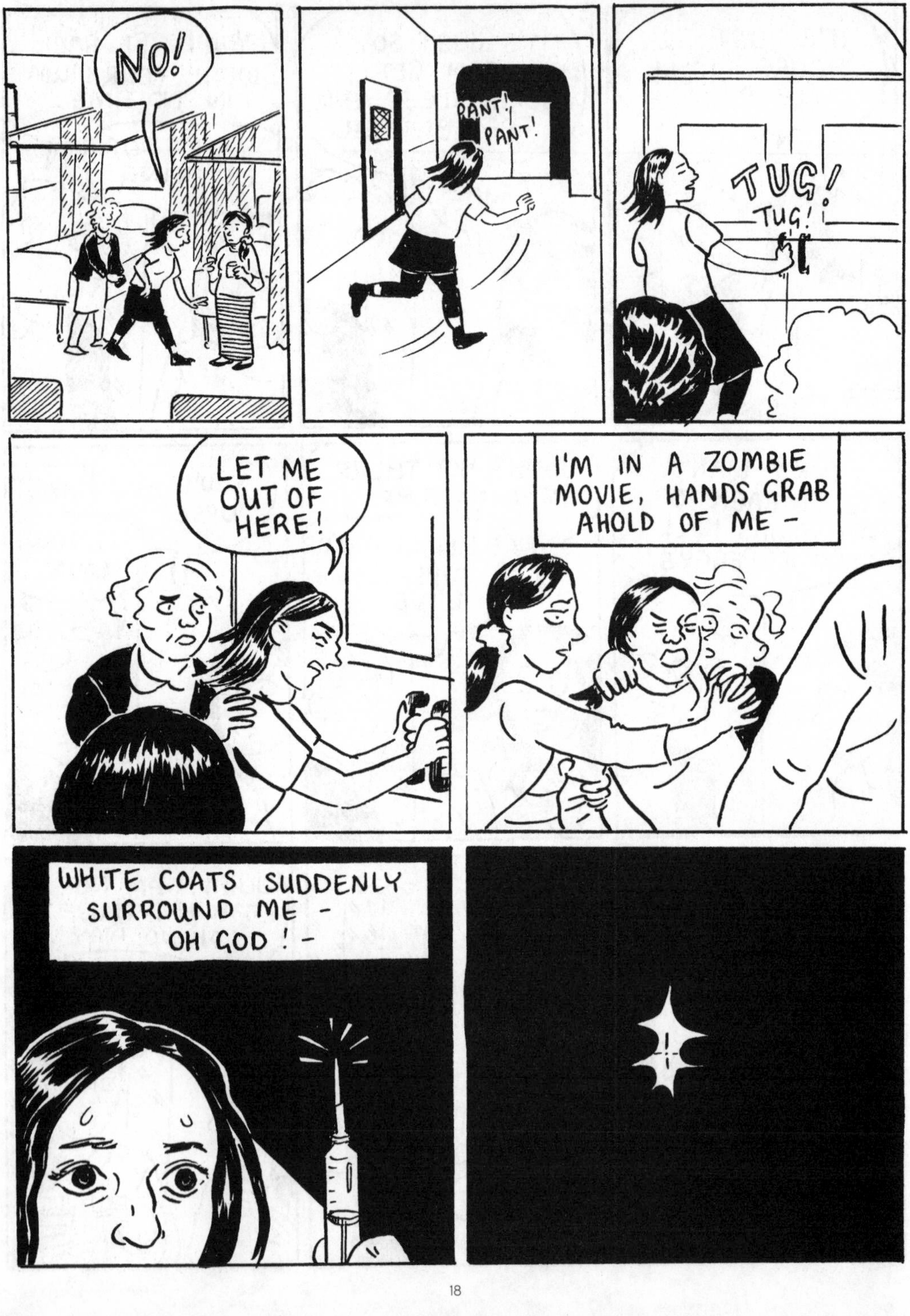

NO!
PANT!
PANT!
TUG!
TUG!
LET ME OUT OF HERE!
I'M IN A ZOMBIE MOVIE, HANDS GRAB AHOLD OF ME -
WHITE COATS SUDDENLY SURROUND ME - OH GOD ! -

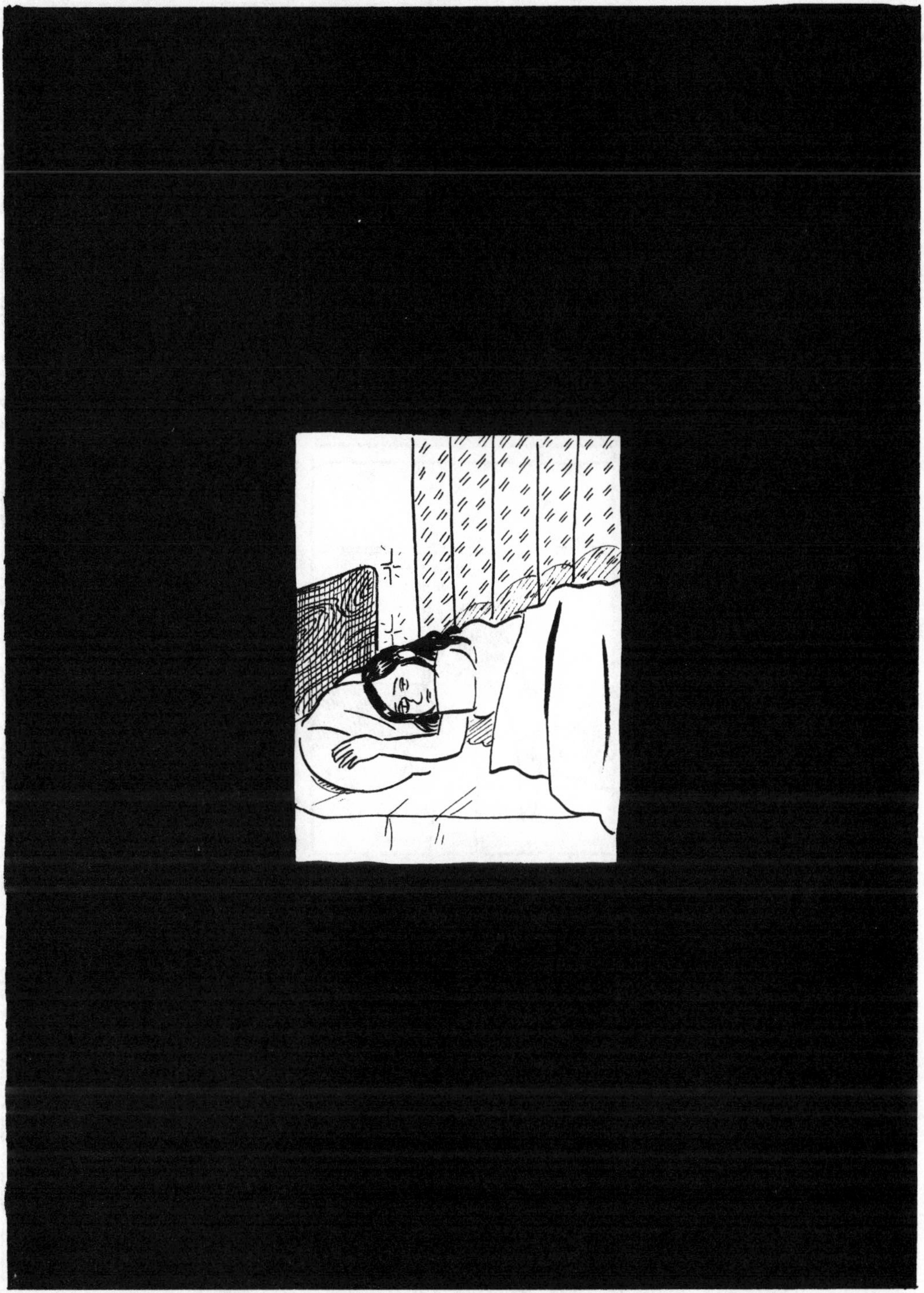

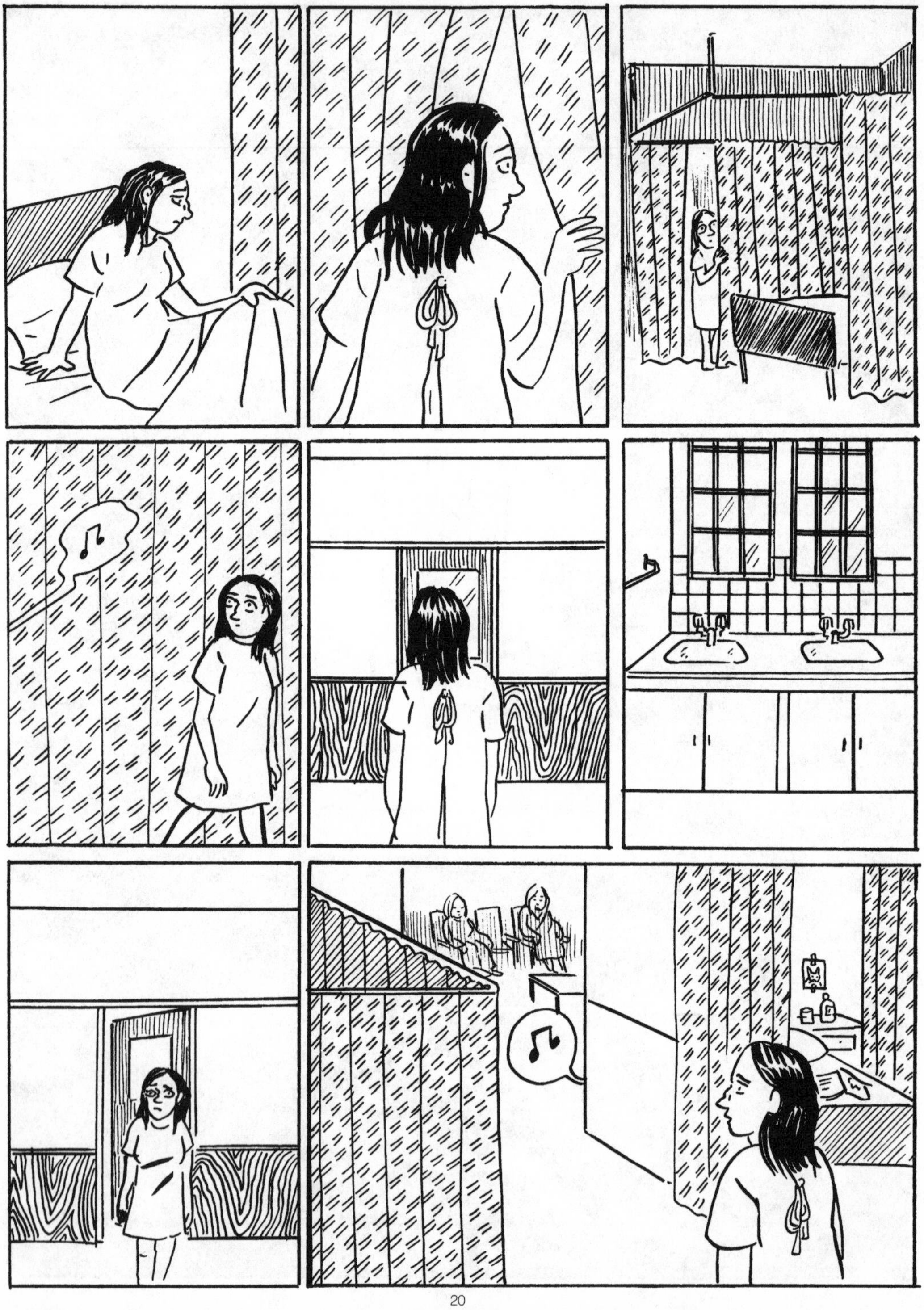

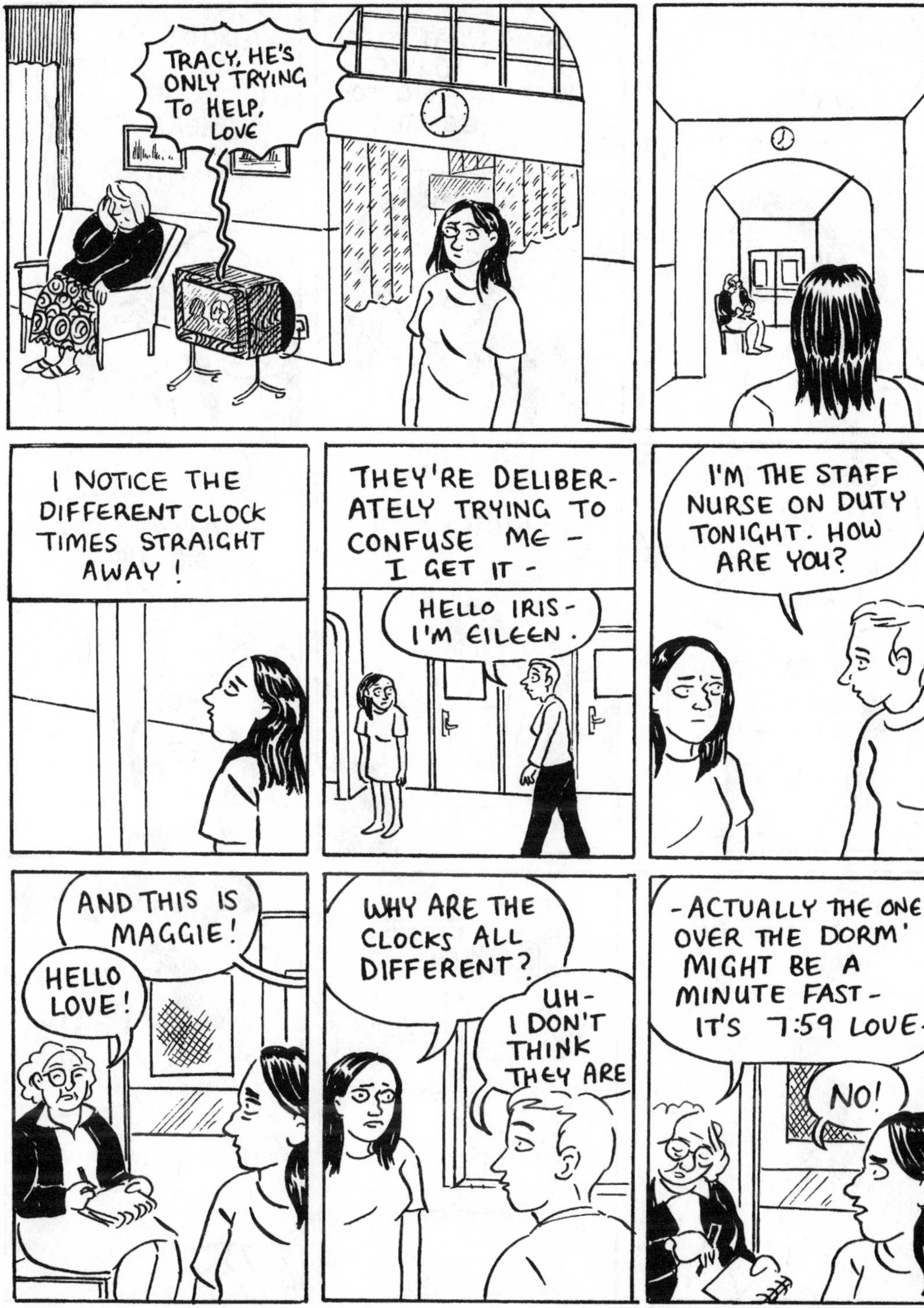
TRACY, HE'S ONLY TRYING TO HELP, LOVE
I NOTICE THE DIFFERENT CLOCK TIMES STRAIGHT AWAY!
THEY'RE DELIBERATELY TRYING TO CONFUSE ME - I GET IT -
HELLO IRIS - I'M EILEEN.
I'M THE STAFF NURSE ON DUTY TONIGHT. HOW ARE YOU?
AND THIS IS MAGGIE!
HELLO LOVE!
WHY ARE THE CLOCKS ALL DIFFERENT?
UH- I DON'T THINK THEY ARE
-ACTUALLY THE ONE OVER THE DORM' MIGHT BE A MINUTE FAST - IT'S 7:59 LOVE-
NO!

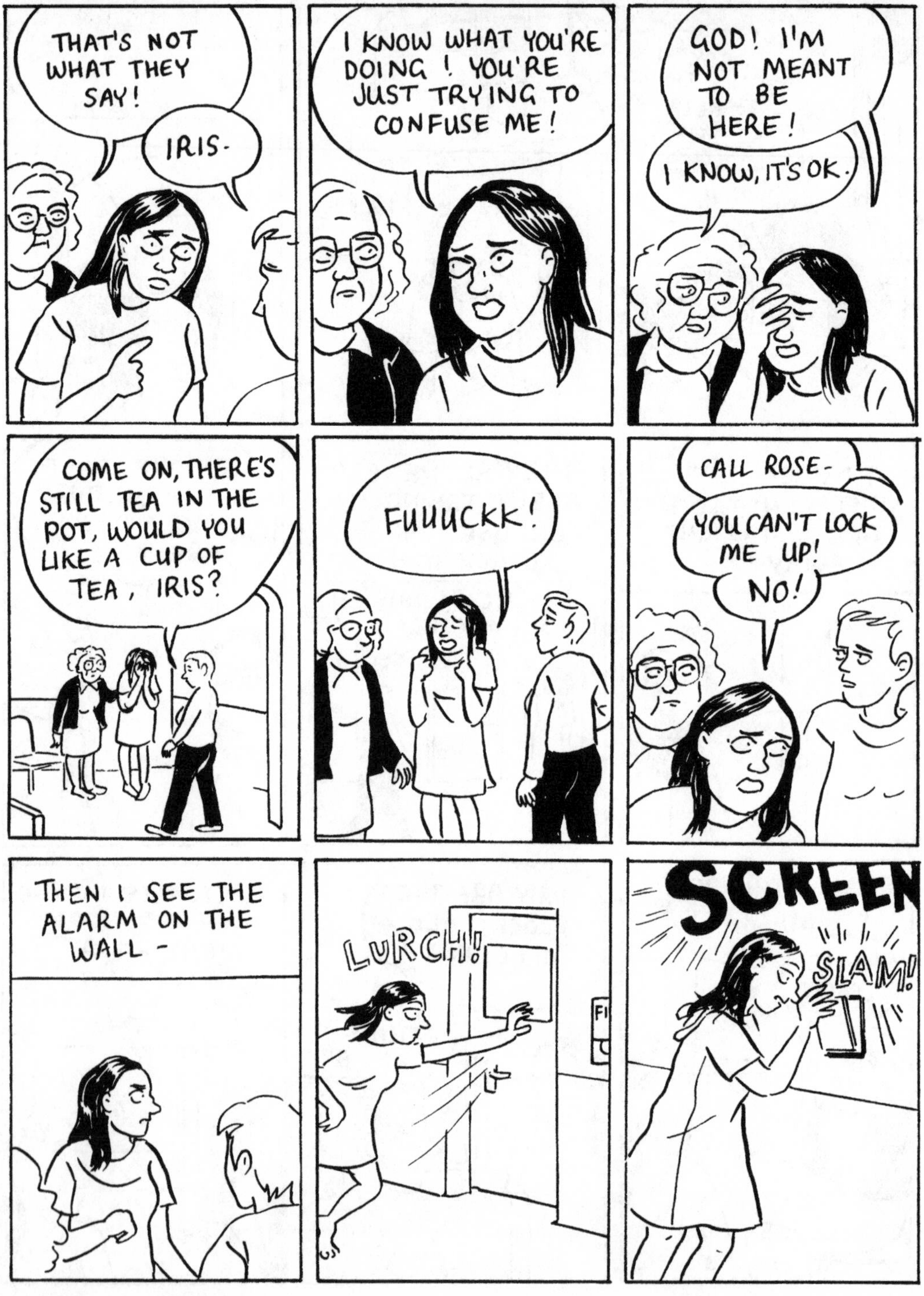
THAT'S NOT WHAT THEY SAY!
IRIS-
I KNOW WHAT YOU'RE DOING! YOU'RE JUST TRYING TO CONFUSE ME!
GOD! I'M NOT MEANT TO BE HERE!
I KNOW, IT'S OK.
COME ON, THERE'S STILL TEA IN THE POT, WOULD YOU LIKE A CUP OF TEA, IRIS?
FUUUCKK!
CALL ROSE-
YOU CAN'T LOCK ME UP! NO!
THEN I SEE THE ALARM ON THE WALL -
LURCH!
SCREEN
SLAM!

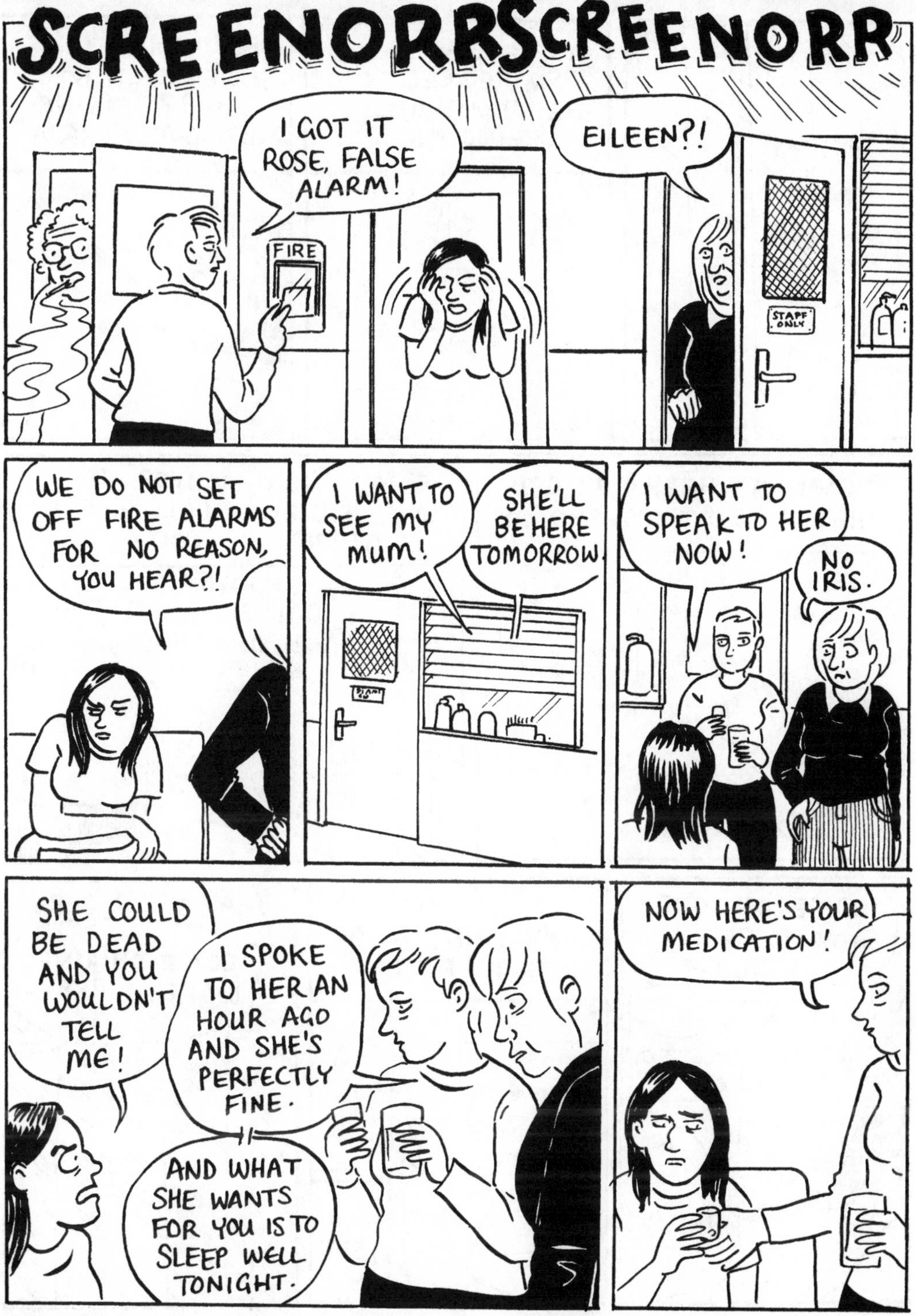
SCREENORRSCREENORR
I GOT IT ROSE, FALSE ALARM!
FIRE
EILEEN?!
STAFF ONLY
WE DO NOT SET OFF FIRE ALARMS FOR NO REASON, YOU HEAR?!
I WANT TO SEE MY MUM!
SHE'LL BE HERE TOMORROW.
I WANT TO SPEAK TO HER NOW!
NO IRIS.
SHE COULD BE DEAD AND YOU WOULDN'T TELL ME!
I SPOKE TO HER AN HOUR AGO AND SHE'S PERFECTLY FINE.
AND WHAT SHE WANTS FOR YOU IS TO SLEEP WELL TONIGHT.
NOW HERE'S YOUR MEDICATION!

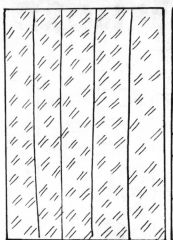

THERE WAS A SNAKE-EYE, THE WHOLE TIME, SEEING ME.

CLINK CLINK

HOW COULD I HAVE BEEN SO DUMB? SETTING OFF THAT ALARM?

FOR ALL TO HEAR? OH GOD, WHAT HAVE I TRIGGERED?

THAT 'GUN' LIGHTER IS WHY I DIDN'T CALL GLEN. SO STUPID, OH GOD.

I SHOULD HAVE CALLED HIM! HE COULD HAVE SAVED ME.

COME ON LOVE, TIME TO GET DRESSED—

I'M NOT HAVING ANYTHING TO DO WITH THAT TEA.

THAT'S FOR SURE.

COME ON JUNE, WAKEY-WAKEY—

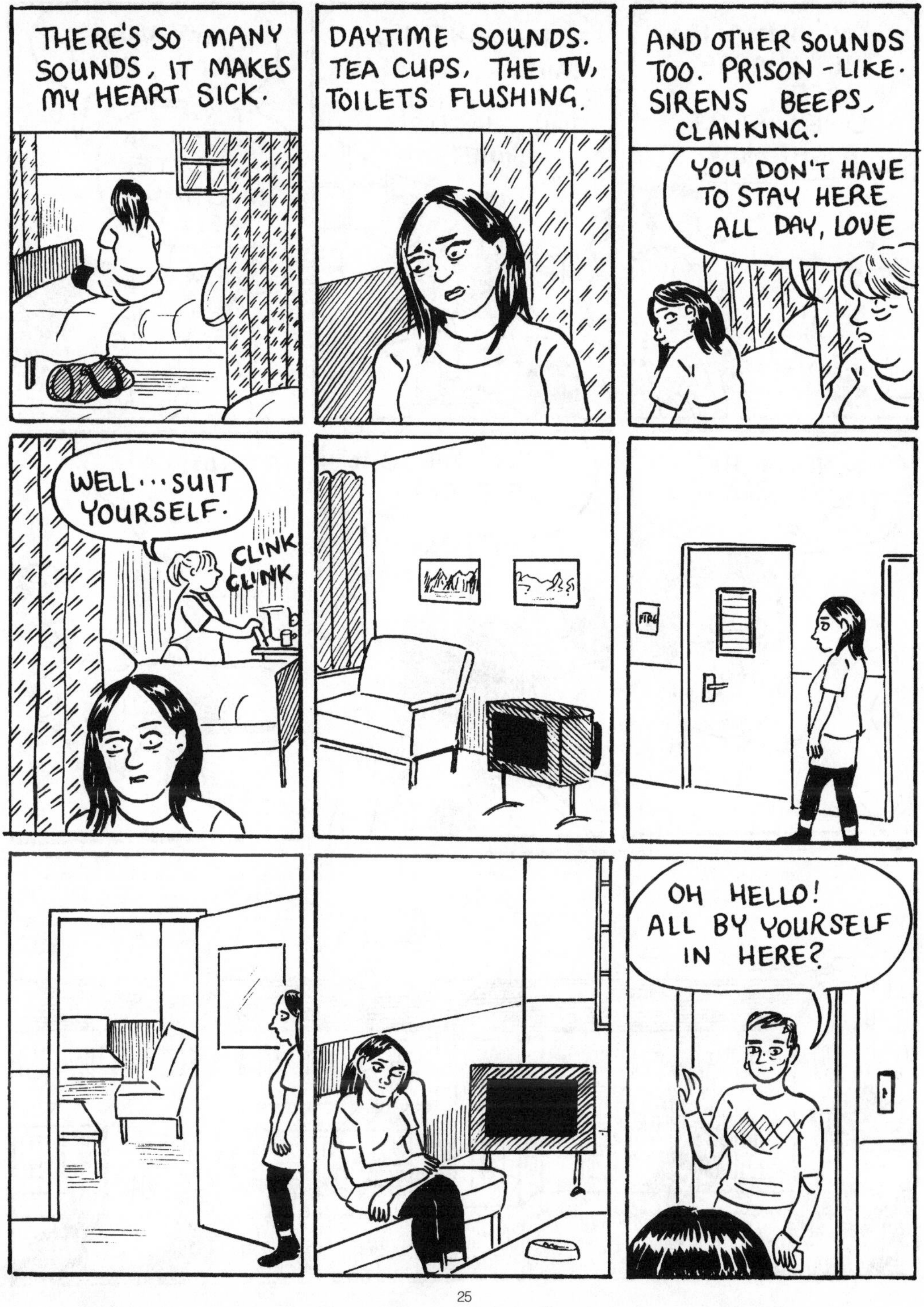

THERE'S SO MANY SOUNDS, IT MAKES MY HEART SICK.
DAYTIME SOUNDS. TEA CUPS, THE TV, TOILETS FLUSHING.
AND OTHER SOUNDS TOO. PRISON-LIKE. SIRENS BEEPS, CLANKING.
YOU DON'T HAVE TO STAY HERE ALL DAY, LOVE
WELL... SUIT YOURSELF.
CLINK
CLINK
OH HELLO! ALL BY YOURSELF IN HERE?

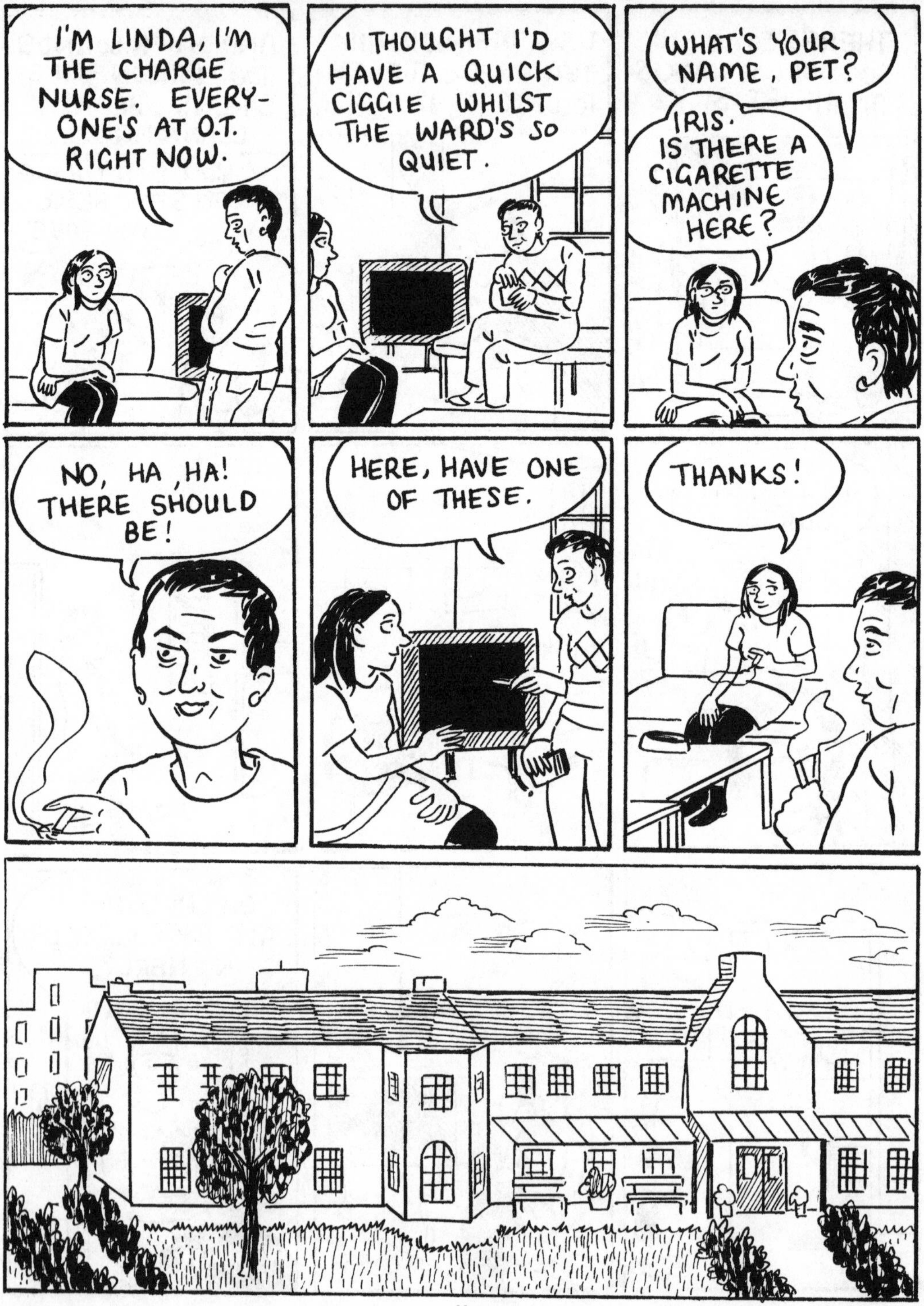
I'M LINDA, I'M THE CHARGE NURSE. EVERY-ONE'S AT O.T. RIGHT NOW.
I THOUGHT I'D HAVE A QUICK CIGGIE WHILST THE WARD'S SO QUIET.
WHAT'S YOUR NAME, PET?
IRIS. IS THERE A CIGARETTE MACHINE HERE?
NO, HA, HA! THERE SHOULD BE!
HERE, HAVE ONE OF THESE.
THANKS!

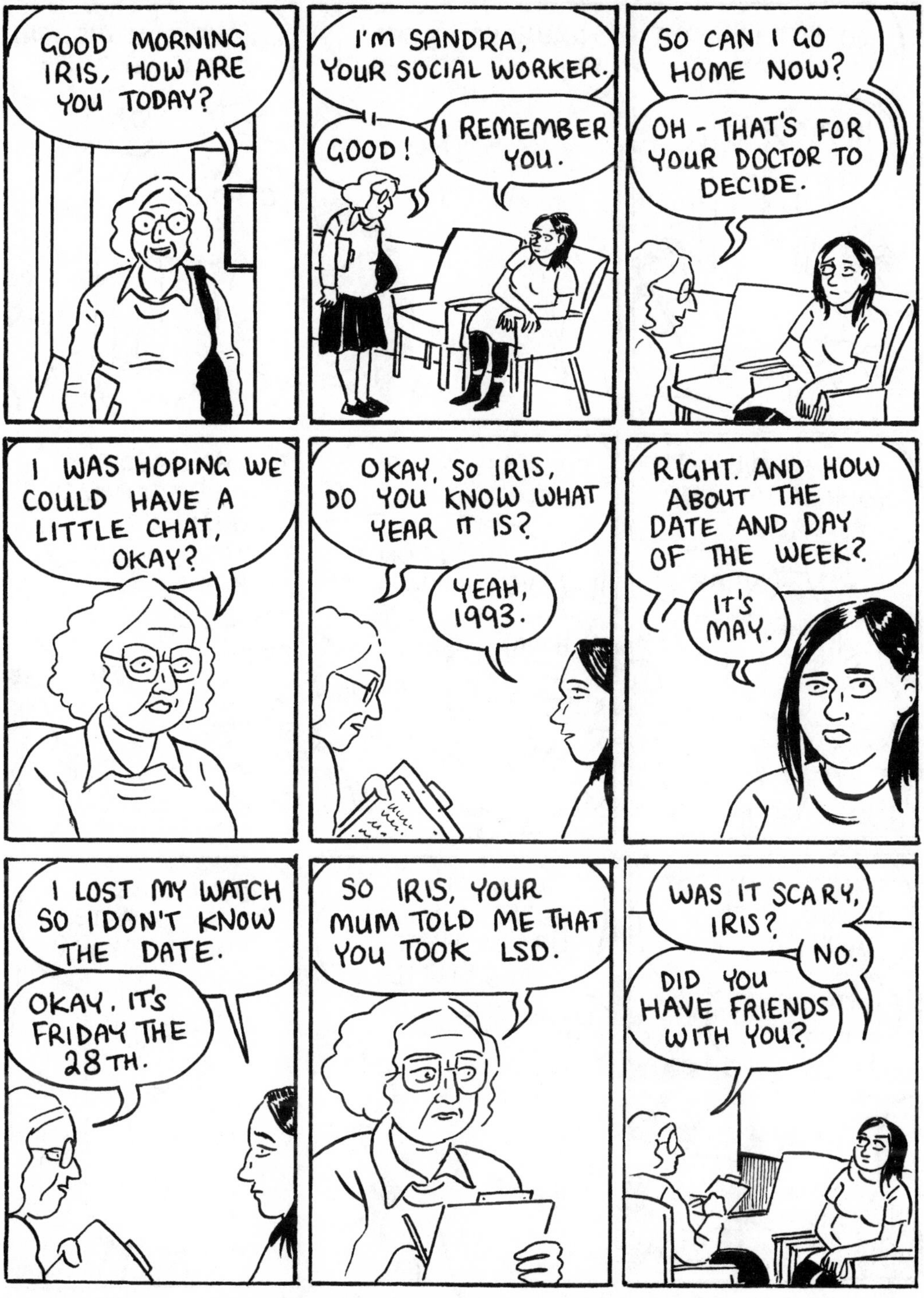
GOOD MORNING IRIS, HOW ARE YOU TODAY?
I'M SANDRA, YOUR SOCIAL WORKER.
GOOD!
I REMEMBER YOU.
SO CAN I GO HOME NOW?
OH - THAT'S FOR YOUR DOCTOR TO DECIDE.
I WAS HOPING WE COULD HAVE A LITTLE CHAT, OKAY?
OKAY, SO IRIS, DO YOU KNOW WHAT YEAR IT IS?
YEAH, 1993.
RIGHT. AND HOW ABOUT THE DATE AND DAY OF THE WEEK?
IT'S MAY.
I LOST MY WATCH SO I DON'T KNOW THE DATE.
OKAY. IT'S FRIDAY THE 28TH.
SO IRIS, YOUR MUM TOLD ME THAT YOU TOOK LSD.
WAS IT SCARY, IRIS?
NO.
DID YOU HAVE FRIENDS WITH YOU?

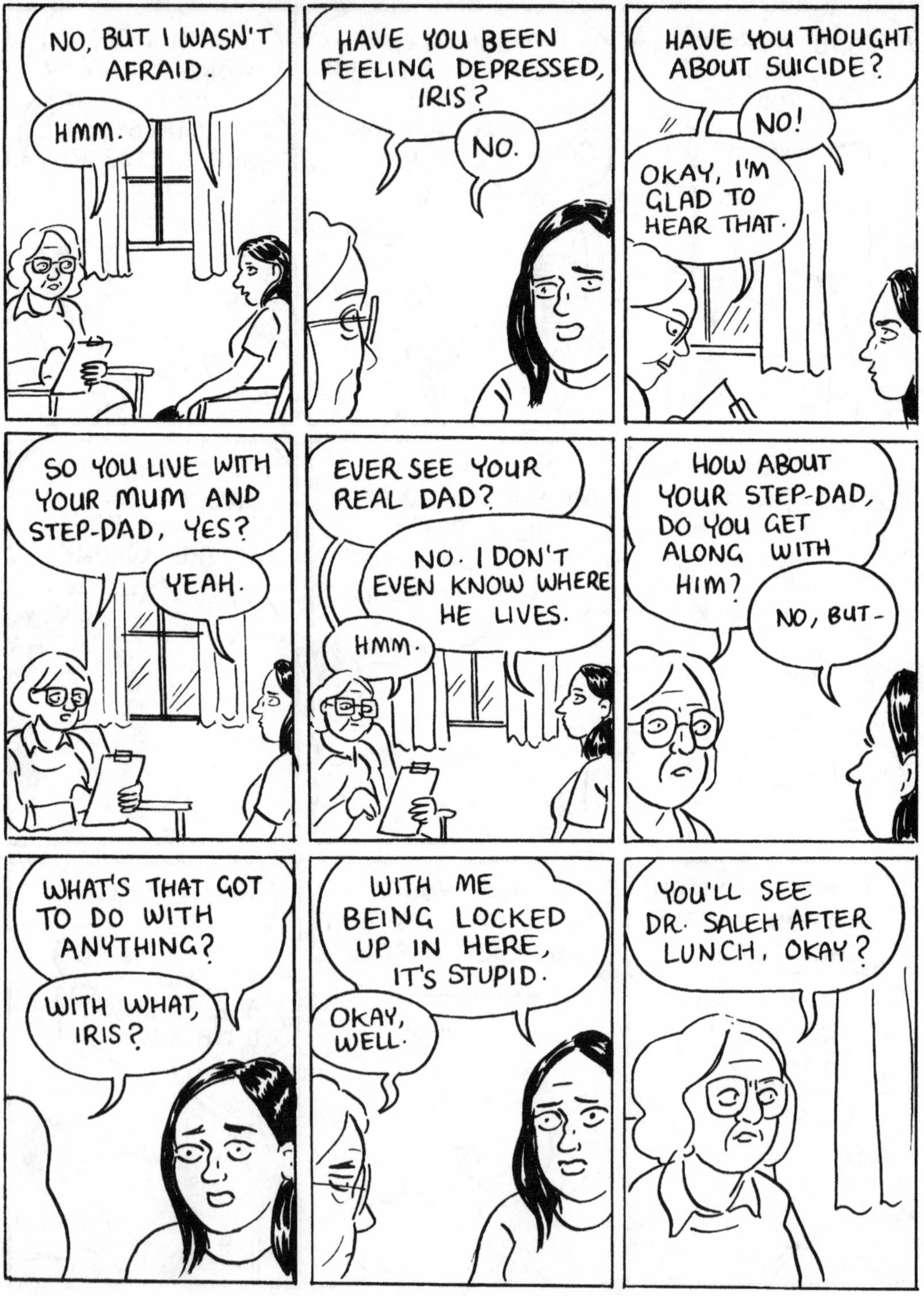
NO, BUT I WASN'T AFRAID.
HMM.
HAVE YOU BEEN FEELING DEPRESSED, IRIS?
NO.
HAVE YOU THOUGHT ABOUT SUICIDE?
NO!
OKAY, I'M GLAD TO HEAR THAT.
SO YOU LIVE WITH YOUR MUM AND STEP-DAD, YES?
YEAH.
EVER SEE YOUR REAL DAD?
NO. I DON'T EVEN KNOW WHERE HE LIVES.
HMM.
HOW ABOUT YOUR STEP-DAD, DO YOU GET ALONG WITH HIM?
NO, BUT-
WHAT'S THAT GOT TO DO WITH ANYTHING?
WITH WHAT, IRIS?
WITH ME BEING LOCKED UP IN HERE, IT'S STUPID.
OKAY, WELL.
YOU'LL SEE DR. SALEH AFTER LUNCH, OKAY?

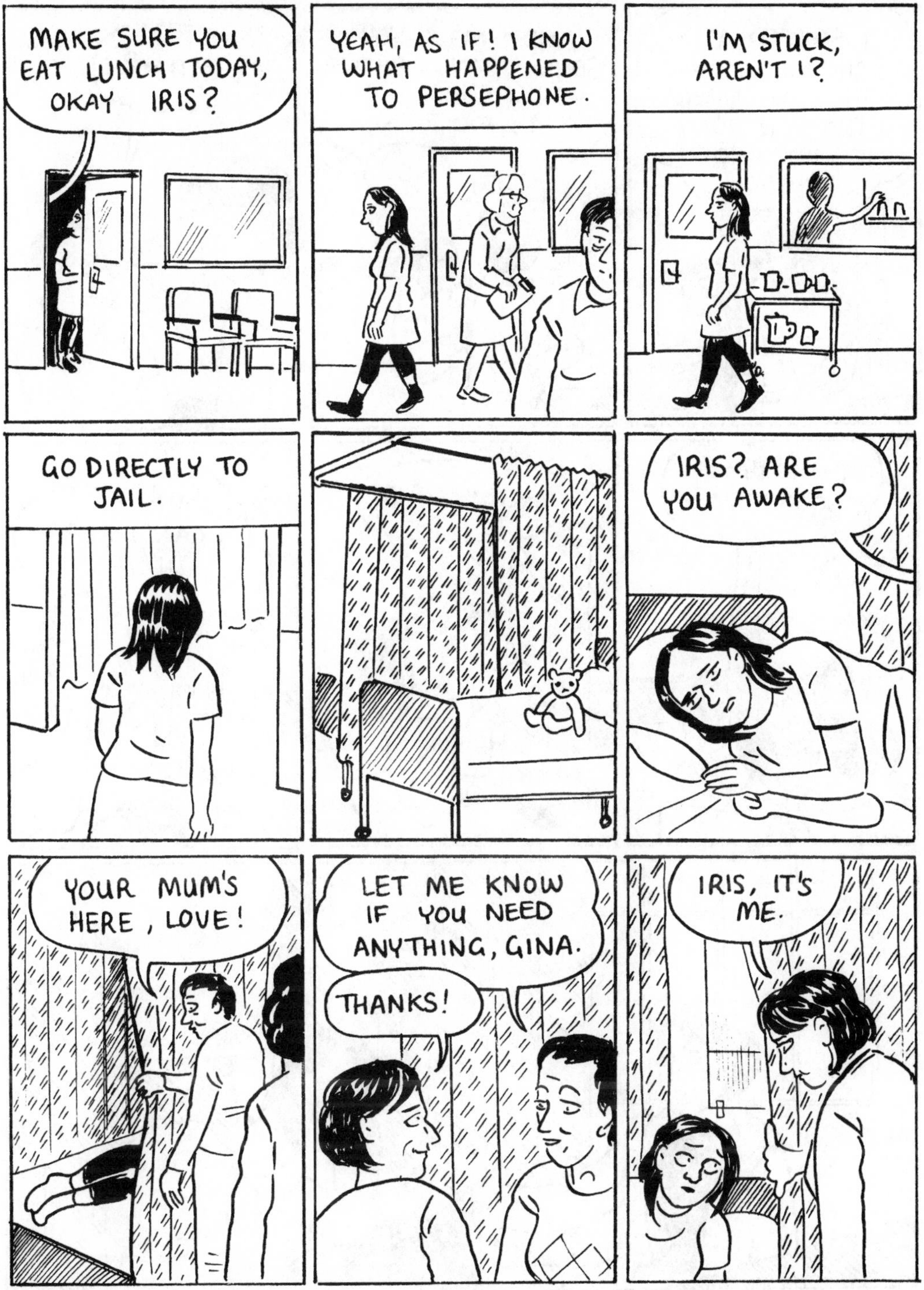
MAKE SURE YOU EAT LUNCH TODAY, OKAY IRIS?
YEAH, AS IF! I KNOW WHAT HAPPENED TO PERSEPHONE.
I'M STUCK, AREN'T I?
GO DIRECTLY TO JAIL.
IRIS? ARE YOU AWAKE?
YOUR MUM'S HERE, LOVE!
LET ME KNOW IF YOU NEED ANYTHING, GINA.
THANKS!
IRIS, IT'S ME.

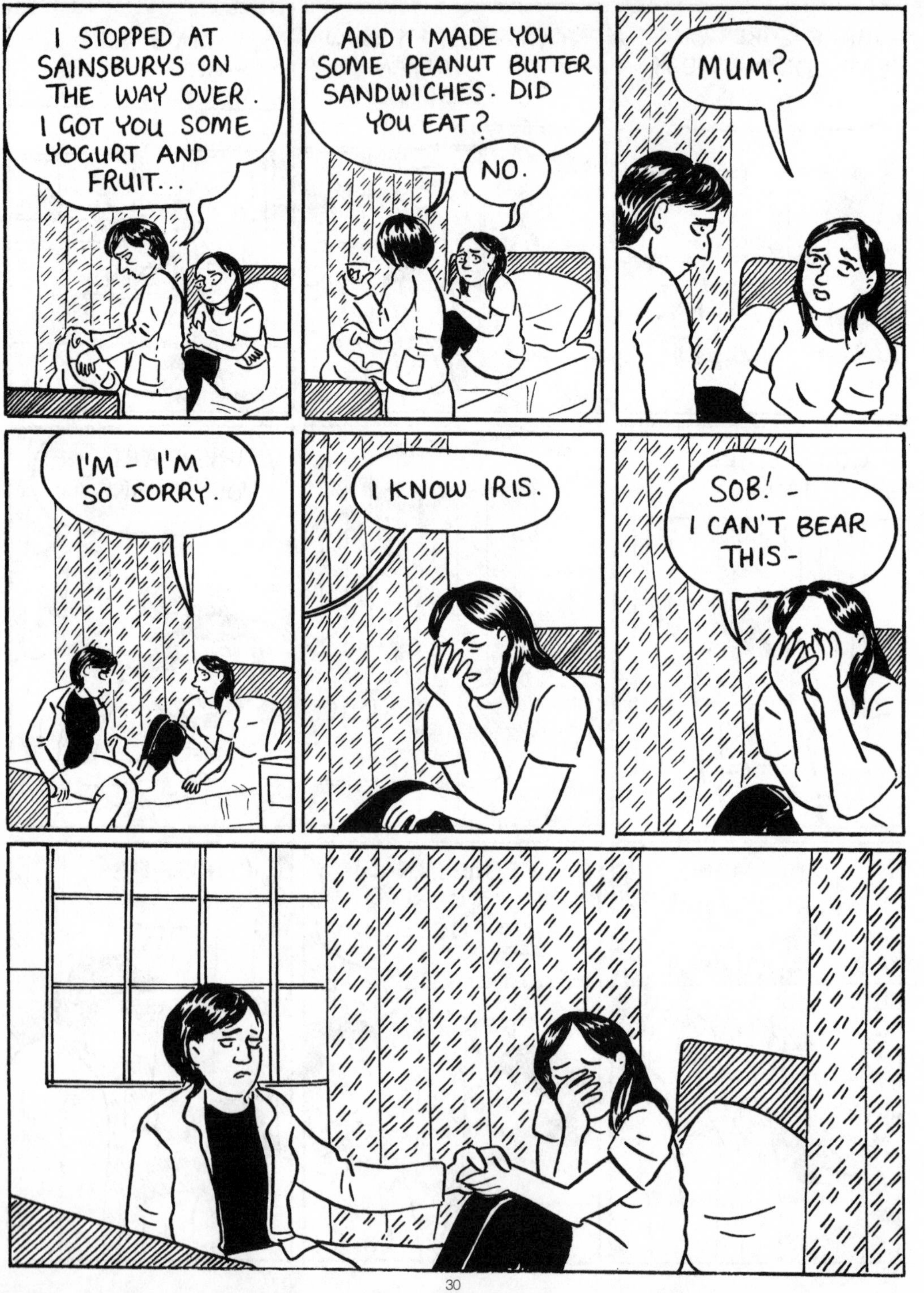
I STOPPED AT SAINSBURYS ON THE WAY OVER. I GOT YOU SOME YOGURT AND FRUIT...
AND I MADE YOU SOME PEANUT BUTTER SANDWICHES. DID YOU EAT?
NO.
MUM?
I'M - I'M SO SORRY.
I KNOW IRIS.
SOB! - I CAN'T BEAR THIS -

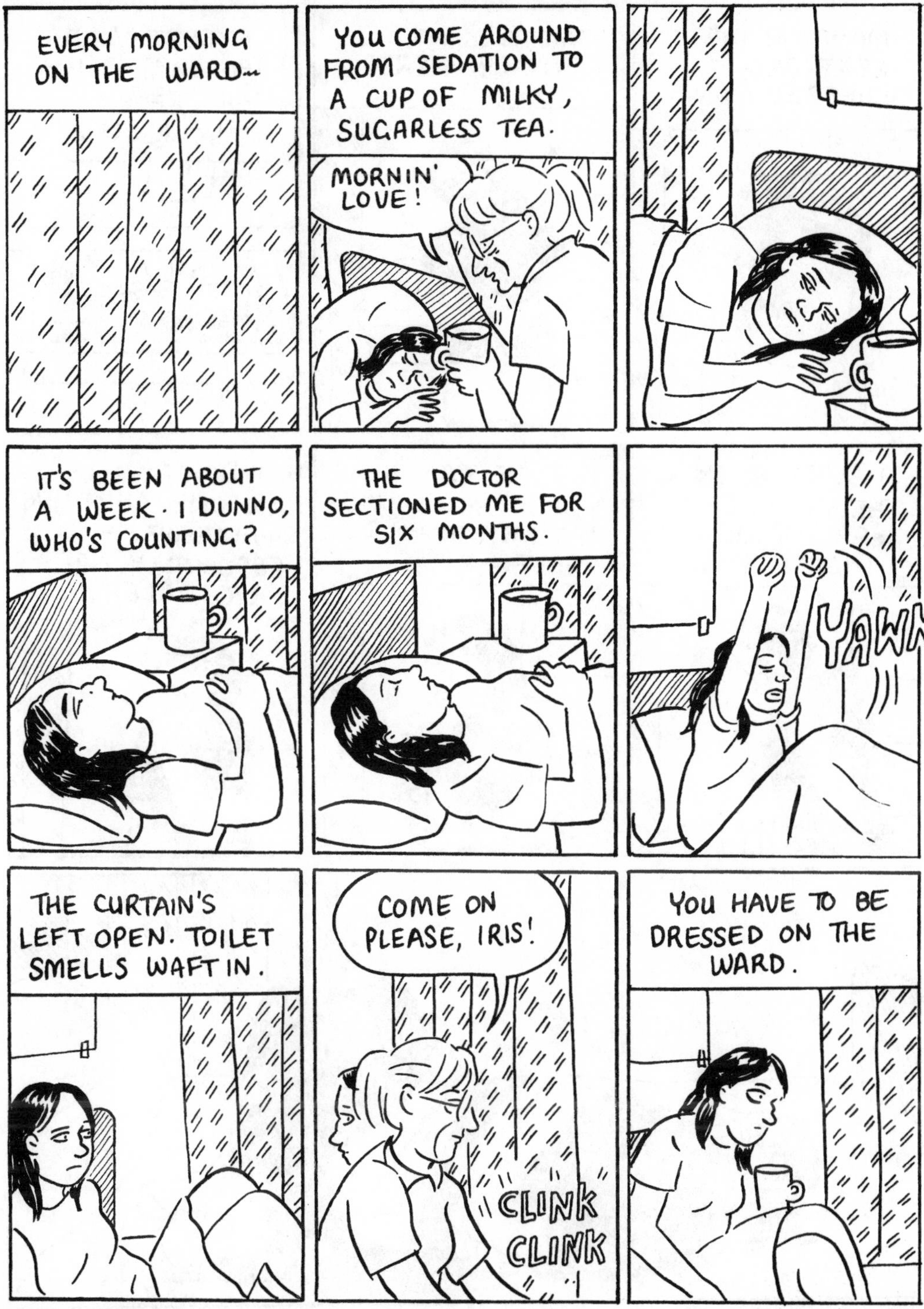
EVERY MORNING ON THE WARD...
YOU COME AROUND FROM SEDATION TO A CUP OF MILKY, SUGARLESS TEA.
MORNIN' LOVE!
IT'S BEEN ABOUT A WEEK. I DUNNO, WHO'S COUNTING?
THE DOCTOR SECTIONED ME FOR SIX MONTHS.
YAWN
THE CURTAIN'S LEFT OPEN. TOILET SMELLS WAFT IN.
COME ON PLEASE, IRIS!
CLINK
CLINK
YOU HAVE TO BE DRESSED ON THE WARD.

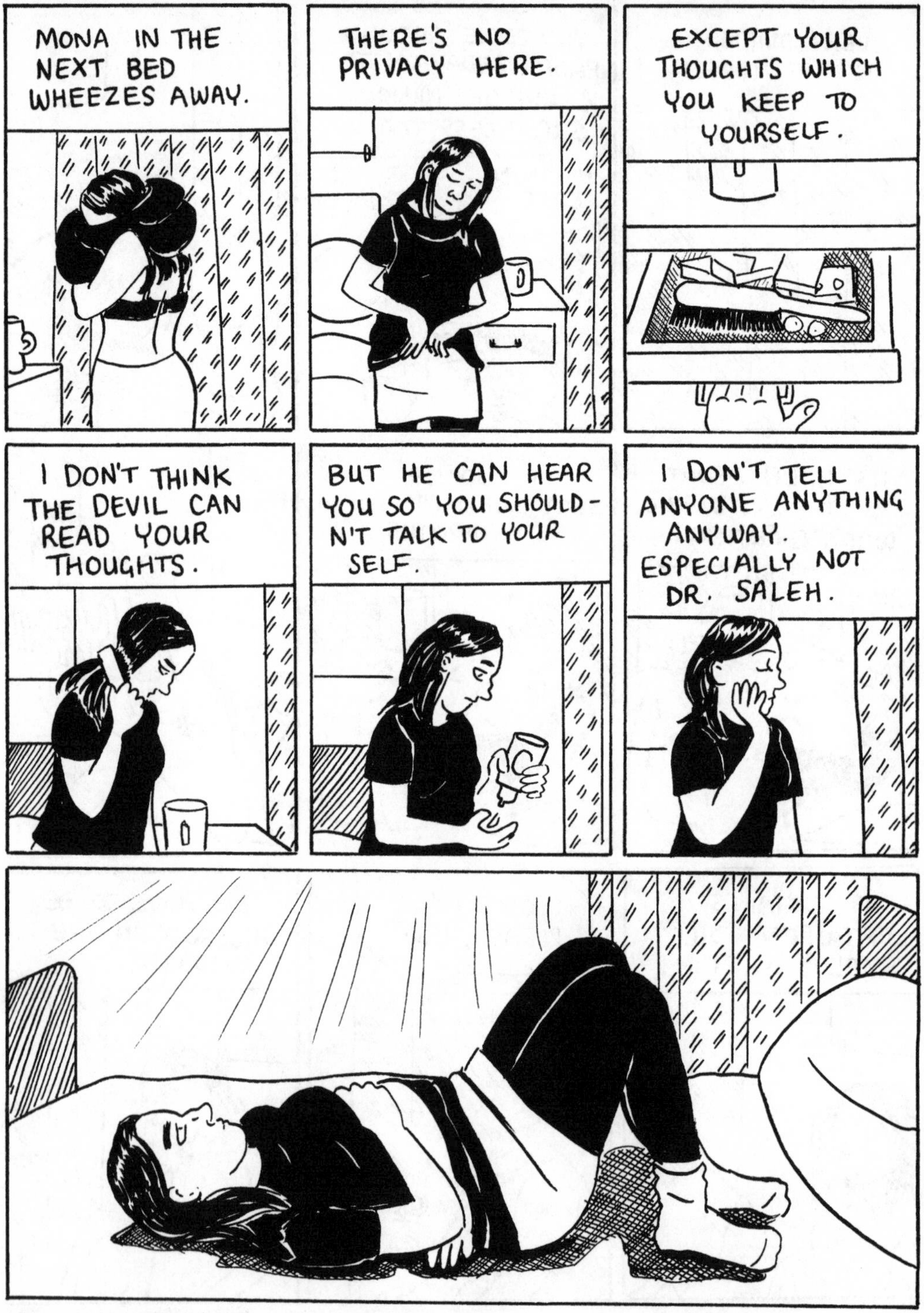
MONA IN THE NEXT BED WHEEZES AWAY.
THERE'S NO PRIVACY HERE.
EXCEPT YOUR THOUGHTS WHICH YOU KEEP TO YOURSELF.
I DON'T THINK THE DEVIL CAN READ YOUR THOUGHTS.
BUT HE CAN HEAR YOU SO YOU SHOULD-N'T TALK TO YOUR SELF.
I DON'T TELL ANYONE ANYTHING ANYWAY. ESPECIALLY NOT DR. SALEH.

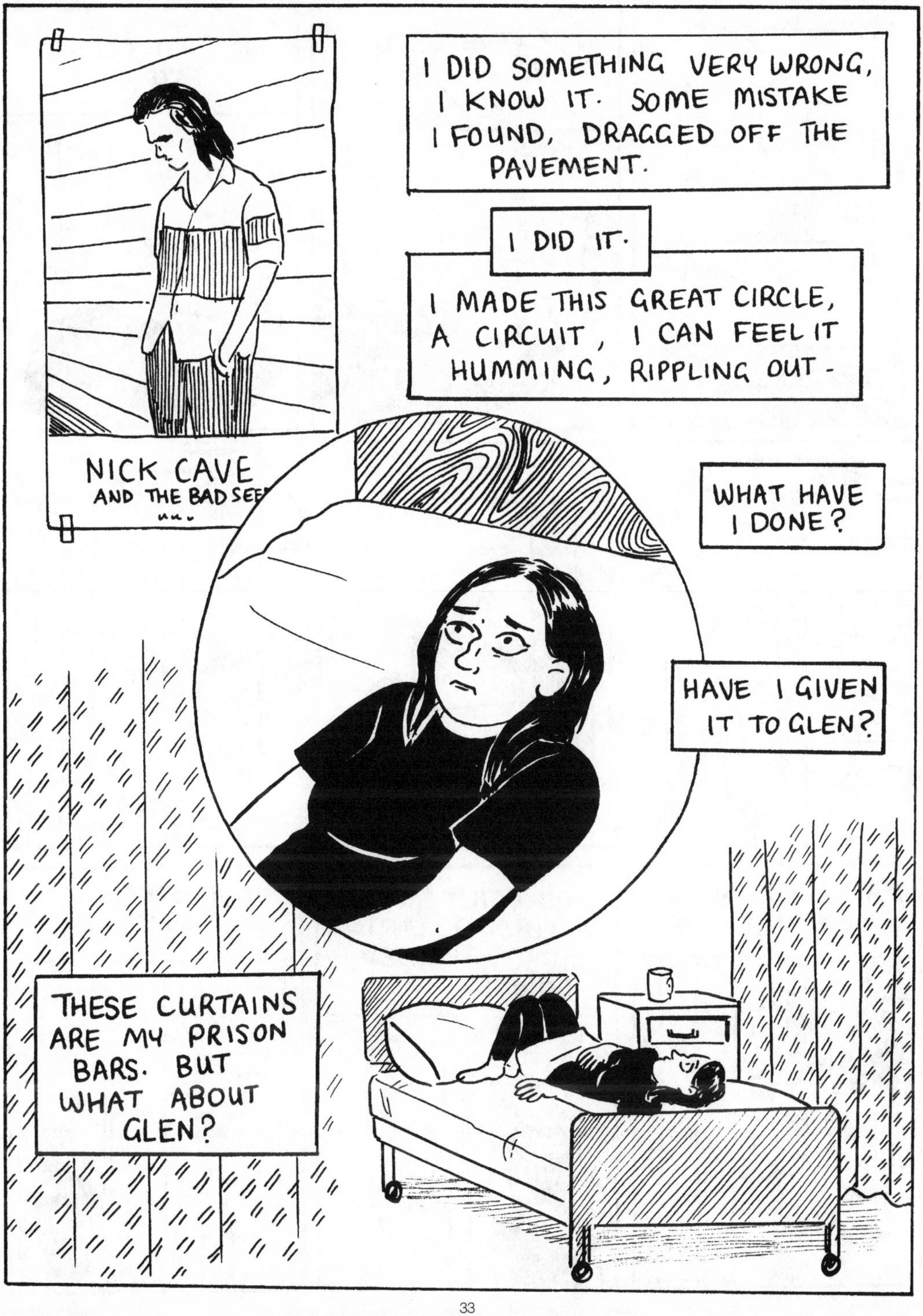
NICK CAVE
AND THE BAD SEE
I DID SOMETHING VERY WRONG, I KNOW IT. SOME MISTAKE I FOUND, DRAGGED OFF THE PAVEMENT.
I DID IT.
I MADE THIS GREAT CIRCLE, A CIRCUIT, I CAN FEEL IT HUMMING, RIPPLING OUT -
WHAT HAVE I DONE?
HAVE I GIVEN IT TO GLEN?
THESE CURTAINS ARE MY PRISON BARS. BUT WHAT ABOUT GLEN?

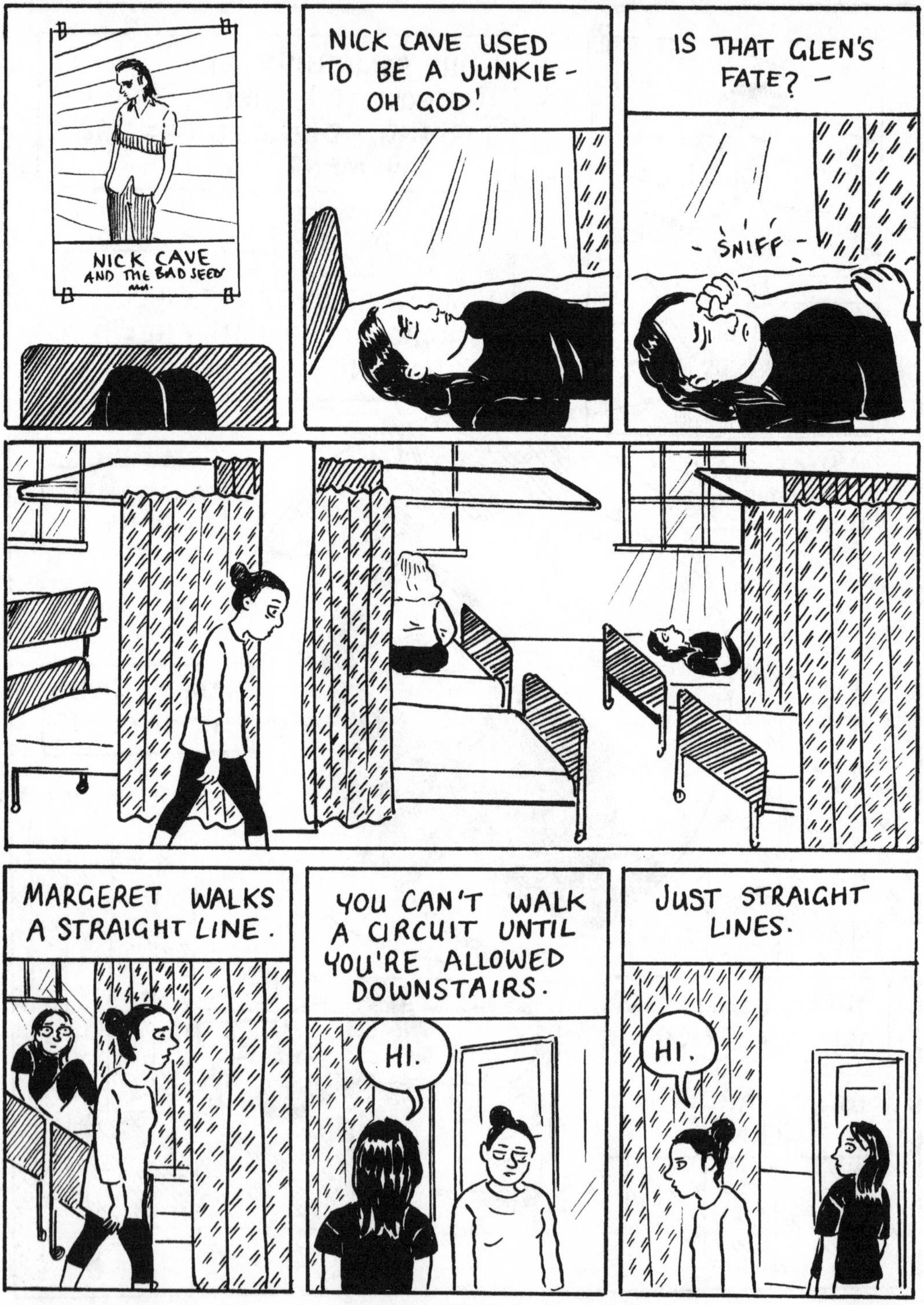

NICK CAVE
AND THE BAD SEEDS
NICK CAVE USED TO BE A JUNKIE - OH GOD!
IS THAT GLEN'S FATE? -
- SNIFF -
MARGERET WALKS A STRAIGHT LINE.
YOU CAN'T WALK A CIRCUIT UNTIL YOU'RE ALLOWED DOWNSTAIRS.
HI.
JUST STRAIGHT LINES.
HI.

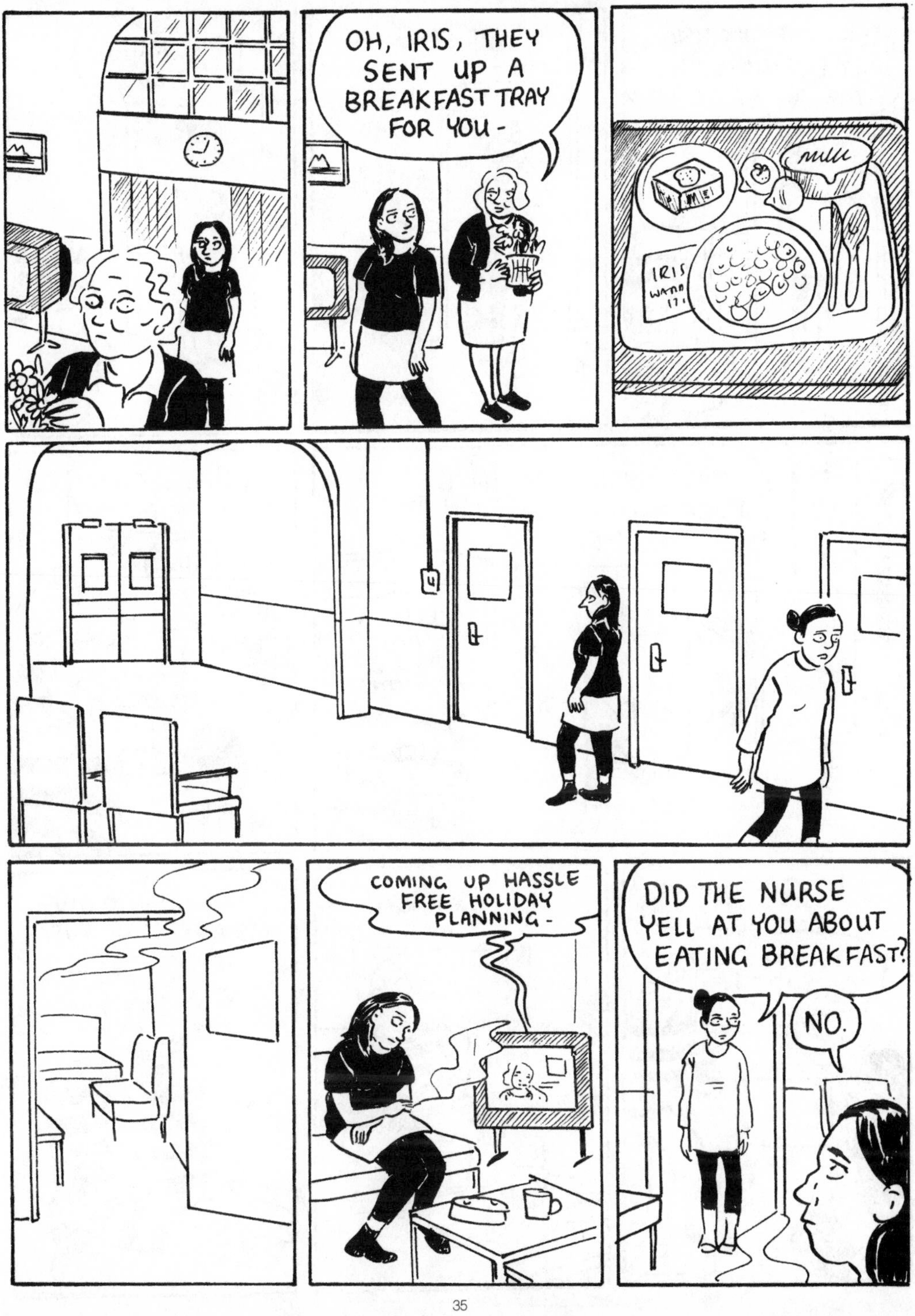
OH, IRIS, THEY SENT UP A BREAKFAST TRAY FOR YOU -
IRIS
COMING UP HASSLE FREE HOLIDAY PLANNING -
DID THE NURSE YELL AT YOU ABOUT EATING BREAKFAST?
NO.

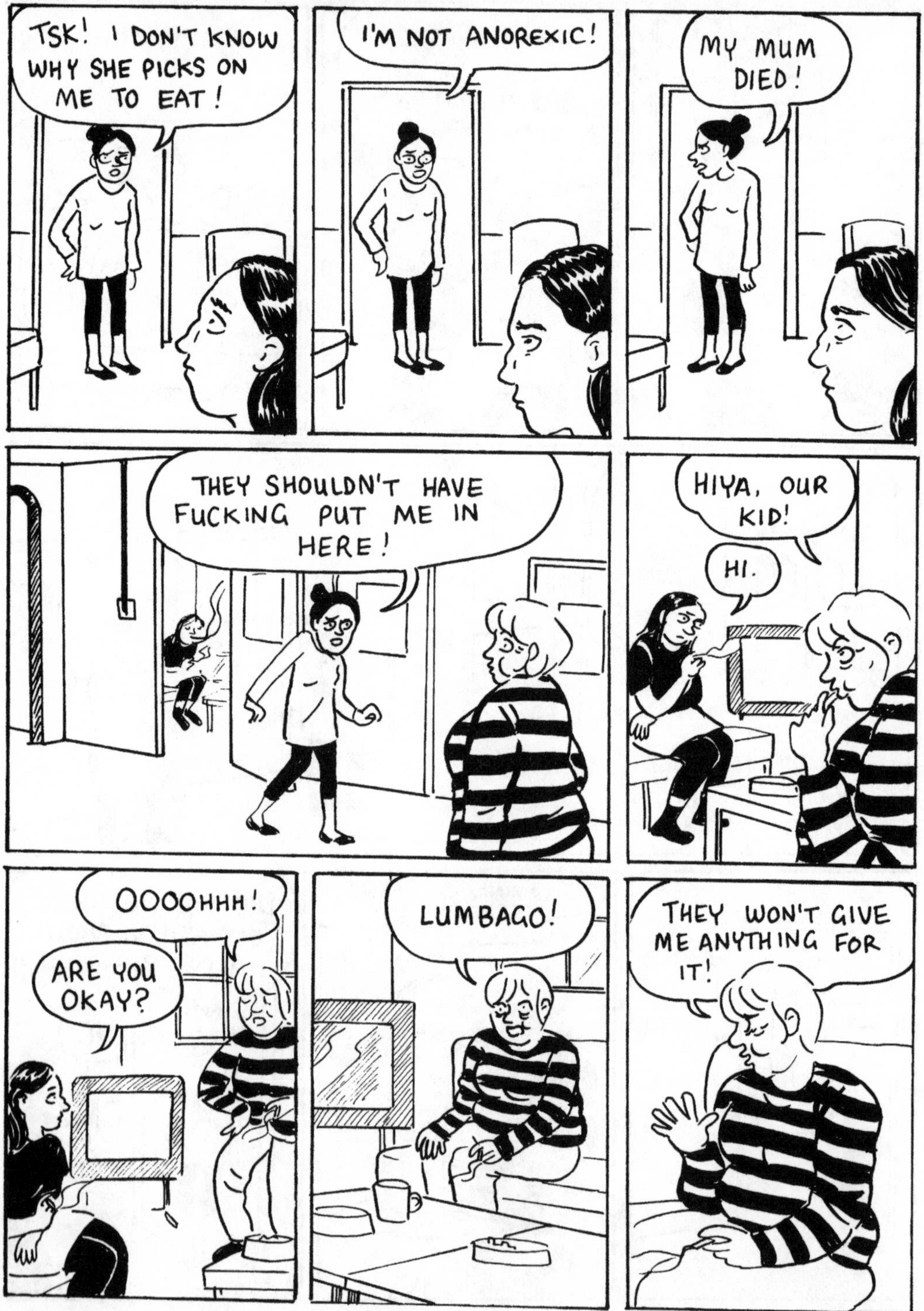
TSK! I DON'T KNOW WHY SHE PICKS ON ME TO EAT!
I'M NOT ANOREXIC!
MY MUM DIED!
THEY SHOULDN'T HAVE FUCKING PUT ME IN HERE!
HIYA, OUR KID!
HI.
OOOOHHH!
ARE YOU OKAY?
LUMBAGO!
THEY WON'T GIVE ME ANYTHING FOR IT!

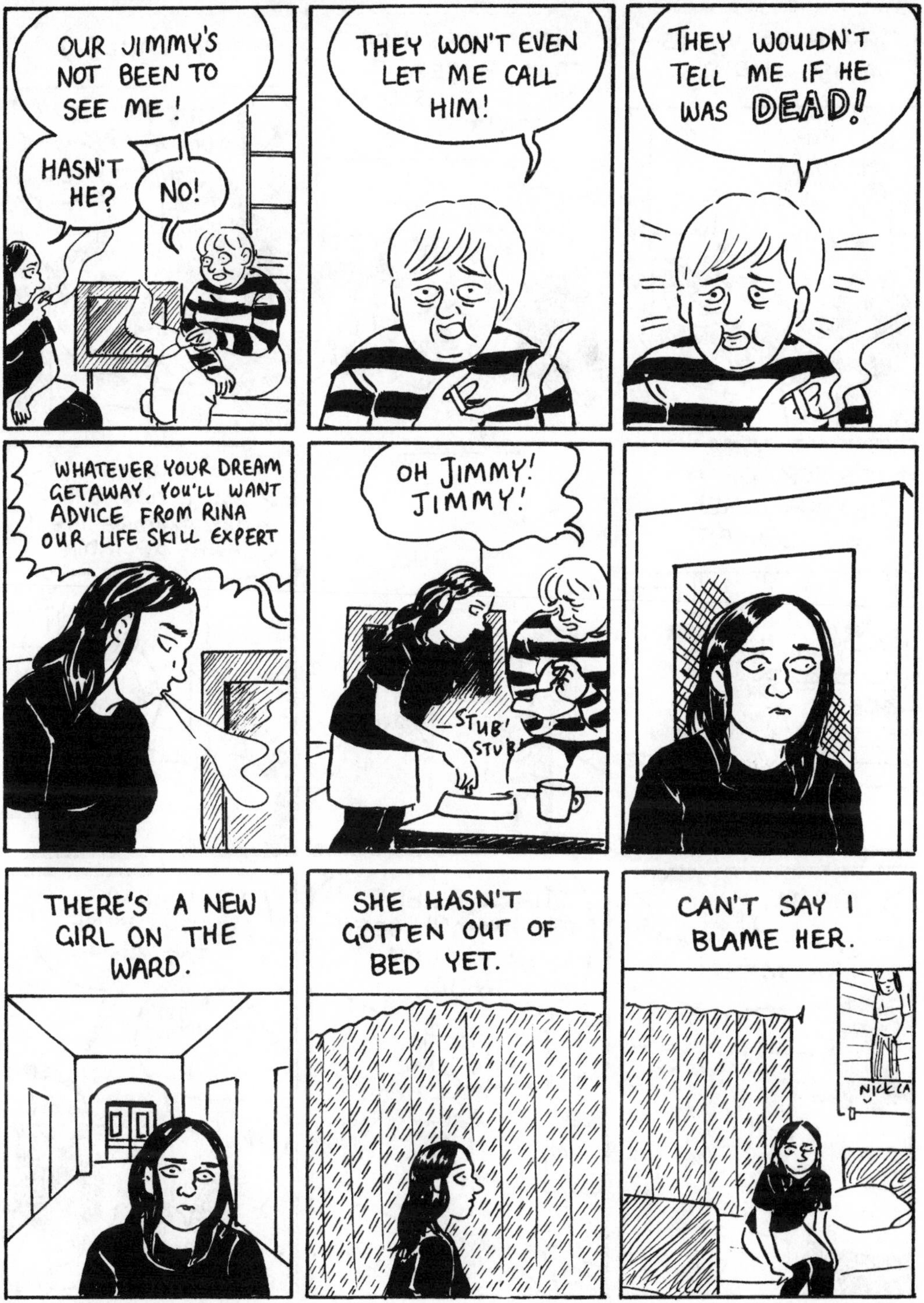
OUR JIMMY'S NOT BEEN TO SEE ME!
HASN'T HE?
NO!
THEY WON'T EVEN LET ME CALL HIM!
THEY WOULDN'T TELL ME IF HE WAS DEAD!
WHATEVER YOUR DREAM GETAWAY, YOU'LL WANT ADVICE FROM RINA OUR LIFE SKILL EXPERT
OH JIMMY! JIMMY!
STUB! STUB!
THERE'S A NEW GIRL ON THE WARD.
SHE HASN'T GOTTEN OUT OF BED YET.
CAN'T SAY I BLAME HER.
NICOLA

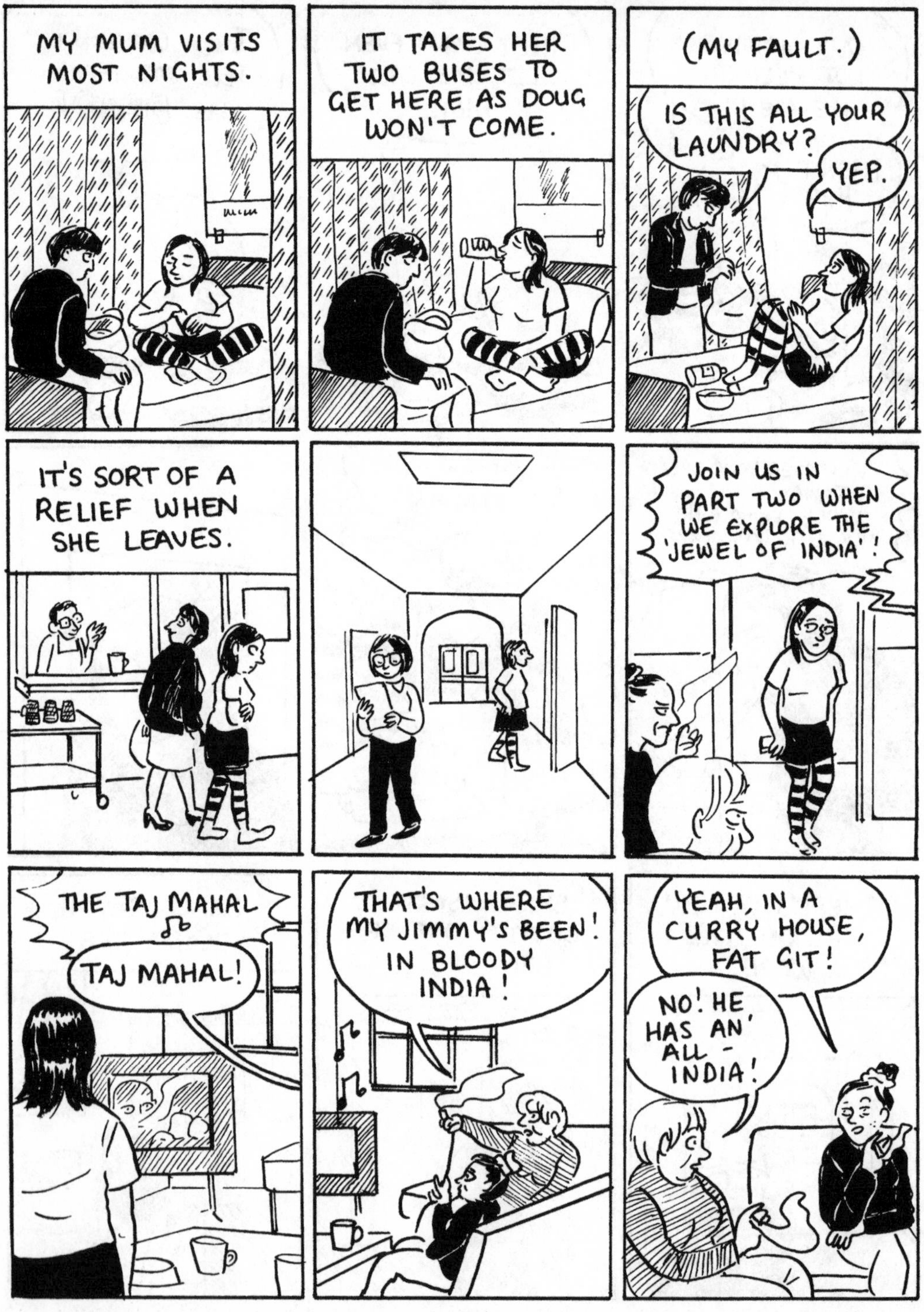
MY MUM VISITS MOST NIGHTS.
IT TAKES HER TWO BUSES TO GET HERE AS DOUG WON'T COME.
(MY FAULT.)
IS THIS ALL YOUR LAUNDRY?
YEP.
IT'S SORT OF A RELIEF WHEN SHE LEAVES.
JOIN US IN PART TWO WHEN WE EXPLORE THE 'JEWEL OF INDIA'!
THE TAJ MAHAL
TAJ MAHAL!
THAT'S WHERE MY JIMMY'S BEEN! IN BLOODY INDIA!
YEAH, IN A CURRY HOUSE, FAT GIT!
NO! HE HAS AN' ALL-INDIA!

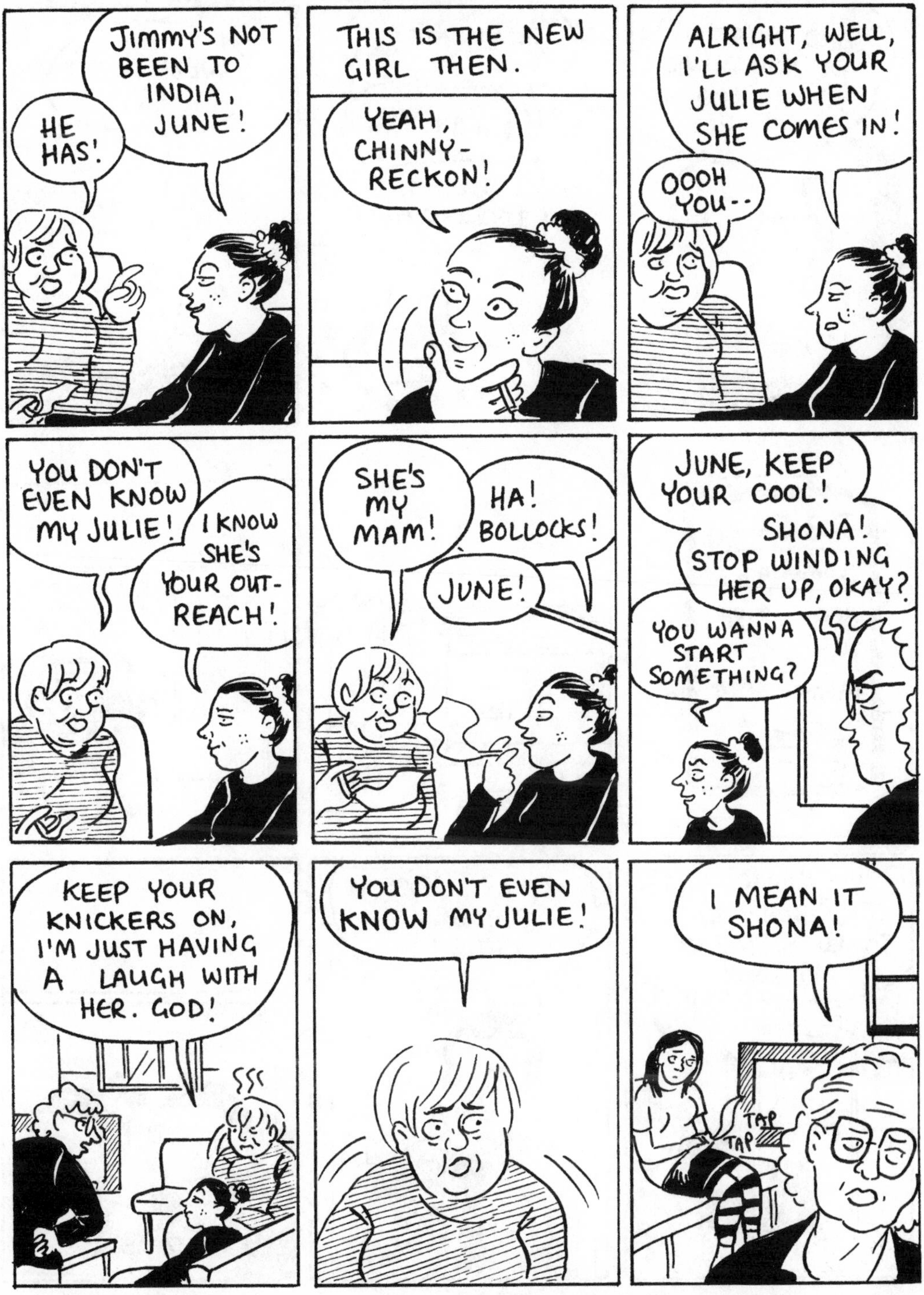
JIMMY'S NOT BEEN TO INDIA, JUNE!
HE HAS!
THIS IS THE NEW GIRL THEN.
YEAH, CHINNY-RECKON!
ALRIGHT, WELL, I'LL ASK YOUR JULIE WHEN SHE COMES IN!
OOOH YOU..
YOU DON'T EVEN KNOW MY JULIE!
I KNOW SHE'S YOUR OUT-REACH!
SHE'S MY MAM!
HA! BOLLOCKS!
JUNE!
JUNE, KEEP YOUR COOL!
SHONA! STOP WINDING HER UP, OKAY?
YOU WANNA START SOMETHING?
KEEP YOUR KNICKERS ON, I'M JUST HAVING A LAUGH WITH HER. GOD!
YOU DON'T EVEN KNOW MY JULIE!
I MEAN IT SHONA!
TAP
TAP

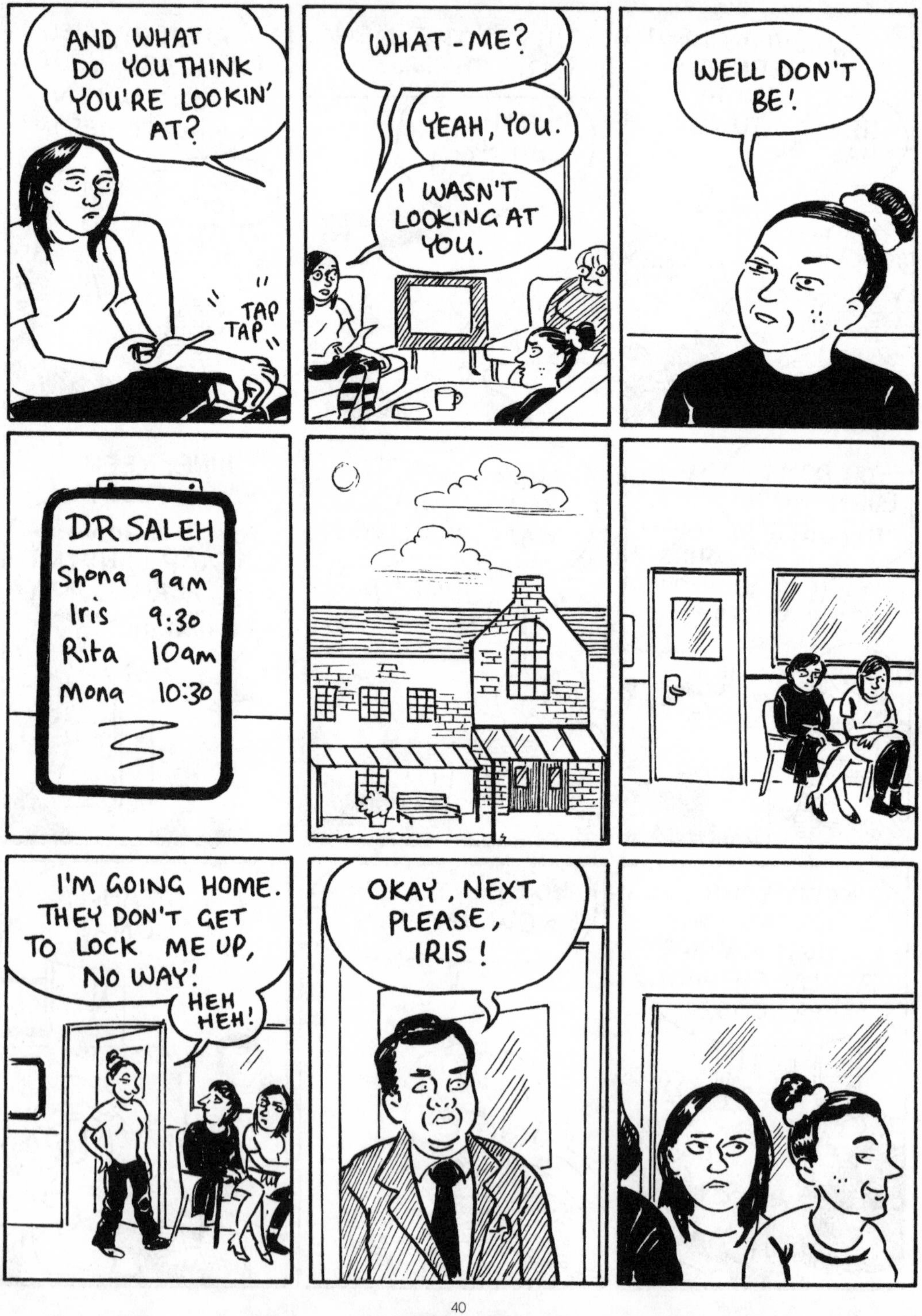
AND WHAT DO YOU THINK YOU'RE LOOKIN' AT?
TAP TAP
WHAT-ME?
YEAH, YOU.
I WASN'T LOOKING AT YOU.
WELL DON'T BE!
DR SALEH
Shona 9am
Iris 9:30
Rita 10am
Mona 10:30
I'M GOING HOME. THEY DON'T GET TO LOCK ME UP, NO WAY!
HEH HEH!
OKAY, NEXT PLEASE, IRIS!

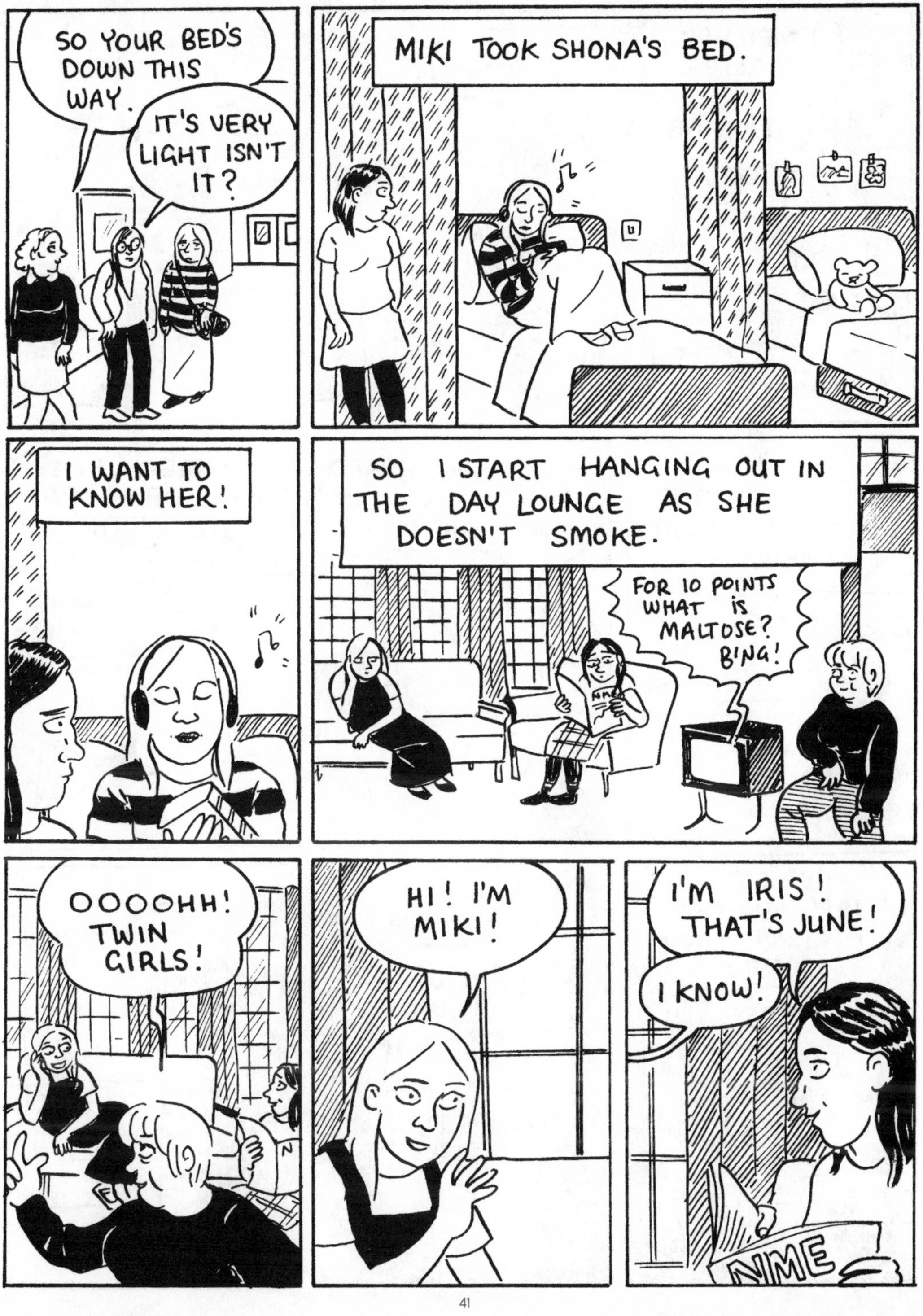
SO YOUR BED'S DOWN THIS WAY.
IT'S VERY LIGHT ISN'T IT?
MIKI TOOK SHONA'S BED.
I WANT TO KNOW HER!
SO I START HANGING OUT IN THE DAY LOUNGE AS SHE DOESN'T SMOKE.
FOR 10 POINTS WHAT IS MALTOSE? BING!
OOOOHH! TWIN GIRLS!
HI! I'M MIKI!
I'M IRIS! THAT'S JUNE!
I KNOW!
NME

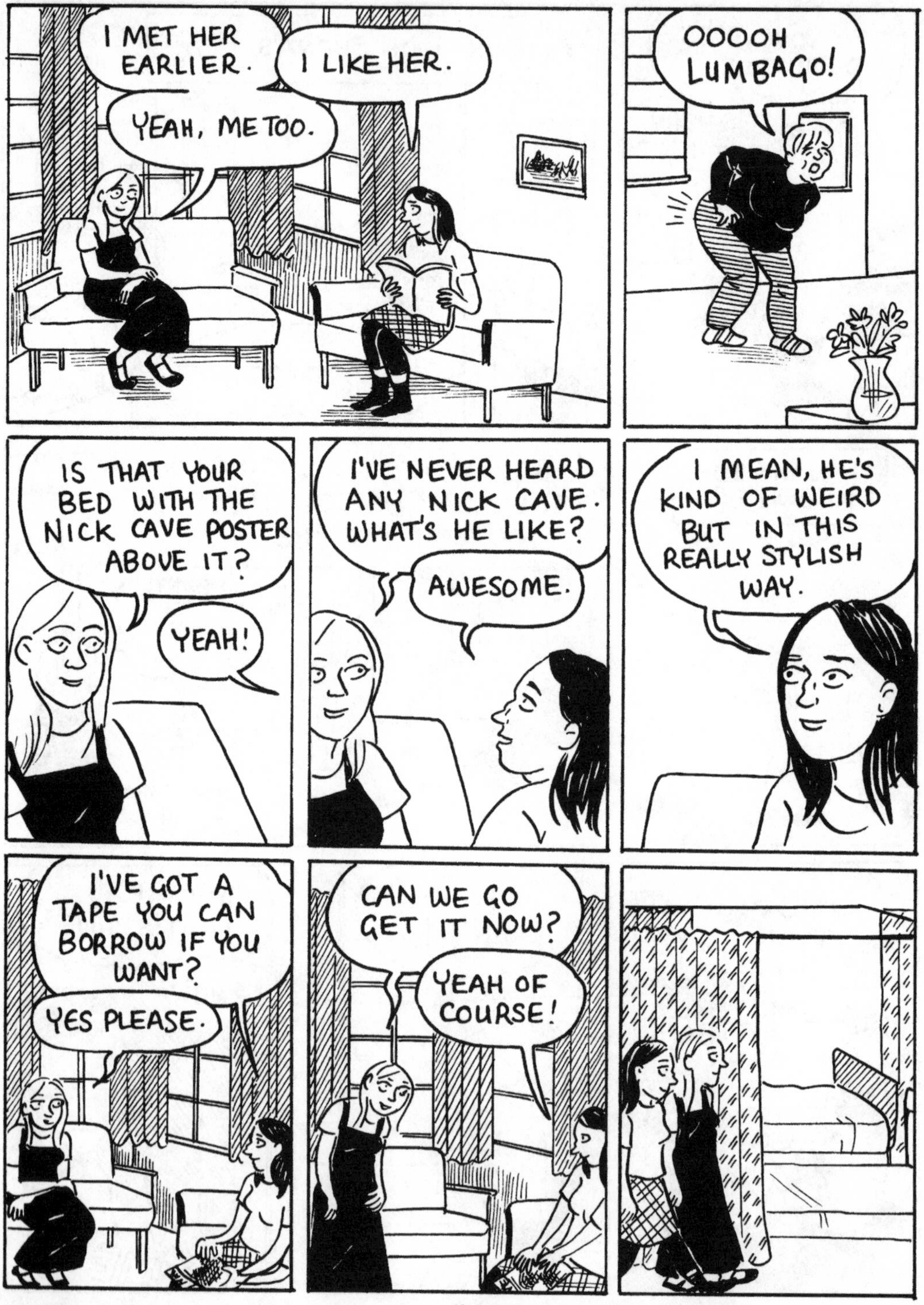
I MET HER EARLIER.
I LIKE HER.
YEAH, ME TOO.
OOOOH LUMBAGO!
IS THAT YOUR BED WITH THE NICK CAVE POSTER ABOVE IT?
YEAH!
I'VE NEVER HEARD ANY NICK CAVE. WHAT'S HE LIKE?
AWESOME.
I MEAN, HE'S KIND OF WEIRD BUT IN THIS REALLY STYLISH WAY.
I'VE GOT A TAPE YOU CAN BORROW IF YOU WANT?
YES PLEASE.
CAN WE GO GET IT NOW?
YEAH OF COURSE!

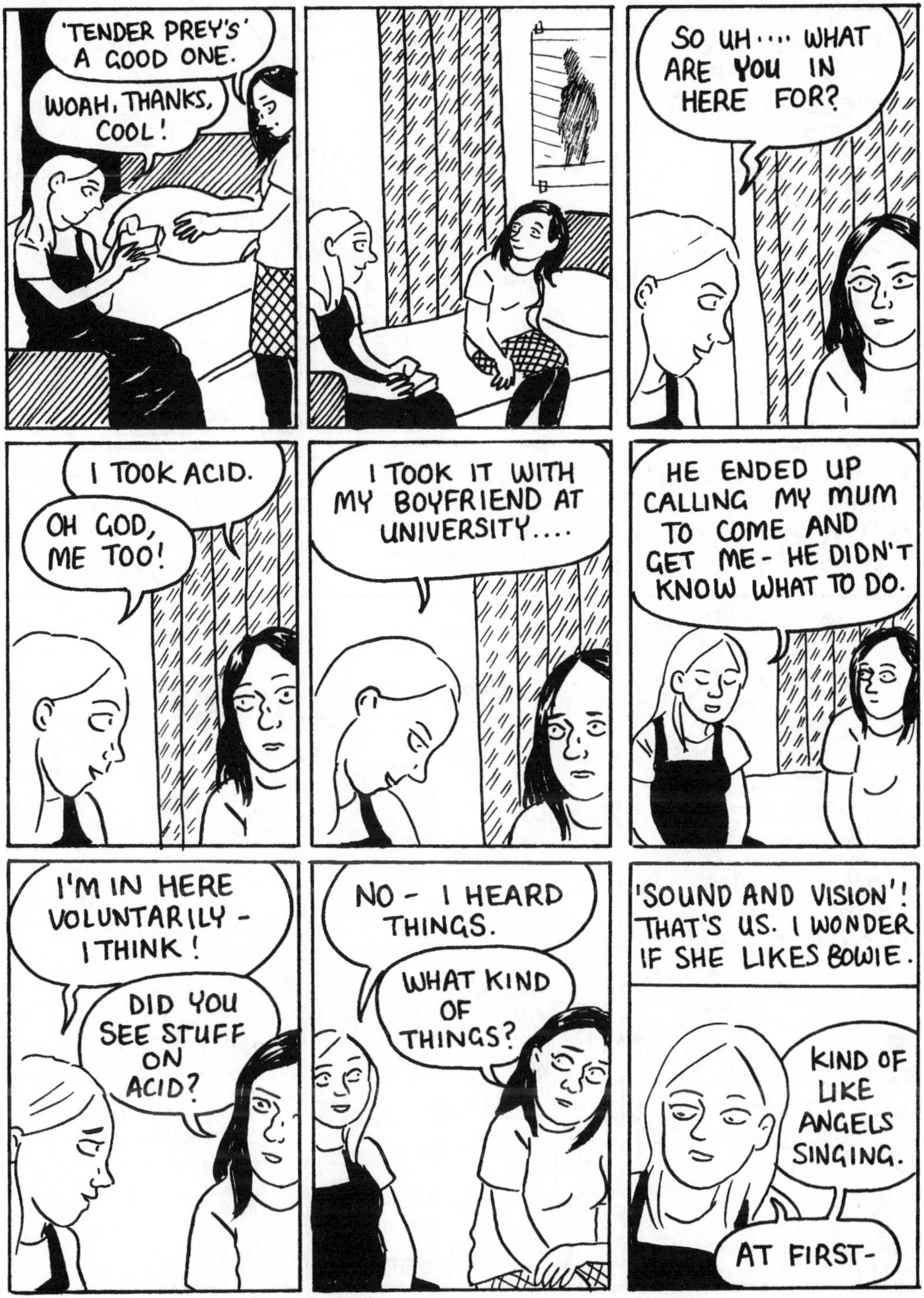
'TENDER PREY'S' A GOOD ONE.
WOAH, THANKS, COOL!
SO UH.... WHAT ARE YOU IN HERE FOR?
I TOOK ACID.
OH GOD, ME TOO!
I TOOK IT WITH MY BOYFRIEND AT UNIVERSITY....
HE ENDED UP CALLING MY MUM TO COME AND GET ME- HE DIDN'T KNOW WHAT TO DO.
I'M IN HERE VOLUNTARILY - I THINK!
DID YOU SEE STUFF ON ACID?
NO - I HEARD THINGS.
WHAT KIND OF THINGS?
'SOUND AND VISION'! THAT'S US. I WONDER IF SHE LIKES BOWIE.
KIND OF LIKE ANGELS SINGING.
AT FIRST-

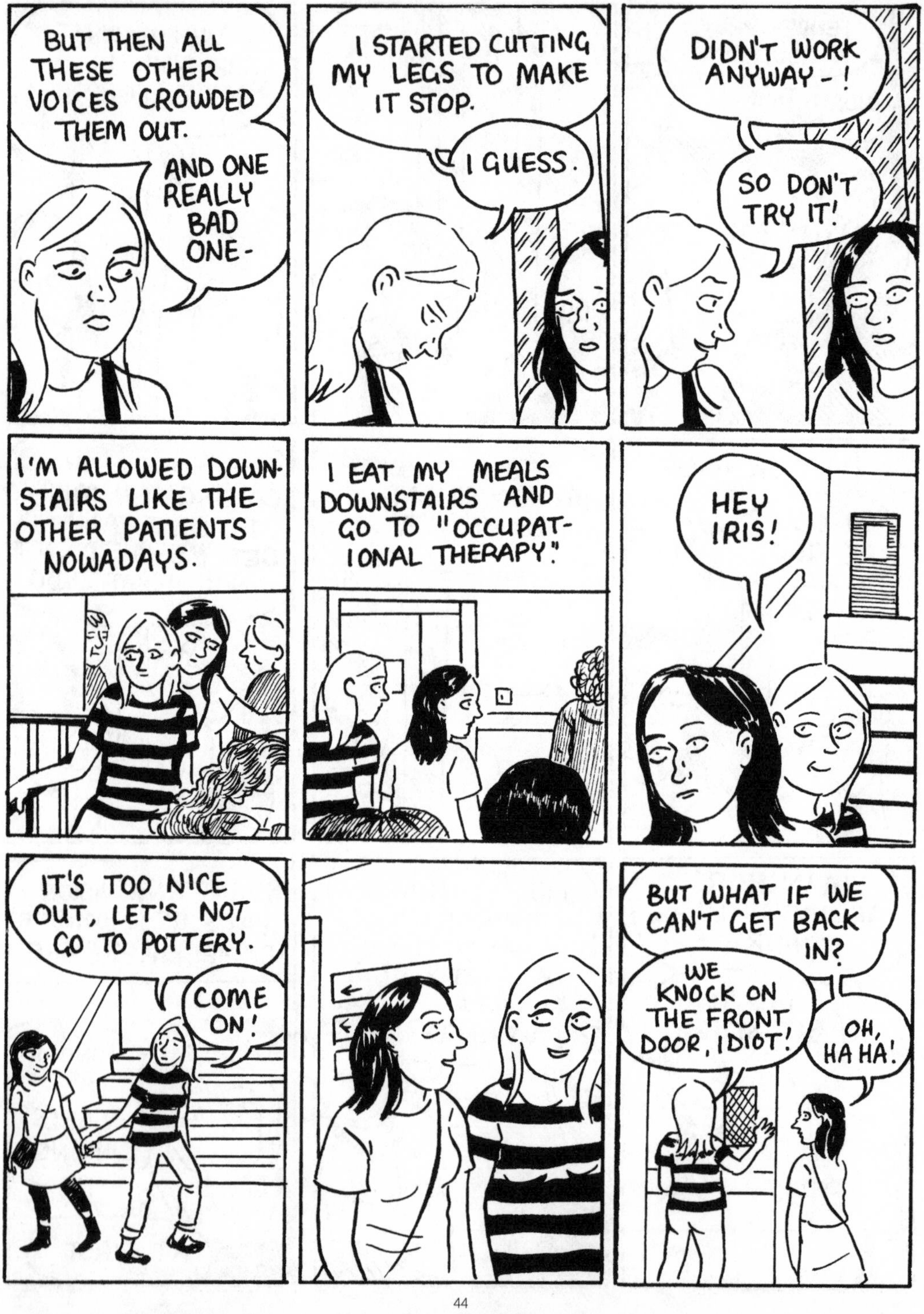

BUT THEN ALL THESE OTHER VOICES CROWDED THEM OUT.
AND ONE REALLY BAD ONE-
I STARTED CUTTING MY LEGS TO MAKE IT STOP.
I GUESS.
DIDN'T WORK ANYWAY-!
SO DON'T TRY IT!
I'M ALLOWED DOWN-STAIRS LIKE THE OTHER PATIENTS NOWADAYS.
I EAT MY MEALS DOWNSTAIRS AND GO TO "OCCUPAT-IONAL THERAPY."
HEY IRIS!
IT'S TOO NICE OUT, LET'S NOT GO TO POTTERY.
COME ON!
BUT WHAT IF WE CAN'T GET BACK IN?
WE KNOCK ON THE FRONT DOOR, IDIOT!
OH, HA HA!

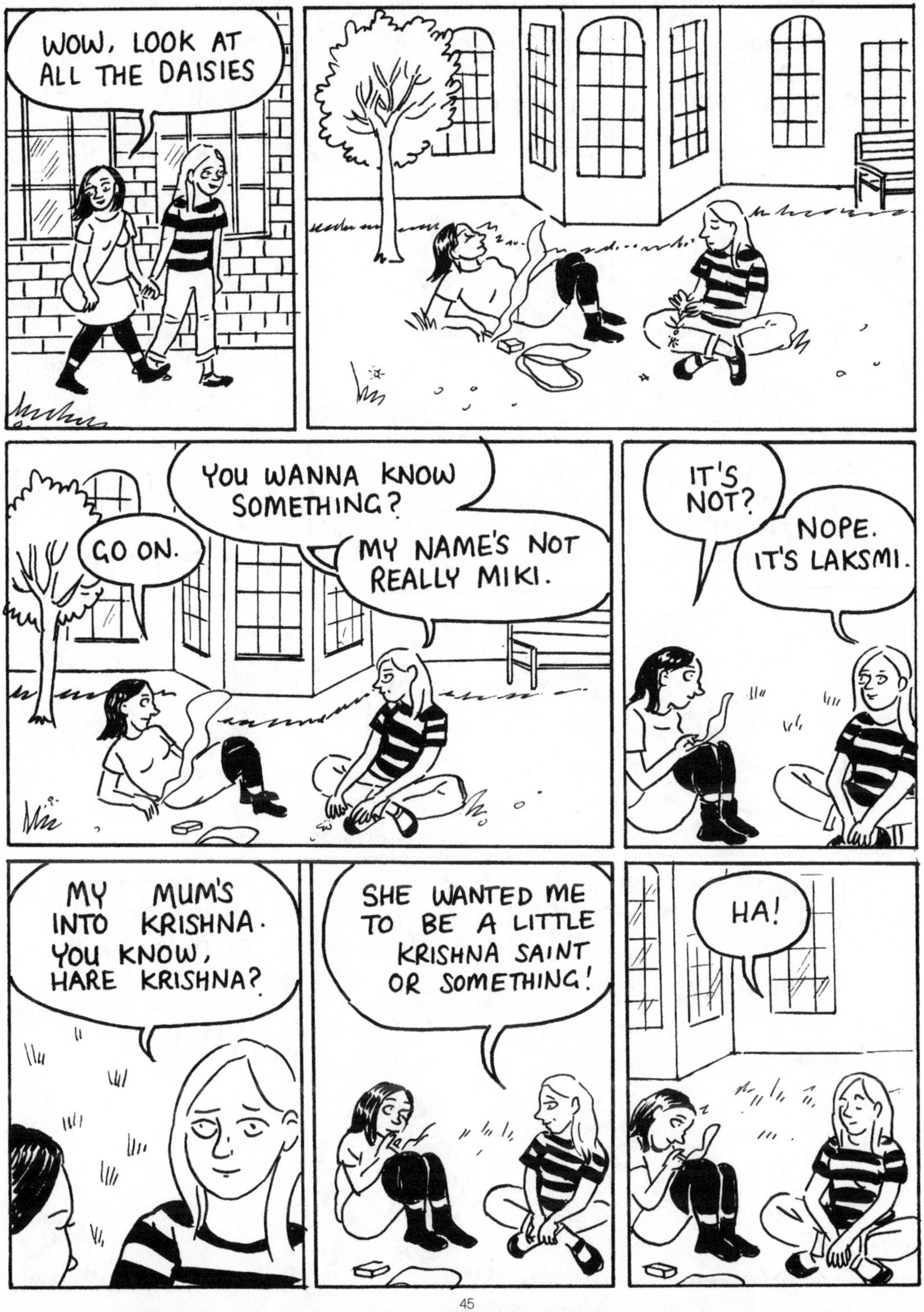
WOW, LOOK AT ALL THE DAISIES
YOU WANNA KNOW SOMETHING?
GO ON.
MY NAME'S NOT REALLY MIKI.
IT'S NOT?
NOPE. IT'S LAKSMI.
MY MUM'S INTO KRISHNA. YOU KNOW, HARE KRISHNA?
SHE WANTED ME TO BE A LITTLE KRISHNA SAINT OR SOMETHING!
HA!

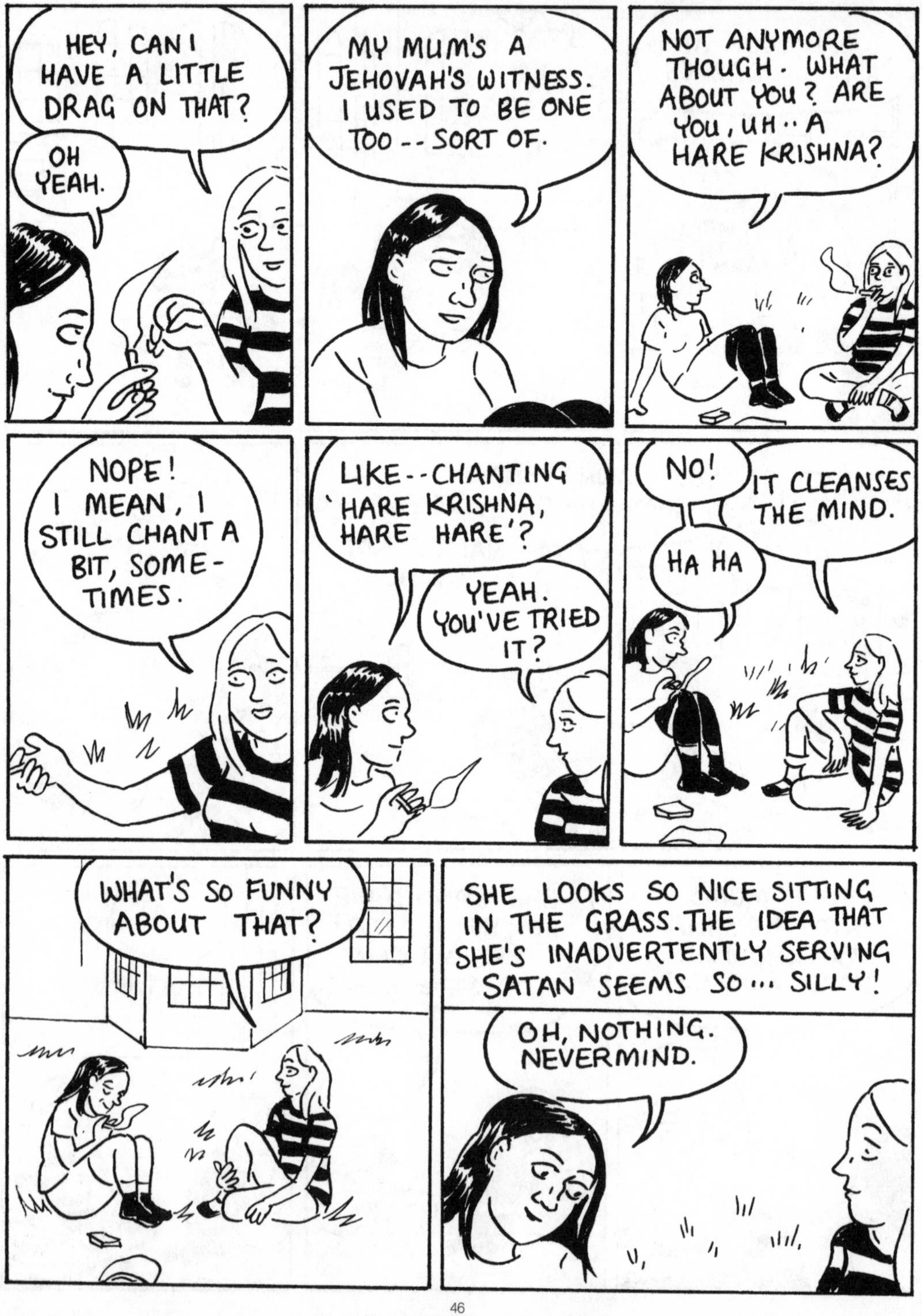
HEY, CAN I HAVE A LITTLE DRAG ON THAT?
OH YEAH.
MY MUM'S A JEHOVAH'S WITNESS. I USED TO BE ONE TOO -- SORT OF.
NOT ANYMORE THOUGH. WHAT ABOUT YOU? ARE YOU, UH.. A HARE KRISHNA?
NOPE! I MEAN, I STILL CHANT A BIT, SOME-TIMES.
LIKE--CHANTING 'HARE KRISHNA, HARE HARE'?
YEAH. YOU'VE TRIED IT?
NO!
HA HA
IT CLEANSES THE MIND.
WHAT'S SO FUNNY ABOUT THAT?
SHE LOOKS SO NICE SITTING IN THE GRASS. THE IDEA THAT SHE'S INADVERTENTLY SERVING SATAN SEEMS SO... SILLY!
OH, NOTHING. NEVERMIND.

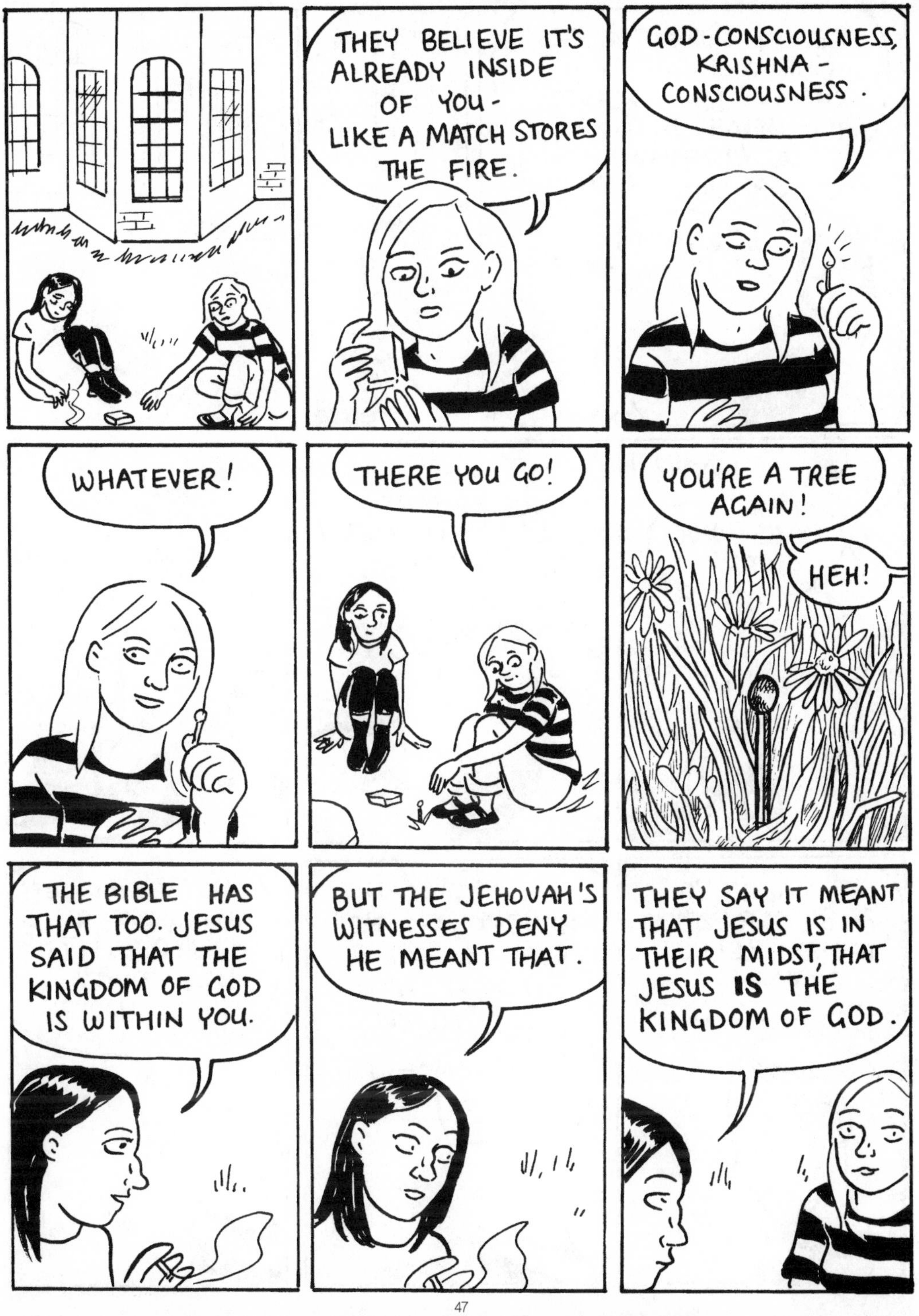
THEY BELIEVE IT'S ALREADY INSIDE OF YOU - LIKE A MATCH STORES THE FIRE.
GOD-CONSCIOUSNESS, KRISHNA-CONSCIOUSNESS.
WHATEVER!
THERE YOU GO!
YOU'RE A TREE AGAIN!
HEH!
THE BIBLE HAS THAT TOO. JESUS SAID THAT THE KINGDOM OF GOD IS WITHIN YOU.
BUT THE JEHOVAH'S WITNESSES DENY HE MEANT THAT.
THEY SAY IT MEANT THAT JESUS IS IN THEIR MIDST, THAT JESUS **IS** THE KINGDOM OF GOD.

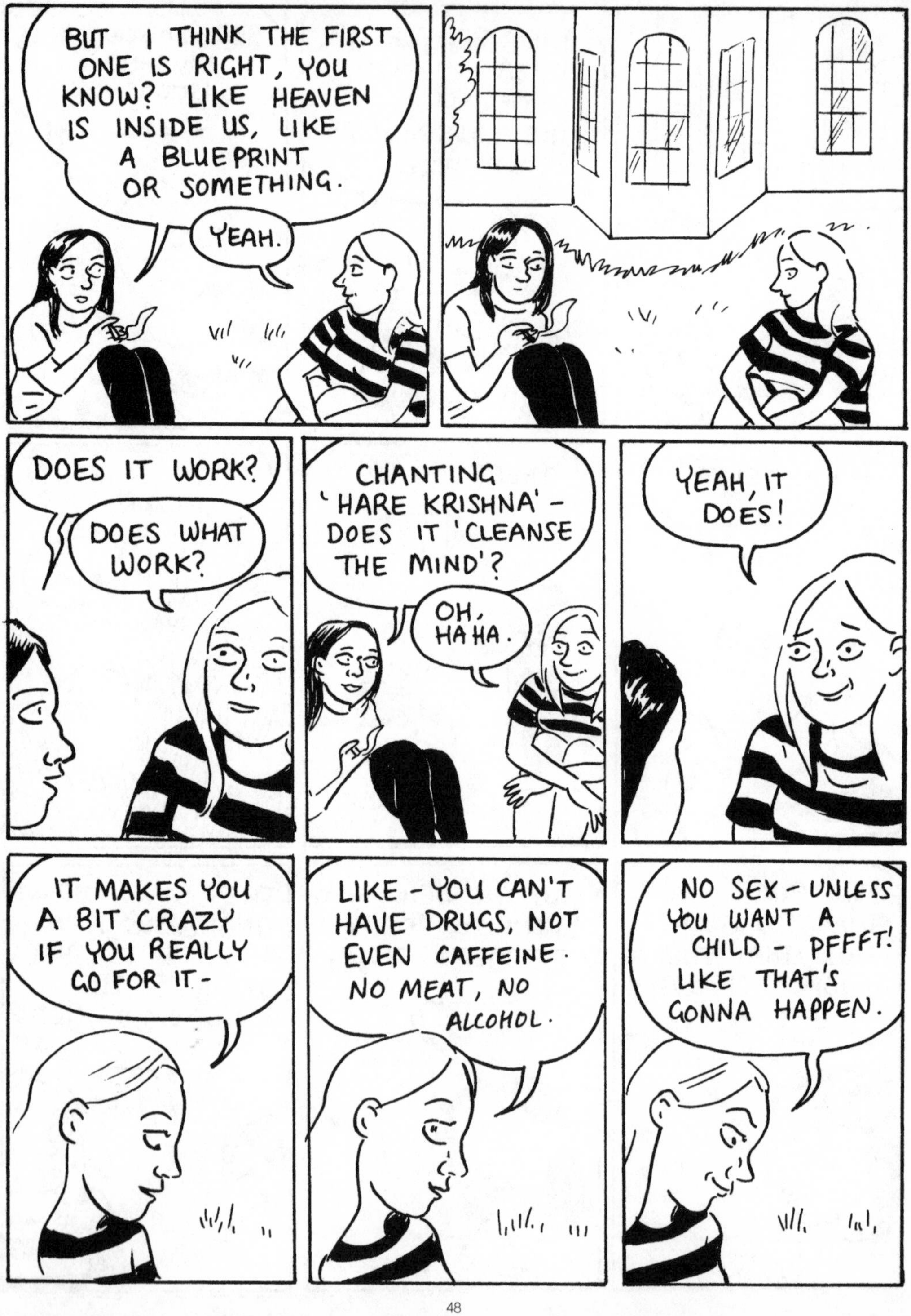
BUT I THINK THE FIRST ONE IS RIGHT, YOU KNOW? LIKE HEAVEN IS INSIDE US, LIKE A BLUEPRINT OR SOMETHING.
YEAH.
DOES IT WORK?
DOES WHAT WORK?
CHANTING 'HARE KRISHNA' - DOES IT 'CLEANSE THE MIND'?
OH, HA HA.
YEAH, IT DOES!
IT MAKES YOU A BIT CRAZY IF YOU REALLY GO FOR IT -
LIKE - YOU CAN'T HAVE DRUGS, NOT EVEN CAFFEINE. NO MEAT, NO ALCOHOL.
NO SEX - UNLESS YOU WANT A CHILD - PFFFT! LIKE THAT'S GONNA HAPPEN.

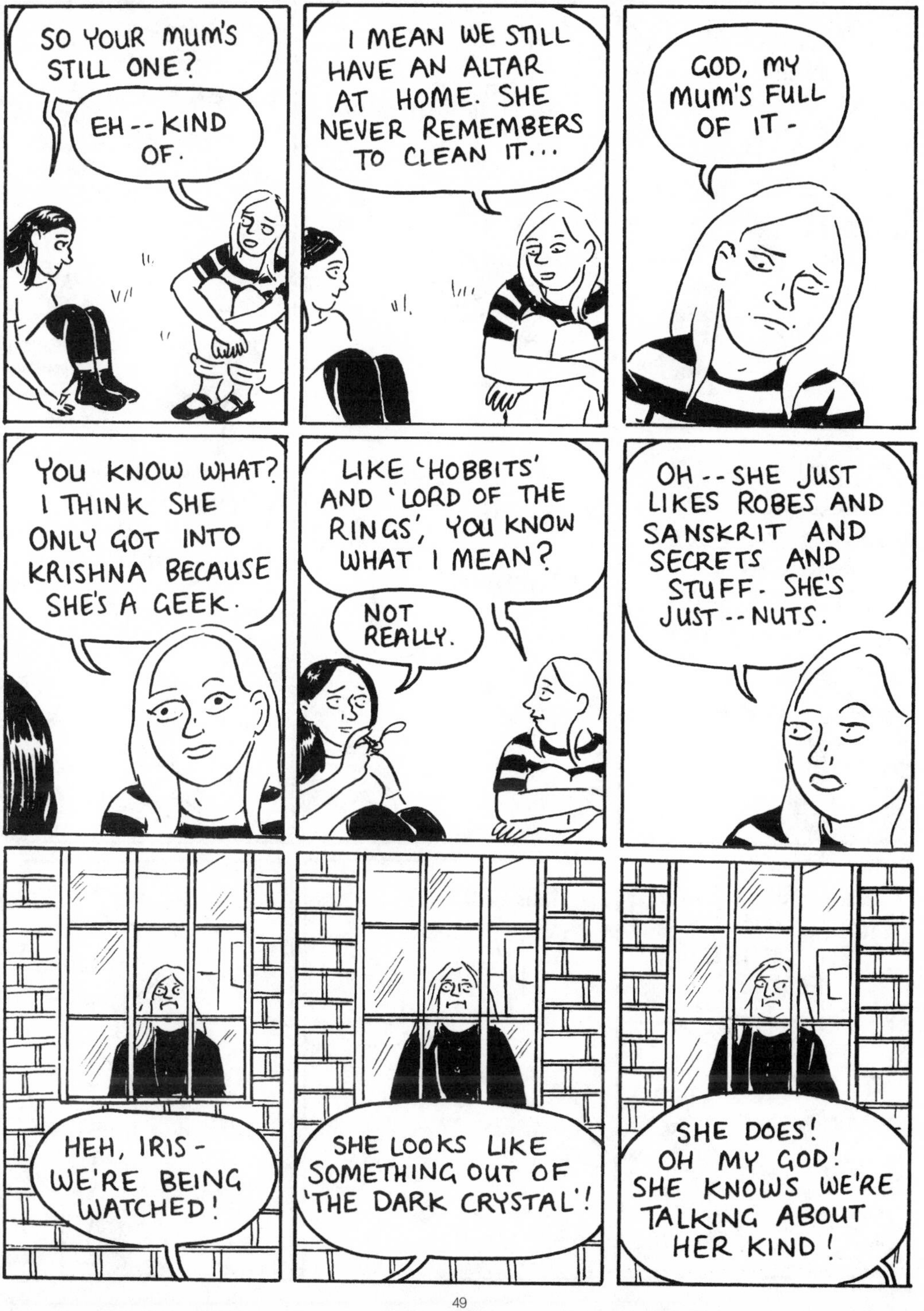
SO YOUR MUM'S STILL ONE?
EH -- KIND OF.
I MEAN WE STILL HAVE AN ALTAR AT HOME. SHE NEVER REMEMBERS TO CLEAN IT...
GOD, MY MUM'S FULL OF IT -
YOU KNOW WHAT? I THINK SHE ONLY GOT INTO KRISHNA BECAUSE SHE'S A GEEK.
LIKE 'HOBBITS' AND 'LORD OF THE RINGS', YOU KNOW WHAT I MEAN?
NOT REALLY.
OH -- SHE JUST LIKES ROBES AND SANSKRIT AND SECRETS AND STUFF. SHE'S JUST -- NUTS.
HEH, IRIS - WE'RE BEING WATCHED!
SHE LOOKS LIKE SOMETHING OUT OF 'THE DARK CRYSTAL'!
SHE DOES! OH MY GOD! SHE KNOWS WE'RE TALKING ABOUT HER KIND!

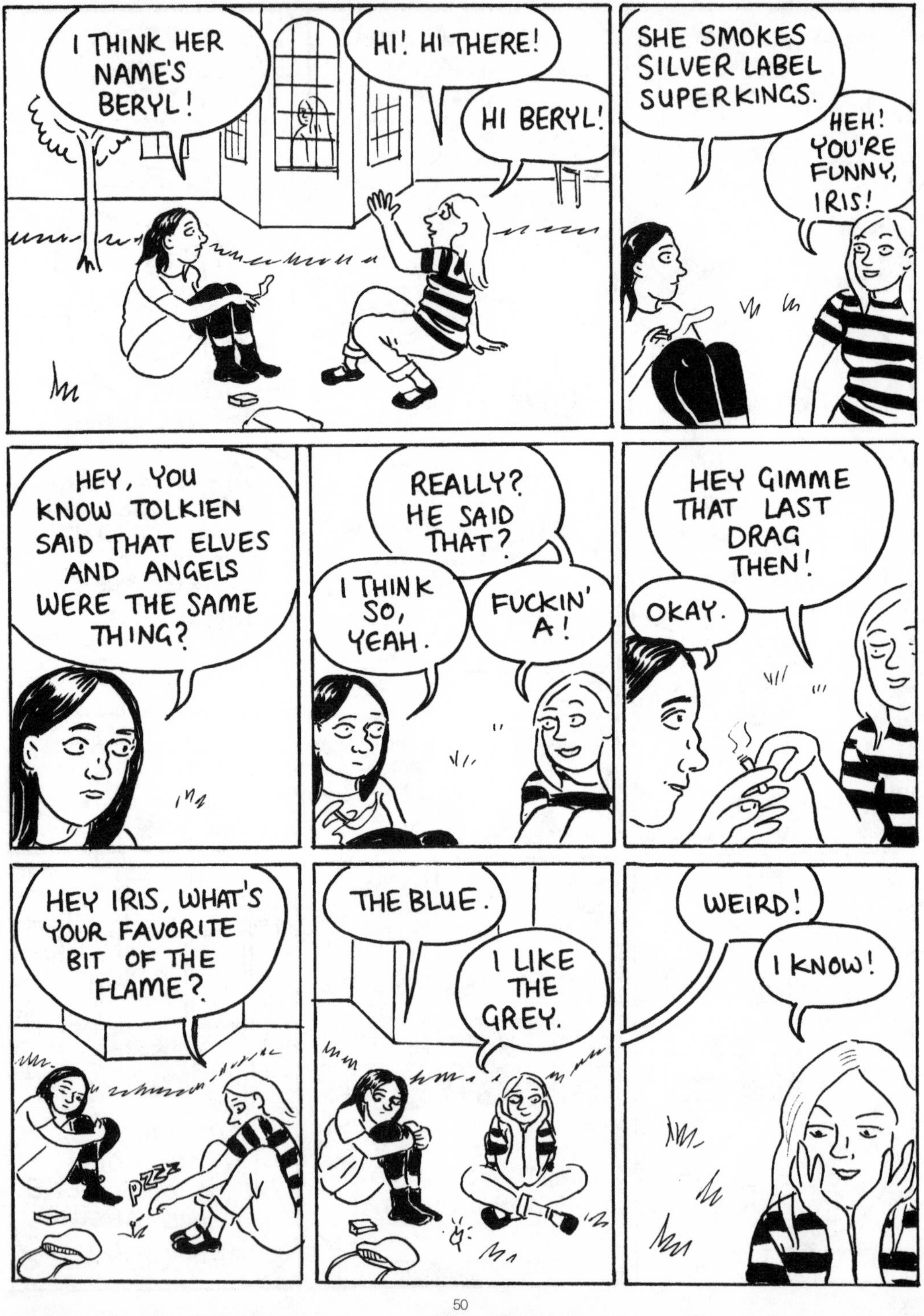
I THINK HER NAME'S BERYL!
HI! HI THERE!
HI BERYL!
SHE SMOKES SILVER LABEL SUPERKINGS.
HEH! YOU'RE FUNNY, IRIS!
HEY, YOU KNOW TOLKIEN SAID THAT ELVES AND ANGELS WERE THE SAME THING?
REALLY? HE SAID THAT?
I THINK SO, YEAH.
FUCKIN' A!
HEY GIMME THAT LAST DRAG THEN!
OKAY.
HEY IRIS, WHAT'S YOUR FAVORITE BIT OF THE FLAME?
PZZZ
THE BLUE.
I LIKE THE GREY.
WEIRD!
I KNOW!

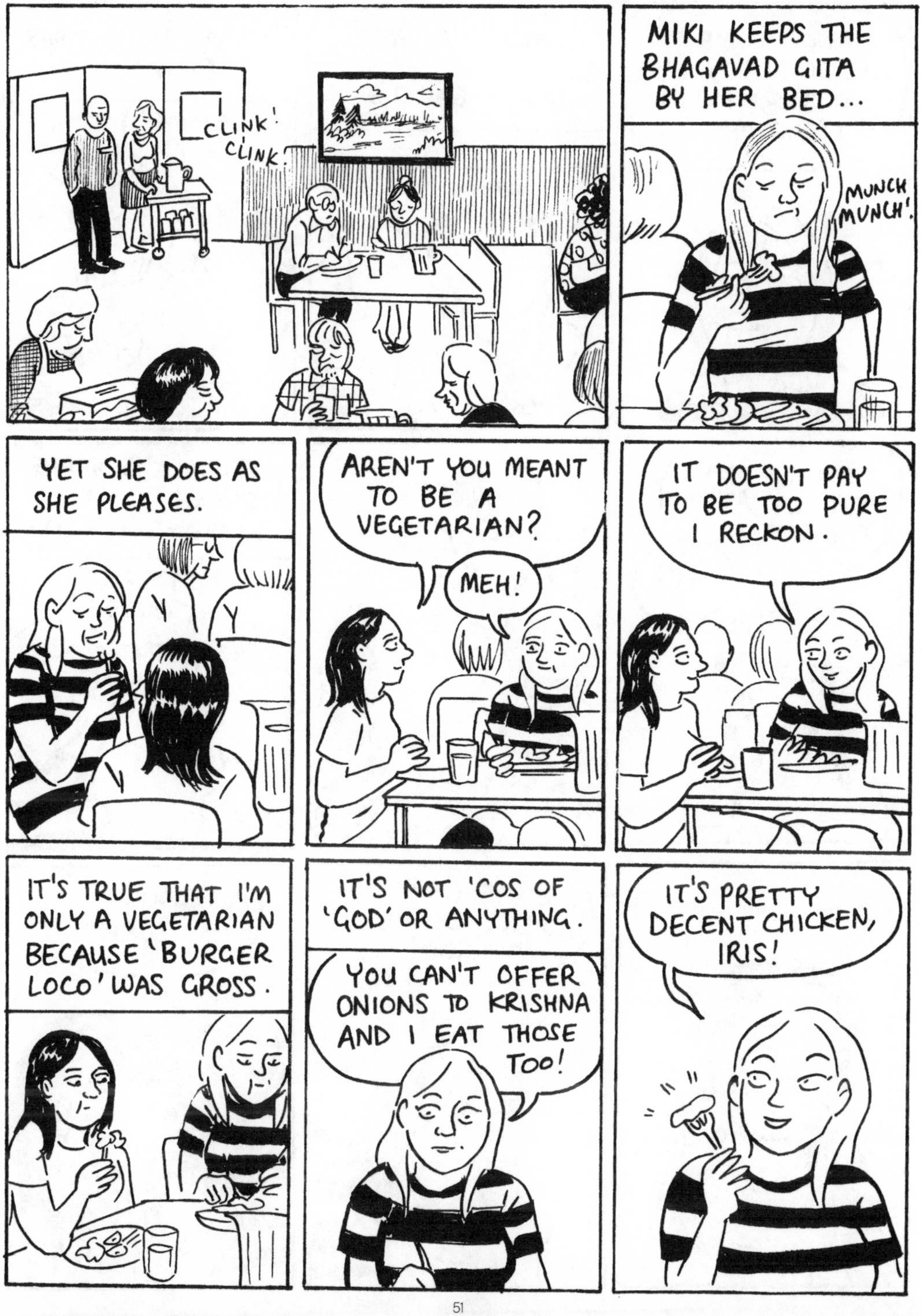
CLINK!
CLINK!
MIKI KEEPS THE BHAGAVAD GITA BY HER BED...
MUNCH MUNCH!
YET SHE DOES AS SHE PLEASES.
AREN'T YOU MEANT TO BE A VEGETARIAN?
MEH!
IT DOESN'T PAY TO BE TOO PURE I RECKON.
IT'S TRUE THAT I'M ONLY A VEGETARIAN BECAUSE 'BURGER LOCO' WAS GROSS.
IT'S NOT 'COS OF 'GOD' OR ANYTHING.
YOU CAN'T OFFER ONIONS TO KRISHNA AND I EAT THOSE TOO!
IT'S PRETTY DECENT CHICKEN, IRIS!

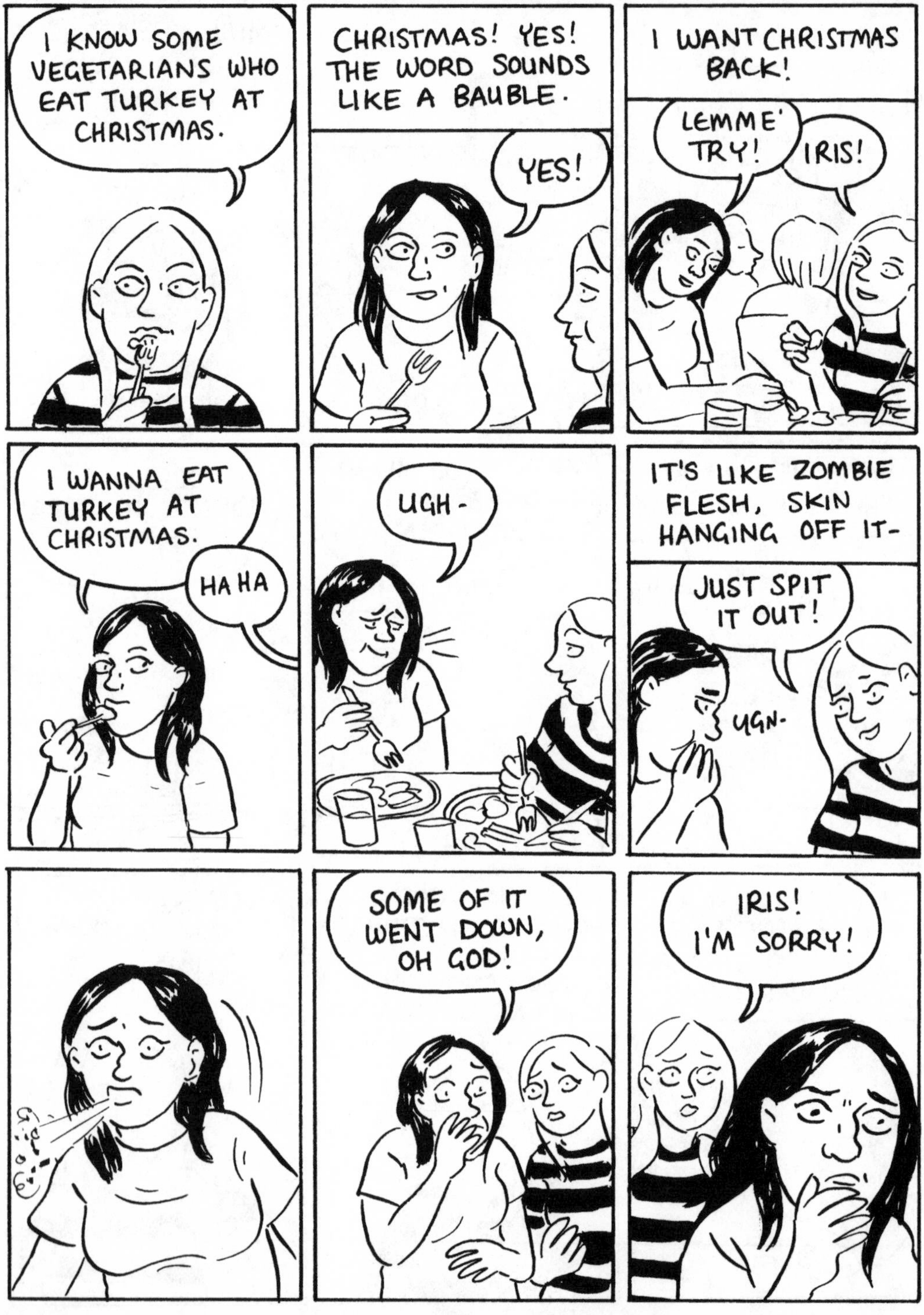
I KNOW SOME VEGETARIANS WHO EAT TURKEY AT CHRISTMAS.
CHRISTMAS! YES! THE WORD SOUNDS LIKE A BAUBLE.
YES!
I WANT CHRISTMAS BACK!
LEMME' TRY!
IRIS!
I WANNA EAT TURKEY AT CHRISTMAS.
HA HA
UGH-
IT'S LIKE ZOMBIE FLESH, SKIN HANGING OFF IT-
JUST SPIT IT OUT!
UGN-
SOME OF IT WENT DOWN, OH GOD!
IRIS! I'M SORRY!

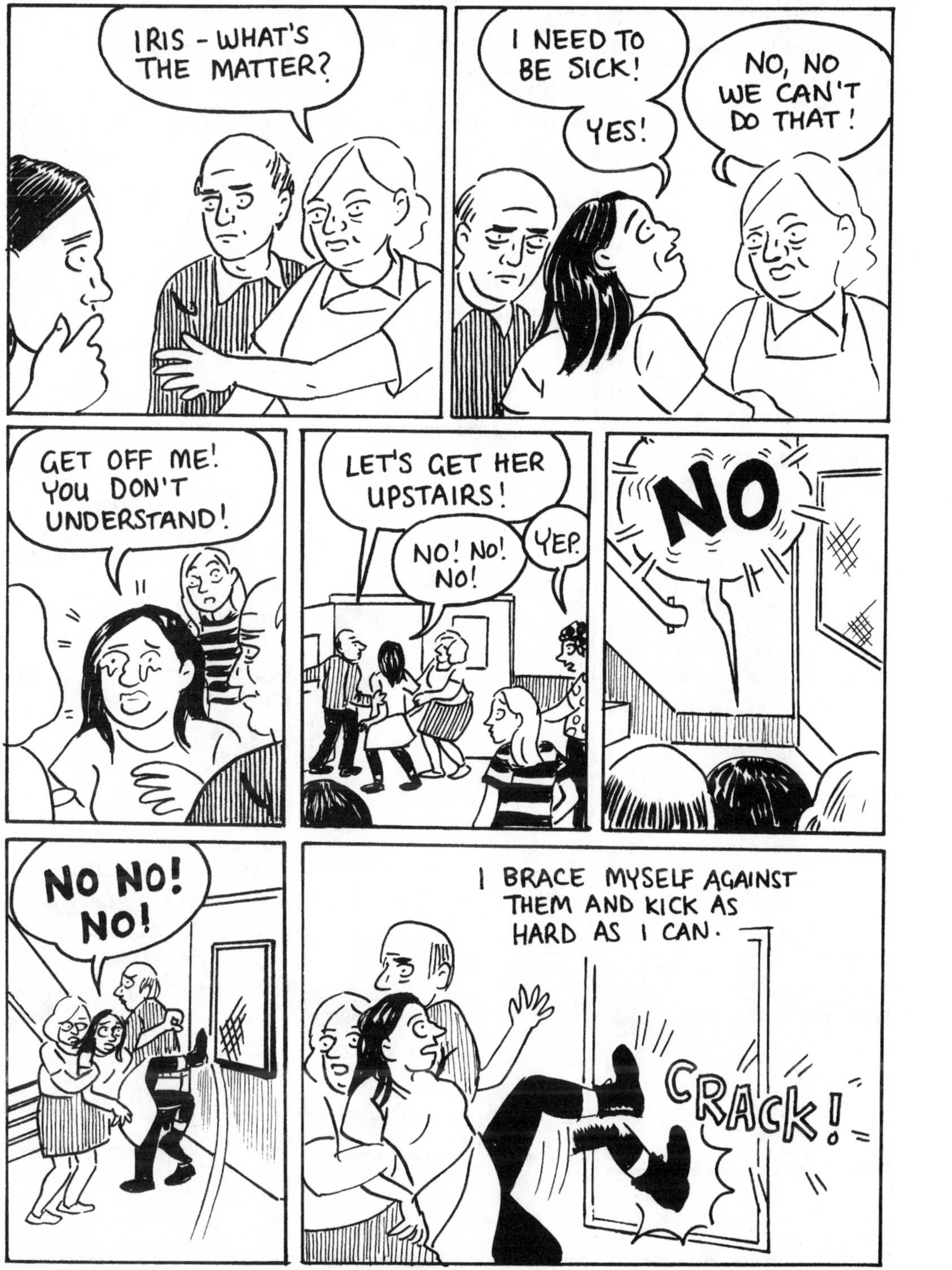
IRIS - WHAT'S THE MATTER?
I NEED TO BE SICK!
YES!
NO, NO WE CAN'T DO THAT!
GET OFF ME! YOU DON'T UNDERSTAND!
LET'S GET HER UPSTAIRS!
NO! NO! NO!
YEP.
NO
NO NO! NO!
I BRACE MYSELF AGAINST THEM AND KICK AS HARD AS I CAN.
CRACK!

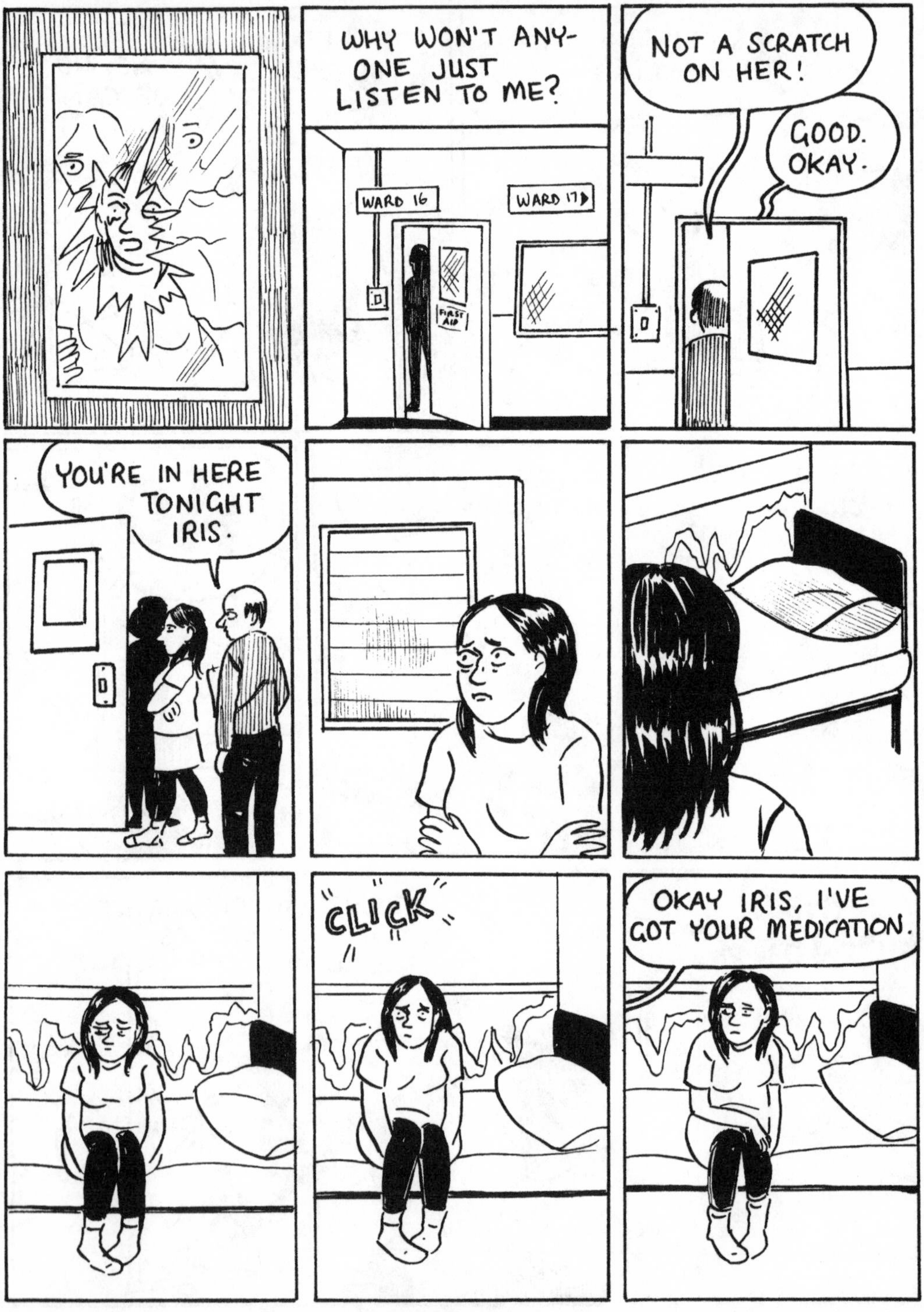
WHY WON'T ANYONE JUST LISTEN TO ME?
WARD 16
WARD 17
FIRST AID
NOT A SCRATCH ON HER!
GOOD. OKAY.
YOU'RE IN HERE TONIGHT IRIS.
CLICK
OKAY IRIS, I'VE GOT YOUR MEDICATION.

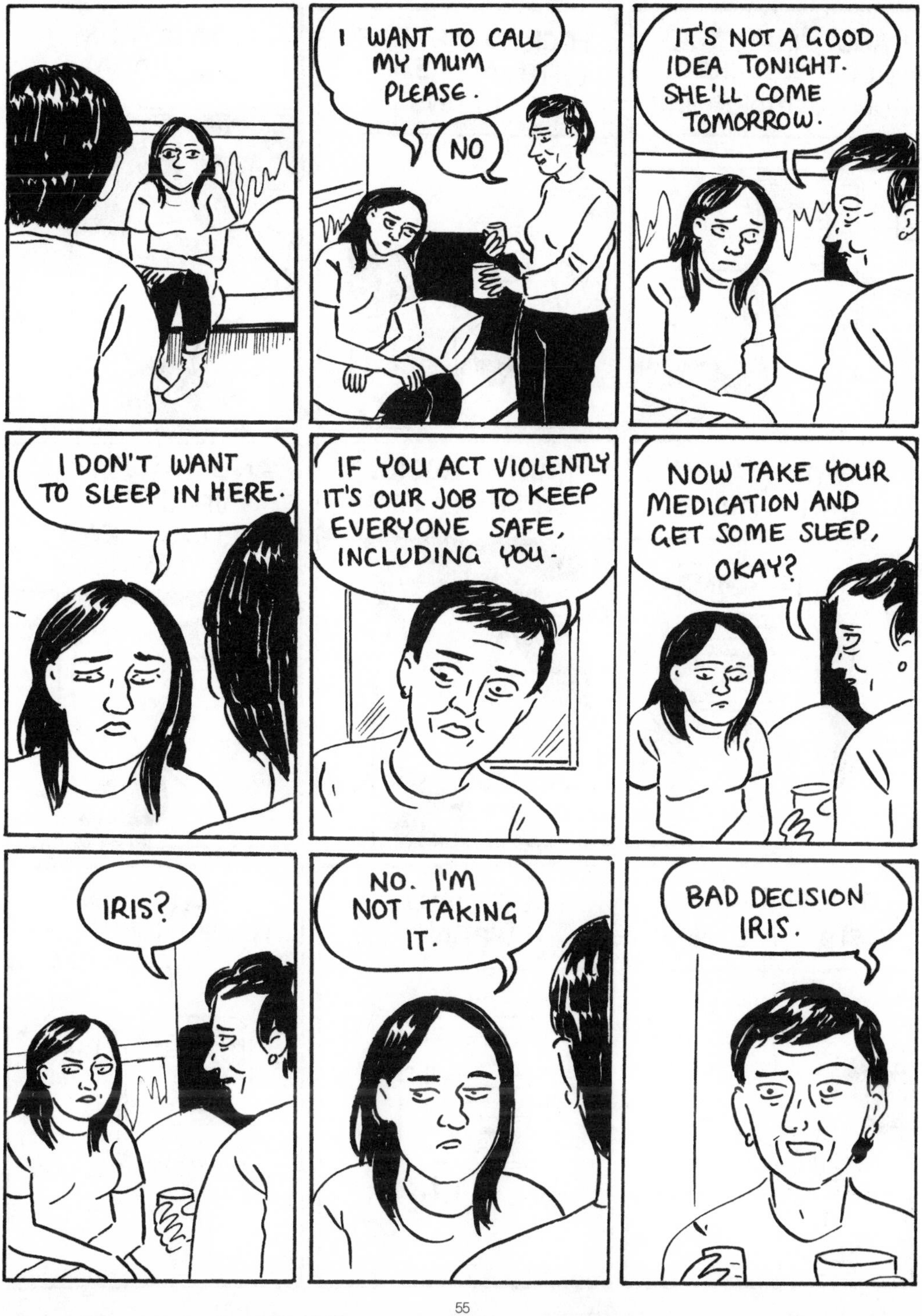
I WANT TO CALL MY MUM PLEASE.
NO
IT'S NOT A GOOD IDEA TONIGHT. SHE'LL COME TOMORROW.
I DON'T WANT TO SLEEP IN HERE.
IF YOU ACT VIOLENTLY IT'S OUR JOB TO KEEP EVERYONE SAFE, INCLUDING YOU.
NOW TAKE YOUR MEDICATION AND GET SOME SLEEP, OKAY?
IRIS?
NO. I'M NOT TAKING IT.
BAD DECISION IRIS.

AND THEN THE DOOR IS LOCKED UNTIL MORNING.
LOCKED IN HERE WITH MY BAD DECISIONS.
I HATE THIS PINK ROOM.
I HATE IT'S WEIRD NOISES.
EXPELAIR
WHIRRRRRR
THINGS WERE ALREADY BAD-
AND NOW? NOW I'VE EATEN ACTUAL DEAD FLESH.
IT'S DISSOLVING INSIDE ME NOW.
WHAT WILL HAPPEN?
EXPEL AIR
CLICK!
WHAT WILL HAPPEN TO ME?
EXPEL AIR

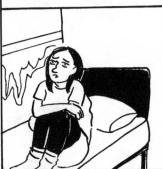

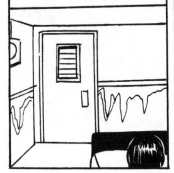

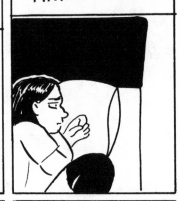

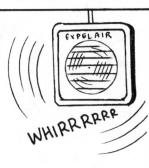

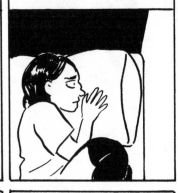

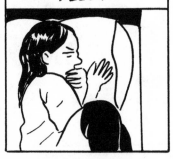

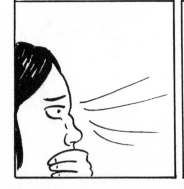

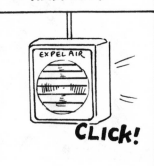

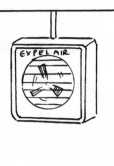

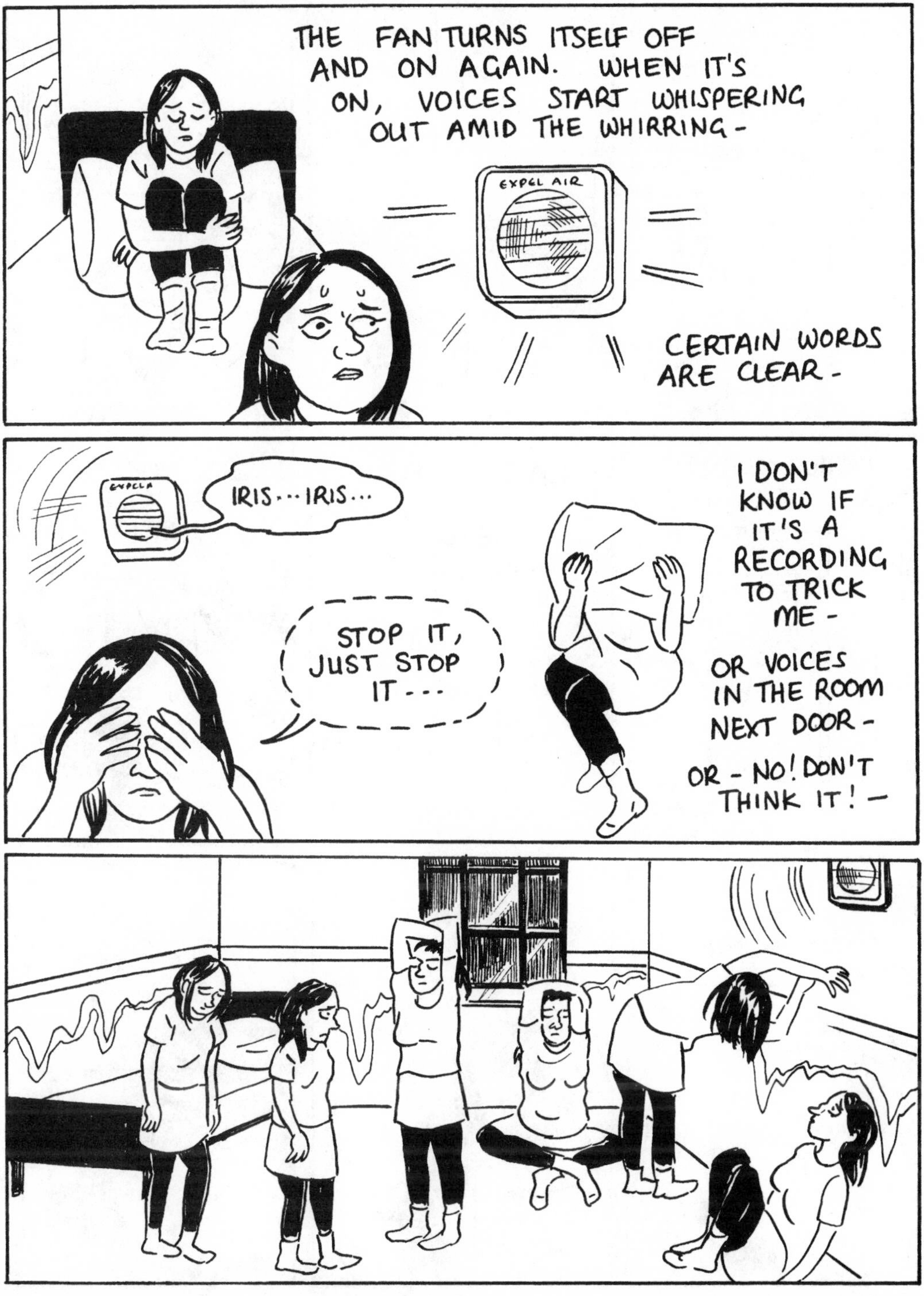
THE FAN TURNS ITSELF OFF AND ON AGAIN. WHEN IT'S ON, VOICES START WHISPERING OUT AMID THE WHIRRING-
EXPEL AIR
CERTAIN WORDS ARE CLEAR-
IRIS... IRIS...
STOP IT, JUST STOP IT...
I DON'T KNOW IF IT'S A RECORDING TO TRICK ME-
OR VOICES IN THE ROOM NEXT DOOR-
OR - NO! DON'T THINK IT! -

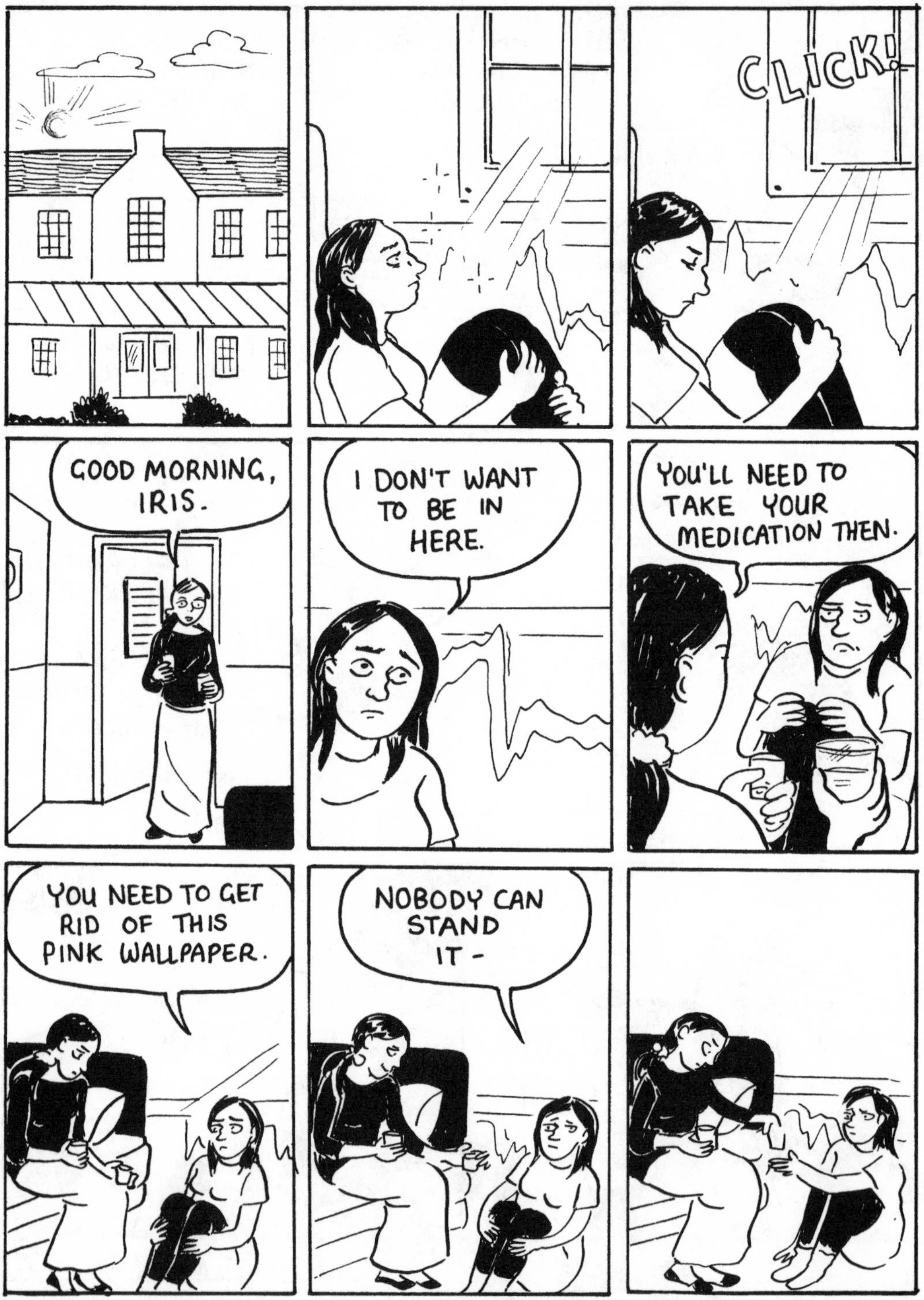
CLICK!
GOOD MORNING, IRIS.
I DON'T WANT TO BE IN HERE.
YOU'LL NEED TO TAKE YOUR MEDICATION THEN.
YOU NEED TO GET RID OF THIS PINK WALLPAPER.
NOBODY CAN STAND IT -

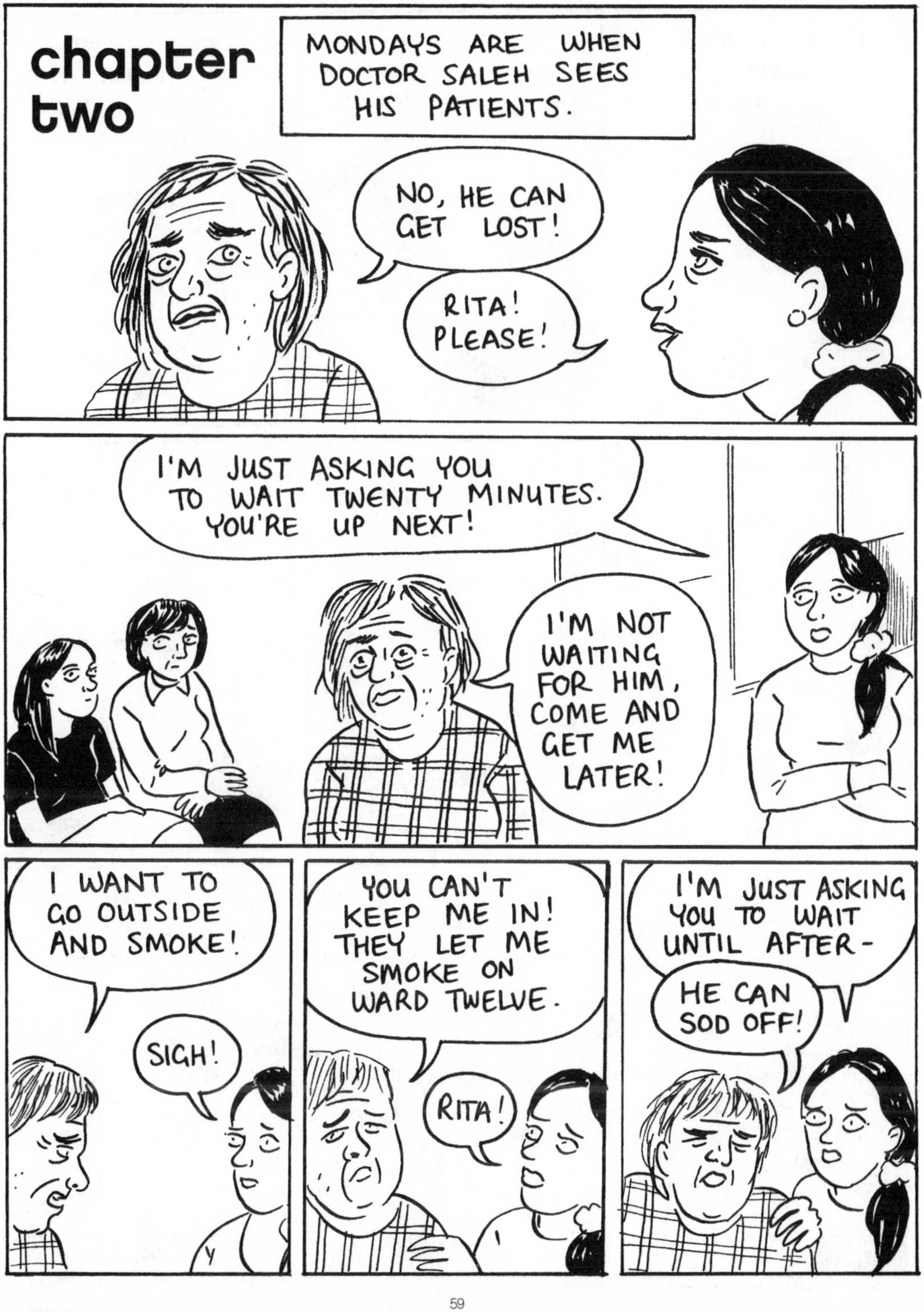
chapter two
MONDAYS ARE WHEN DOCTOR SALEH SEES HIS PATIENTS.
NO, HE CAN GET LOST!
RITA! PLEASE!
I'M JUST ASKING YOU TO WAIT TWENTY MINUTES. YOU'RE UP NEXT!
I'M NOT WAITING FOR HIM, COME AND GET ME LATER!
I WANT TO GO OUTSIDE AND SMOKE!
SIGH!
YOU CAN'T KEEP ME IN! THEY LET ME SMOKE ON WARD TWELVE.
RITA!
I'M JUST ASKING YOU TO WAIT UNTIL AFTER-
HE CAN SOD OFF!

AH, IRIS, MRS. NEUFIELD - HOW ARE WE BOTH?
THIS IS DOCTOR SALEH, I DON'T LIKE HIM MUCH.
THERE'S SOMETHING STALE ABOUT HIM. HE CAN'T SMILE PROPERLY.
.... PURSUE THE BEST TREAT-MENT... BLAH BLAH ..
I KNOW NOT TO TELL HIM ANYTHING.
THAT WE WORK TOGETHER TO GET YOU WELL-
IRIS- WHEN YOU WON'T TALK TO ME, IT IS NOT PRODUCTIVE, IS IT?
NOD
WE GO AROUND IN CIRCLES, YOU SEE?
YES! CIRCLES!
SNICKER!
IS THERE ANY AUDITORY INTERFERENCE, HEARING VOICES AND SO FORTH?
YES, I CAN HEAR YOU!

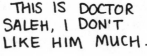

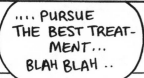

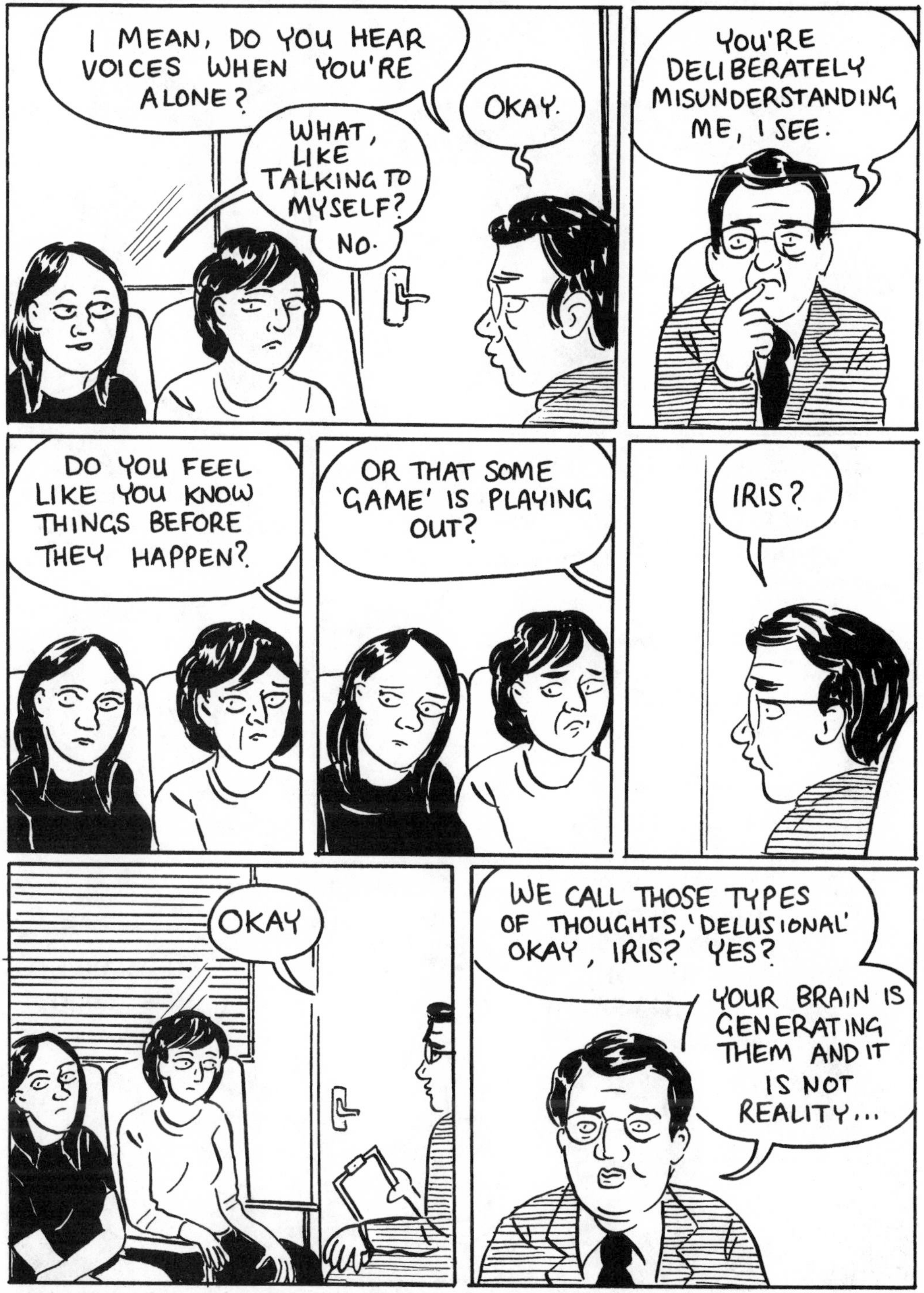
I MEAN, DO YOU HEAR VOICES WHEN YOU'RE ALONE?
WHAT, LIKE TALKING TO MYSELF? NO.
OKAY.
YOU'RE DELIBERATELY MISUNDERSTANDING ME, I SEE.
DO YOU FEEL LIKE YOU KNOW THINGS BEFORE THEY HAPPEN?
OR THAT SOME 'GAME' IS PLAYING OUT?
IRIS?
OKAY
WE CALL THOSE TYPES OF THOUGHTS, 'DELUSIONAL' OKAY, IRIS? YES?
YOUR BRAIN IS GENERATING THEM AND IT IS NOT REALITY...

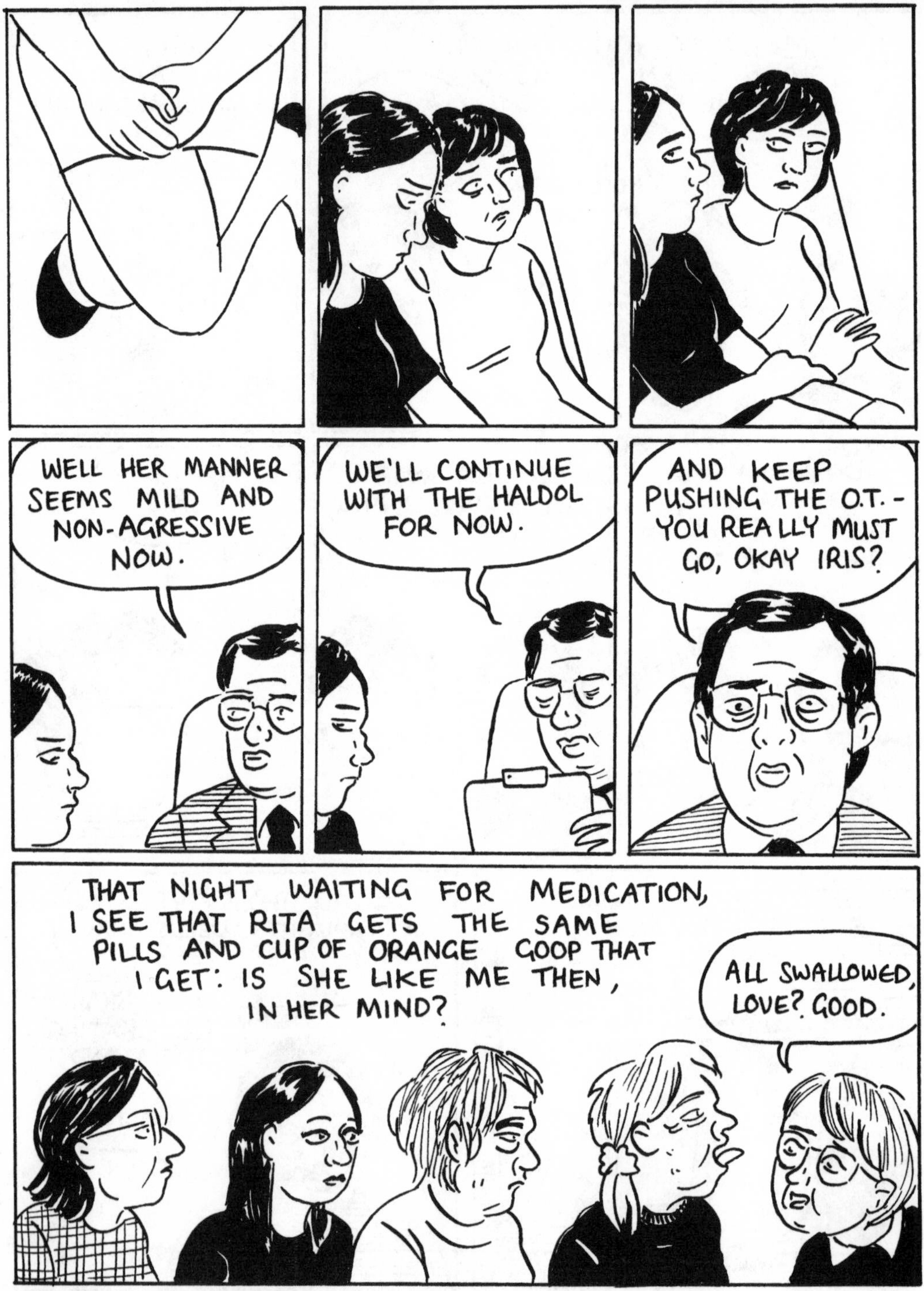
WELL HER MANNER SEEMS MILD AND NON-AGRESSIVE NOW.
WE'LL CONTINUE WITH THE HALDOL FOR NOW.
AND KEEP PUSHING THE O.T. - YOU REALLY MUST GO, OKAY IRIS?
THAT NIGHT WAITING FOR MEDICATION, I SEE THAT RITA GETS THE SAME PILLS AND CUP OF ORANGE GOOP THAT I GET: IS SHE LIKE ME THEN, IN HER MIND?
ALL SWALLOWED, LOVE? GOOD.

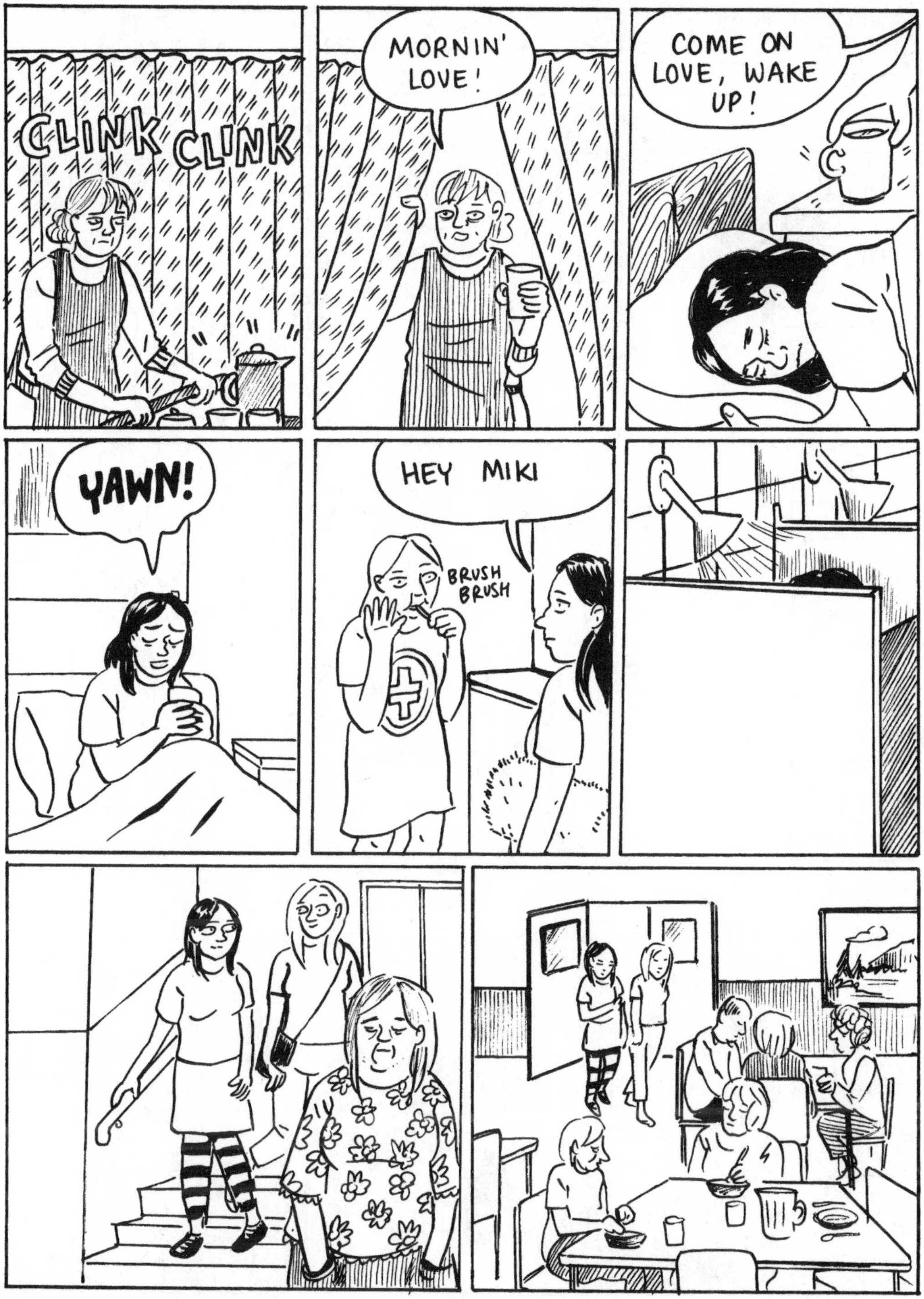
CLINK CLINK
MORNIN' LOVE!
COME ON LOVE, WAKE UP!
YAWN!
HEY MIKI
BRUSH BRUSH

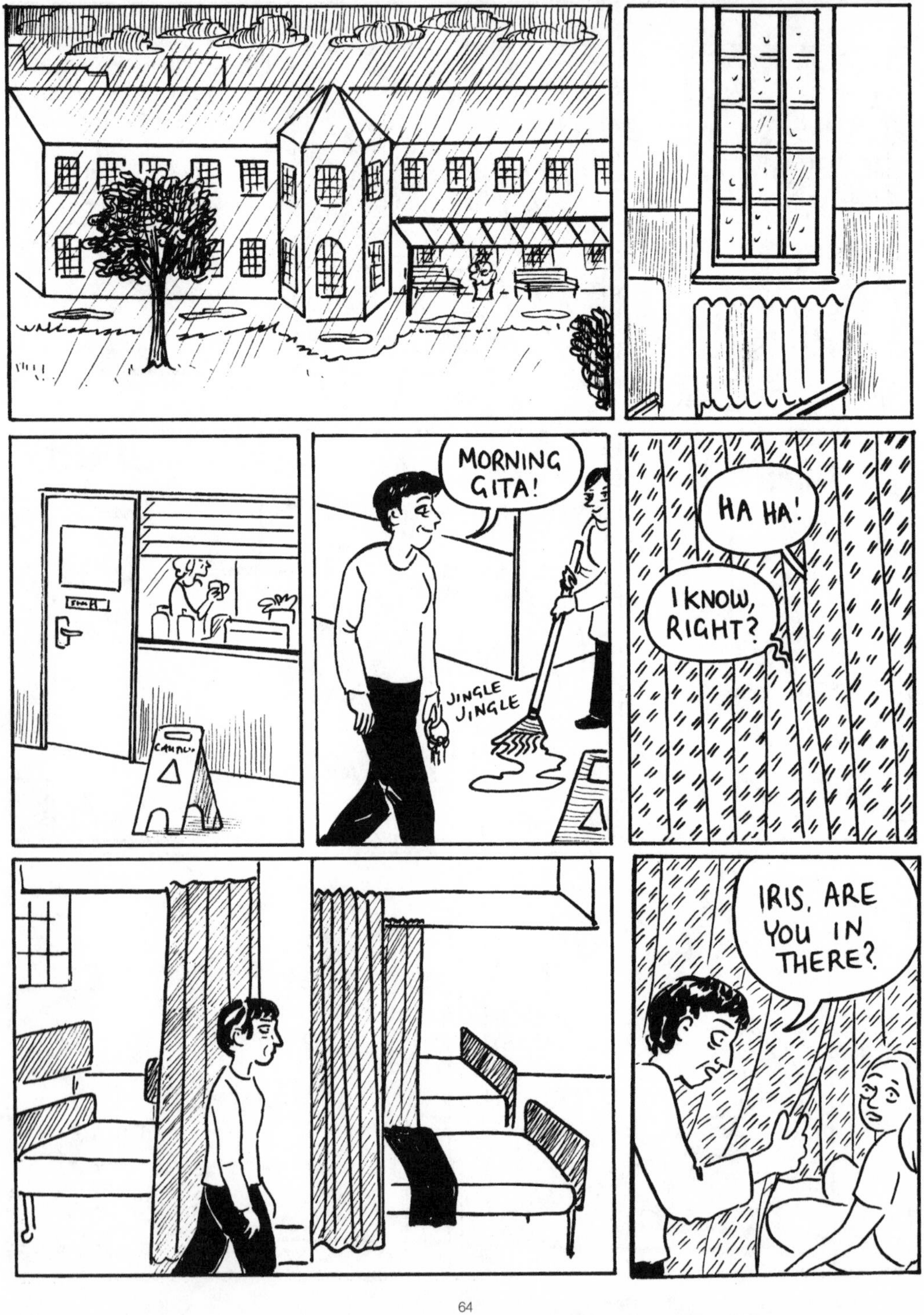
MORNING GITA!
JINGLE JINGLE
HA HA!
I KNOW, RIGHT?
IRIS, ARE YOU IN THERE?

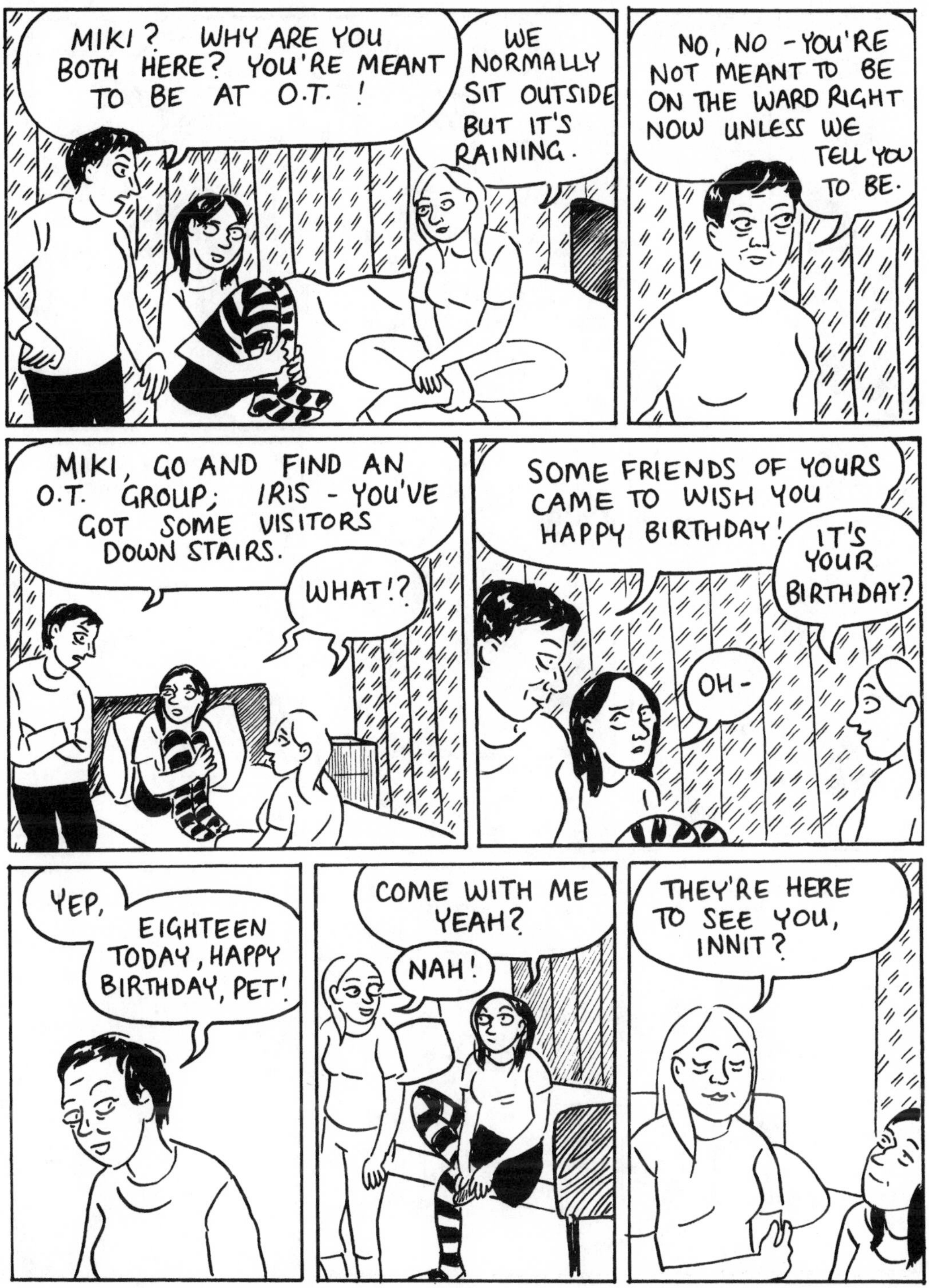
MIKI? WHY ARE YOU BOTH HERE? YOU'RE MEANT TO BE AT O.T.!
WE NORMALLY SIT OUTSIDE BUT IT'S RAINING.
NO, NO - YOU'RE NOT MEANT TO BE ON THE WARD RIGHT NOW UNLESS WE TELL YOU TO BE.
MIKI, GO AND FIND AN O.T. GROUP; IRIS - YOU'VE GOT SOME VISITORS DOWN STAIRS.
WHAT!?
SOME FRIENDS OF YOURS CAME TO WISH YOU HAPPY BIRTHDAY!
IT'S YOUR BIRTHDAY?
OH-
YEP, EIGHTEEN TODAY, HAPPY BIRTHDAY, PET!
COME WITH ME YEAH?
NAH!
THEY'RE HERE TO SEE YOU, INNIT?

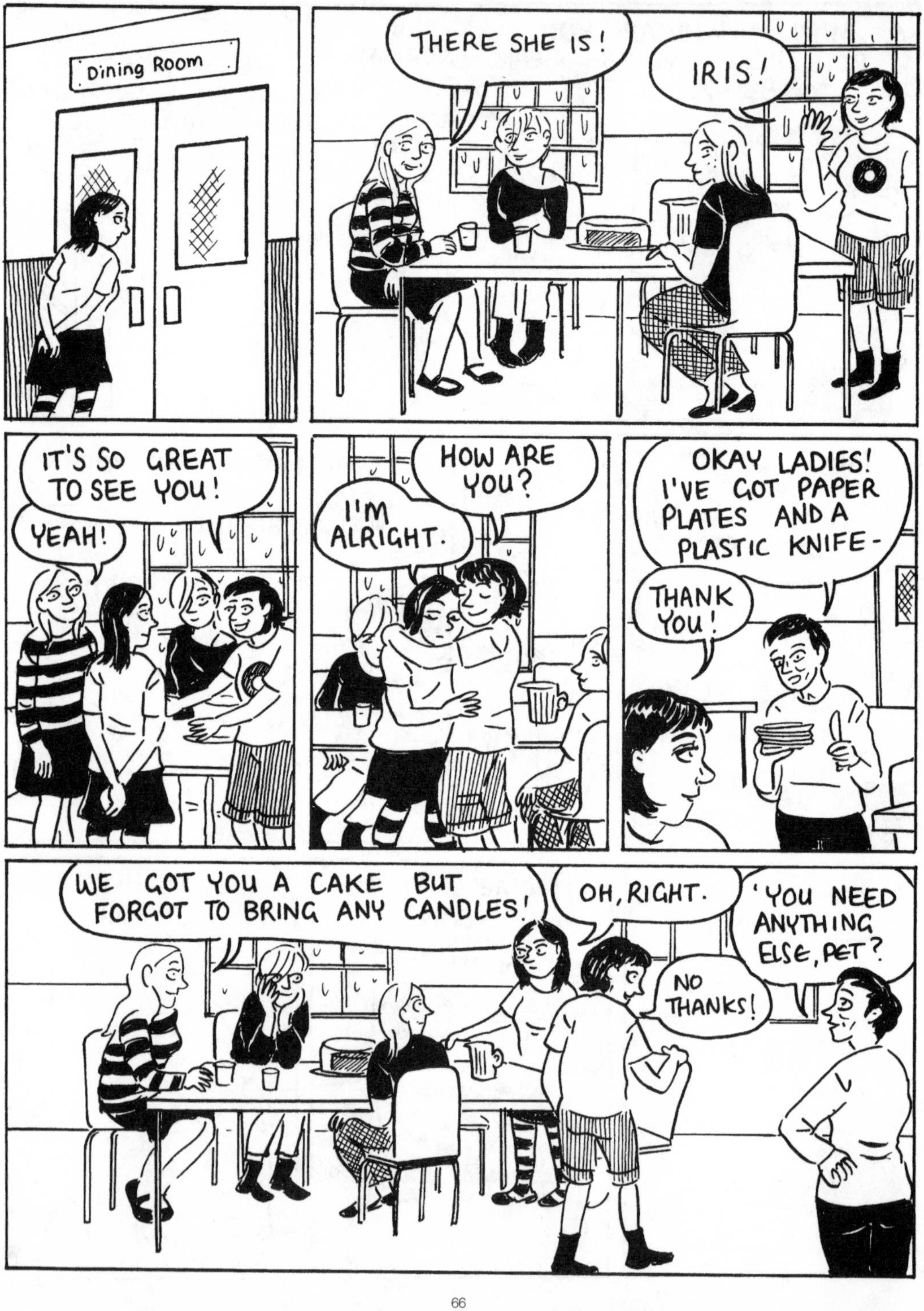
Dining Room
THERE SHE IS!
IRIS!
IT'S SO GREAT TO SEE YOU!
YEAH!
HOW ARE YOU?
I'M ALRIGHT.
OKAY LADIES! I'VE GOT PAPER PLATES AND A PLASTIC KNIFE-
THANK YOU!
WE GOT YOU A CAKE BUT FORGOT TO BRING ANY CANDLES!
OH, RIGHT.
'YOU NEED ANYTHING ELSE, PET?
NO THANKS!

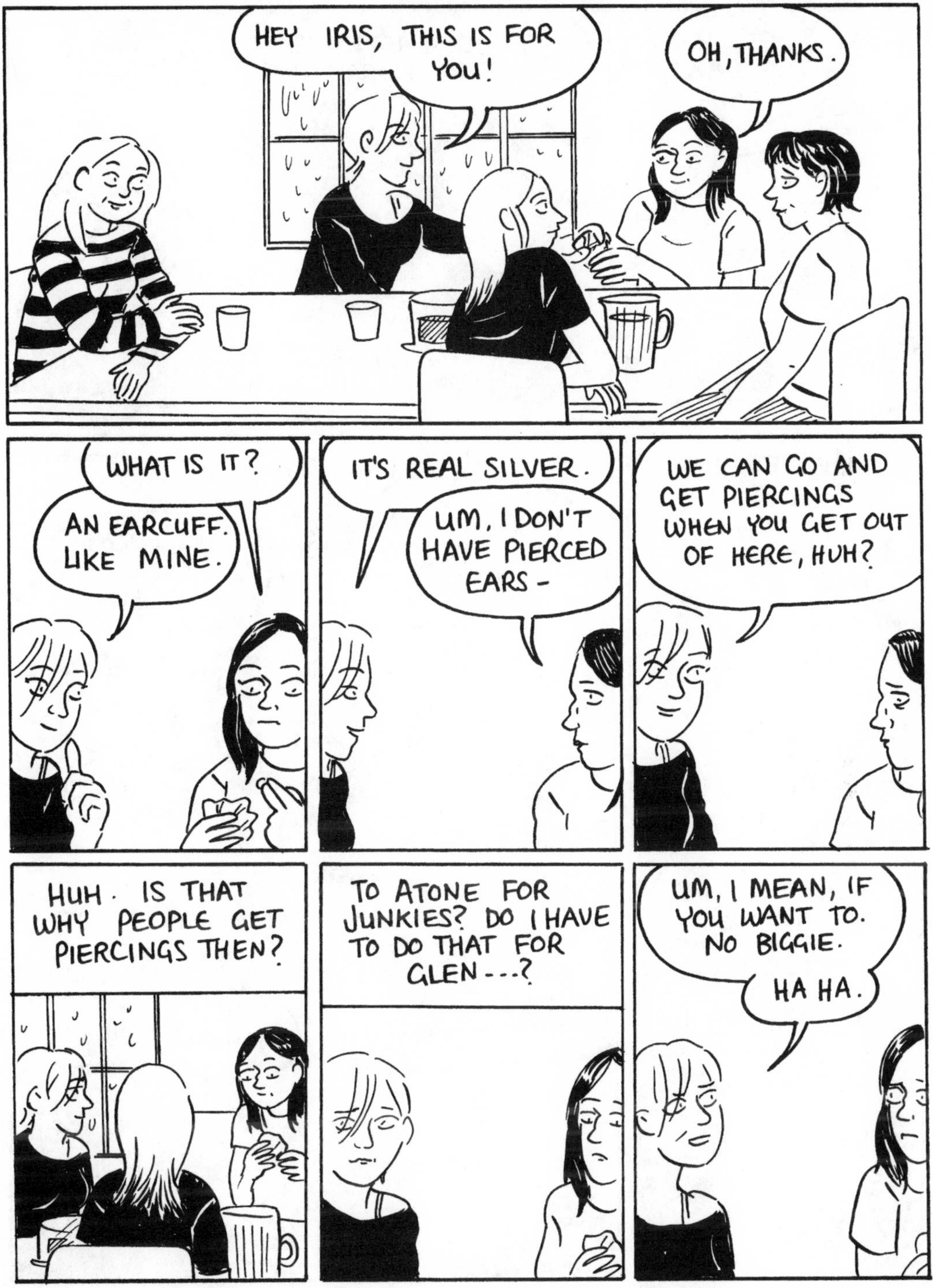
HEY IRIS, THIS IS FOR YOU!
OH, THANKS.
WHAT IS IT?
AN EARCUFF. LIKE MINE.
IT'S REAL SILVER.
UM, I DON'T HAVE PIERCED EARS -
WE CAN GO AND GET PIERCINGS WHEN YOU GET OUT OF HERE, HUH?
HUH. IS THAT WHY PEOPLE GET PIERCINGS THEN?
TO ATONE FOR JUNKIES? DO I HAVE TO DO THAT FOR GLEN---?
UM, I MEAN, IF YOU WANT TO. NO BIGGIE.
HA HA.

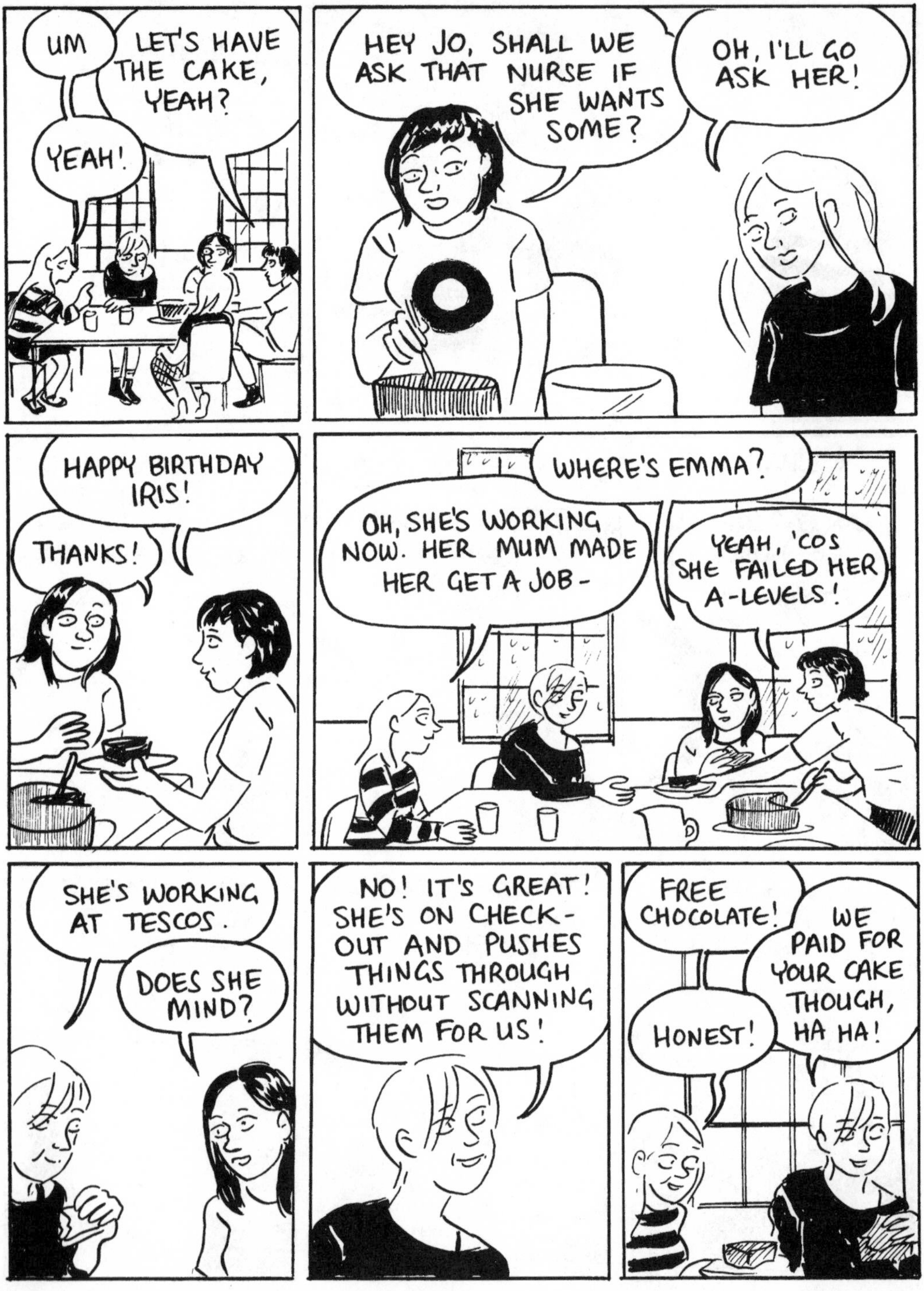
UM
LET'S HAVE THE CAKE, YEAH?
YEAH!
HEY JO, SHALL WE ASK THAT NURSE IF SHE WANTS SOME?
OH, I'LL GO ASK HER!
HAPPY BIRTHDAY IRIS!
THANKS!
WHERE'S EMMA?
OH, SHE'S WORKING NOW. HER MUM MADE HER GET A JOB -
YEAH, 'COS SHE FAILED HER A-LEVELS!
SHE'S WORKING AT TESCOS.
DOES SHE MIND?
NO! IT'S GREAT! SHE'S ON CHECK-OUT AND PUSHES THINGS THROUGH WITHOUT SCANNING THEM FOR US!
FREE CHOCOLATE!
HONEST!
WE PAID FOR YOUR CAKE THOUGH, HA HA!

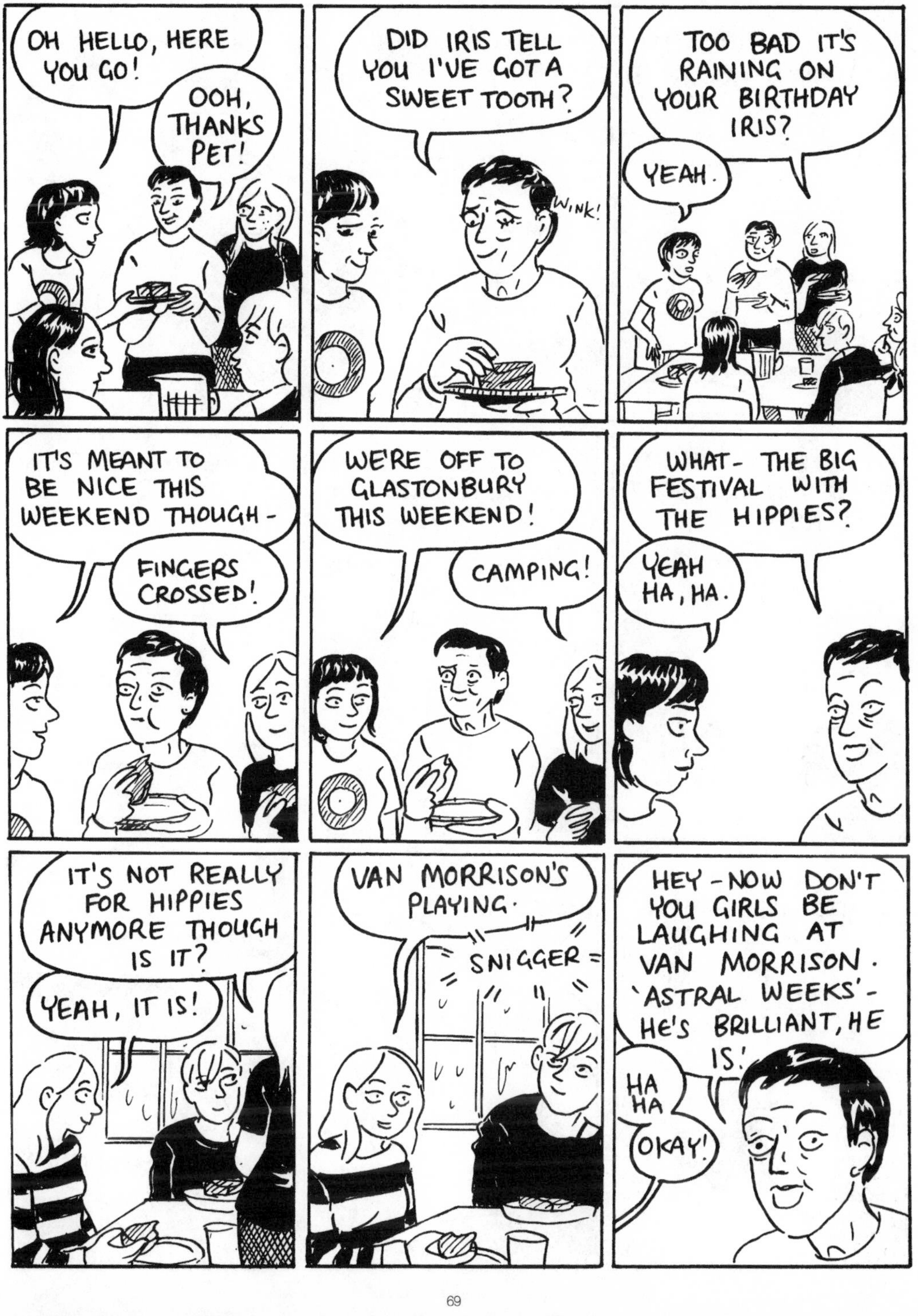
OH HELLO, HERE YOU GO!
OOH, THANKS PET!
DID IRIS TELL YOU I'VE GOT A SWEET TOOTH?
WINK!
TOO BAD IT'S RAINING ON YOUR BIRTHDAY IRIS?
YEAH.
IT'S MEANT TO BE NICE THIS WEEKEND THOUGH -
FINGERS CROSSED!
WE'RE OFF TO GLASTONBURY THIS WEEKEND!
CAMPING!
WHAT - THE BIG FESTIVAL WITH THE HIPPIES?
YEAH HA, HA.
IT'S NOT REALLY FOR HIPPIES ANYMORE THOUGH IS IT?
YEAH, IT IS!
VAN MORRISON'S PLAYING.
SNIGGER
HEY - NOW DON'T YOU GIRLS BE LAUGHING AT VAN MORRISON. 'ASTRAL WEEKS' - HE'S BRILLIANT, HE IS!
HA HA
OKAY!

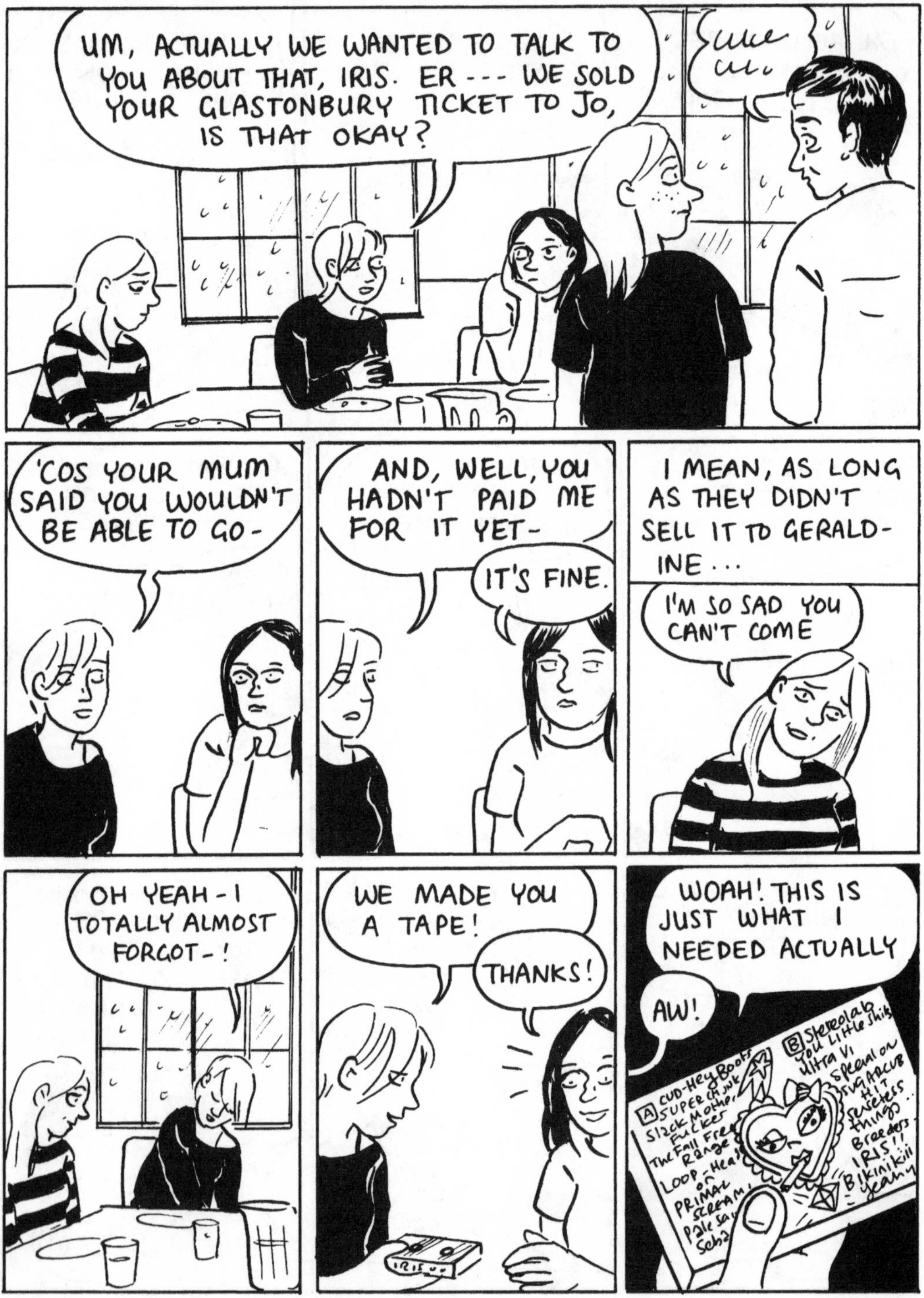
UM, ACTUALLY WE WANTED TO TALK TO YOU ABOUT THAT, IRIS. ER --- WE SOLD YOUR GLASTONBURY TICKET TO JO, IS THAT OKAY?
'COS YOUR MUM SAID YOU WOULDN'T BE ABLE TO GO-
AND, WELL, YOU HADN'T PAID ME FOR IT YET-
IT'S FINE.
I MEAN, AS LONG AS THEY DIDN'T SELL IT TO GERALD-INE...
I'M SO SAD YOU CAN'T COME
OH YEAH - I TOTALLY ALMOST FORGOT-!
WE MADE YOU A TAPE!
THANKS!
WOAH! THIS IS JUST WHAT I NEEDED ACTUALLY
AW!
A CUD-Hey Boots
SUPERCHUNK
Slack Mother Fucker
The Fall
Range
Loop
or
PRIMAL SCREAM!
B Stereolab
You Little
Ultra Vi
Special on
SUGARCUB
HIT
Senseless things...
Breeders
IRIS!!
Bikinikill
yeah
IRIS

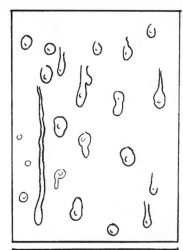

THE CONVERSATION DRIFTS AWAY WITHOUT ME. I FIND MYSELF LISTENING TO THE RAIN.

AND THE BUZZ FLUORESCENT LIGHT TUBES ABOVE.

FUNNY HOW YOU CAN DO THAT, BLUR PEOPLE OUT.

I MEAN - I HAVEN'T ACCEPTED YET SO -

BUT I'VE DONE IT BEFORE I GUESS- IT'S LIKE LISTENING TO MUSIC AND PICKING OUT JUST THE BASSLINE OR SOMETHING..

THERE'S ALWAYS 'CLEARING' -

YEAH -

IT'S LIKE SWAPPING A COOL CITY FOR A LESS COOL CITY BUT THE COURSE IS WHAT I REALLY WANT -

RIGHT.

I THINK I'M PRETTY MUCH DECIDED - IT AND LEICESTER'S OKAY

YEAH.

I WISH I'D KNOWN YOU WERE COMING!

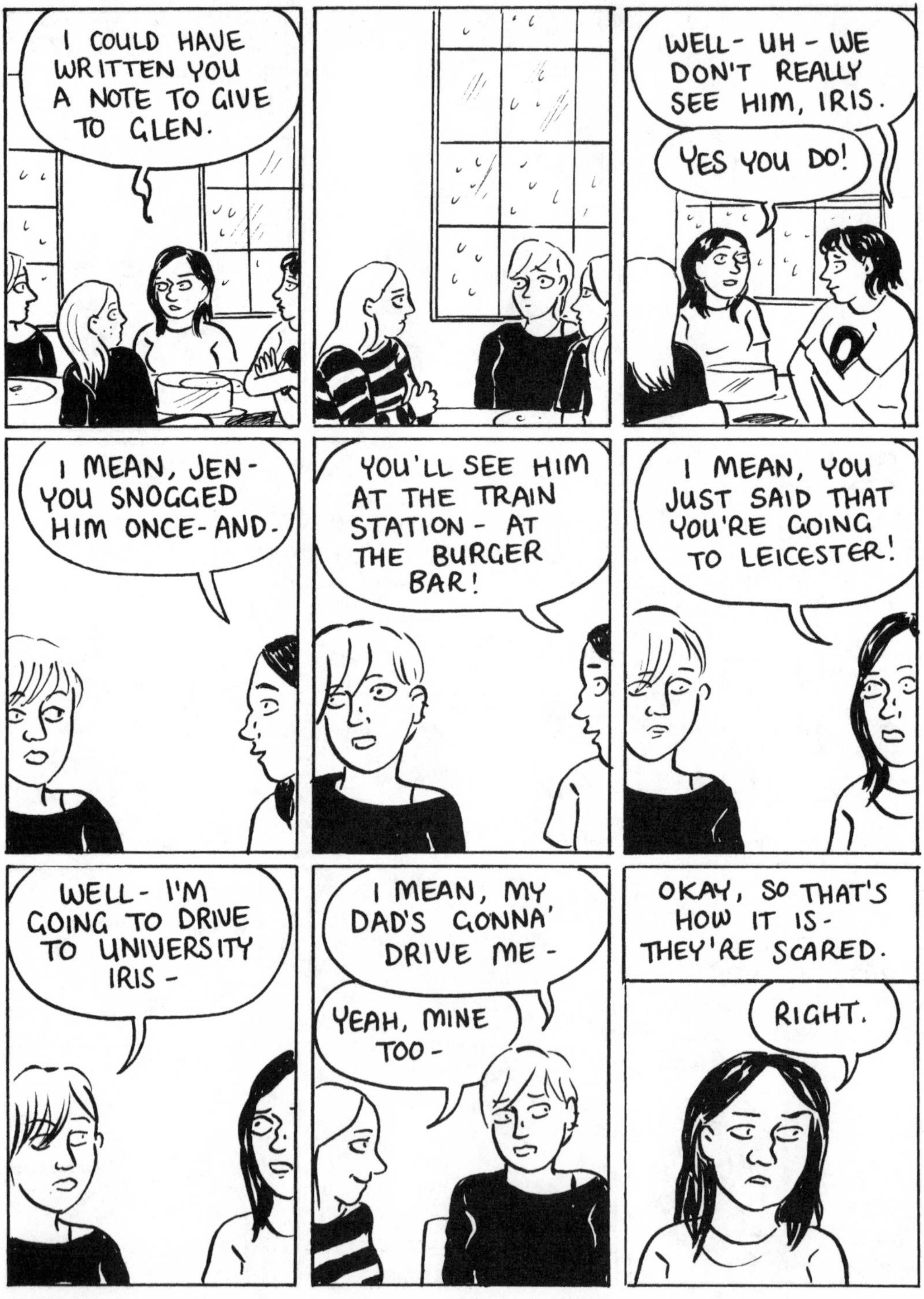
I COULD HAVE WRITTEN YOU A NOTE TO GIVE TO GLEN.
WELL- UH - WE DON'T REALLY SEE HIM, IRIS.
YES YOU DO!
I MEAN, JEN- YOU SNOGGED HIM ONCE-AND-
YOU'LL SEE HIM AT THE TRAIN STATION - AT THE BURGER BAR!
I MEAN, YOU JUST SAID THAT YOU'RE GOING TO LEICESTER!
WELL- I'M GOING TO DRIVE TO UNIVERSITY IRIS -
I MEAN, MY DAD'S GONNA' DRIVE ME -
YEAH, MINE TOO -
OKAY, SO THAT'S HOW IT IS- THEY'RE SCARED.
RIGHT.

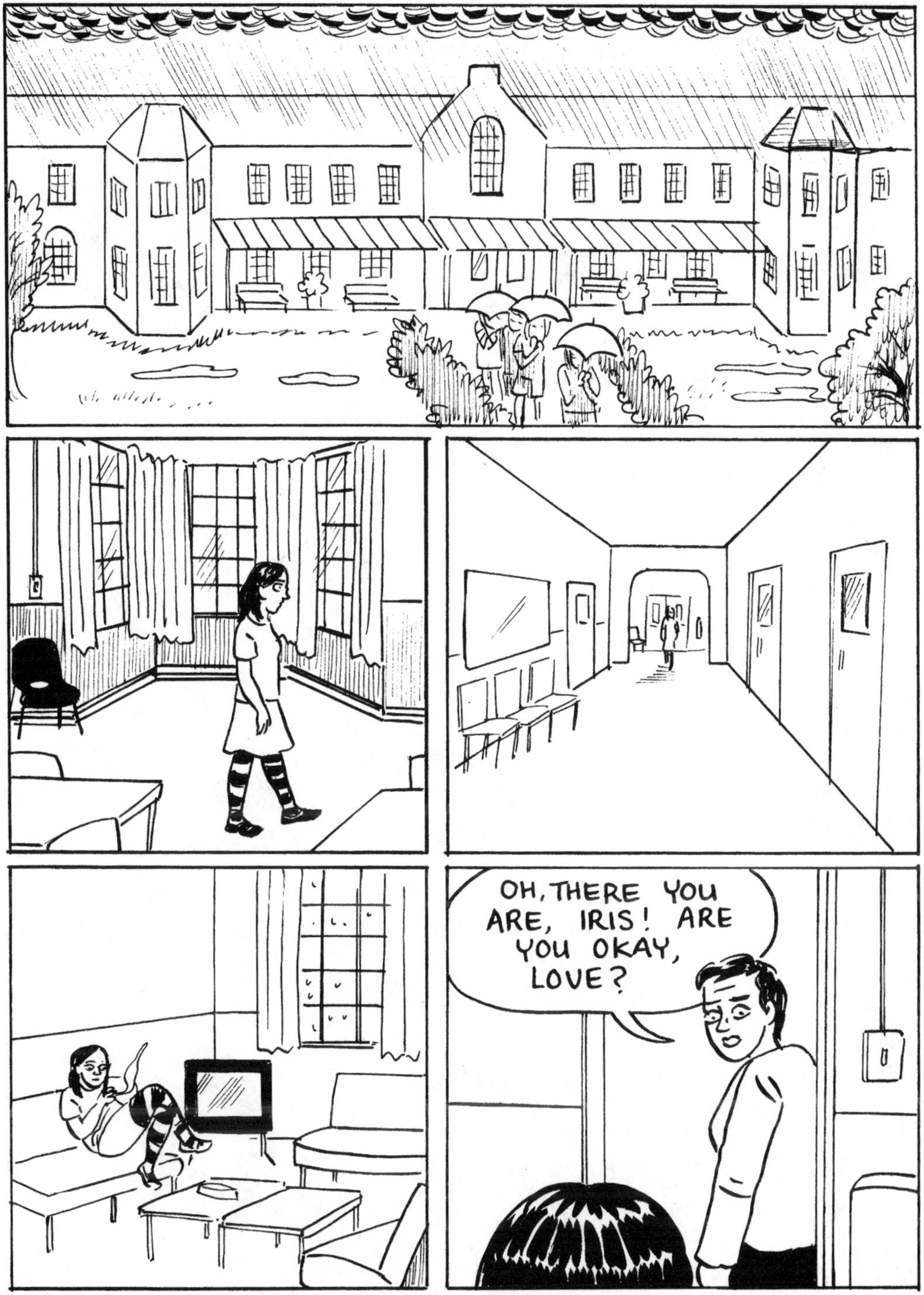
OH, THERE YOU ARE, IRIS! ARE YOU OKAY, LOVE?

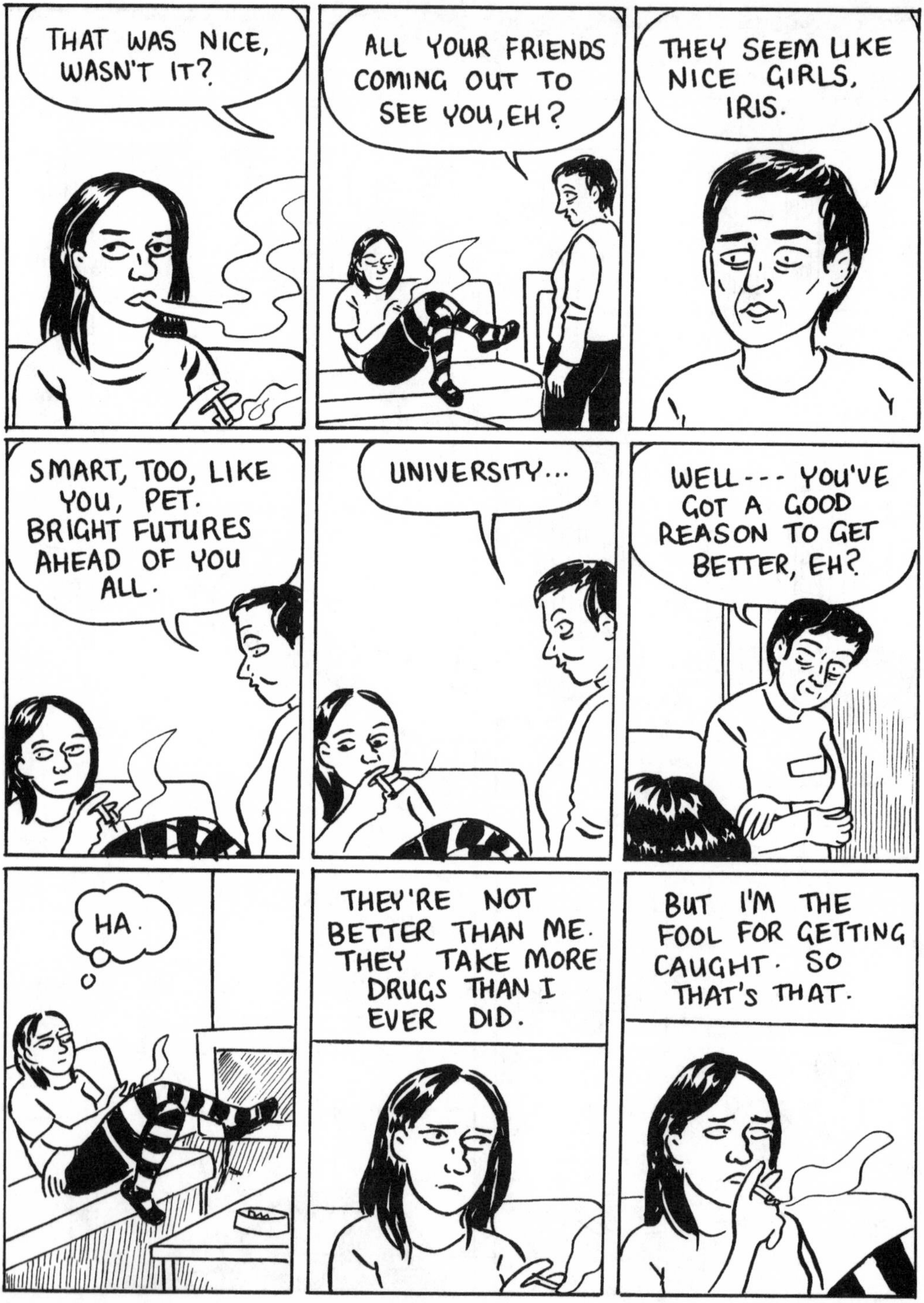
THAT WAS NICE, WASN'T IT?
ALL YOUR FRIENDS COMING OUT TO SEE YOU, EH?
THEY SEEM LIKE NICE GIRLS, IRIS.
SMART, TOO, LIKE YOU, PET. BRIGHT FUTURES AHEAD OF YOU ALL.
UNIVERSITY...
WELL--- YOU'VE GOT A GOOD REASON TO GET BETTER, EH?
HA.
THEY'RE NOT BETTER THAN ME. THEY TAKE MORE DRUGS THAN I EVER DID.
BUT I'M THE FOOL FOR GETTING CAUGHT. SO THAT'S THAT.

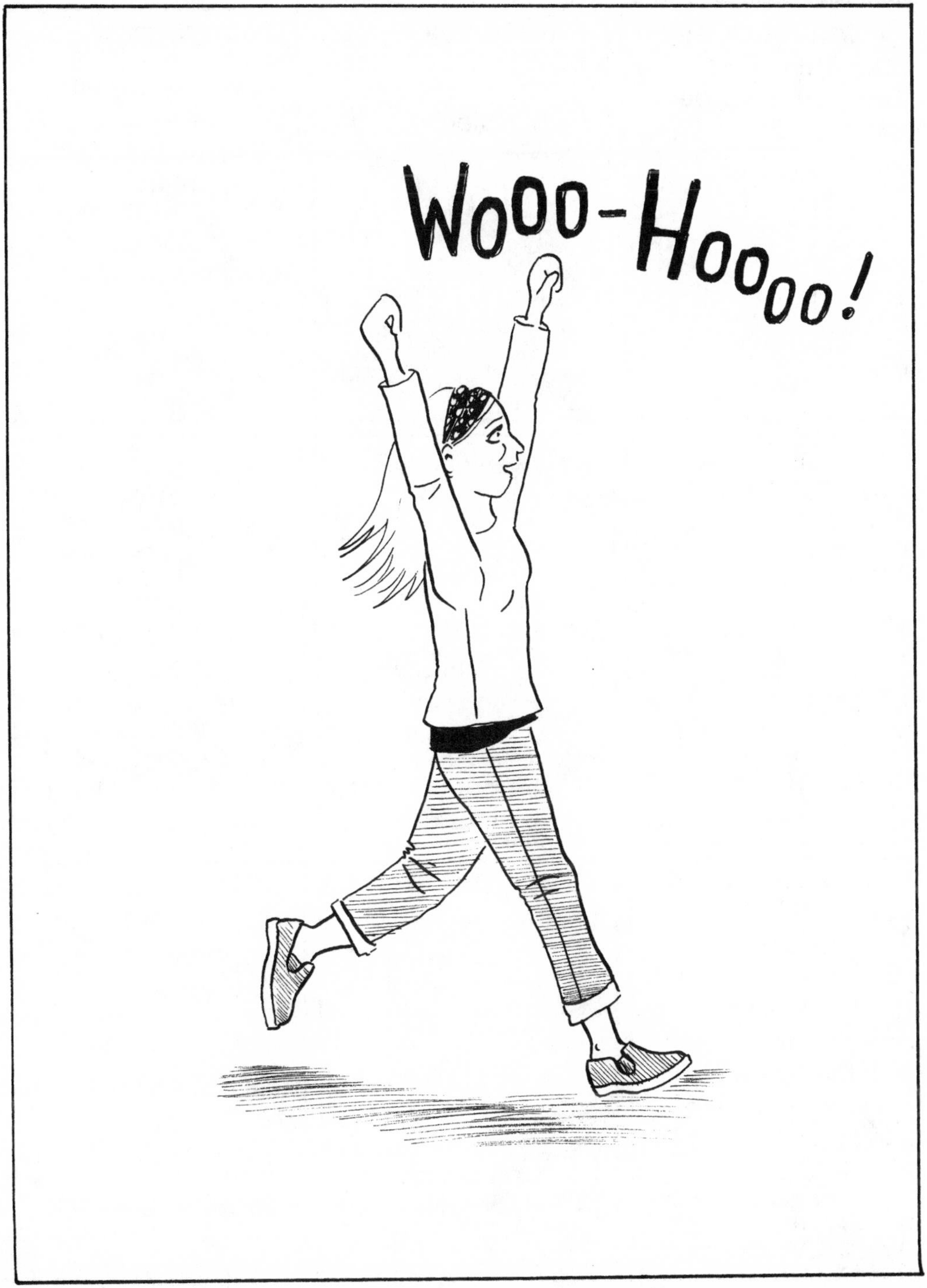
WOOO-HOOOOO!

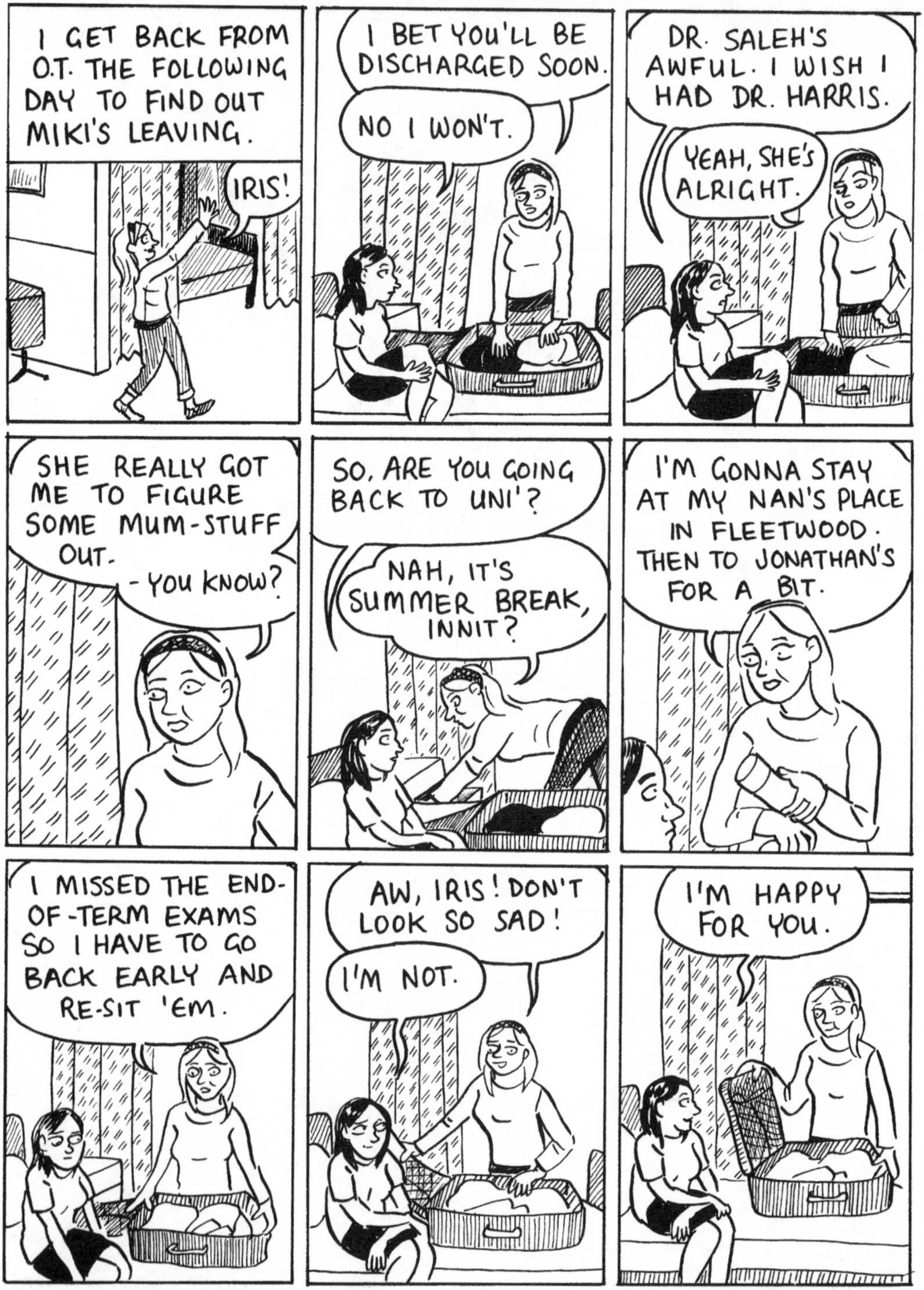
I GET BACK FROM O.T. THE FOLLOWING DAY TO FIND OUT MIKI'S LEAVING.
IRIS!
I BET YOU'LL BE DISCHARGED SOON.
NO I WON'T.
DR. SALEH'S AWFUL. I WISH I HAD DR. HARRIS.
YEAH, SHE'S ALRIGHT.
SHE REALLY GOT ME TO FIGURE SOME MUM-STUFF OUT.
- YOU KNOW?
SO, ARE YOU GOING BACK TO UNI'?
NAH, IT'S SUMMER BREAK, INNIT?
I'M GONNA STAY AT MY NAN'S PLACE IN FLEETWOOD. THEN TO JONATHAN'S FOR A BIT.
I MISSED THE END-OF-TERM EXAMS SO I HAVE TO GO BACK EARLY AND RE-SIT 'EM.
AW, IRIS! DON'T LOOK SO SAD!
I'M NOT.
I'M HAPPY FOR YOU.

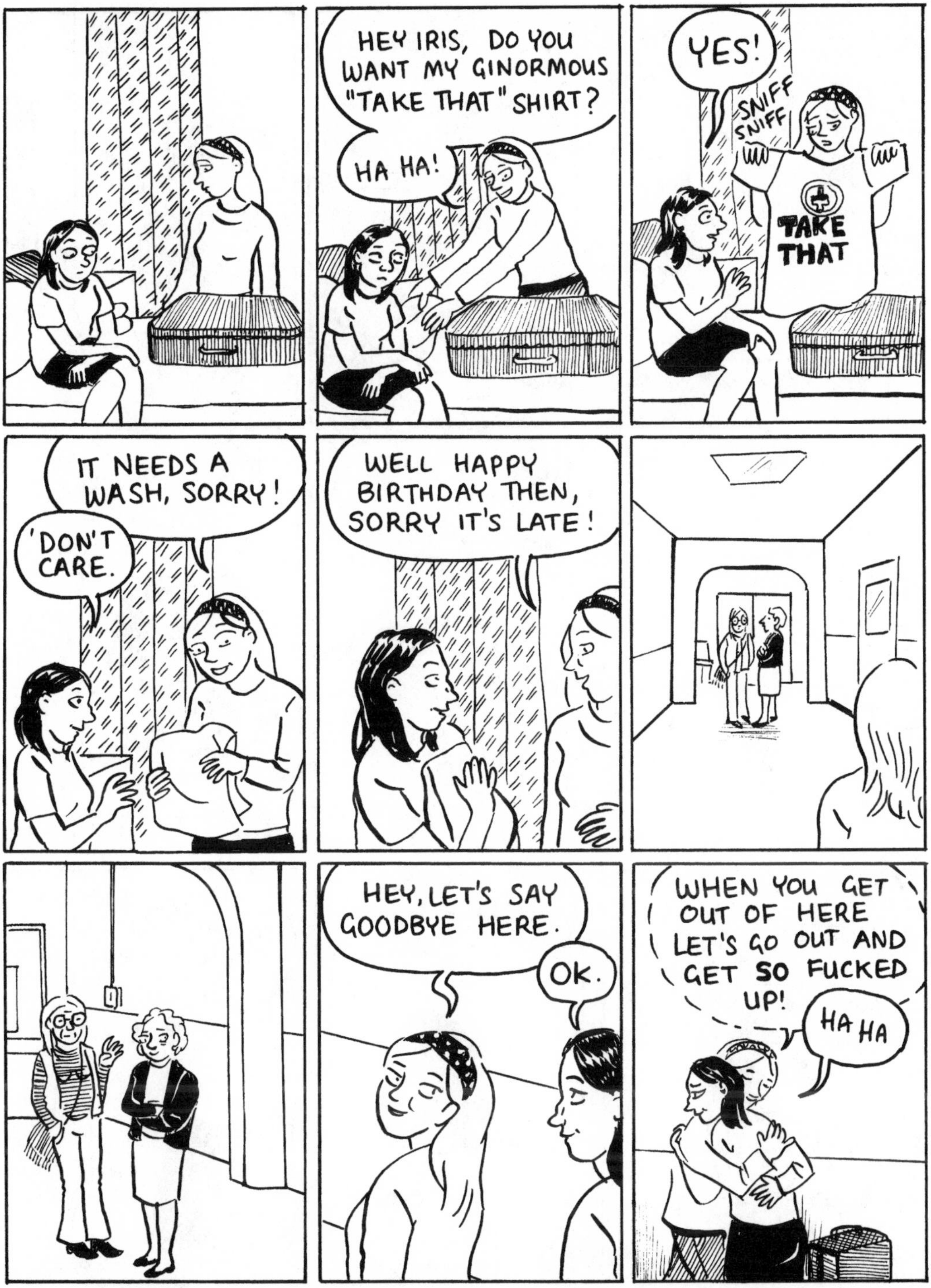
HEY IRIS, DO YOU WANT MY GINORMOUS "TAKE THAT" SHIRT?
HA HA!
YES!
SNIFF SNIFF
TAKE THAT
IT NEEDS A WASH, SORRY!
'DON'T CARE.
WELL HAPPY BIRTHDAY THEN, SORRY IT'S LATE!
HEY, LET'S SAY GOODBYE HERE.
OK.
WHEN YOU GET OUT OF HERE LET'S GO OUT AND GET SO FUCKED UP!
HA HA

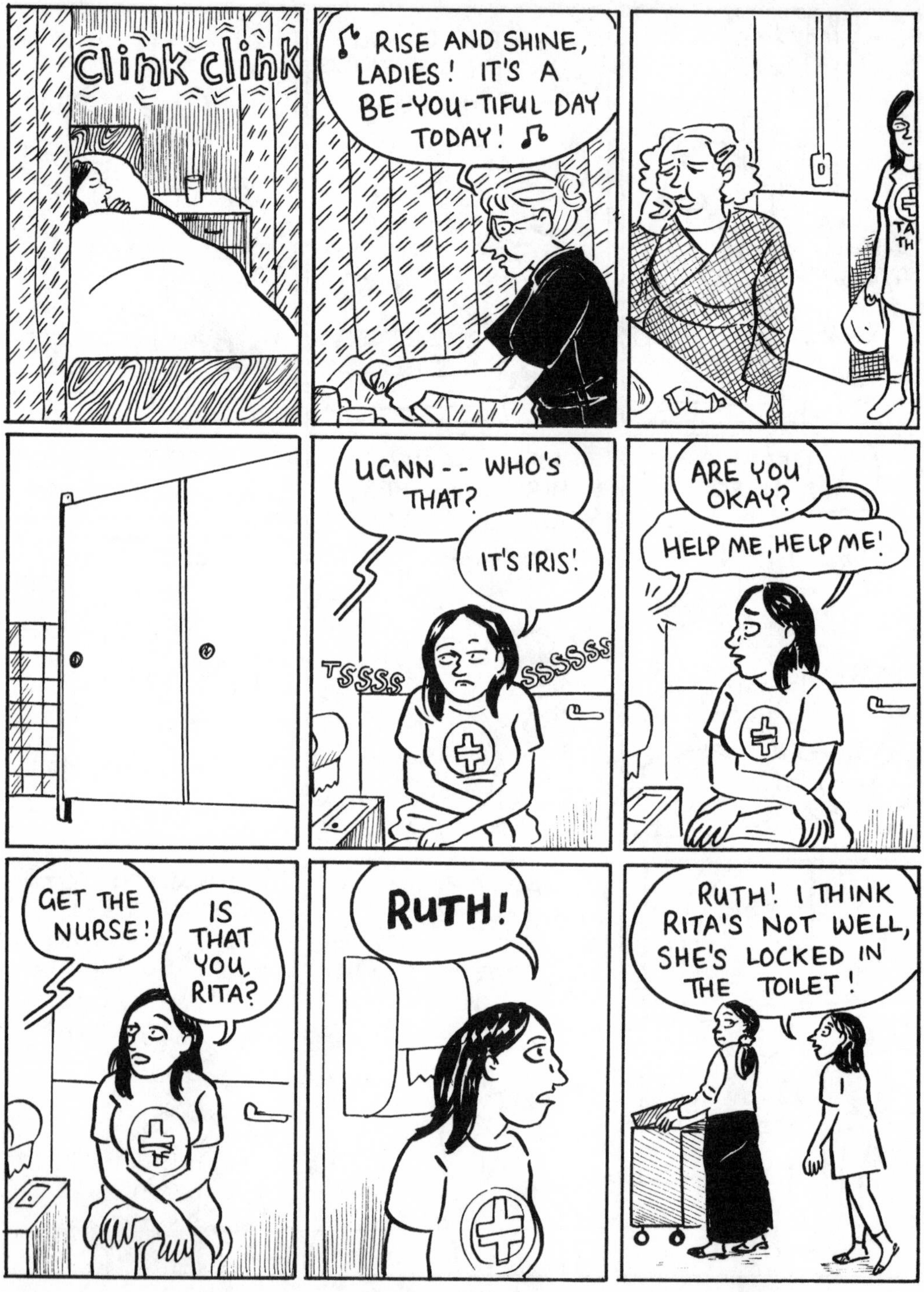
CLINK CLINK
RISE AND SHINE, LADIES! IT'S A BE-YOU-TIFUL DAY TODAY!
UGNN-- WHO'S THAT?
IT'S IRIS!
TSSSS
SSSSSS
ARE YOU OKAY?
HELP ME, HELP ME!
GET THE NURSE!
IS THAT YOU, RITA?
RUTH!
RUTH! I THINK RITA'S NOT WELL, SHE'S LOCKED IN THE TOILET!

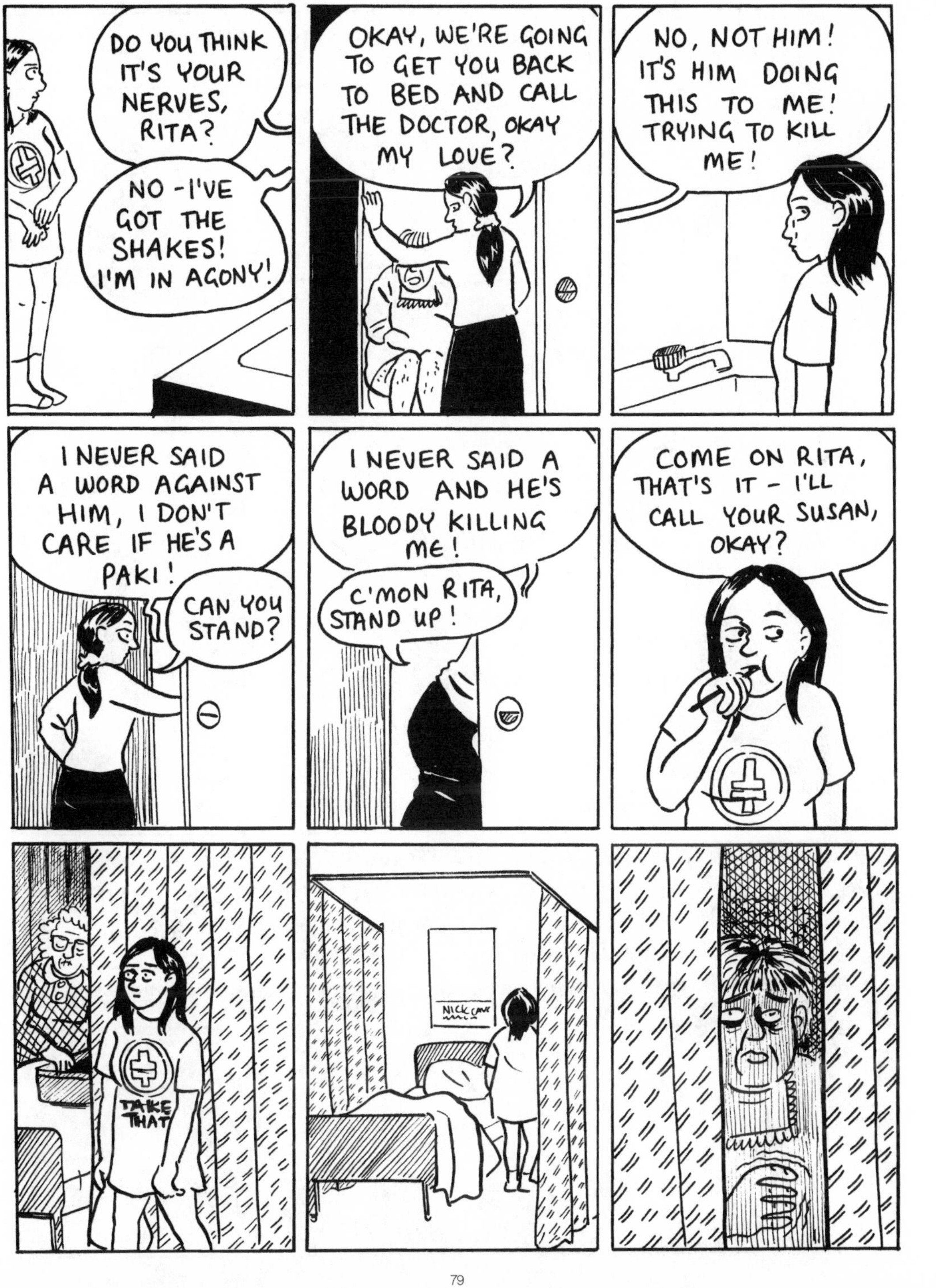
DO YOU THINK IT'S YOUR NERVES, RITA?
NO - I'VE GOT THE SHAKES! I'M IN AGONY!
OKAY, WE'RE GOING TO GET YOU BACK TO BED AND CALL THE DOCTOR, OKAY MY LOVE?
NO, NOT HIM! IT'S HIM DOING THIS TO ME! TRYING TO KILL ME!
I NEVER SAID A WORD AGAINST HIM, I DON'T CARE IF HE'S A PAKI!
CAN YOU STAND?
I NEVER SAID A WORD AND HE'S BLOODY KILLING ME!
C'MON RITA, STAND UP!
COME ON RITA, THAT'S IT - I'LL CALL YOUR SUSAN, OKAY?
TAKE THAT
NICK CAVE

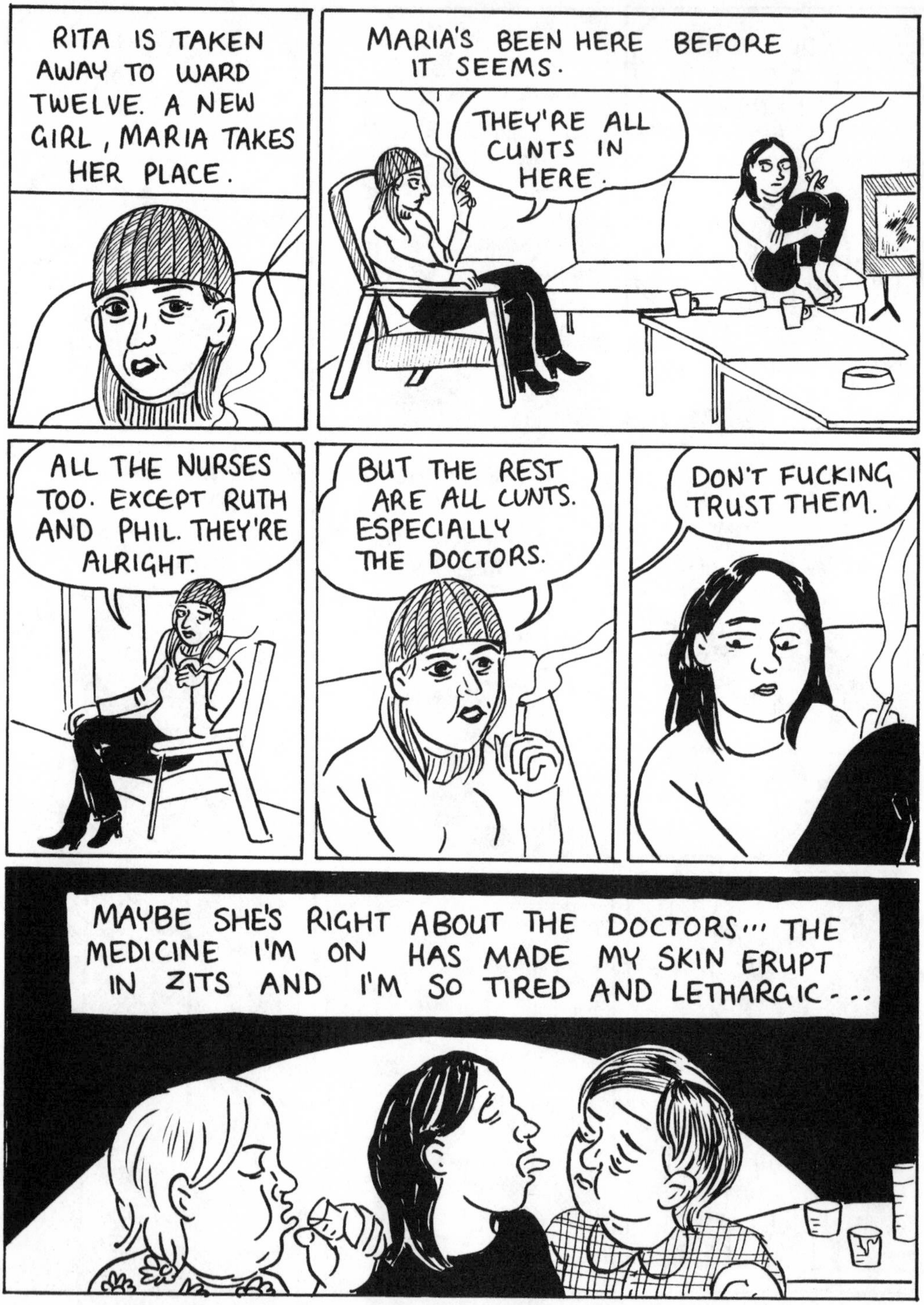

RITA IS TAKEN AWAY TO WARD TWELVE. A NEW GIRL, MARIA TAKES HER PLACE.
MARIA'S BEEN HERE BEFORE IT SEEMS.
THEY'RE ALL CUNTS IN HERE.
ALL THE NURSES TOO. EXCEPT RUTH AND PHIL. THEY'RE ALRIGHT.
BUT THE REST ARE ALL CUNTS. ESPECIALLY THE DOCTORS.
DON'T FUCKING TRUST THEM.
MAYBE SHE'S RIGHT ABOUT THE DOCTORS... THE MEDICINE I'M ON HAS MADE MY SKIN ERUPT IN ZITS AND I'M SO TIRED AND LETHARGIC...

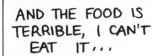
AND THE FOOD IS TERRIBLE, I CAN'T EAT IT...

IRIS, IT'S YOUR SPECIALLY ORDERED MEAL.

CAN YOU AT LEAST TRY IT PLEASE?

NO! I WON'T! I HATE CHEESE!

THEN SWITCH TO THE VEGAN OPTION. YOU'VE GOT TO EAT, IRIS!

I WOLF DOWN THE FOOD MY MUM BRINGS AT NIGHT.

I GOT SOME MAGAZINES FOR YOU.

NICI BUN.

I CAN'T READ ANYMORE. MY EYES ARE ALL BLURRY.

THE NURSES SAID IT'S THE MEDICATION.

WELL, I CAN GET YOU SOME READING SPECS!

COOL ONES, LIKE JARVIS COCKER'S!

HA.

I NEED LIP BALM TOO. MY MOUTH'S SO SORE, MUM.

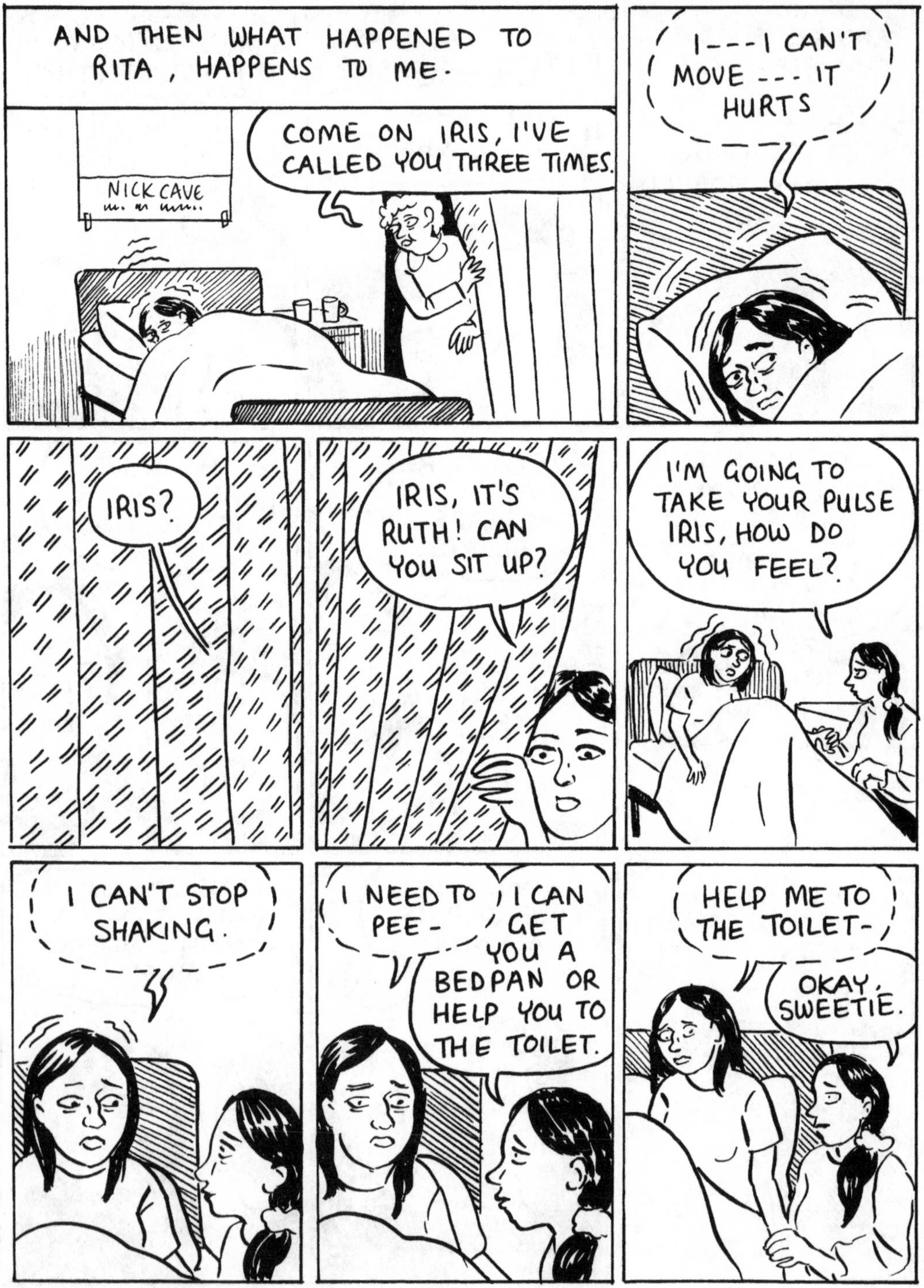
AND THEN WHAT HAPPENED TO RITA, HAPPENS TO ME.
NICK CAVE
COME ON IRIS, I'VE CALLED YOU THREE TIMES.
I---I CAN'T MOVE --- IT HURTS
IRIS?
IRIS, IT'S RUTH! CAN YOU SIT UP?
I'M GOING TO TAKE YOUR PULSE IRIS, HOW DO YOU FEEL?
I CAN'T STOP SHAKING.
I NEED TO PEE-
I CAN GET YOU A BEDPAN OR HELP YOU TO THE TOILET.
HELP ME TO THE TOILET-
OKAY, SWEETIE.

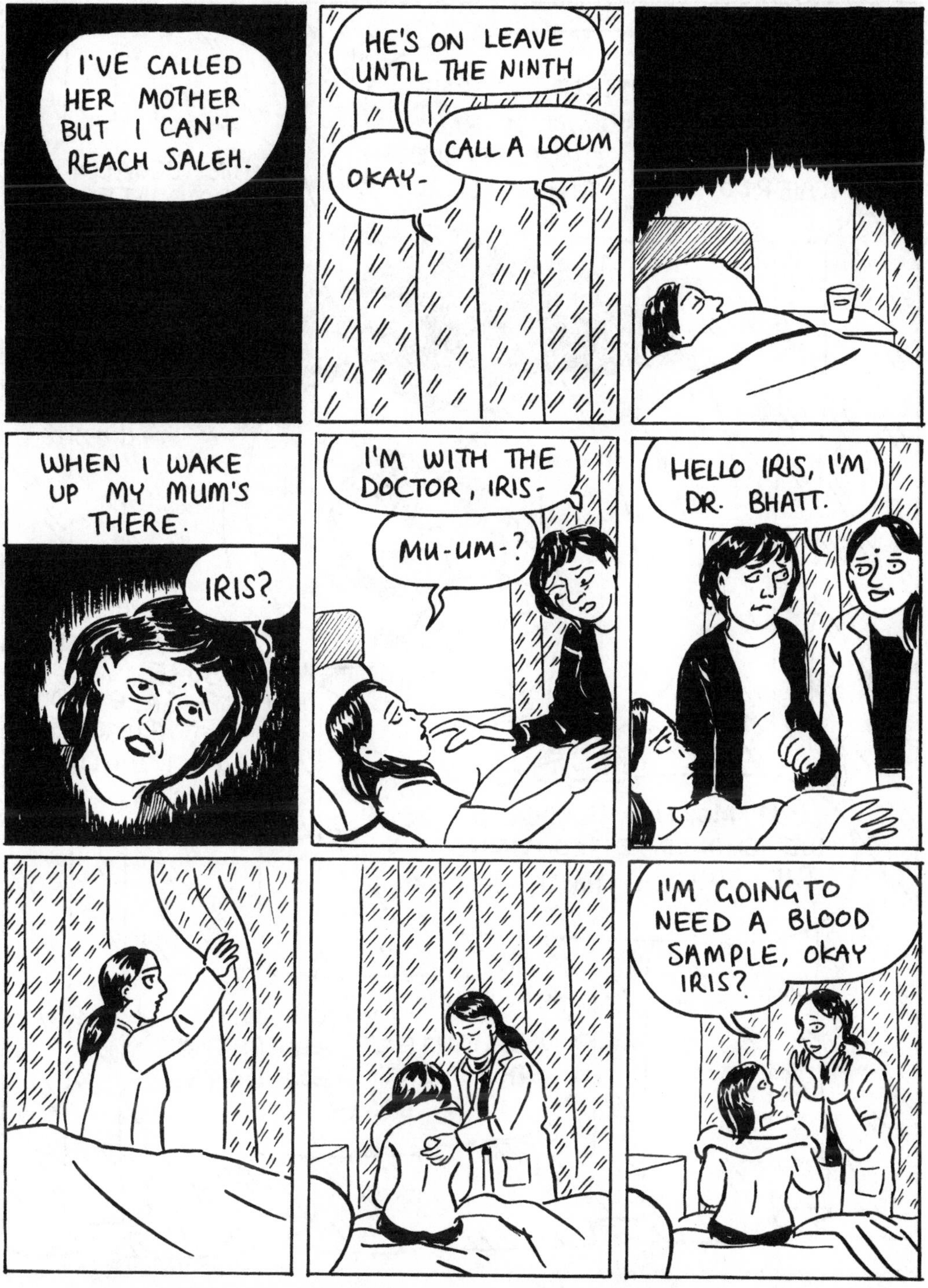
I'VE CALLED HER MOTHER BUT I CAN'T REACH SALEH.
HE'S ON LEAVE UNTIL THE NINTH
OKAY-
CALL A LOCUM
WHEN I WAKE UP MY MUM'S THERE.
IRIS?
I'M WITH THE DOCTOR, IRIS-
MU-UM-?
HELLO IRIS, I'M DR. BHATT.
I'M GOING TO NEED A BLOOD SAMPLE, OKAY IRIS?

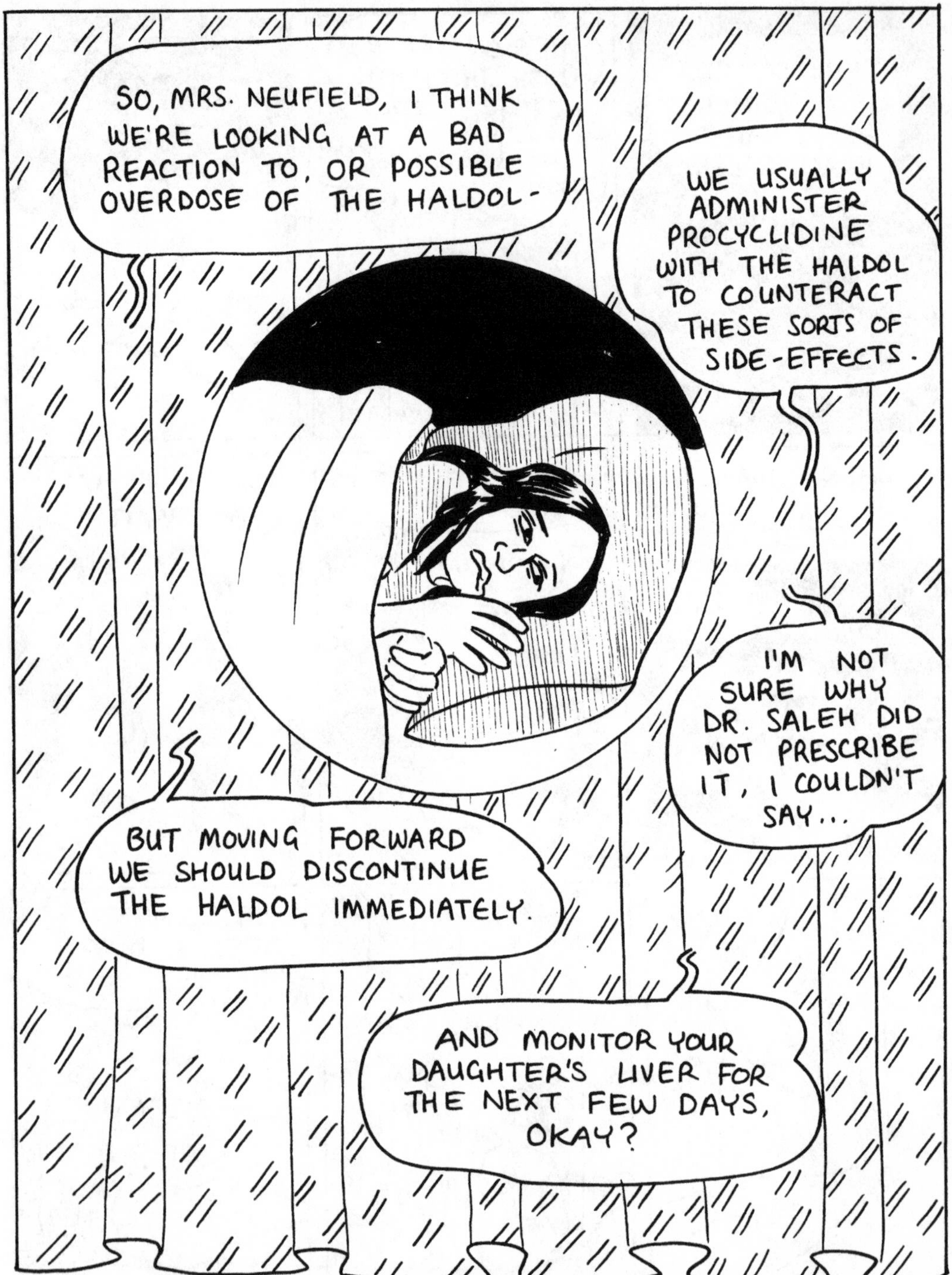
SO, MRS. NEUFIELD, I THINK WE'RE LOOKING AT A BAD REACTION TO, OR POSSIBLE OVERDOSE OF THE HALDOL-
WE USUALLY ADMINISTER PROCYCLIDINE WITH THE HALDOL TO COUNTERACT THESE SORTS OF SIDE-EFFECTS.
I'M NOT SURE WHY DR. SALEH DID NOT PRESCRIBE IT, I COULDN'T SAY...
BUT MOVING FORWARD WE SHOULD DISCONTINUE THE HALDOL IMMEDIATELY.
AND MONITOR YOUR DAUGHTER'S LIVER FOR THE NEXT FEW DAYS, OKAY?

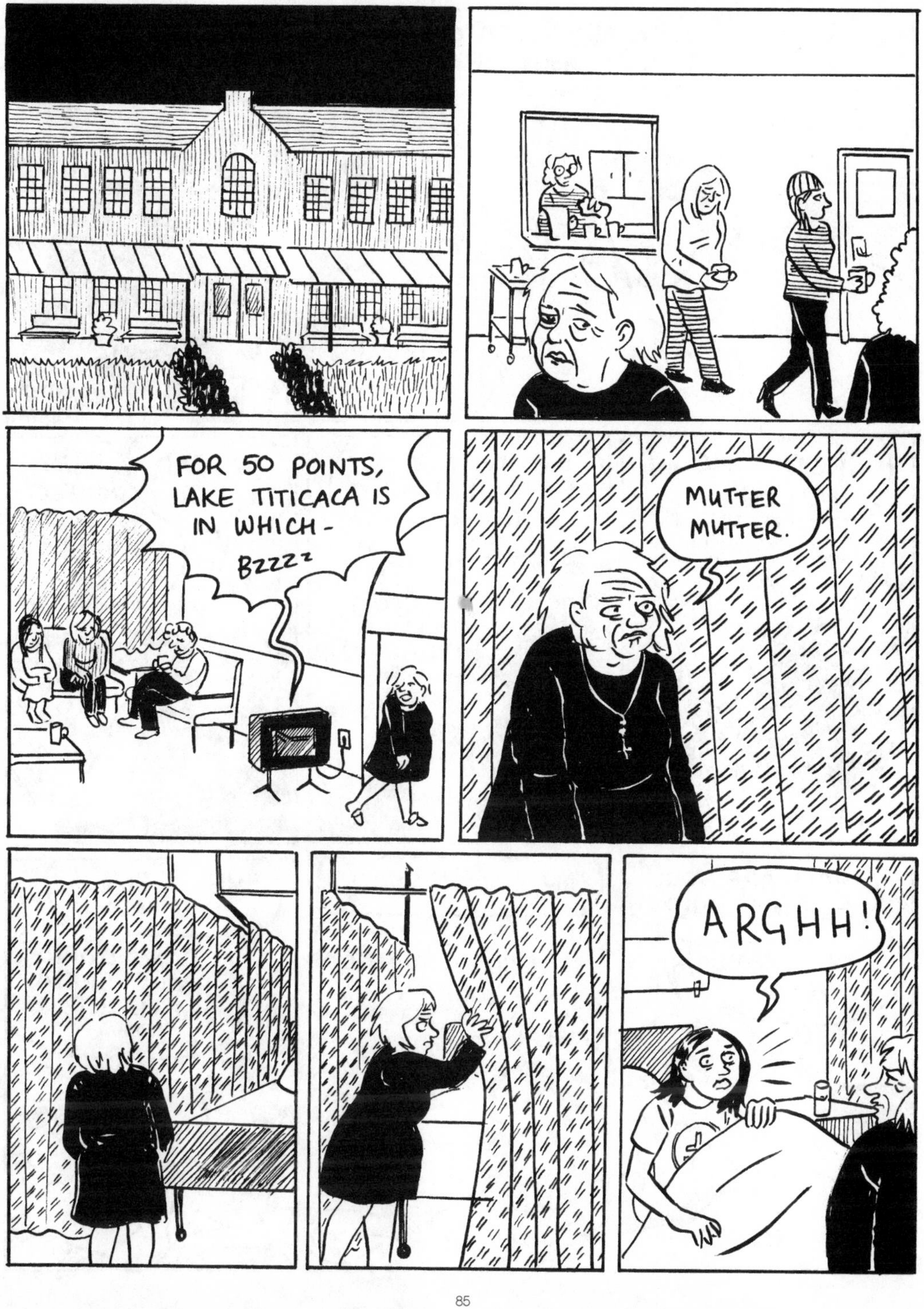
FOR 50 POINTS, LAKE TITICACA IS IN WHICH -
BZZZZ
MUTTER MUTTER.
ARGHH!

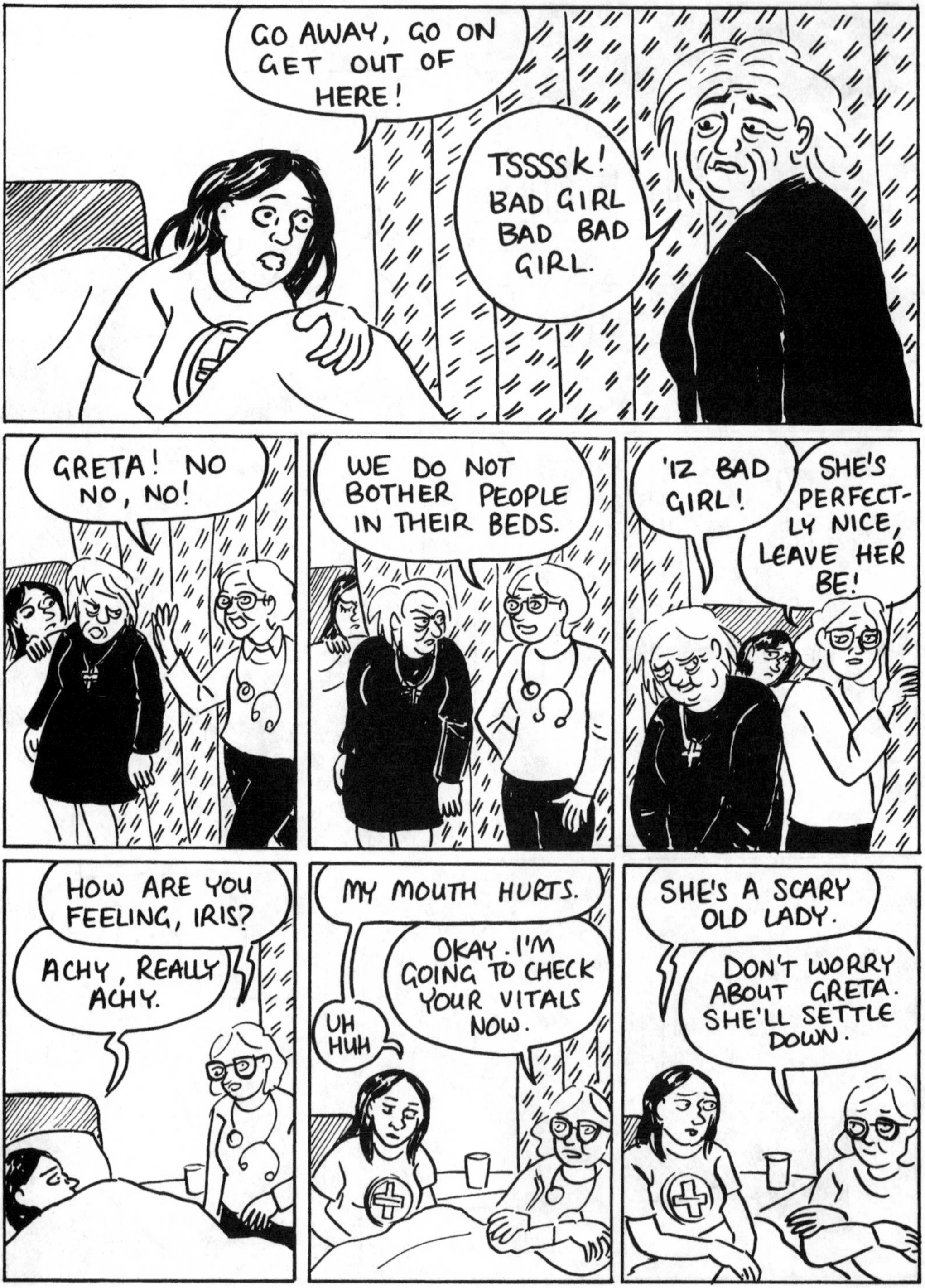

GO AWAY, GO ON GET OUT OF HERE!
TSSSSk! BAD GIRL BAD BAD GIRL.
GRETA! NO NO, NO!
WE DO NOT BOTHER PEOPLE IN THEIR BEDS.
'IZ BAD GIRL!
SHE'S PERFECTLY NICE, LEAVE HER BE!
HOW ARE YOU FEELING, IRIS?
ACHY, REALLY ACHY.
MY MOUTH HURTS.
OKAY. I'M GOING TO CHECK YOUR VITALS NOW.
UH HUH
SHE'S A SCARY OLD LADY.
DON'T WORRY ABOUT GRETA. SHE'LL SETTLE DOWN.

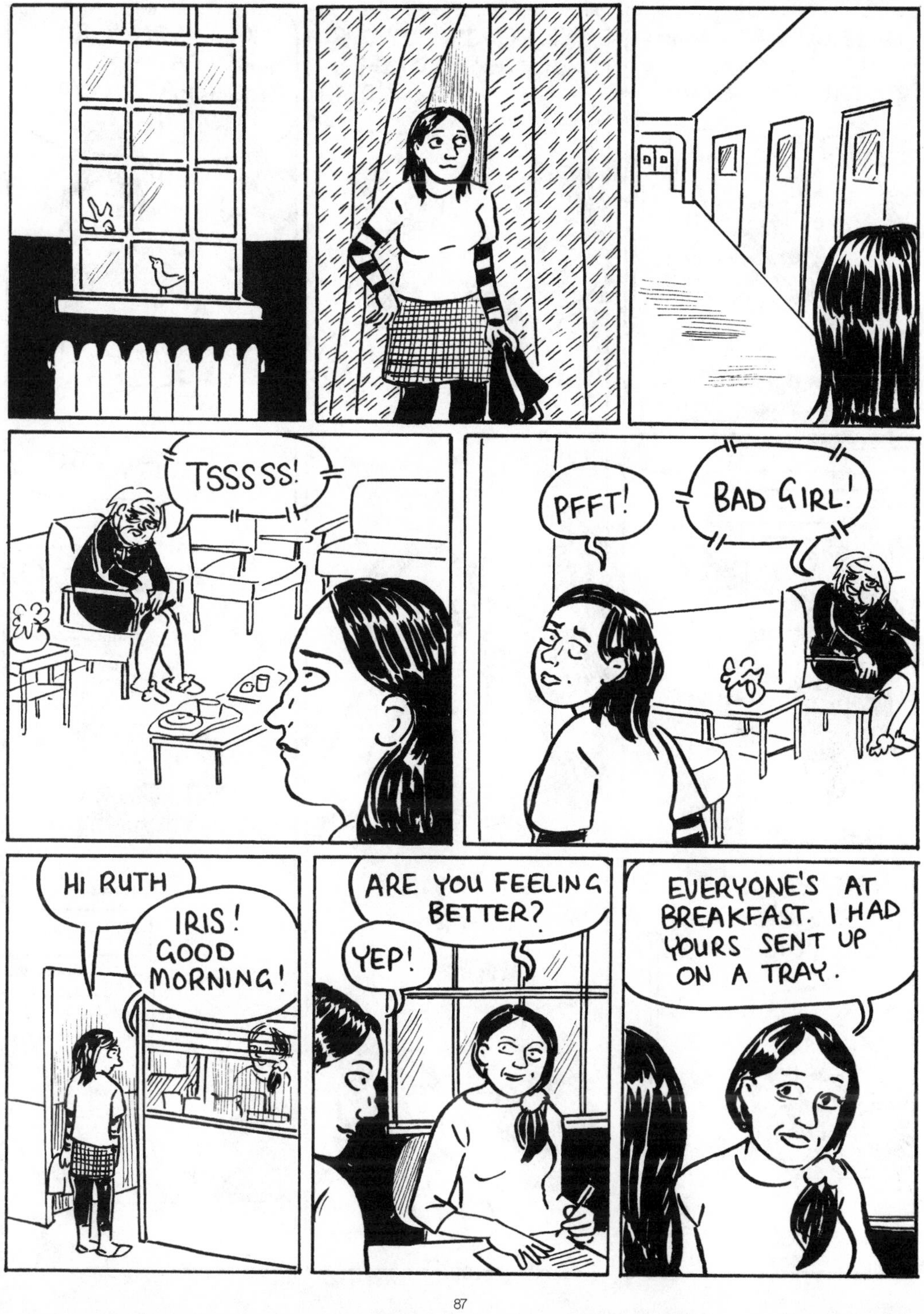
TSSSSS!
PFFT!
BAD GIRL!
HI RUTH
IRIS! GOOD MORNING!
ARE YOU FEELING BETTER?
YEP!
EVERYONE'S AT BREAKFAST. I HAD YOURS SENT UP ON A TRAY.

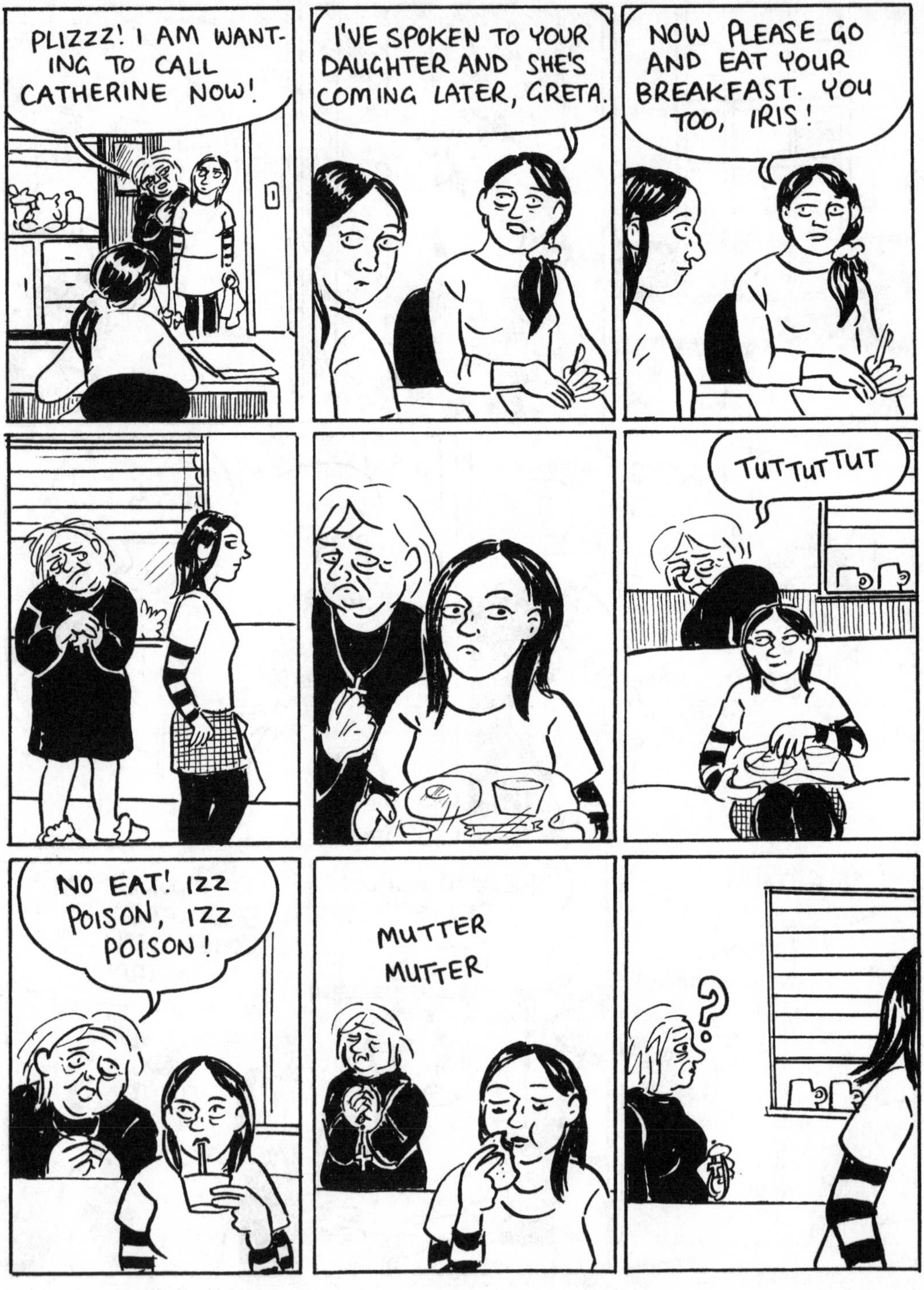
PLIZZZ! I AM WANTING TO CALL CATHERINE NOW!
I'VE SPOKEN TO YOUR DAUGHTER AND SHE'S COMING LATER, GRETA.
NOW PLEASE GO AND EAT YOUR BREAKFAST. YOU TOO, IRIS!
TUT TUT TUT
NO EAT! IZZ POISON, IZZ POISON!
MUTTER MUTTER
?

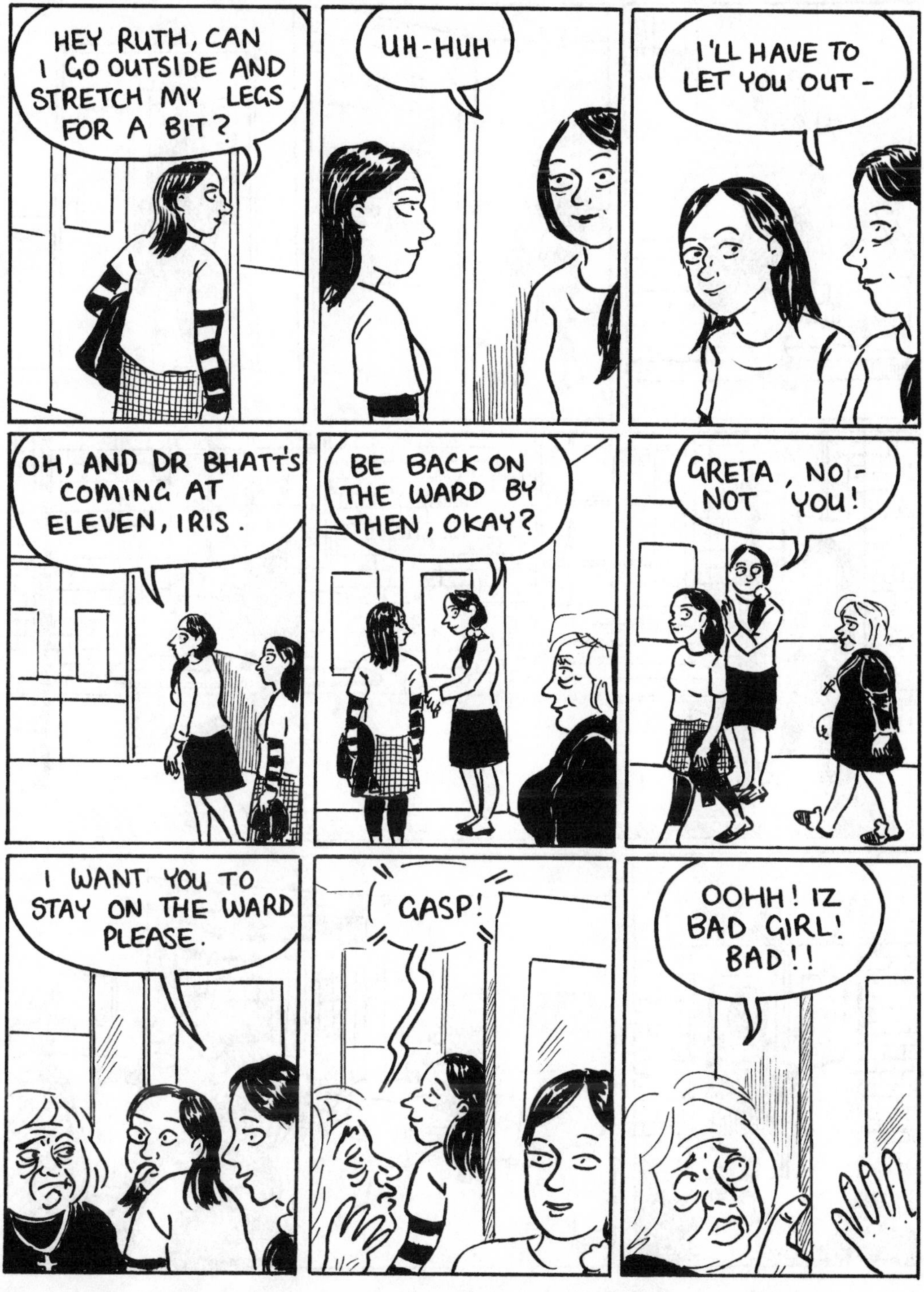
HEY RUTH, CAN I GO OUTSIDE AND STRETCH MY LEGS FOR A BIT?
UH-HUH
I'LL HAVE TO LET YOU OUT -
OH, AND DR BHATT'S COMING AT ELEVEN, IRIS.
BE BACK ON THE WARD BY THEN, OKAY?
GRETA, NO - NOT YOU!
I WANT YOU TO STAY ON THE WARD PLEASE.
GASP!
OOHH! IZ BAD GIRL! BAD!!

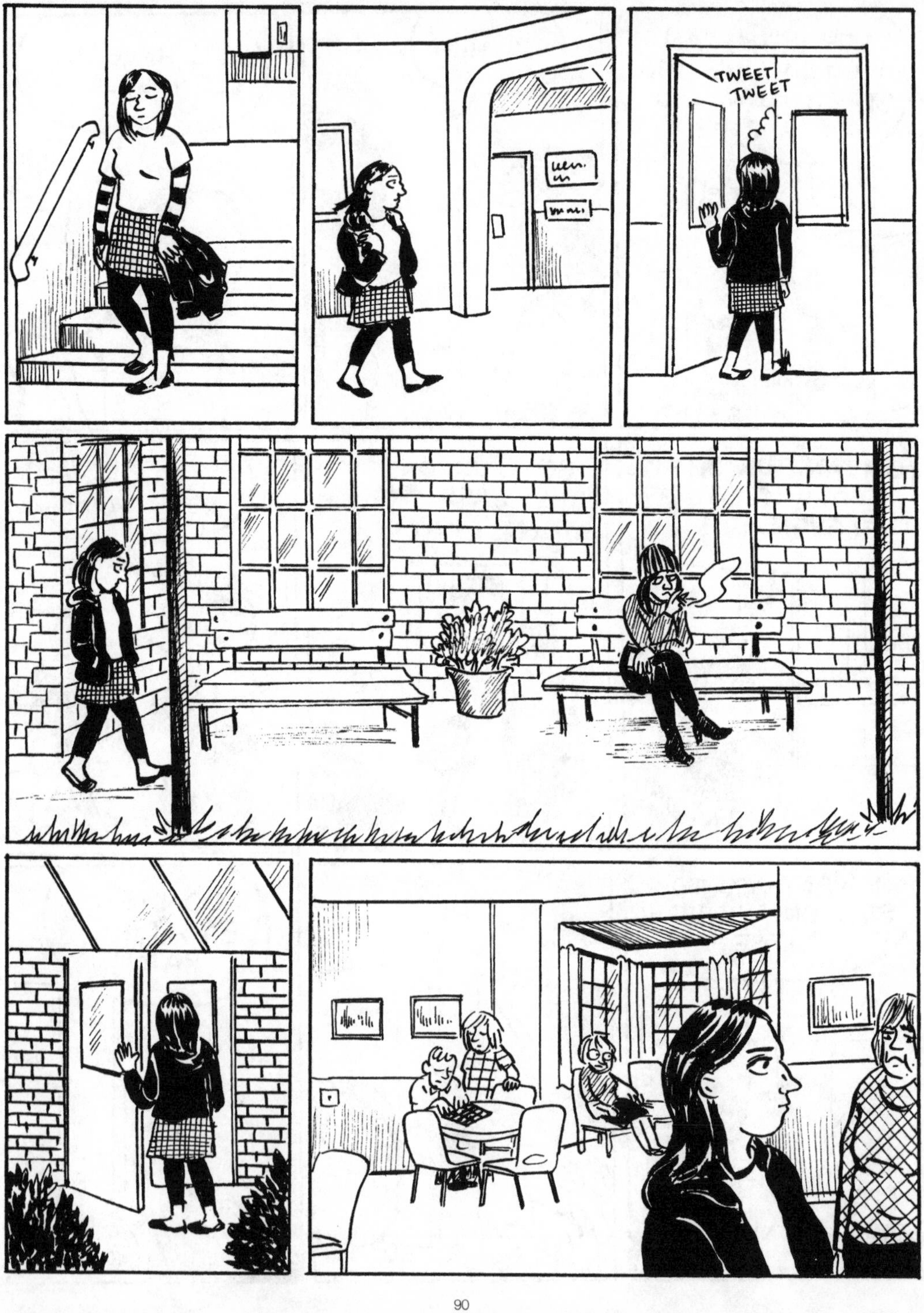
TWEET
TWEET

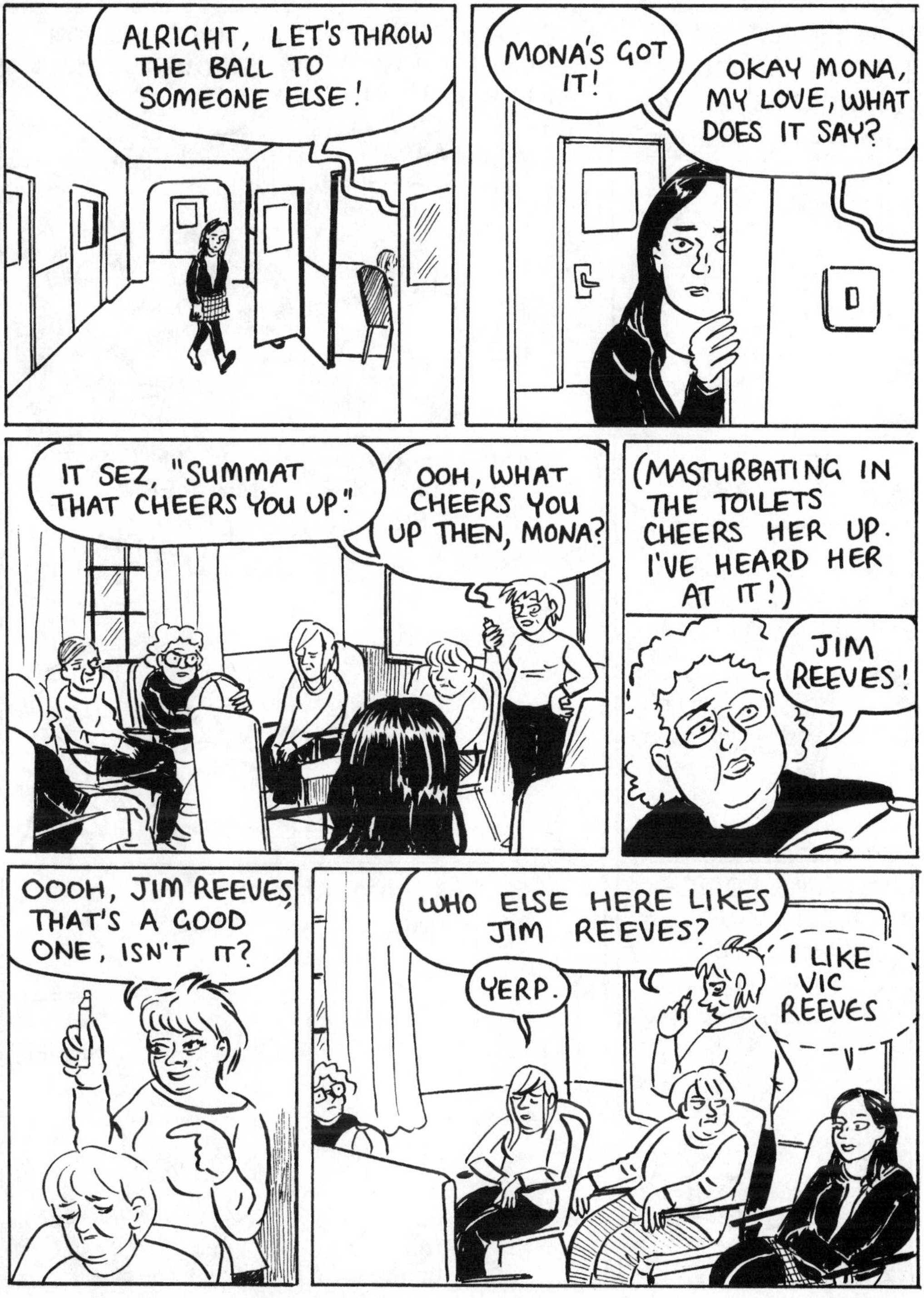
ALRIGHT, LET'S THROW THE BALL TO SOMEONE ELSE!
MONA'S GOT IT!
OKAY MONA, MY LOVE, WHAT DOES IT SAY?
IT SEZ, "SUMMAT THAT CHEERS YOU UP."
OOH, WHAT CHEERS YOU UP THEN, MONA?
(MASTURBATING IN THE TOILETS CHEERS HER UP. I'VE HEARD HER AT IT!)
JIM REEVES!
OOOH, JIM REEVES, THAT'S A GOOD ONE, ISN'T IT?
WHO ELSE HERE LIKES JIM REEVES?
YERP.
I LIKE VIC REEVES

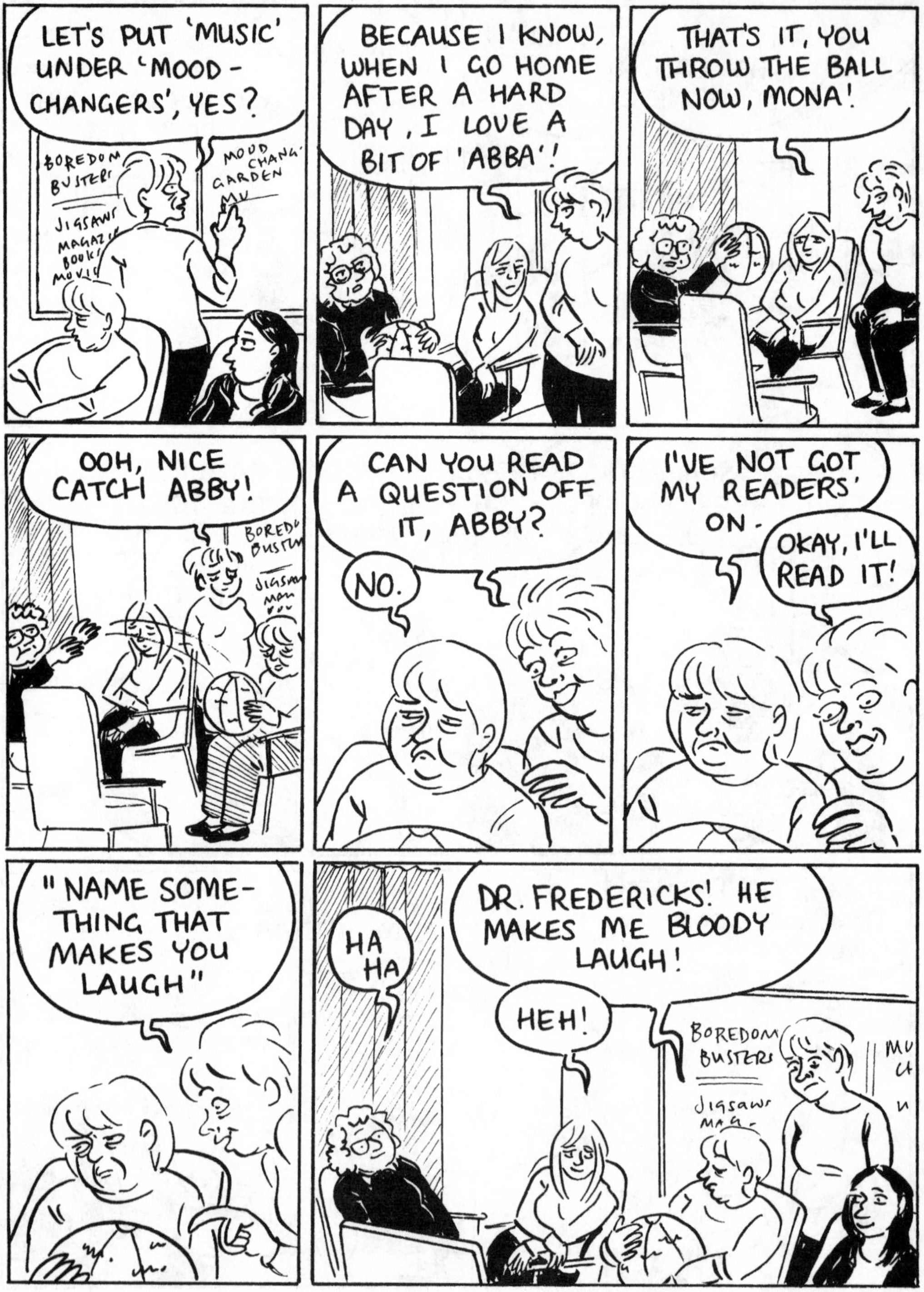
LET'S PUT 'MUSIC' UNDER 'MOOD-CHANGERS', YES?
BOREDOM BUSTERS
JIGSAWS
MOOD CHANG
GARDEN
BECAUSE I KNOW, WHEN I GO HOME AFTER A HARD DAY, I LOVE A BIT OF 'ABBA'!
THAT'S IT, YOU THROW THE BALL NOW, MONA!
OOH, NICE CATCH ABBY!
CAN YOU READ A QUESTION OFF IT, ABBY?
NO.
I'VE NOT GOT MY READERS' ON.
OKAY, I'LL READ IT!
"NAME SOME-THING THAT MAKES YOU LAUGH"
HA HA
DR. FREDERICKS! HE MAKES ME BLOODY LAUGH!
HEH!
BOREDOM BUSTERS
JIGSAWS

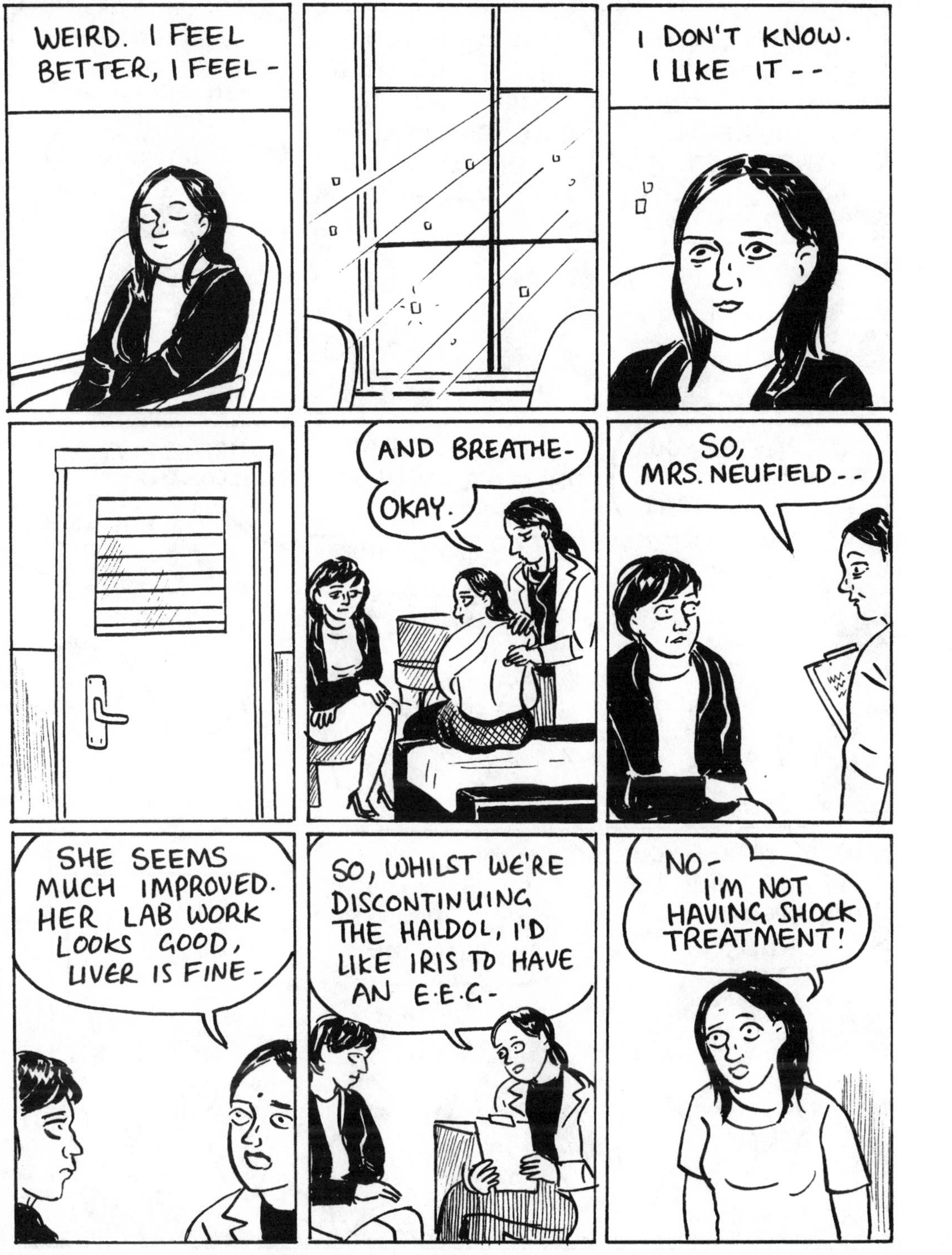
WEIRD. I FEEL BETTER, I FEEL -
I DON'T KNOW. I LIKE IT - -
AND BREATHE-
OKAY.
SO, MRS. NEUFIELD - -
SHE SEEMS MUCH IMPROVED. HER LAB WORK LOOKS GOOD, LIVER IS FINE -
SO, WHILST WE'RE DISCONTINUING THE HALDOL, I'D LIKE IRIS TO HAVE AN E.E.G. -
NO - I'M NOT HAVING SHOCK TREATMENT!

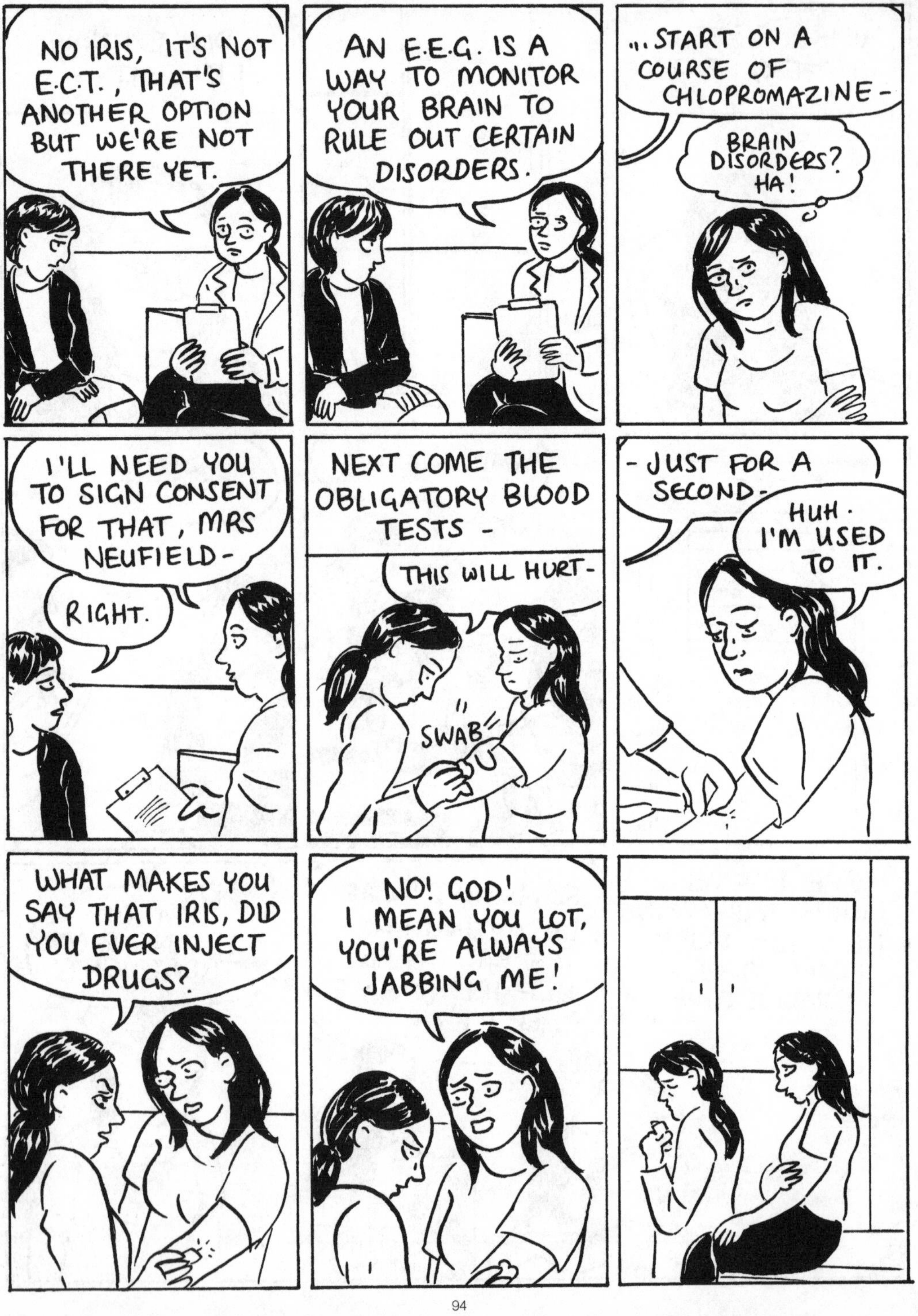
NO IRIS, IT'S NOT E.C.T., THAT'S ANOTHER OPTION BUT WE'RE NOT THERE YET.
AN E.E.G. IS A WAY TO MONITOR YOUR BRAIN TO RULE OUT CERTAIN DISORDERS.
... START ON A COURSE OF CHLOPROMAZINE -
BRAIN DISORDERS? HA!
I'LL NEED YOU TO SIGN CONSENT FOR THAT, MRS NEUFIELD -
RIGHT.
NEXT COME THE OBLIGATORY BLOOD TESTS -
THIS WILL HURT -
SWAB
- JUST FOR A SECOND -
HUH. I'M USED TO IT.
WHAT MAKES YOU SAY THAT IRIS, DID YOU EVER INJECT DRUGS?
NO! GOD! I MEAN YOU LOT, YOU'RE ALWAYS JABBING ME!

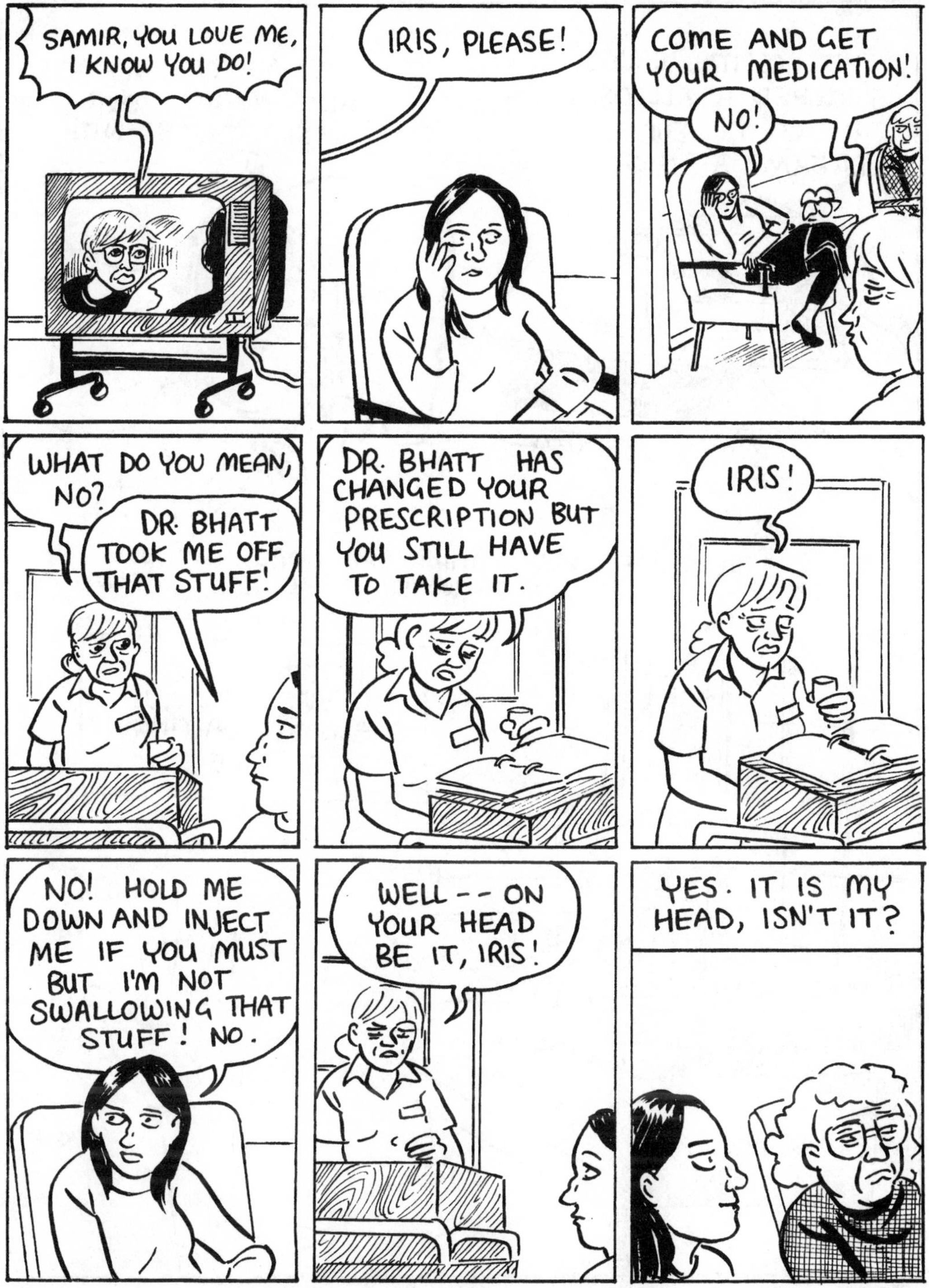
SAMIR, YOU LOVE ME, I KNOW YOU DO!
IRIS, PLEASE!
COME AND GET YOUR MEDICATION!
NO!
WHAT DO YOU MEAN, NO?
DR. BHATT TOOK ME OFF THAT STUFF!
DR. BHATT HAS CHANGED YOUR PRESCRIPTION BUT YOU STILL HAVE TO TAKE IT.
IRIS!
NO! HOLD ME DOWN AND INJECT ME IF YOU MUST BUT I'M NOT SWALLOWING THAT STUFF! NO.
WELL -- ON YOUR HEAD BE IT, IRIS!
YES. IT IS MY HEAD, ISN'T IT?

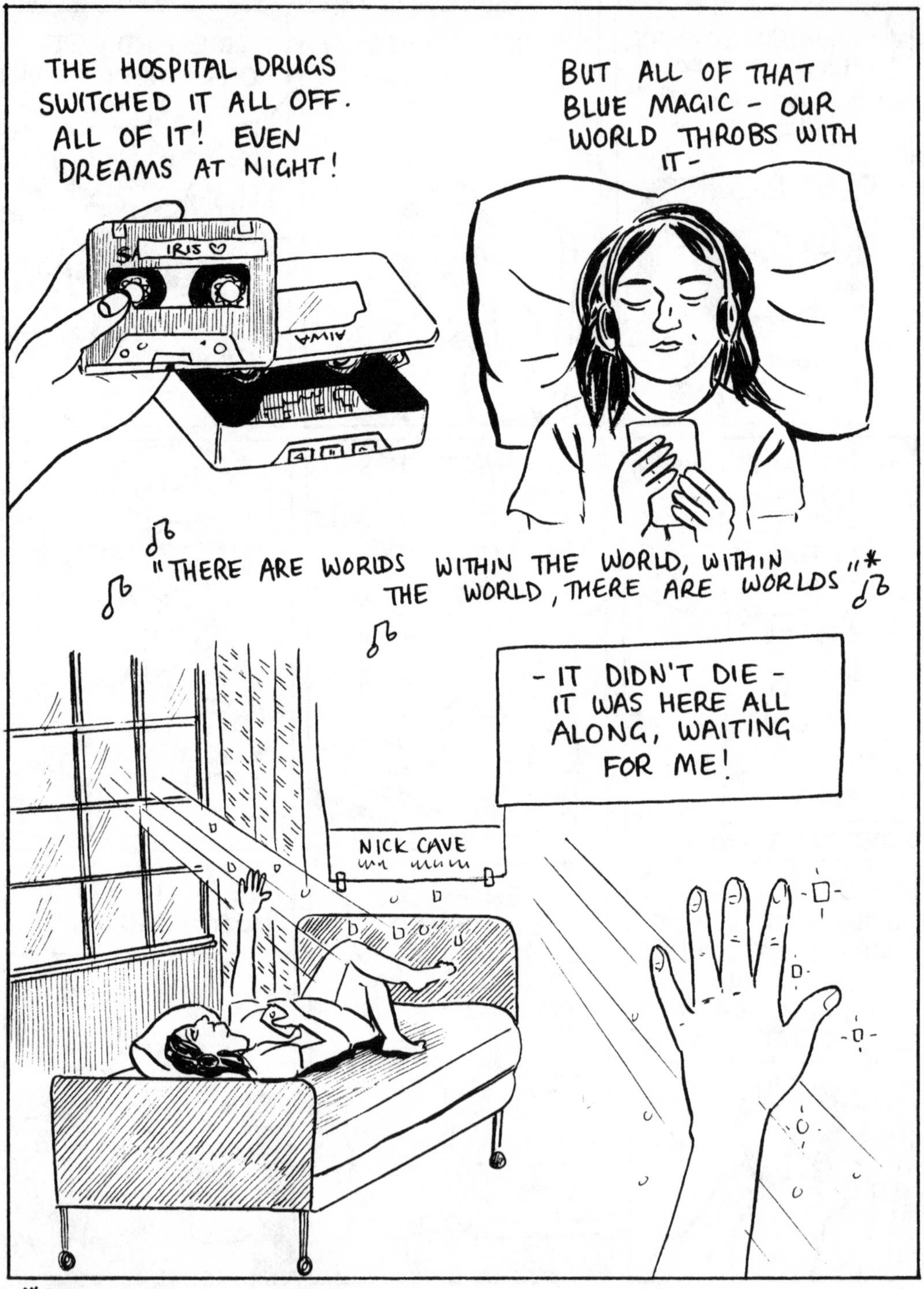
THE HOSPITAL DRUGS SWITCHED IT ALL OFF. ALL OF IT! EVEN DREAMS AT NIGHT!
IRIS ♡
AIWA
BUT ALL OF THAT BLUE MAGIC - OUR WORLD THROBS WITH IT-
"THERE ARE WORLDS WITHIN THE WORLD, WITHIN THE WORLD, THERE ARE WORLDS"*
- IT DIDN'T DIE - IT WAS HERE ALL ALONG, WAITING FOR ME!
NICK CAVE

*STEREOLAB: YOU LITTLE SHITS

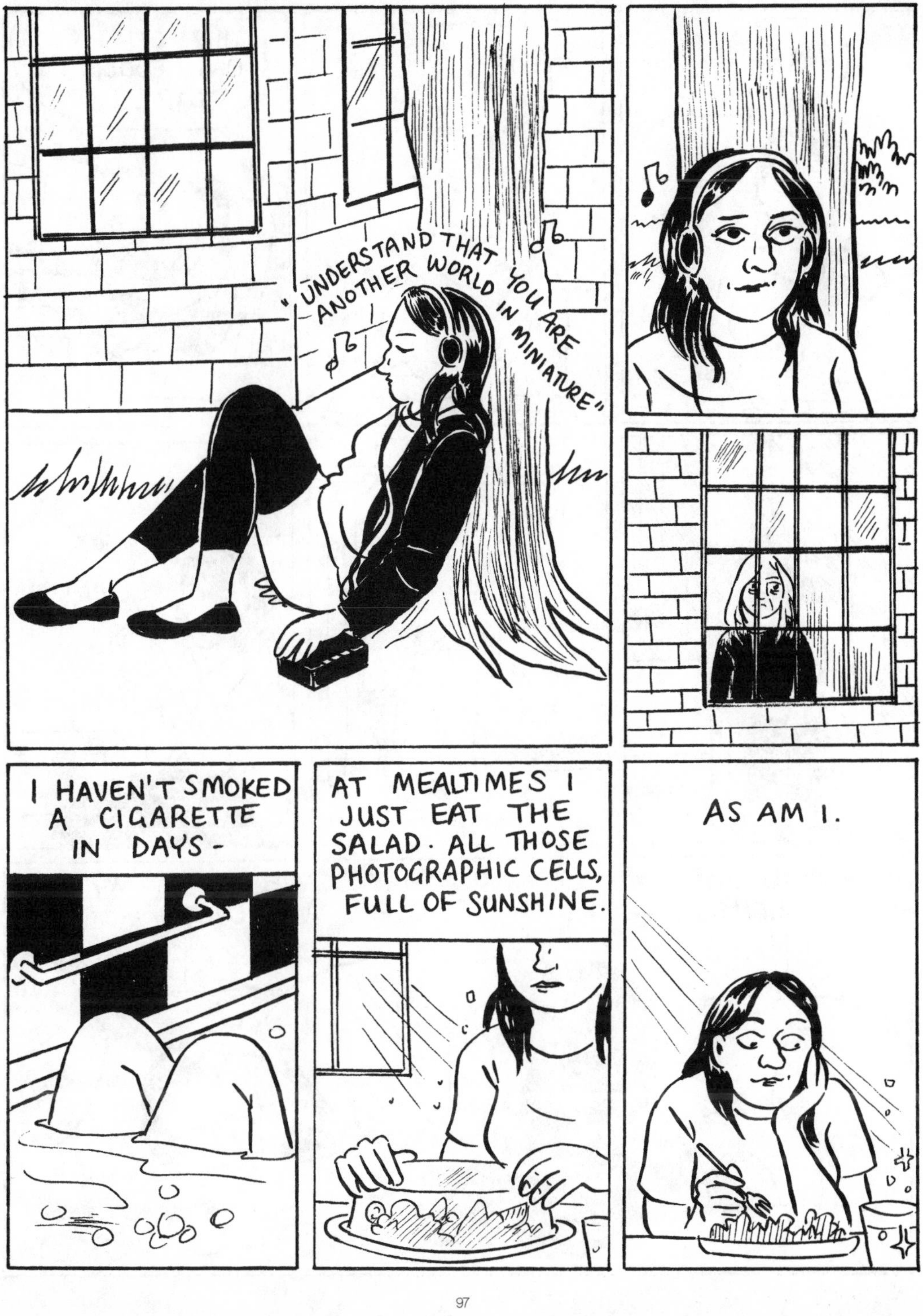
"UNDERSTAND THAT YOU ARE ANOTHER WORLD IN MINIATURE"
I HAVEN'T SMOKED A CIGARETTE IN DAYS -
AT MEALTIMES I JUST EAT THE SALAD. ALL THOSE PHOTOGRAPHIC CELLS, FULL OF SUNSHINE.
AS AM I.

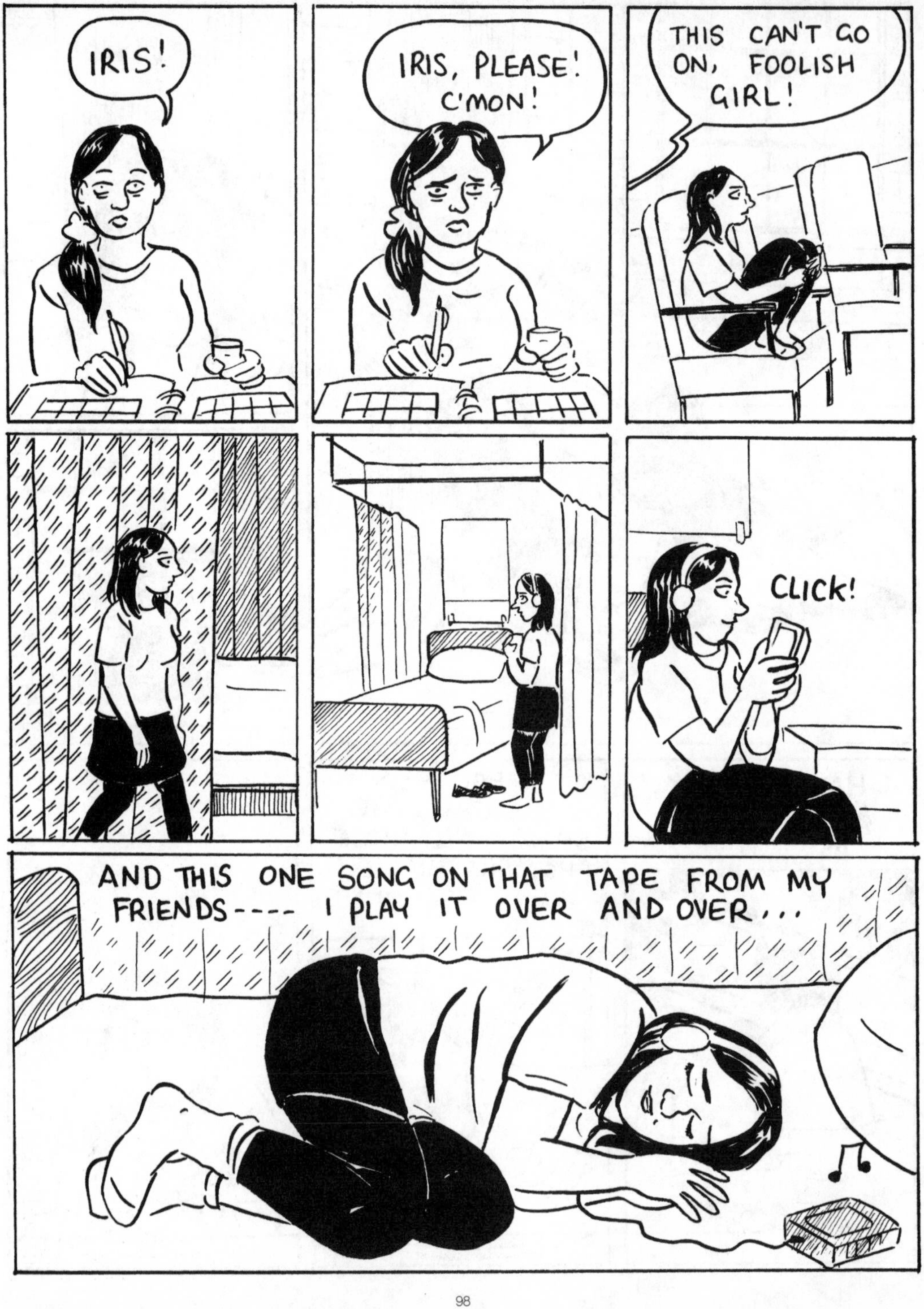
IRIS!
IRIS, PLEASE! C'MON!
THIS CAN'T GO ON, FOOLISH GIRL!
CLICK!
AND THIS ONE SONG ON THAT TAPE FROM MY FRIENDS---- I PLAY IT OVER AND OVER...

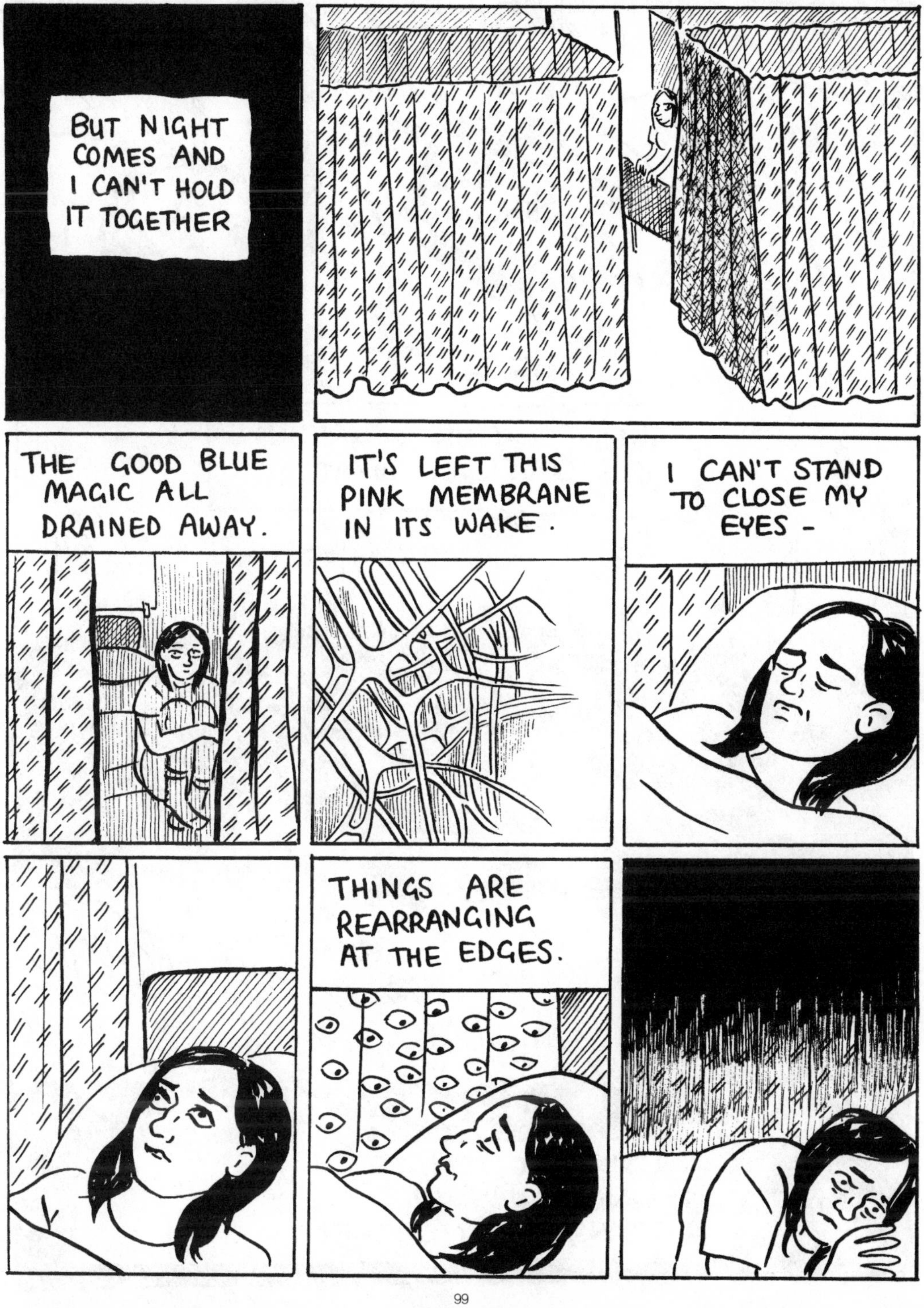
BUT NIGHT COMES AND I CAN'T HOLD IT TOGETHER
THE GOOD BLUE MAGIC ALL DRAINED AWAY.
IT'S LEFT THIS PINK MEMBRANE IN ITS WAKE.
I CAN'T STAND TO CLOSE MY EYES -
THINGS ARE REARRANGING AT THE EDGES.

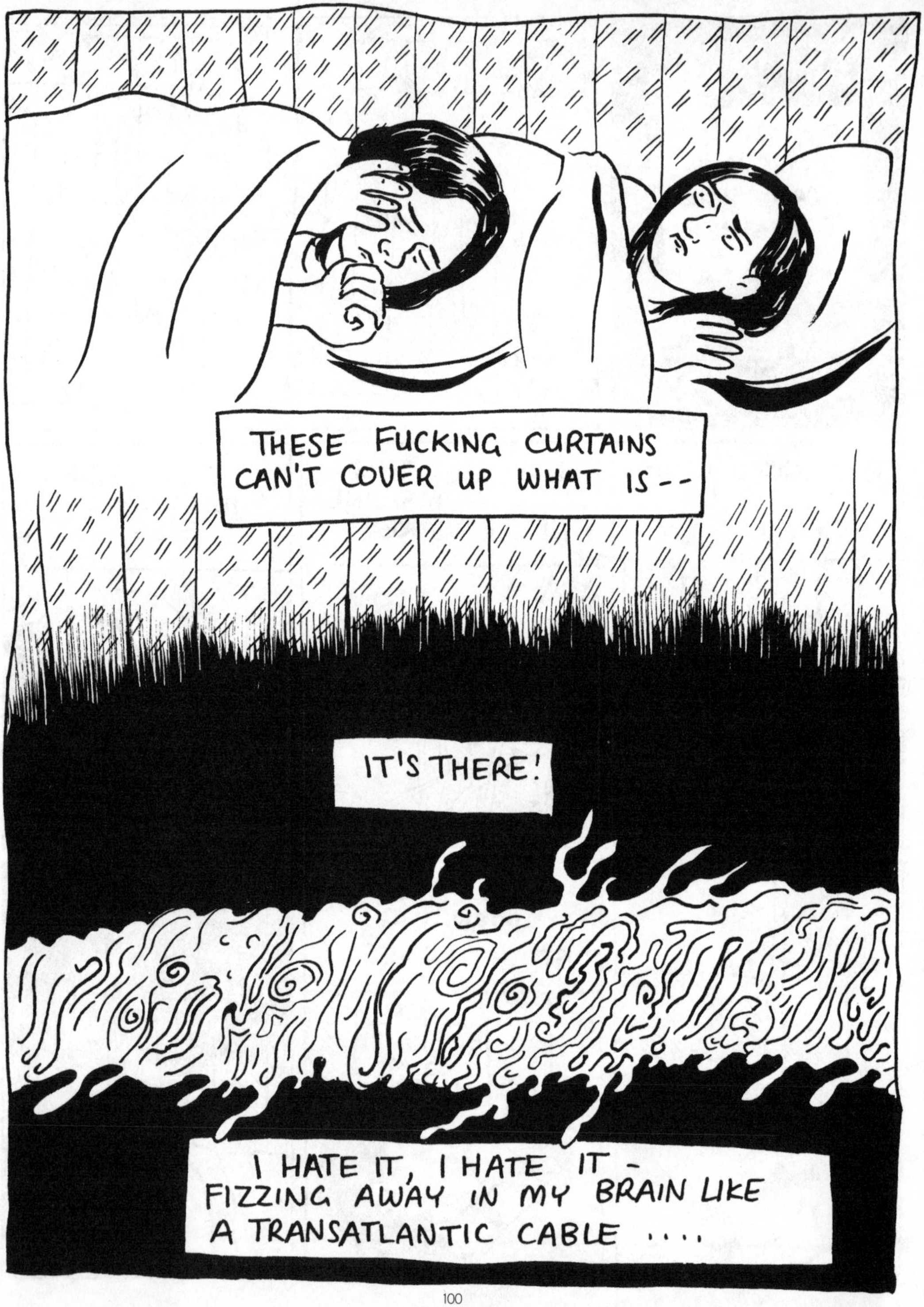
THESE FUCKING CURTAINS CAN'T COVER UP WHAT IS--
IT'S THERE!
I HATE IT, I HATE IT - FIZZING AWAY IN MY BRAIN LIKE A TRANSATLANTIC CABLE ....

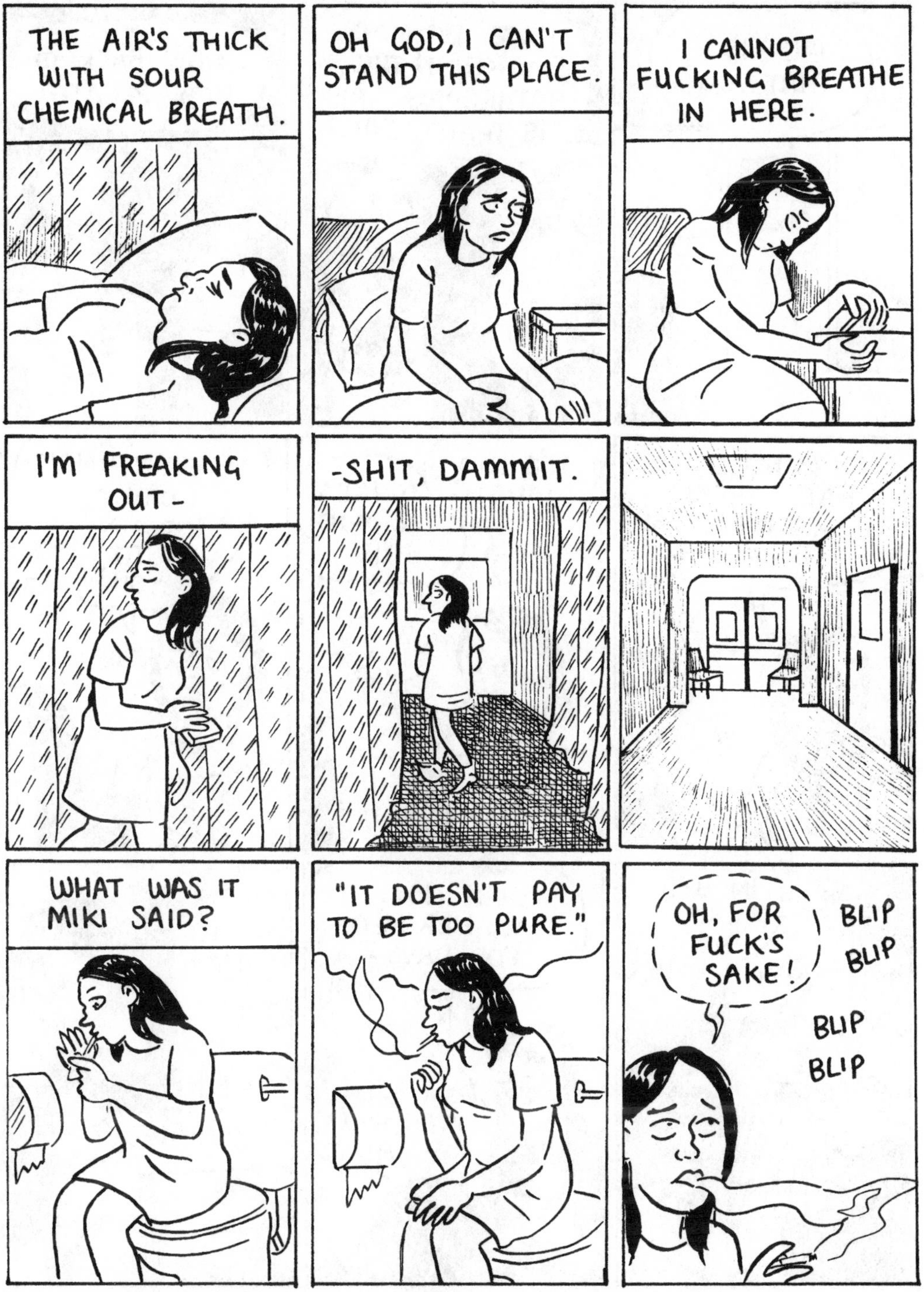
THE AIR'S THICK WITH SOUR CHEMICAL BREATH.
OH GOD, I CAN'T STAND THIS PLACE.
I CANNOT FUCKING BREATHE IN HERE.
I'M FREAKING OUT-
-SHIT, DAMMIT.
WHAT WAS IT MIKI SAID?
"IT DOESN'T PAY TO BE TOO PURE."
OH, FOR FUCK'S SAKE!
BLIP
BLIP
BLIP
BLIP

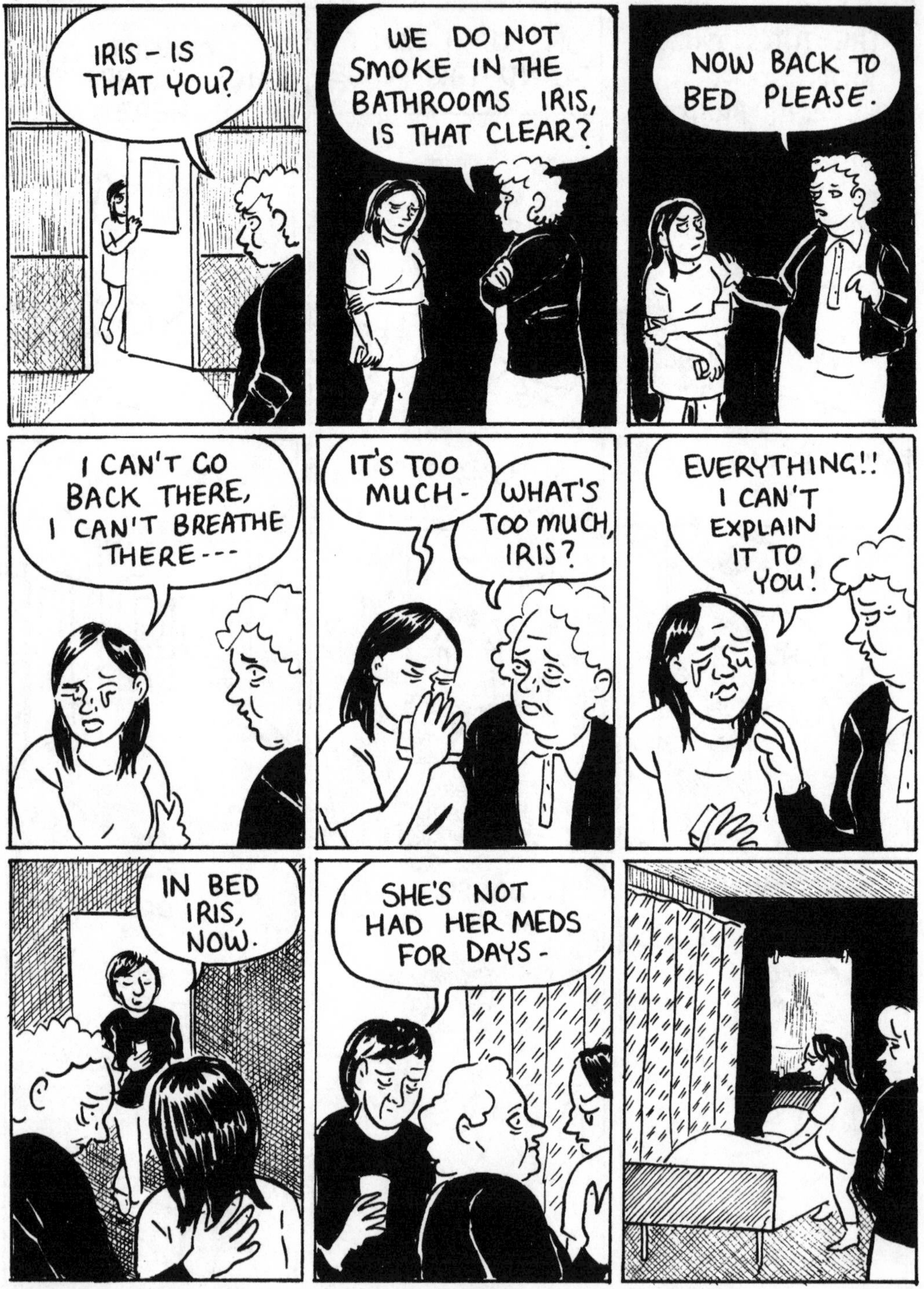
IRIS - IS THAT YOU?
WE DO NOT SMOKE IN THE BATHROOMS IRIS, IS THAT CLEAR?
NOW BACK TO BED PLEASE.
I CAN'T GO BACK THERE, I CAN'T BREATHE THERE---
IT'S TOO MUCH-
WHAT'S TOO MUCH, IRIS?
EVERYTHING!! I CAN'T EXPLAIN IT TO YOU!
IN BED IRIS, NOW.
SHE'S NOT HAD HER MEDS FOR DAYS-

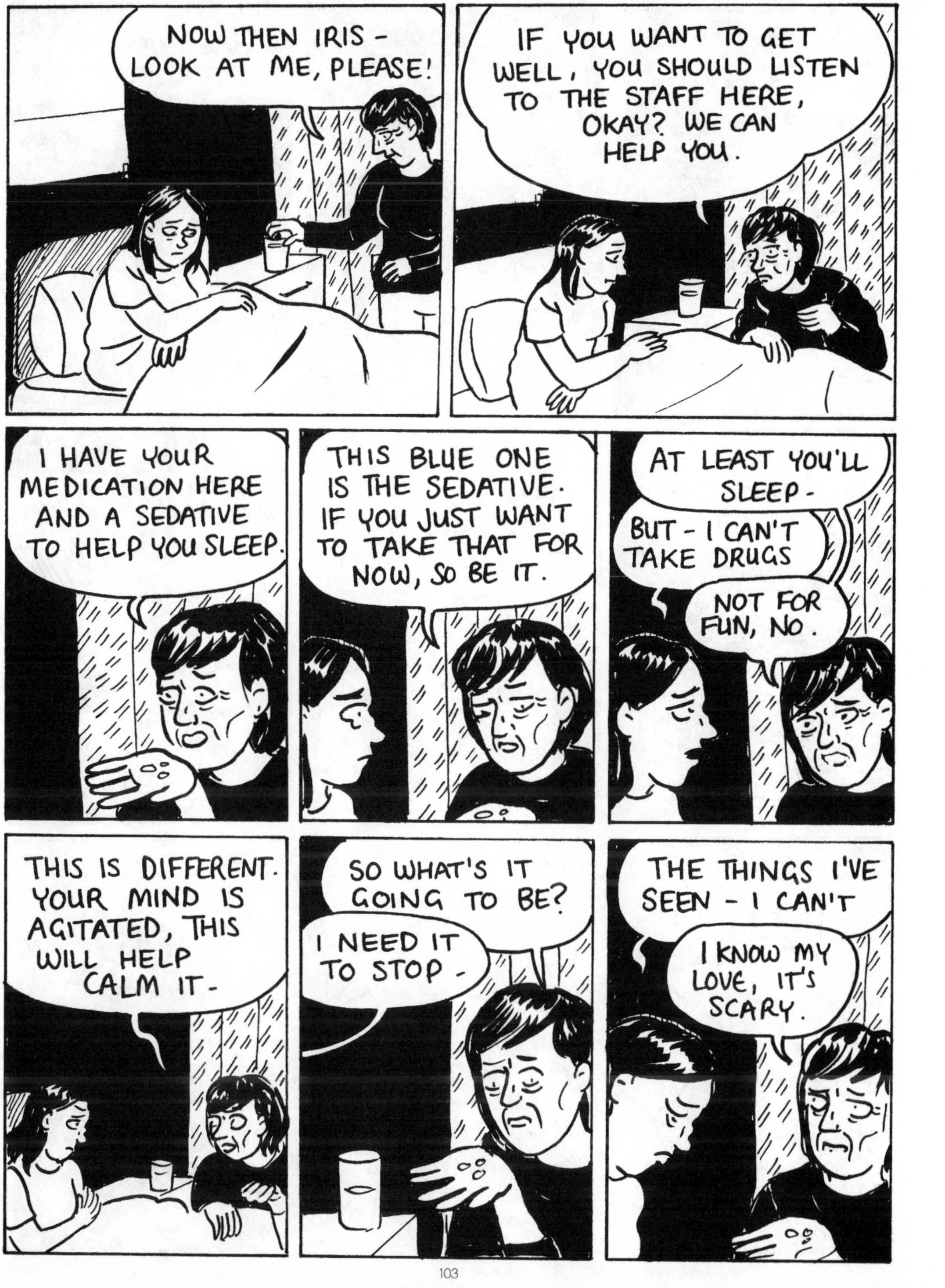
NOW THEN IRIS - LOOK AT ME, PLEASE!
IF YOU WANT TO GET WELL, YOU SHOULD LISTEN TO THE STAFF HERE, OKAY? WE CAN HELP YOU.
I HAVE YOUR MEDICATION HERE AND A SEDATIVE TO HELP YOU SLEEP.
THIS BLUE ONE IS THE SEDATIVE. IF YOU JUST WANT TO TAKE THAT FOR NOW, SO BE IT.
AT LEAST YOU'LL SLEEP -
BUT - I CAN'T TAKE DRUGS
NOT FOR FUN, NO.
THIS IS DIFFERENT. YOUR MIND IS AGITATED, THIS WILL HELP CALM IT -
SO WHAT'S IT GOING TO BE?
I NEED IT TO STOP -
THE THINGS I'VE SEEN - I CAN'T
I KNOW MY LOVE, IT'S SCARY.

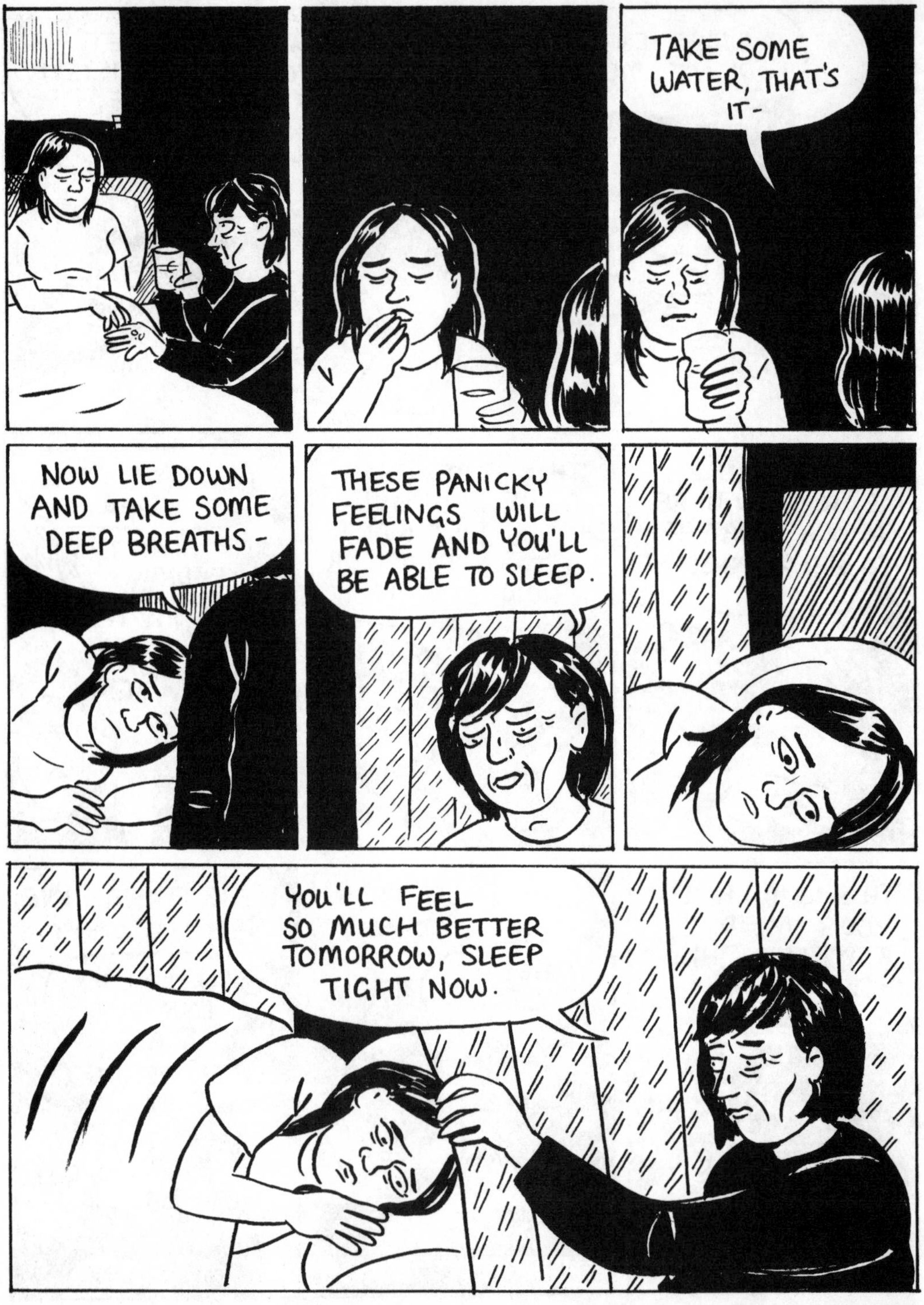
TAKE SOME WATER, THAT'S IT-
NOW LIE DOWN AND TAKE SOME DEEP BREATHS-
THESE PANICKY FEELINGS WILL FADE AND YOU'LL BE ABLE TO SLEEP.
YOU'LL FEEL SO MUCH BETTER TOMORROW, SLEEP TIGHT NOW.

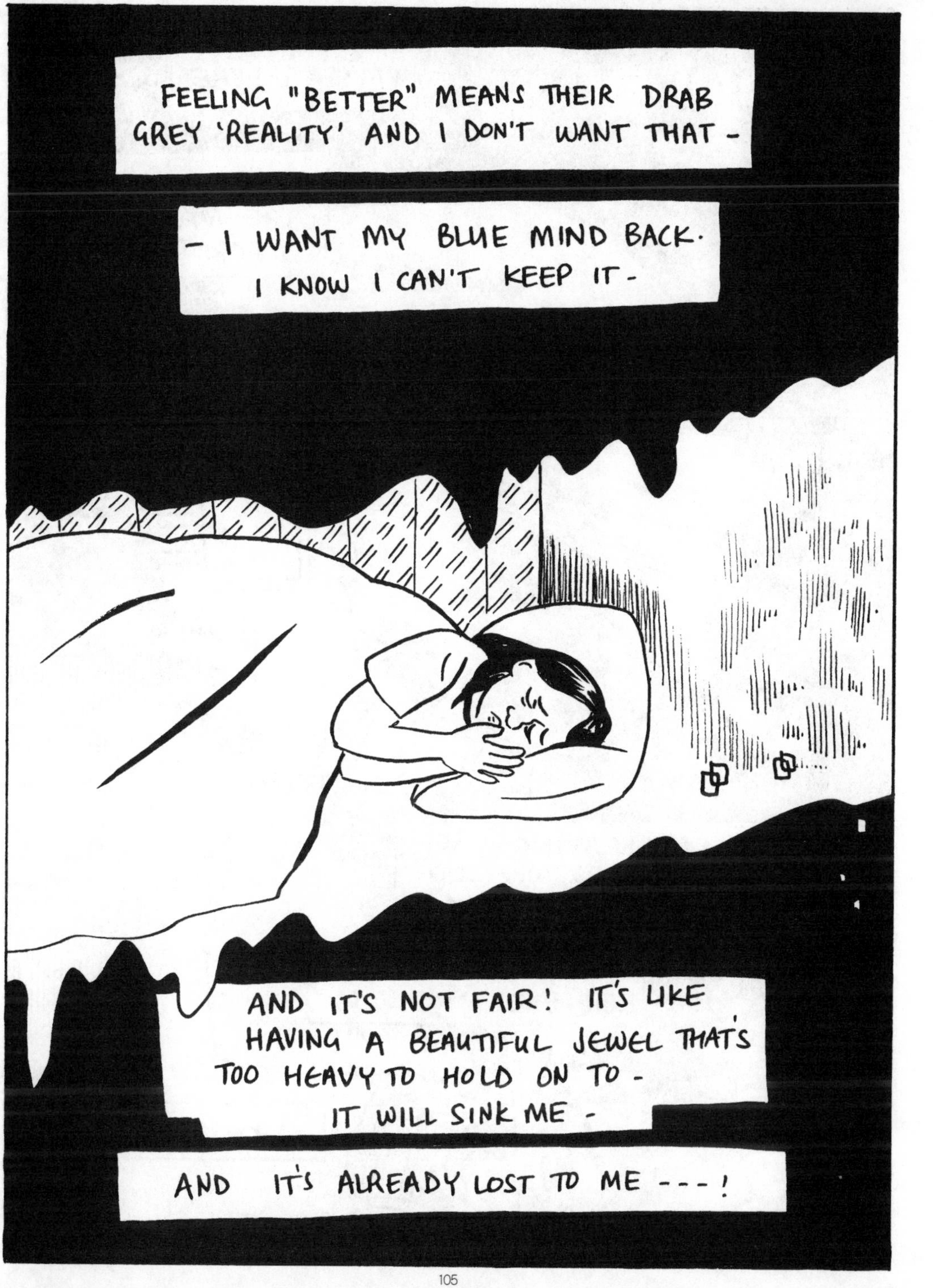
FEELING "BETTER" MEANS THEIR DRAB GREY 'REALITY' AND I DON'T WANT THAT -
- I WANT MY BLUE MIND BACK. I KNOW I CAN'T KEEP IT -
AND IT'S NOT FAIR! IT'S LIKE HAVING A BEAUTIFUL JEWEL THAT'S TOO HEAVY TO HOLD ON TO - IT WILL SINK ME -
AND IT'S ALREADY LOST TO ME ---!

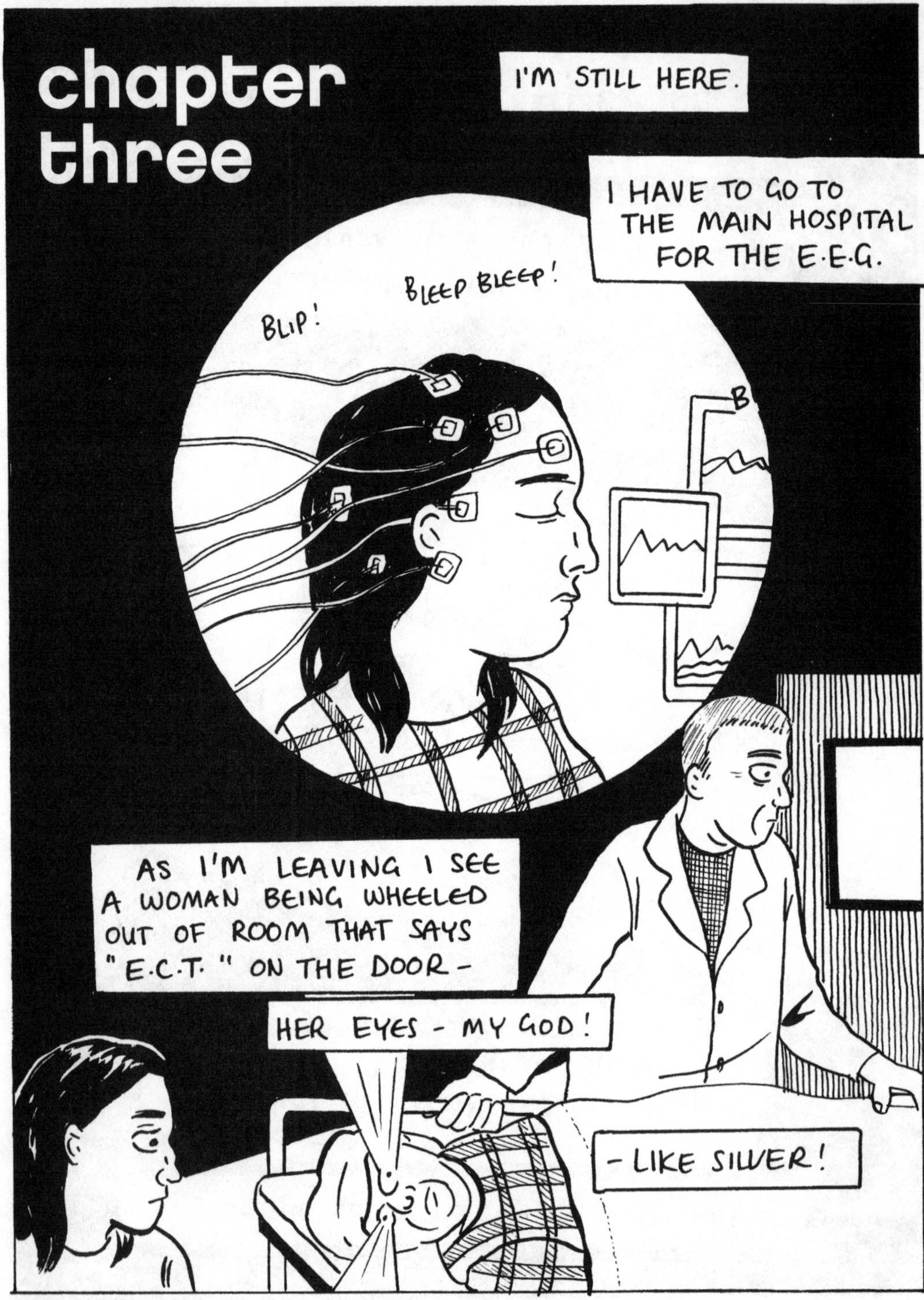
chapter three
I'M STILL HERE.
I HAVE TO GO TO THE MAIN HOSPITAL FOR THE E·E·G.
BLIP!
BLEEP BLEEP!
AS I'M LEAVING I SEE A WOMAN BEING WHEELED OUT OF ROOM THAT SAYS "E·C·T·" ON THE DOOR -
HER EYES - MY GOD!
- LIKE SILVER!

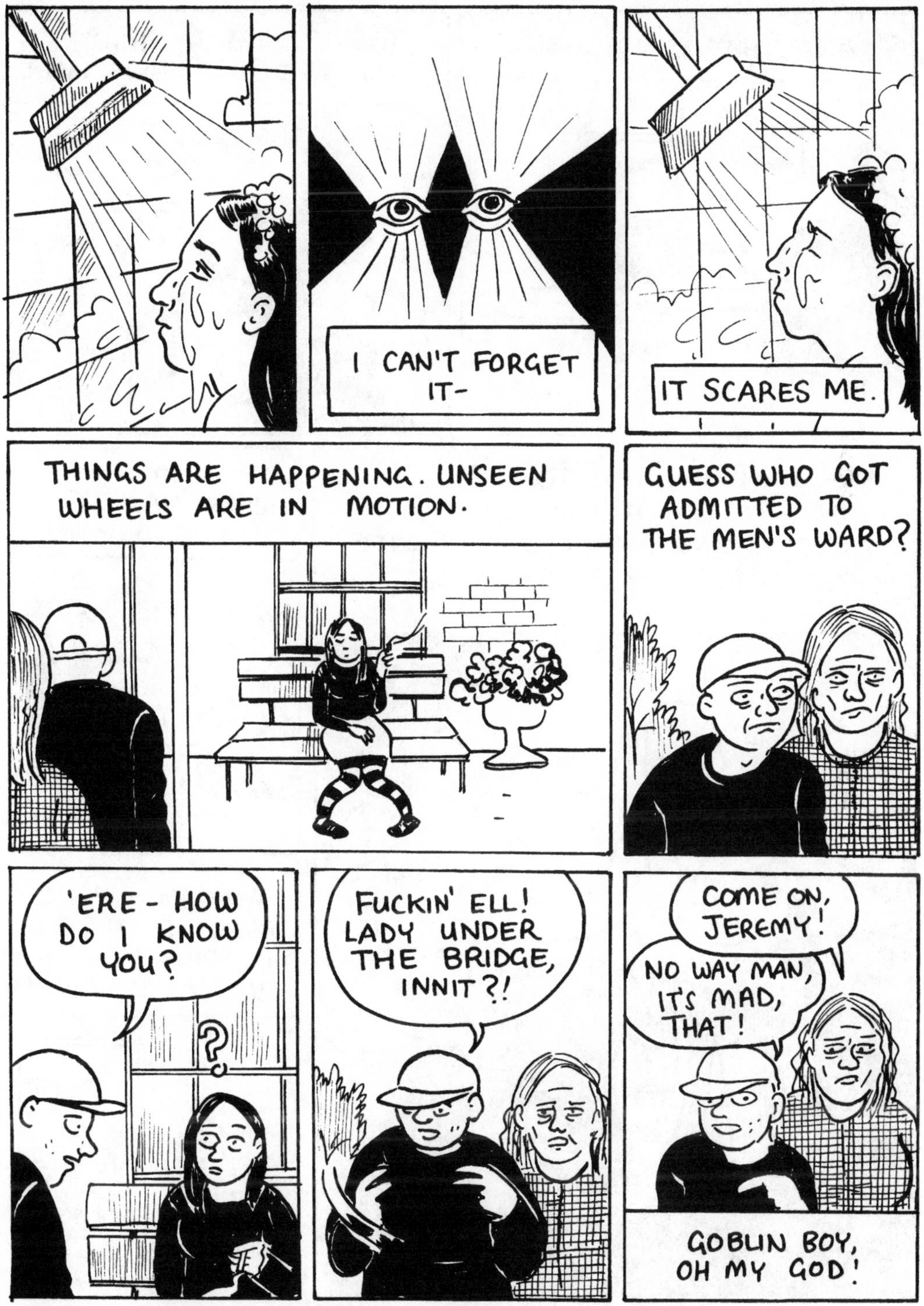
I CAN'T FORGET IT-
IT SCARES ME.
THINGS ARE HAPPENING. UNSEEN WHEELS ARE IN MOTION.
GUESS WHO GOT ADMITTED TO THE MEN'S WARD?
'ERE - HOW DO I KNOW YOU?
?
FUCKIN' ELL! LADY UNDER THE BRIDGE, INNIT?!
COME ON, JEREMY!
NO WAY MAN, IT'S MAD, THAT!
GOBLIN BOY, OH MY GOD!

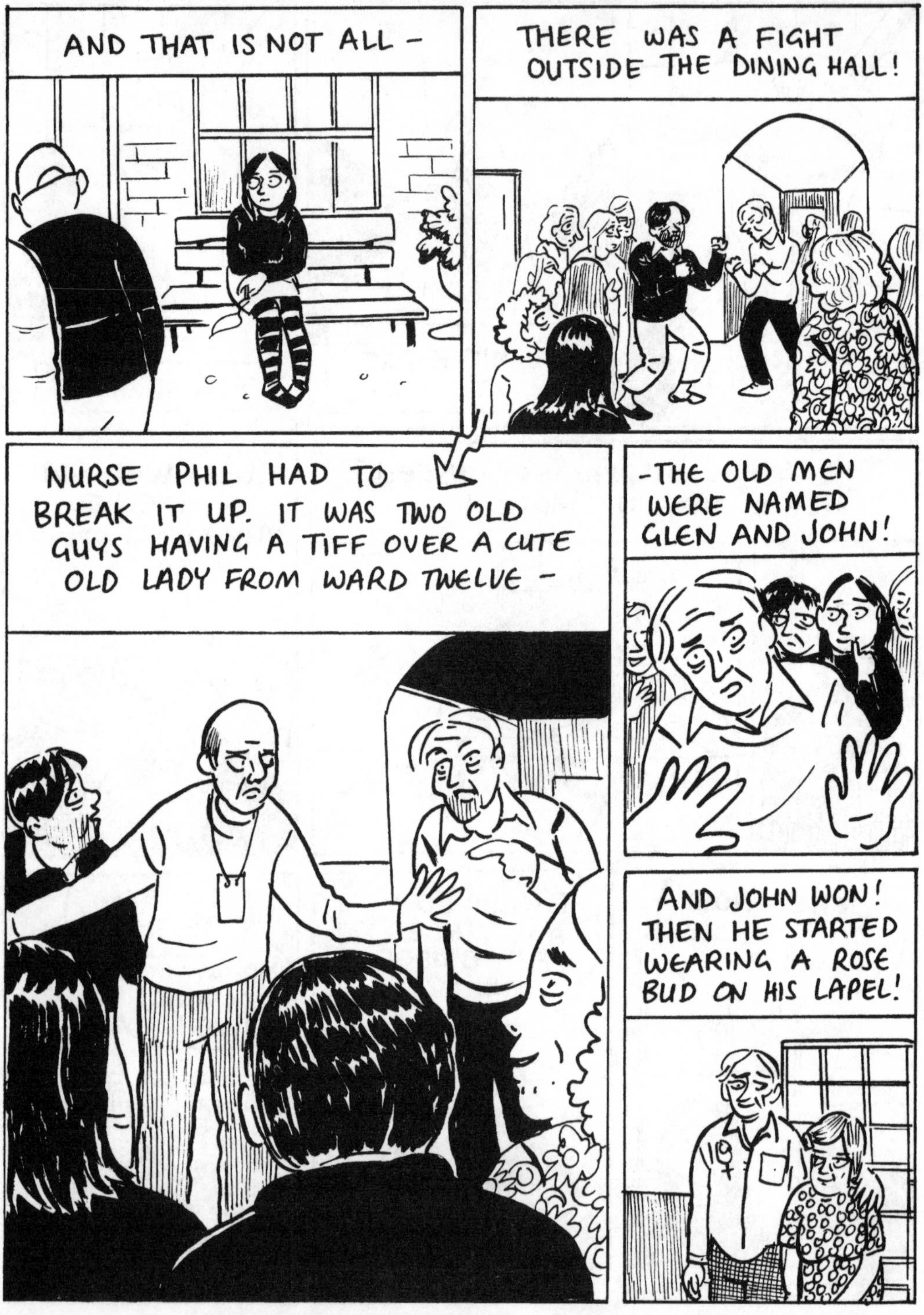
AND THAT IS NOT ALL -
THERE WAS A FIGHT OUTSIDE THE DINING HALL!
NURSE PHIL HAD TO BREAK IT UP. IT WAS TWO OLD GUYS HAVING A TIFF OVER A CUTE OLD LADY FROM WARD TWELVE -
-THE OLD MEN WERE NAMED GLEN AND JOHN!
AND JOHN WON! THEN HE STARTED WEARING A ROSE BUD ON HIS LAPEL!

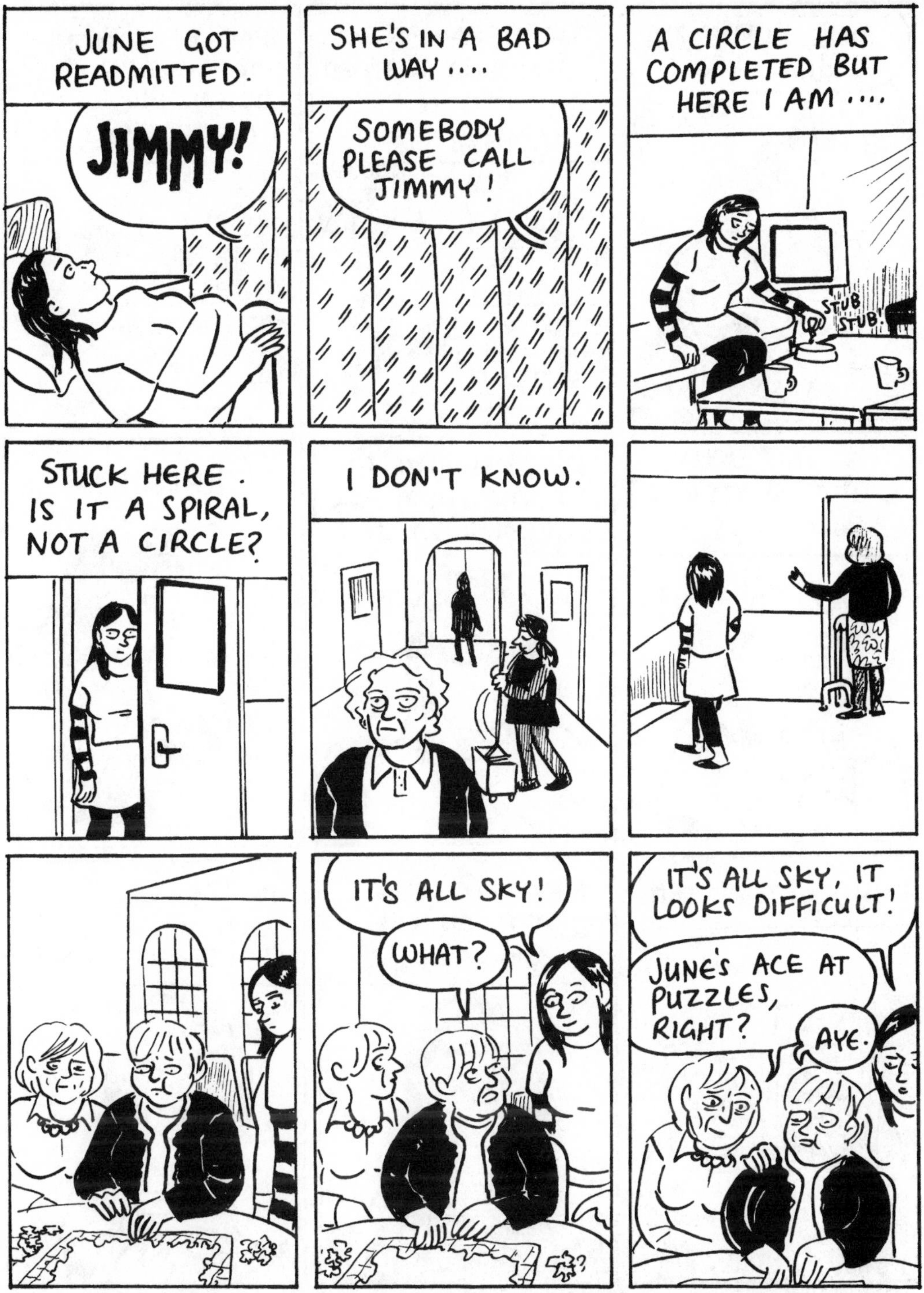
JUNE GOT READMITTED.
JIMMY!
SHE'S IN A BAD WAY....
SOMEBODY PLEASE CALL JIMMY!
A CIRCLE HAS COMPLETED BUT HERE I AM....
STUB STUB!
STUCK HERE. IS IT A SPIRAL, NOT A CIRCLE?
I DON'T KNOW.
IT'S ALL SKY!
WHAT?
IT'S ALL SKY, IT LOOKS DIFFICULT!
JUNE'S ACE AT PUZZLES, RIGHT?
AYE.

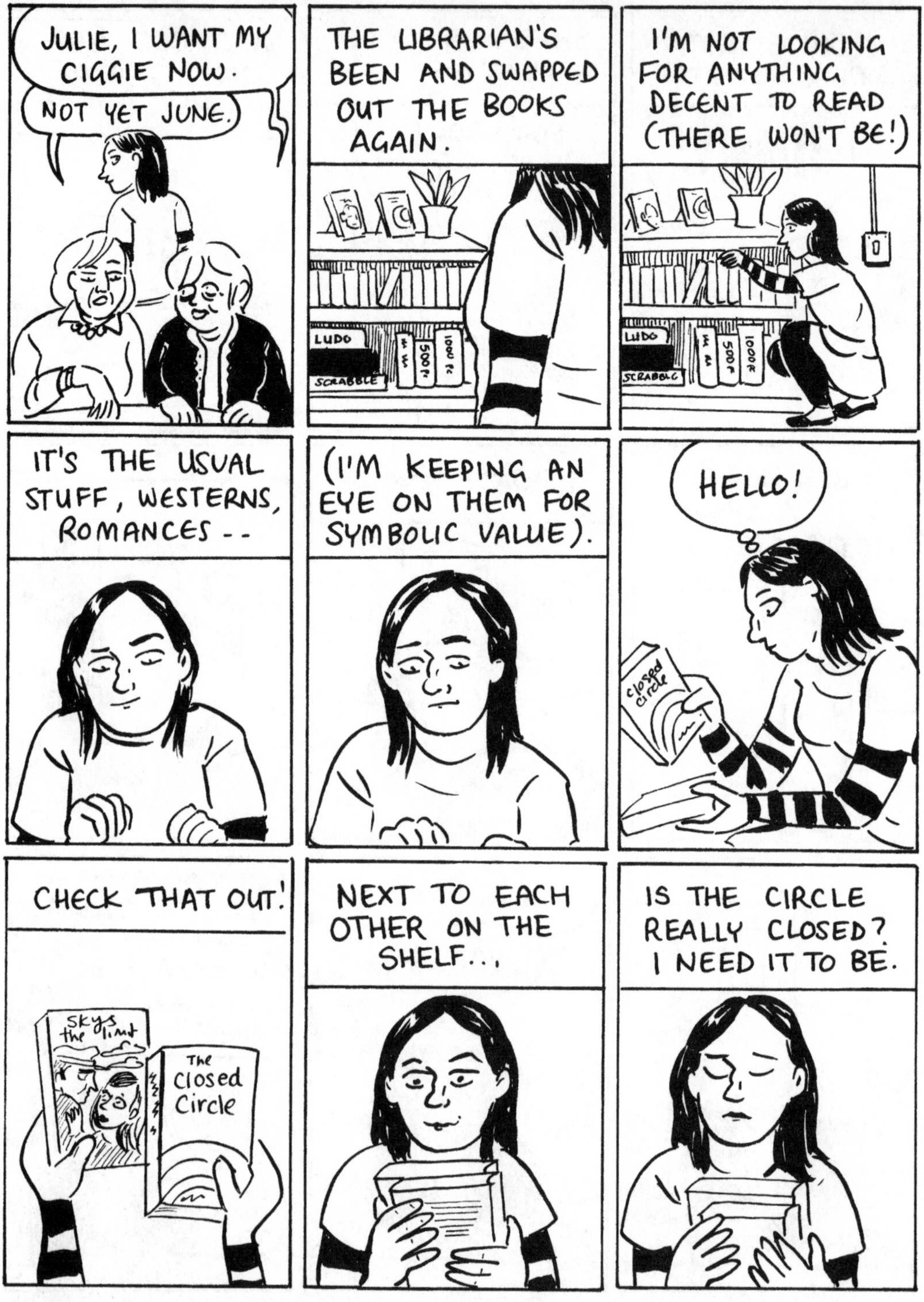

JULIE, I WANT MY CIGGIE NOW.
NOT YET JUNE.
THE LIBRARIAN'S BEEN AND SWAPPED OUT THE BOOKS AGAIN.
LUDO
SCRABBLE
I'M NOT LOOKING FOR ANYTHING DECENT TO READ (THERE WON'T BE!)
IT'S THE USUAL STUFF, WESTERNS, ROMANCES --
(I'M KEEPING AN EYE ON THEM FOR SYMBOLIC VALUE).
HELLO!
closed circle
CHECK THAT OUT!
Skys the limit
The Closed Circle
NEXT TO EACH OTHER ON THE SHELF...
IS THE CIRCLE REALLY CLOSED? I NEED IT TO BE.

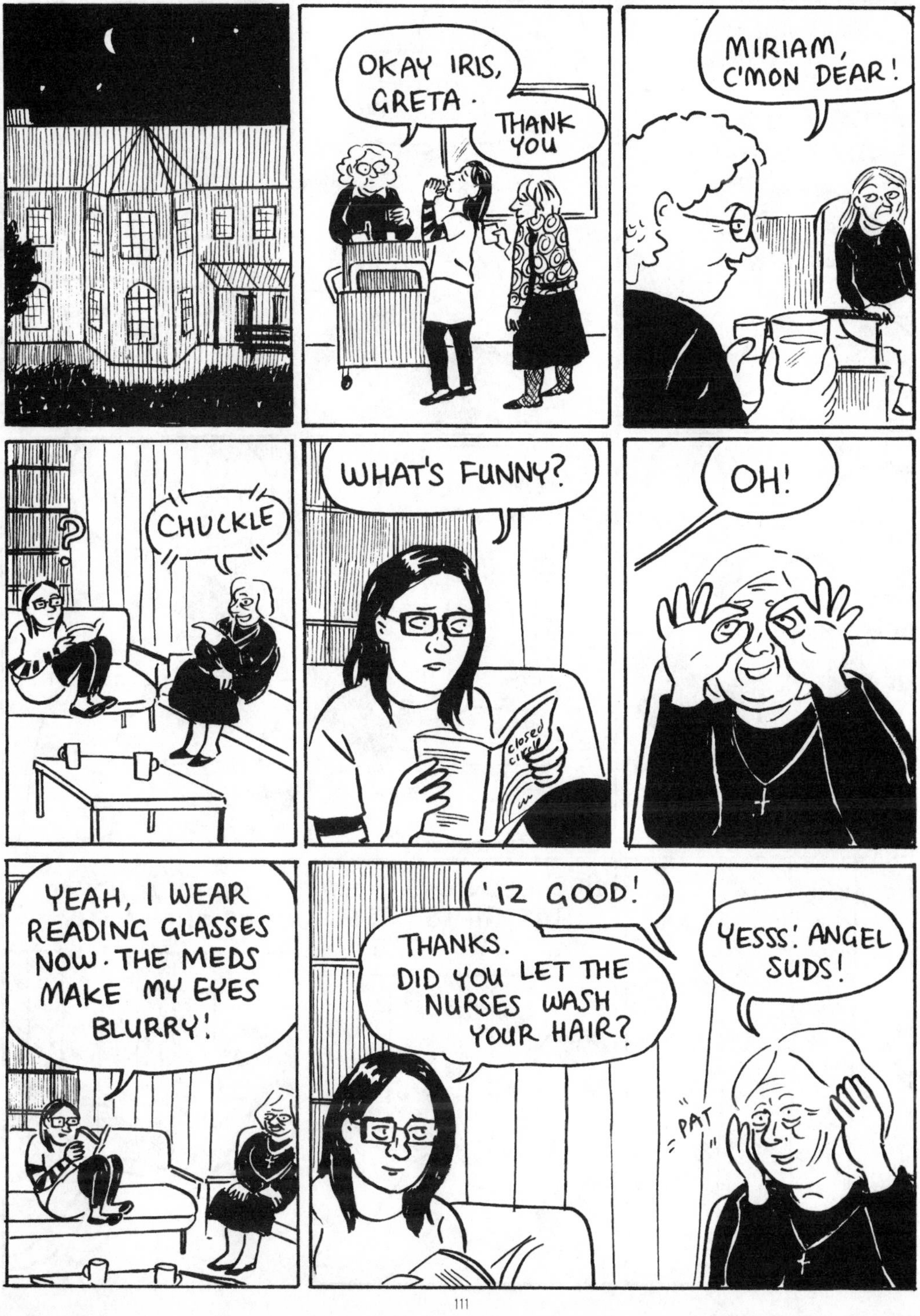

OKAY IRIS, GRETA.
THANK YOU
MIRIAM, C'MON DEAR!
?
CHUCKLE
WHAT'S FUNNY?
closed circle
OH!
YEAH, I WEAR READING GLASSES NOW. THE MEDS MAKE MY EYES BLURRY!
'IZ GOOD!
THANKS. DID YOU LET THE NURSES WASH YOUR HAIR?
YESSS! ANGEL SUDS!
PAT

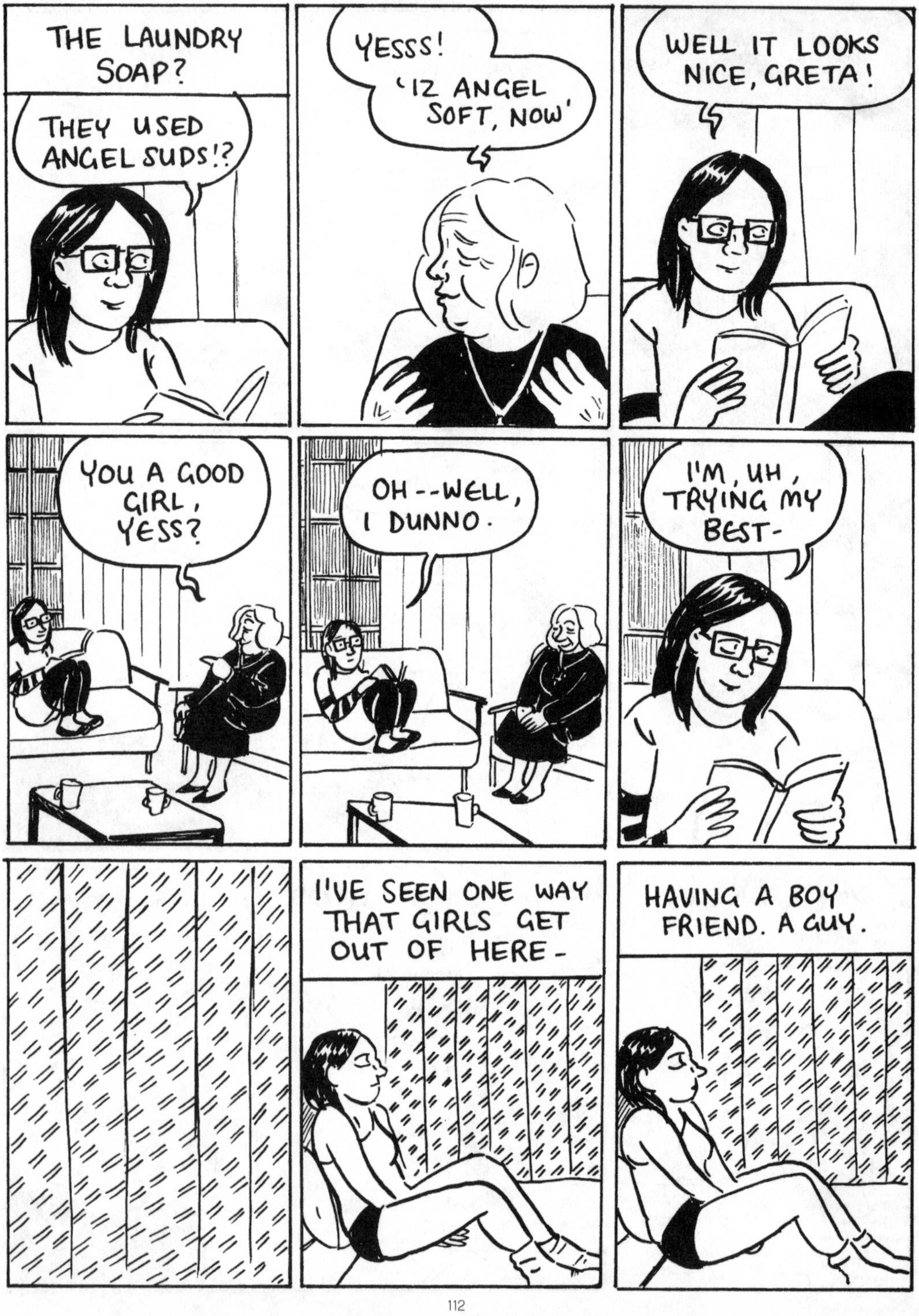
THE LAUNDRY SOAP?
THEY USED ANGEL SUDS!?
YESSS! 'IZ ANGEL SOFT, NOW'
WELL IT LOOKS NICE, GRETA!
YOU A GOOD GIRL, YESS?
OH--WELL, I DUNNO.
I'M, UH, TRYING MY BEST-
I'VE SEEN ONE WAY THAT GIRLS GET OUT OF HERE-
HAVING A BOY FRIEND. A GUY.

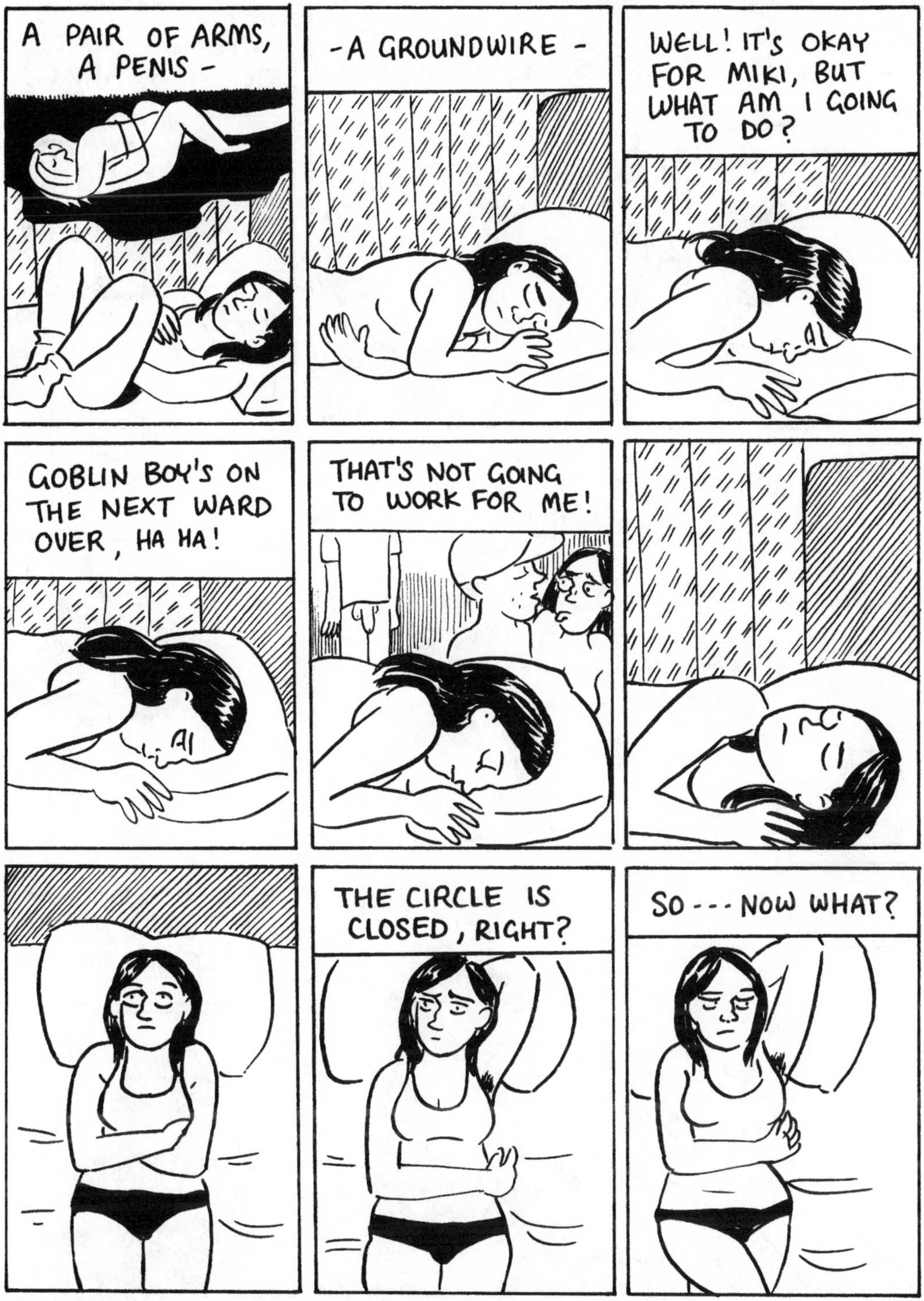
A PAIR OF ARMS, A PENIS -
- A GROUNDWIRE -
WELL! IT'S OKAY FOR MIKI, BUT WHAT AM I GOING TO DO?
GOBLIN BOY'S ON THE NEXT WARD OVER, HA HA!
THAT'S NOT GOING TO WORK FOR ME!
THE CIRCLE IS CLOSED, RIGHT?
SO --- NOW WHAT?

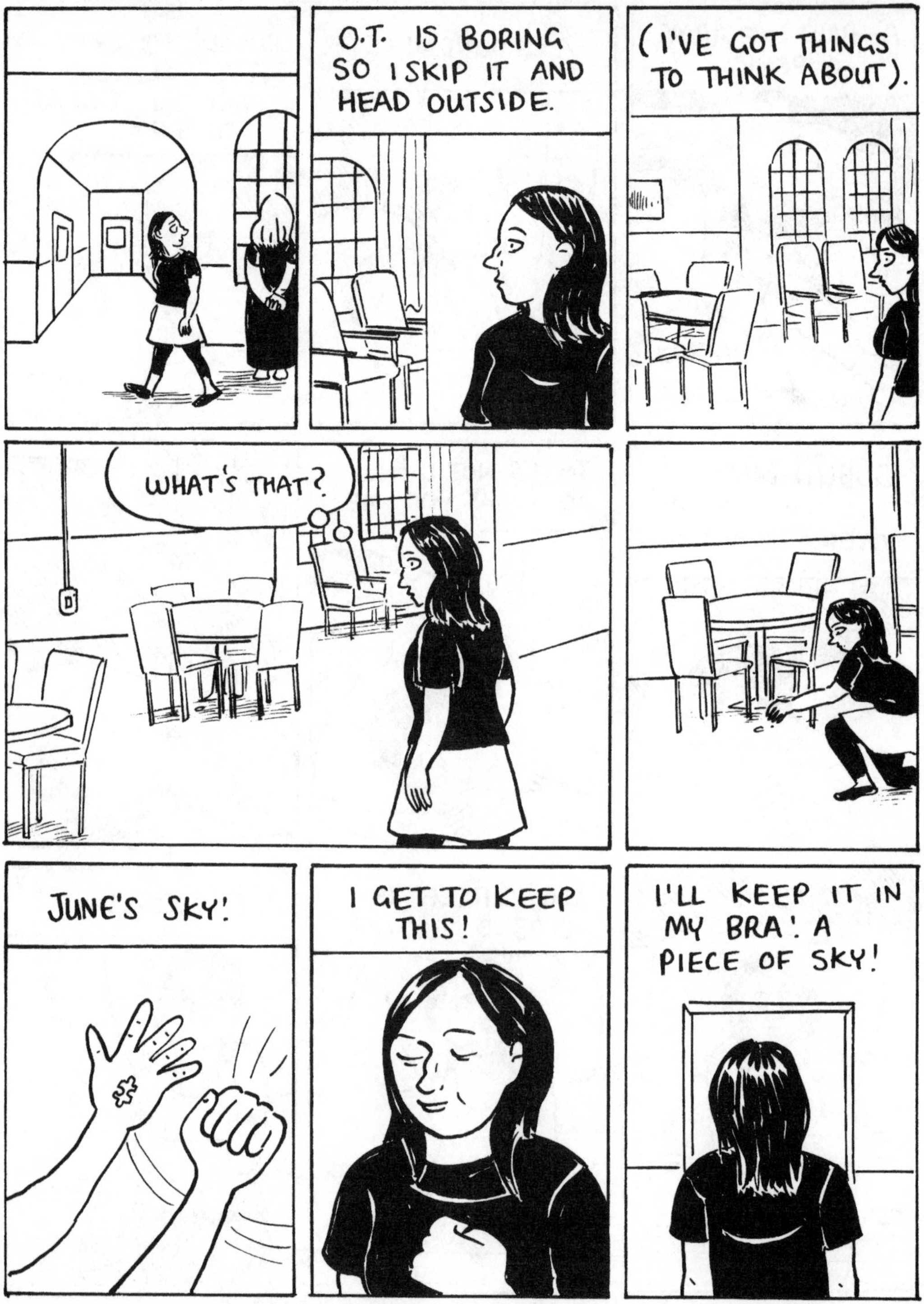
O.T. IS BORING SO I SKIP IT AND HEAD OUTSIDE.
(I'VE GOT THINGS TO THINK ABOUT).
WHAT'S THAT?
JUNE'S SKY!
I GET TO KEEP THIS!
I'LL KEEP IT IN MY BRA! A PIECE OF SKY!

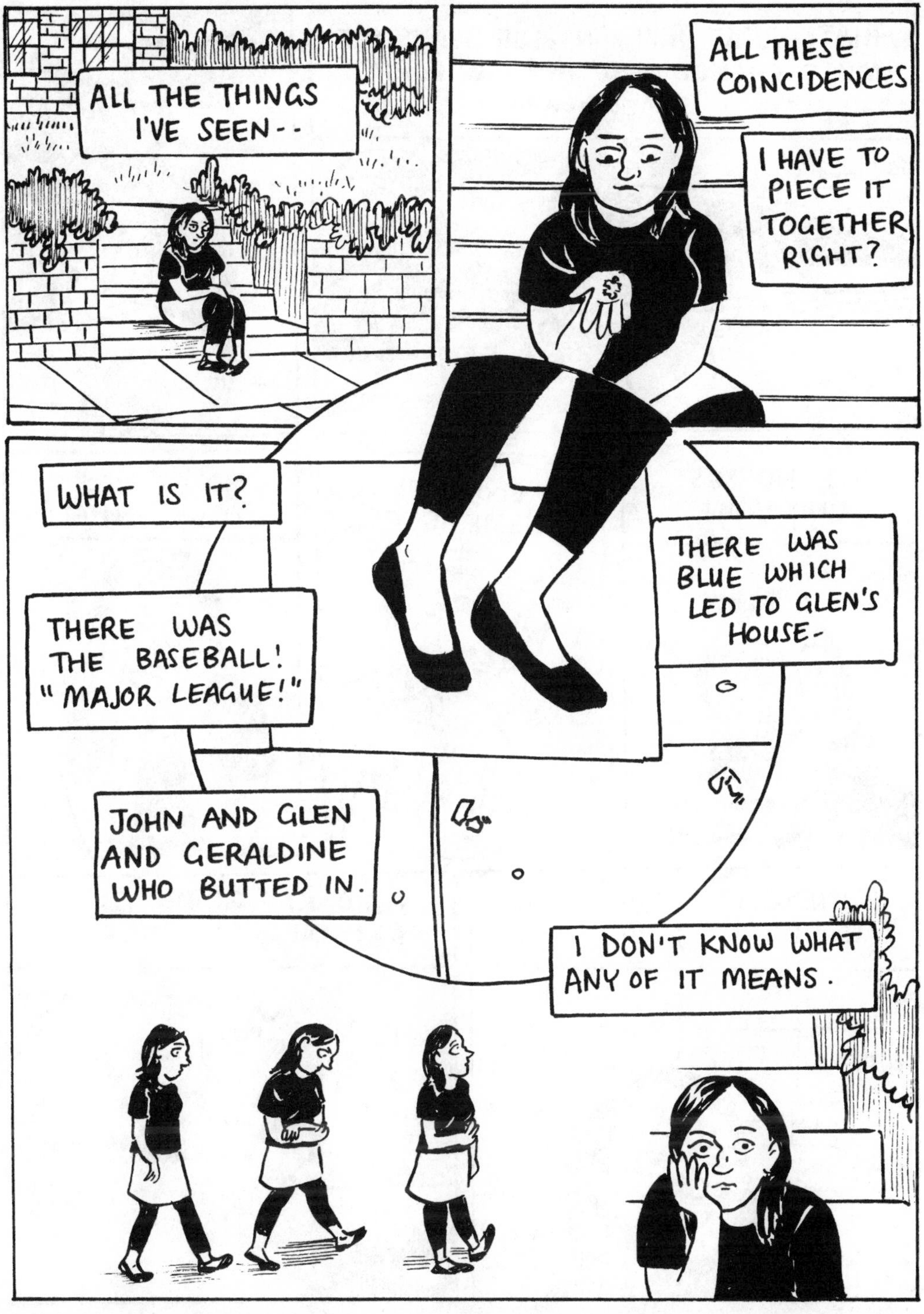
ALL THE THINGS I'VE SEEN--
ALL THESE COINCIDENCES
I HAVE TO PIECE IT TOGETHER RIGHT?
WHAT IS IT?
THERE WAS THE BASEBALL! "MAJOR LEAGUE!"
THERE WAS BLUE WHICH LED TO GLEN'S HOUSE-
JOHN AND GLEN AND GERALDINE WHO BUTTED IN.
I DON'T KNOW WHAT ANY OF IT MEANS.

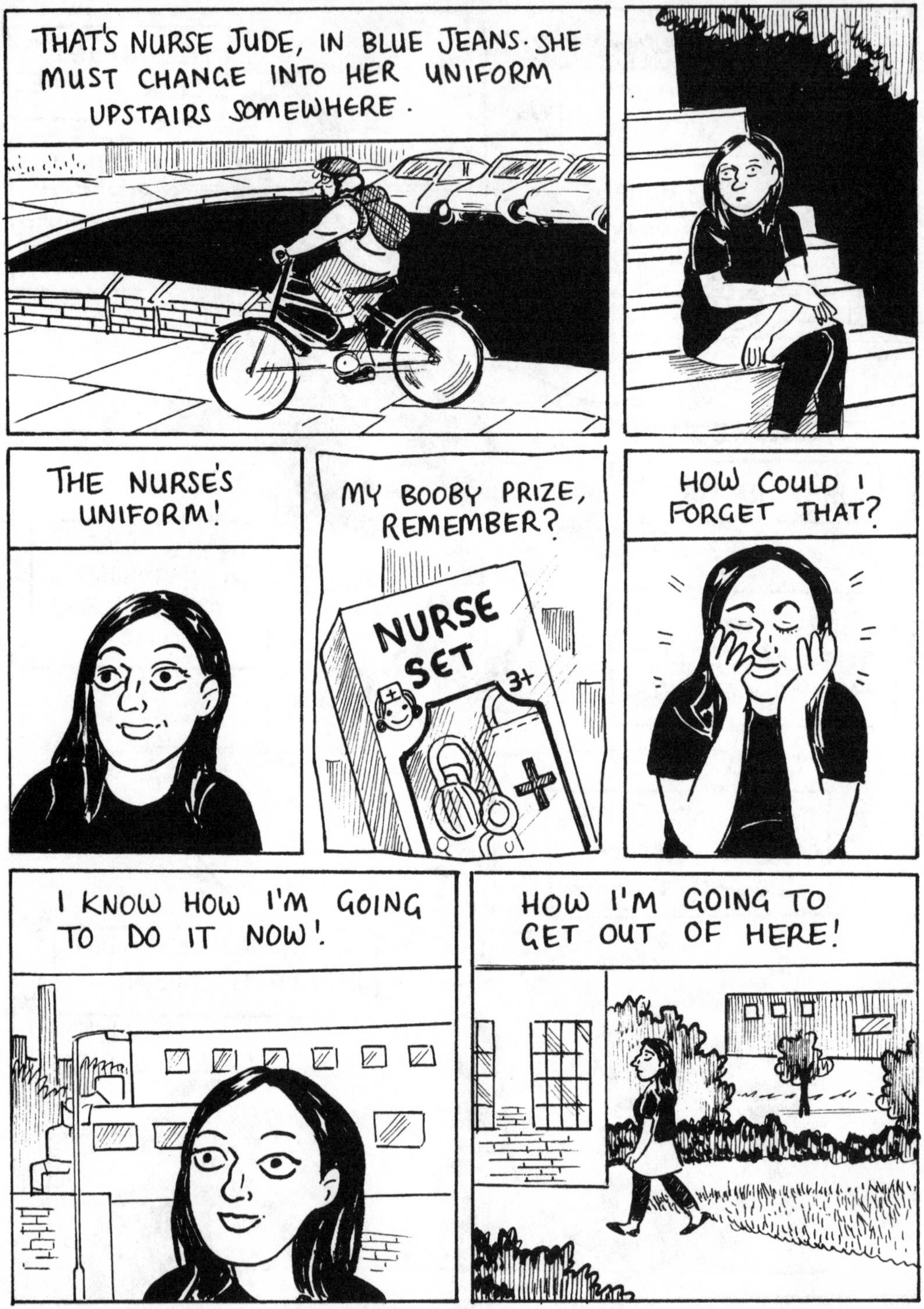
THAT'S NURSE JUDE, IN BLUE JEANS. SHE MUST CHANGE INTO HER UNIFORM UPSTAIRS SOMEWHERE.
THE NURSE'S UNIFORM!
MY BOOBY PRIZE, REMEMBER?
NURSE SET
3+
HOW COULD I FORGET THAT?
I KNOW HOW I'M GOING TO DO IT NOW!
HOW I'M GOING TO GET OUT OF HERE!

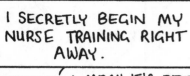 I SECRETLY BEGIN MY NURSE TRAINING RIGHT AWAY.

I MEAN IT'S BETTER NOW JULIE'S BACK—

 I PAY CLOSE ATTENTION.

SHE'S STILL VERY ERRATIC THOUGH.

YES

 UH— CAN WE HELP YOU, IRIS?

NOPE! JUST CLEANING UP THESE CUPS.

 WELL, THANKS

NO PROBLEM

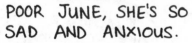 POOR JUNE, SHE'S SO SAD AND ANXIOUS.

 UGHNNNN

OH JUNE! NO!

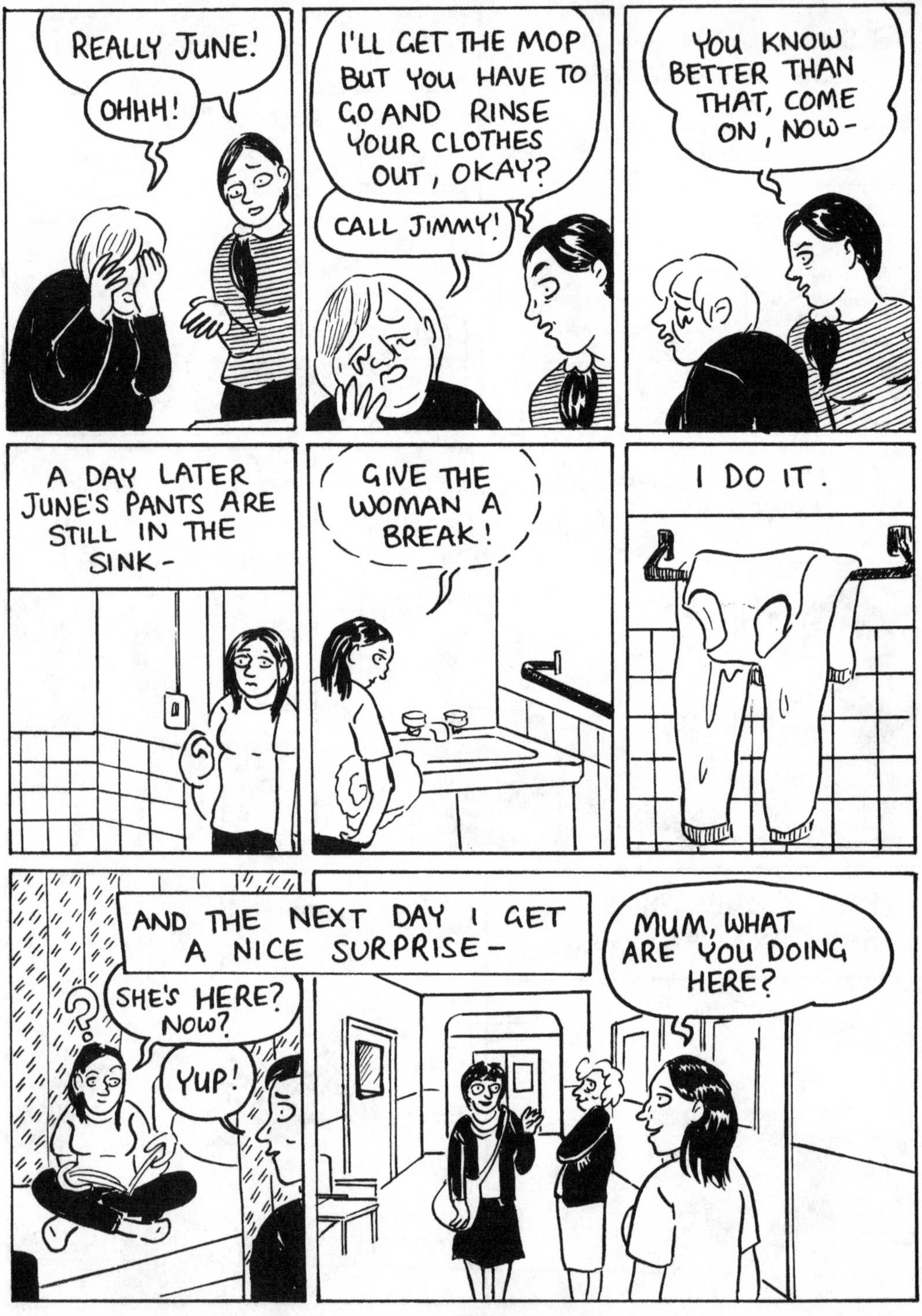
REALLY JUNE!
OHHH!
I'LL GET THE MOP BUT YOU HAVE TO GO AND RINSE YOUR CLOTHES OUT, OKAY?
CALL JIMMY!
YOU KNOW BETTER THAN THAT, COME ON, NOW-
A DAY LATER JUNE'S PANTS ARE STILL IN THE SINK-
GIVE THE WOMAN A BREAK!
I DO IT.
AND THE NEXT DAY I GET A NICE SURPRISE-
SHE'S HERE? NOW?
YUP!
MUM, WHAT ARE YOU DOING HERE?

I TOOK THE DAY OFF WORK SO WE COULD HAVE A DAY OUT!
REALLY?
YEP, IT WAS DR. SALEH'S IDEA.
OKAY!
I'VE GOT A TAXI WAITING OUTSIDE.
OH WOW!
DO YOU WANT TO GO SHOPPING?
YES!
IT CAN BE A BELATED BIRTHDAY TREAT!
I'LL GO GET MY JACKET!
BLUE LINE

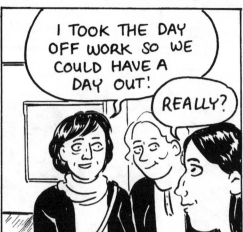

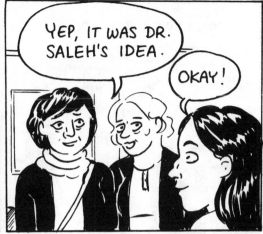

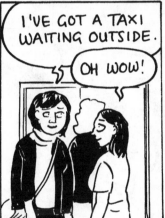

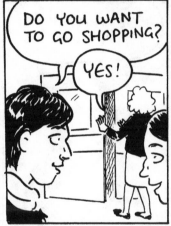

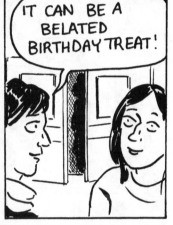

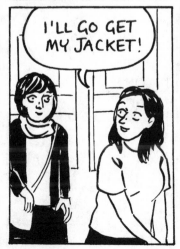

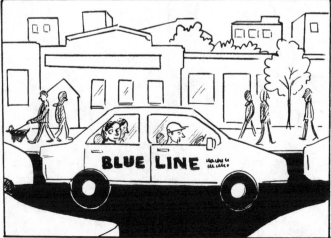

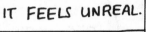

SO HERE I AM LOOSE IN THE WORLD!

IT FEELS UNREAL.

HOW IS IT?

PRETTY GOOD!

BETTER THAN HOSPITAL FOOD!

IRIS—

YEAH?

I-I'VE BEEN WANTING TO TALK TO YOU ABOUT SOME-THING.

IT'S - DOUG. HE'S MOVED OUT!

OH!

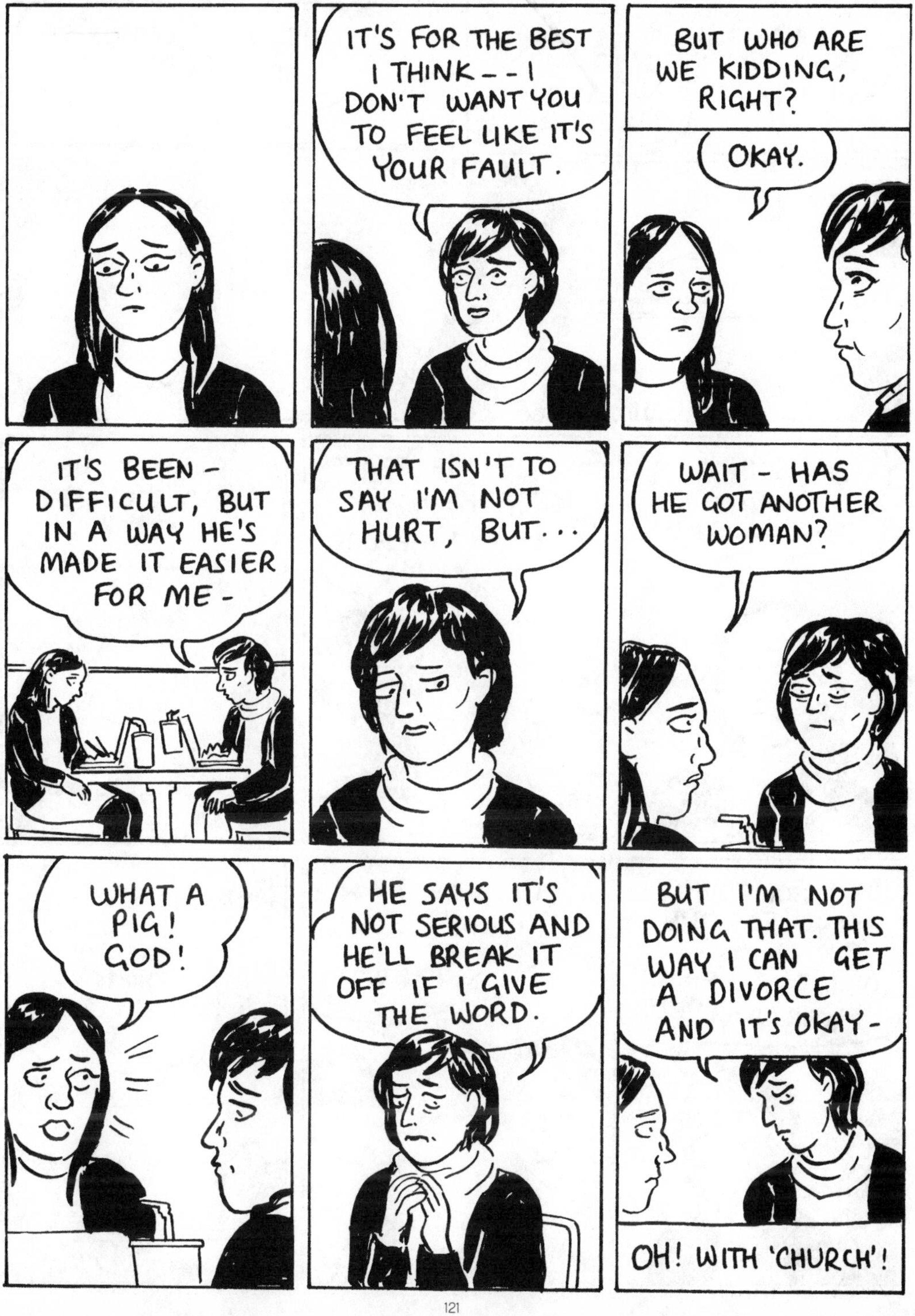
IT'S FOR THE BEST I THINK--I DON'T WANT YOU TO FEEL LIKE IT'S YOUR FAULT.
BUT WHO ARE WE KIDDING, RIGHT?
OKAY.
IT'S BEEN - DIFFICULT, BUT IN A WAY HE'S MADE IT EASIER FOR ME -
THAT ISN'T TO SAY I'M NOT HURT, BUT...
WAIT - HAS HE GOT ANOTHER WOMAN?
WHAT A PIG! GOD!
HE SAYS IT'S NOT SERIOUS AND HE'LL BREAK IT OFF IF I GIVE THE WORD.
BUT I'M NOT DOING THAT. THIS WAY I CAN GET A DIVORCE AND IT'S OKAY-
OH! WITH 'CHURCH'!

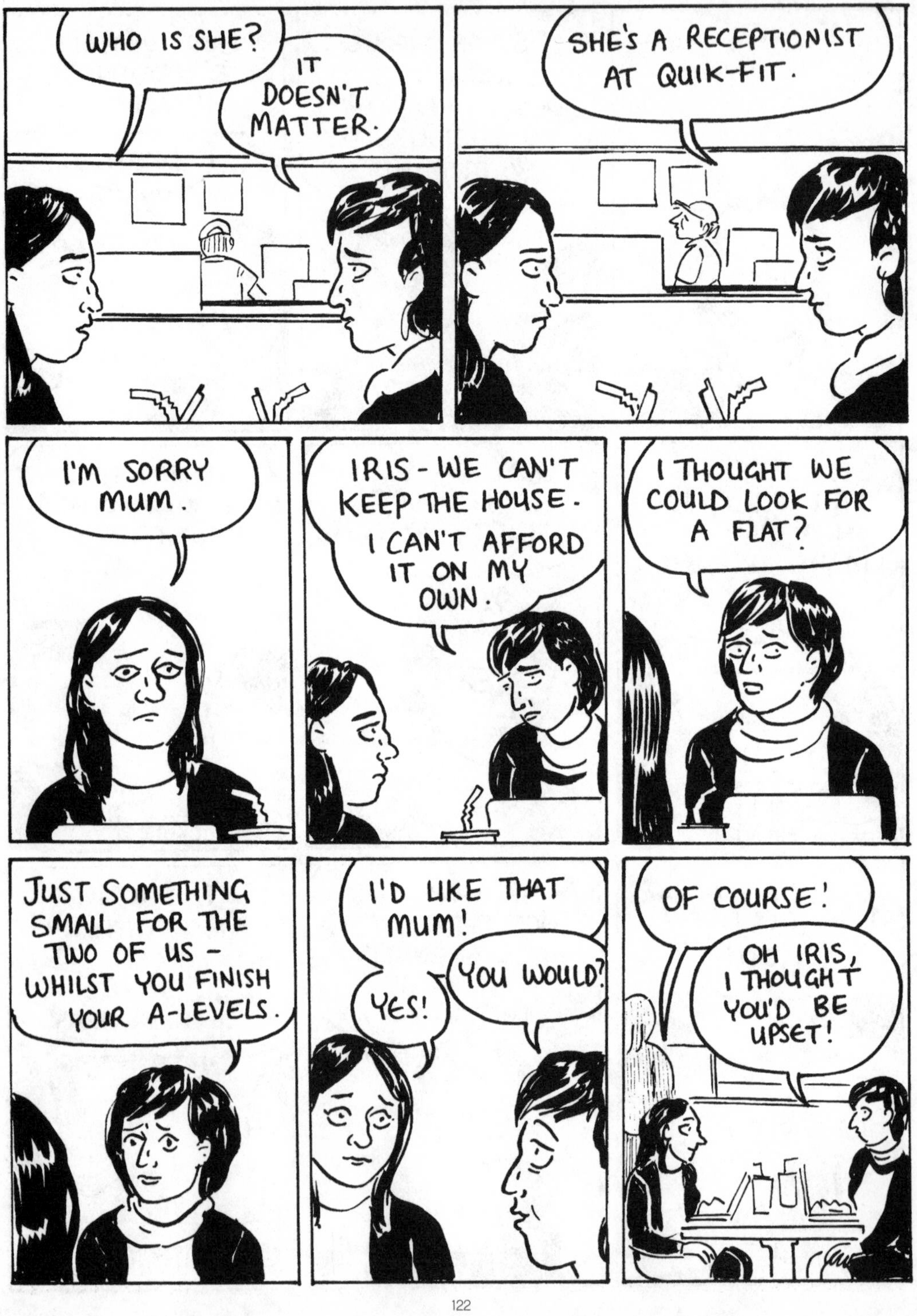
WHO IS SHE?
IT DOESN'T MATTER.
SHE'S A RECEPTIONIST AT QUIK-FIT.
I'M SORRY MUM.
IRIS - WE CAN'T KEEP THE HOUSE.
I CAN'T AFFORD IT ON MY OWN.
I THOUGHT WE COULD LOOK FOR A FLAT?
JUST SOMETHING SMALL FOR THE TWO OF US - WHILST YOU FINISH YOUR A-LEVELS.
I'D LIKE THAT MUM!
YOU WOULD?
YES!
OF COURSE!
OH IRIS, I THOUGHT YOU'D BE UPSET!

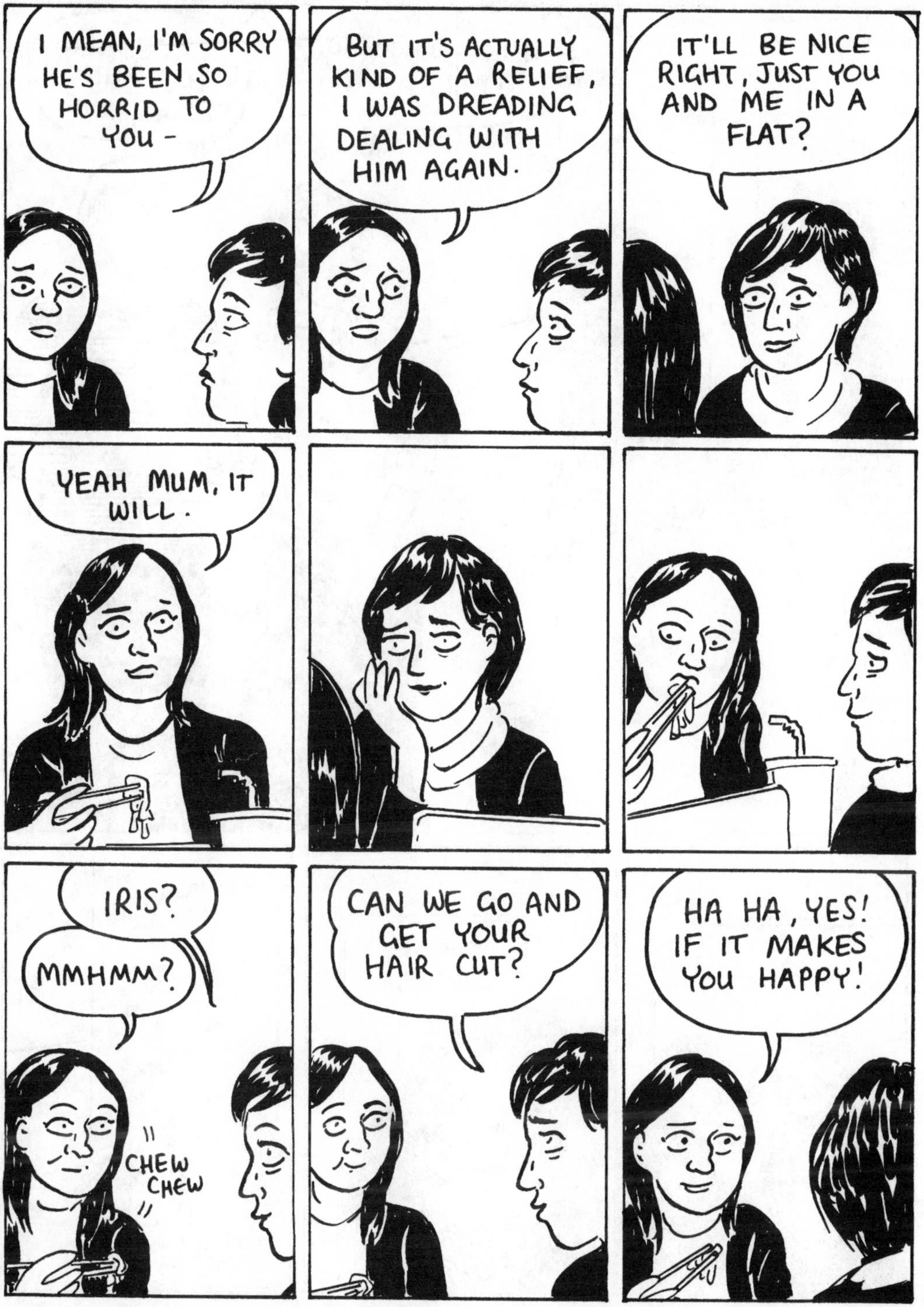
I MEAN, I'M SORRY HE'S BEEN SO HORRID TO YOU -
BUT IT'S ACTUALLY KIND OF A RELIEF, I WAS DREADING DEALING WITH HIM AGAIN.
IT'LL BE NICE RIGHT, JUST YOU AND ME IN A FLAT?
YEAH MUM, IT WILL.
IRIS?
MMHMM?
CHEW CHEW
CAN WE GO AND GET YOUR HAIR CUT?
HA HA, YES! IF IT MAKES YOU HAPPY!

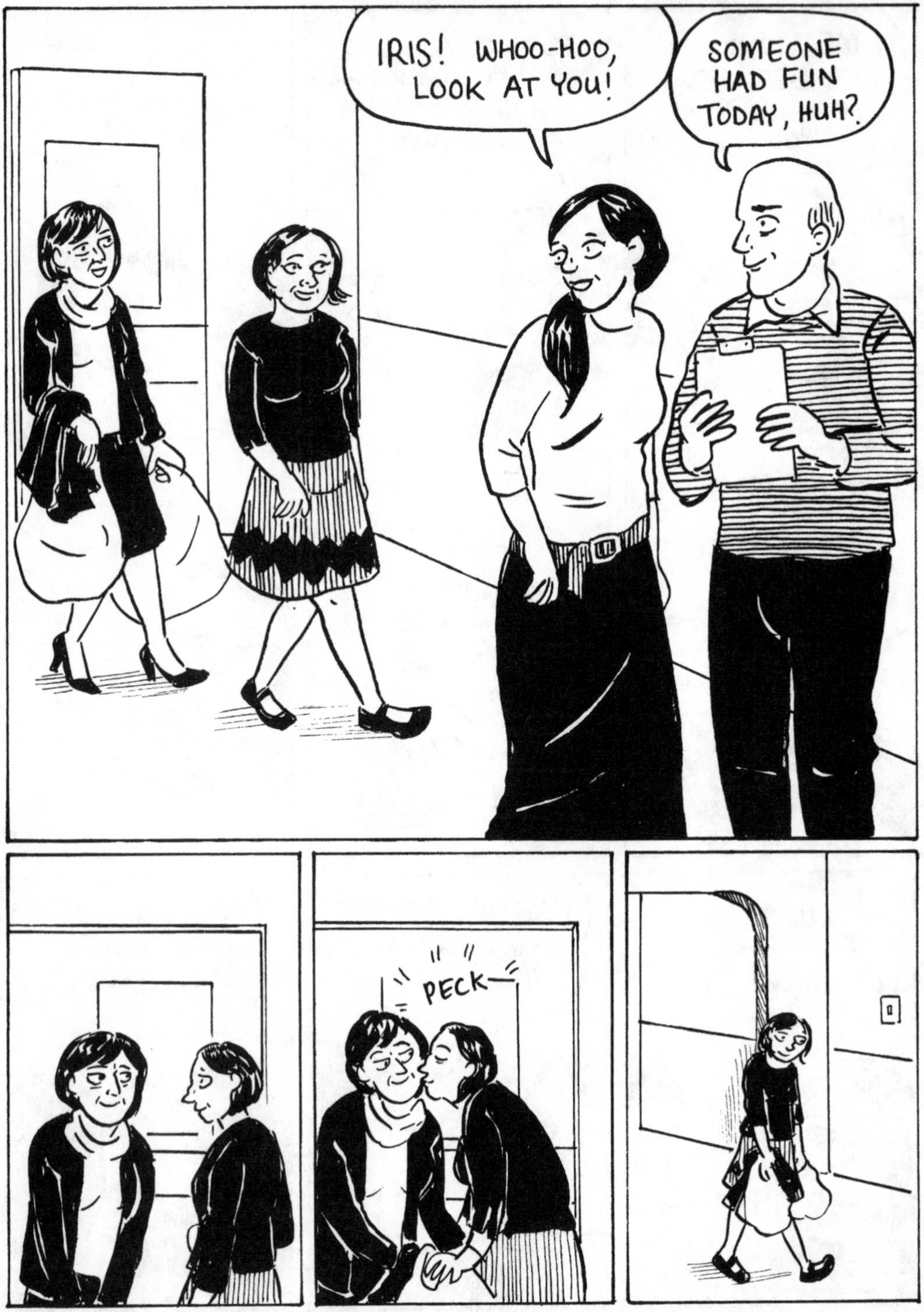
IRIS! WHOO-HOO, LOOK AT YOU!
SOMEONE HAD FUN TODAY, HUH?
PECK

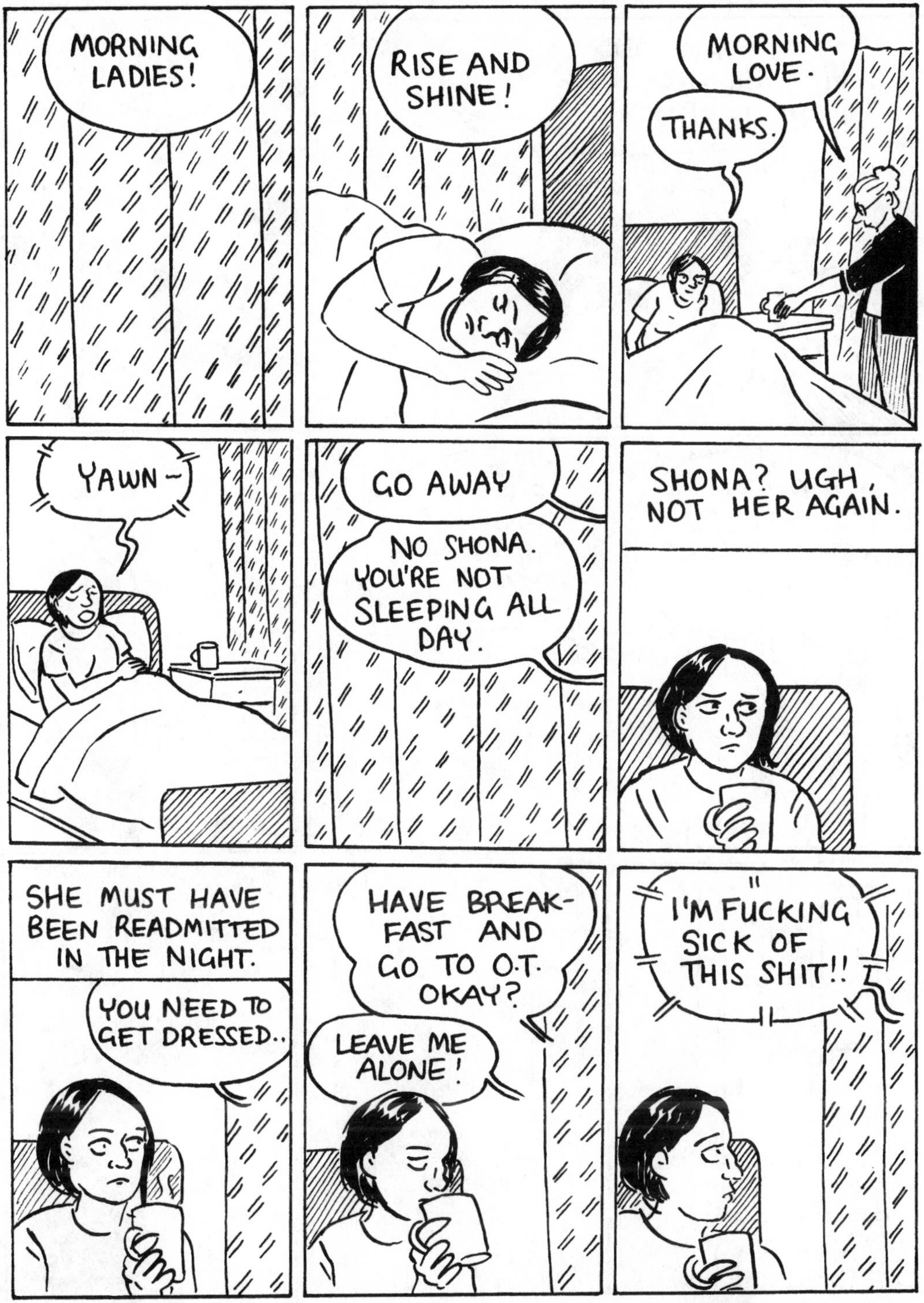
MORNING LADIES!
RISE AND SHINE!
MORNING LOVE.
THANKS.
YAWN~
GO AWAY
NO SHONA. YOU'RE NOT SLEEPING ALL DAY.
SHONA? UGH, NOT HER AGAIN.
SHE MUST HAVE BEEN READMITTED IN THE NIGHT.
YOU NEED TO GET DRESSED..
HAVE BREAK-FAST AND GO TO O.T. OKAY?
LEAVE ME ALONE!
"I'M FUCKING SICK OF THIS SHIT!!

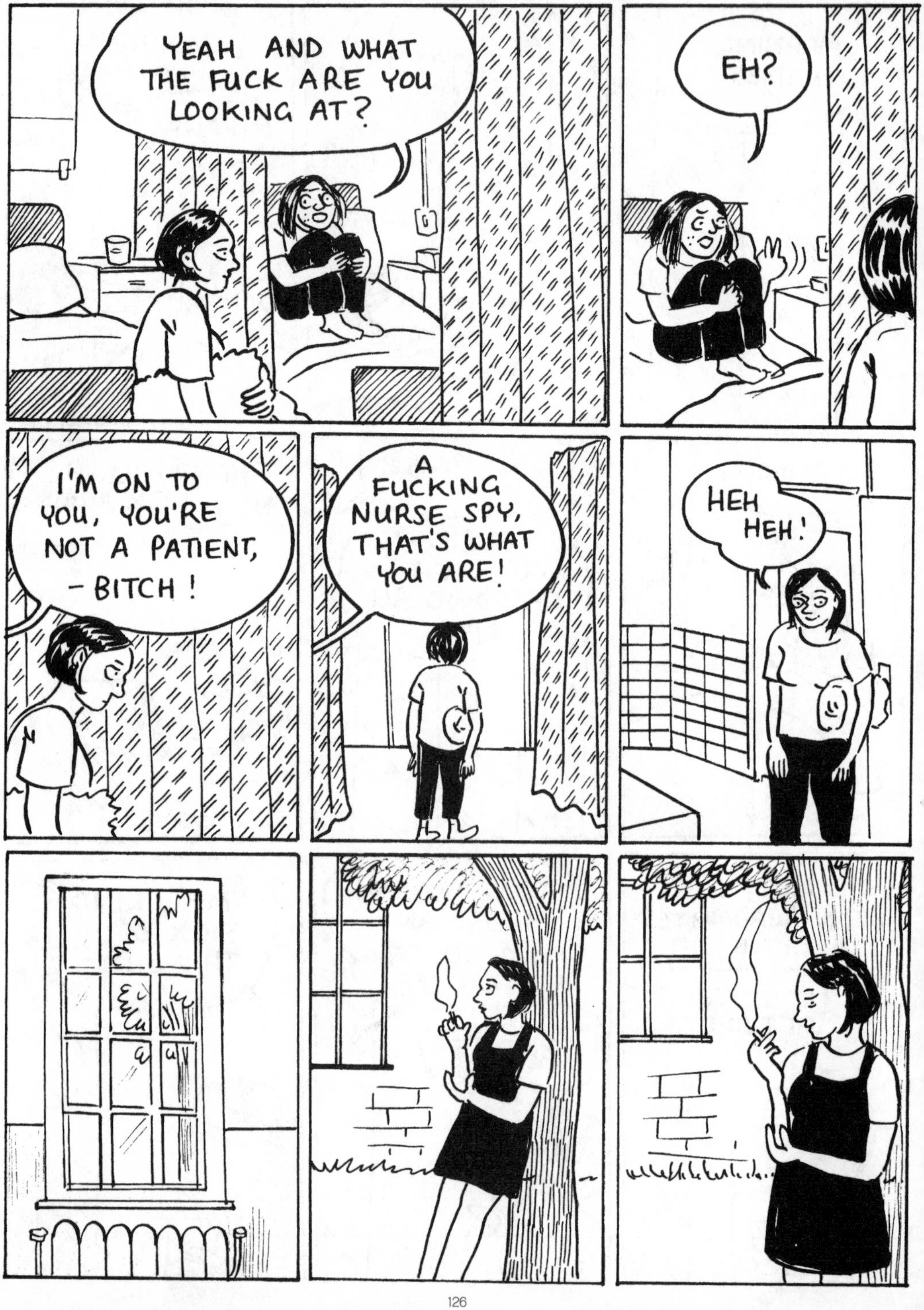
YEAH AND WHAT THE FUCK ARE YOU LOOKING AT?
EH?
I'M ON TO YOU, YOU'RE NOT A PATIENT, - BITCH!
A FUCKING NURSE SPY, THAT'S WHAT YOU ARE!
HEH HEH!

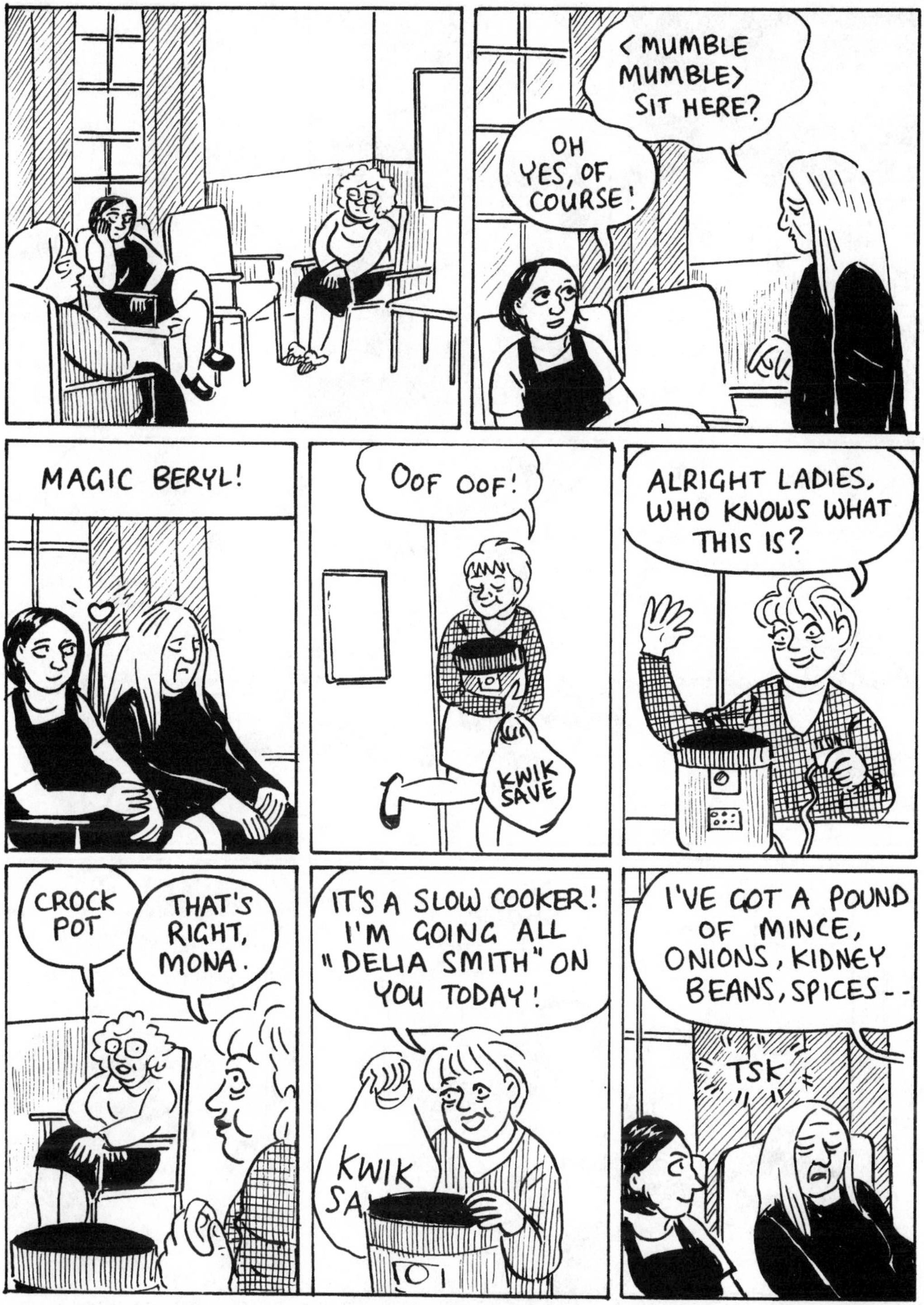
<MUMBLE MUMBLE> SIT HERE?
OH YES, OF COURSE!
MAGIC BERYL!
OOF OOF!
ALRIGHT LADIES, WHO KNOWS WHAT THIS IS?
KWIK SAVE
CROCK POT
THAT'S RIGHT, MONA.
IT'S A SLOW COOKER! I'M GOING ALL "DELIA SMITH" ON YOU TODAY!
I'VE GOT A POUND OF MINCE, ONIONS, KIDNEY BEANS, SPICES--
TSK

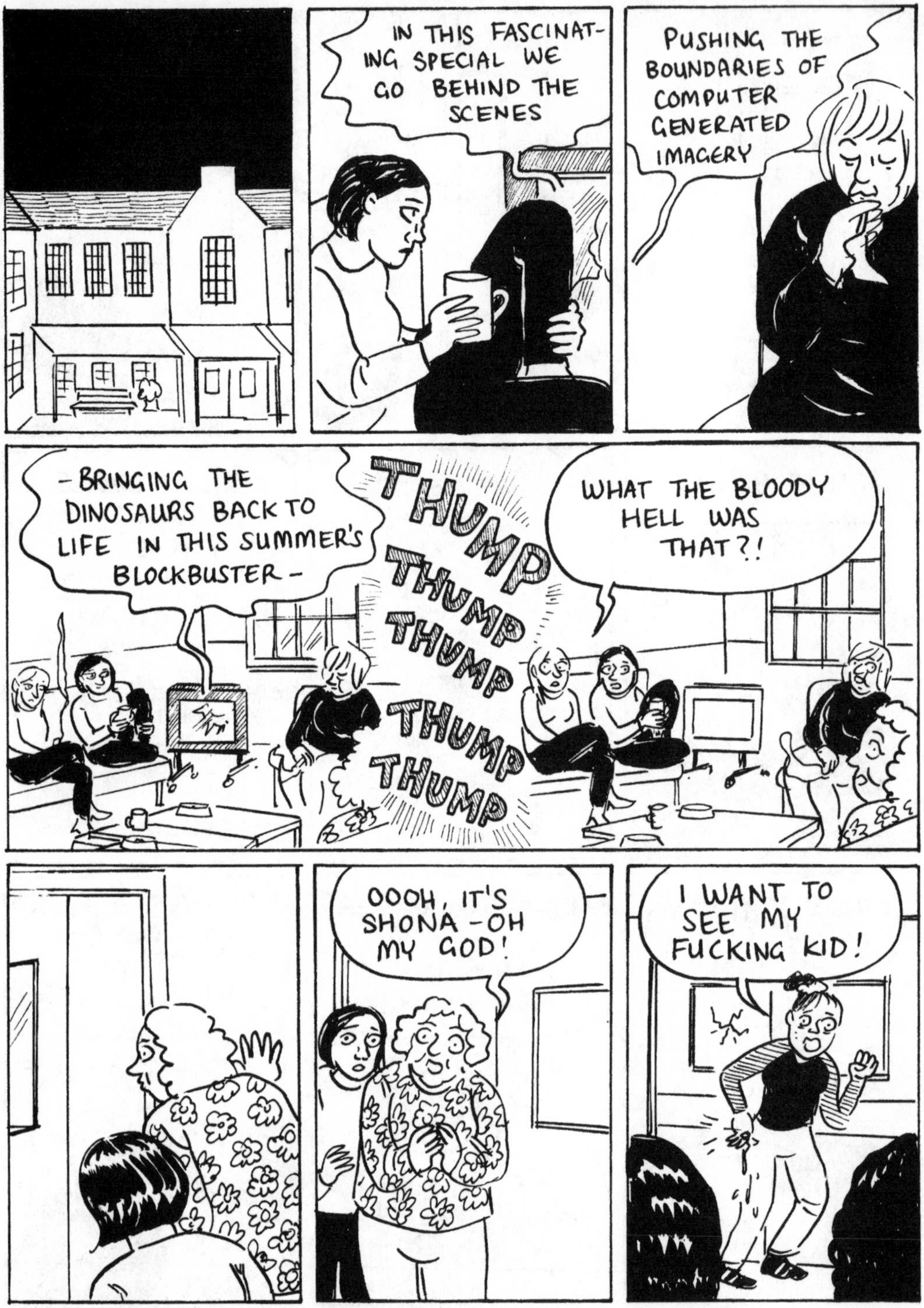
IN THIS FASCINATING SPECIAL WE GO BEHIND THE SCENES
PUSHING THE BOUNDARIES OF COMPUTER GENERATED IMAGERY
-BRINGING THE DINOSAURS BACK TO LIFE IN THIS SUMMER'S BLOCKBUSTER-
THUMP THUMP THUMP THUMP THUMP
WHAT THE BLOODY HELL WAS THAT?!
OOOH, IT'S SHONA -OH MY GOD!
I WANT TO SEE MY FUCKING KID!

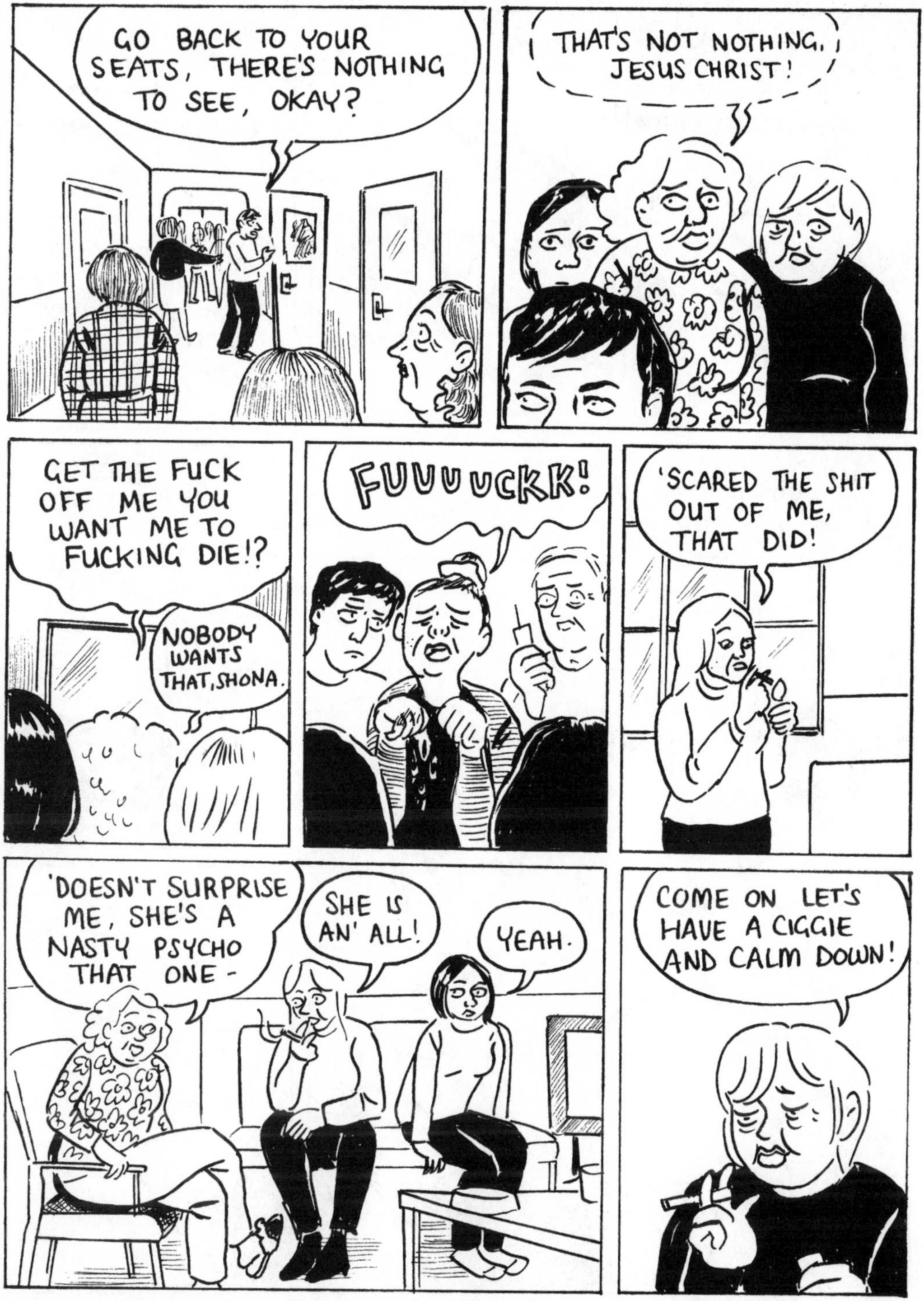
GO BACK TO YOUR SEATS, THERE'S NOTHING TO SEE, OKAY?
THAT'S NOT NOTHING. JESUS CHRIST!
GET THE FUCK OFF ME YOU WANT ME TO FUCKING DIE!?
NOBODY WANTS THAT, SHONA.
FUUUUCKK!
'SCARED THE SHIT OUT OF ME, THAT DID!
'DOESN'T SURPRISE ME, SHE'S A NASTY PSYCHO THAT ONE -
SHE IS AN' ALL!
YEAH.
COME ON LET'S HAVE A CIGGIE AND CALM DOWN!

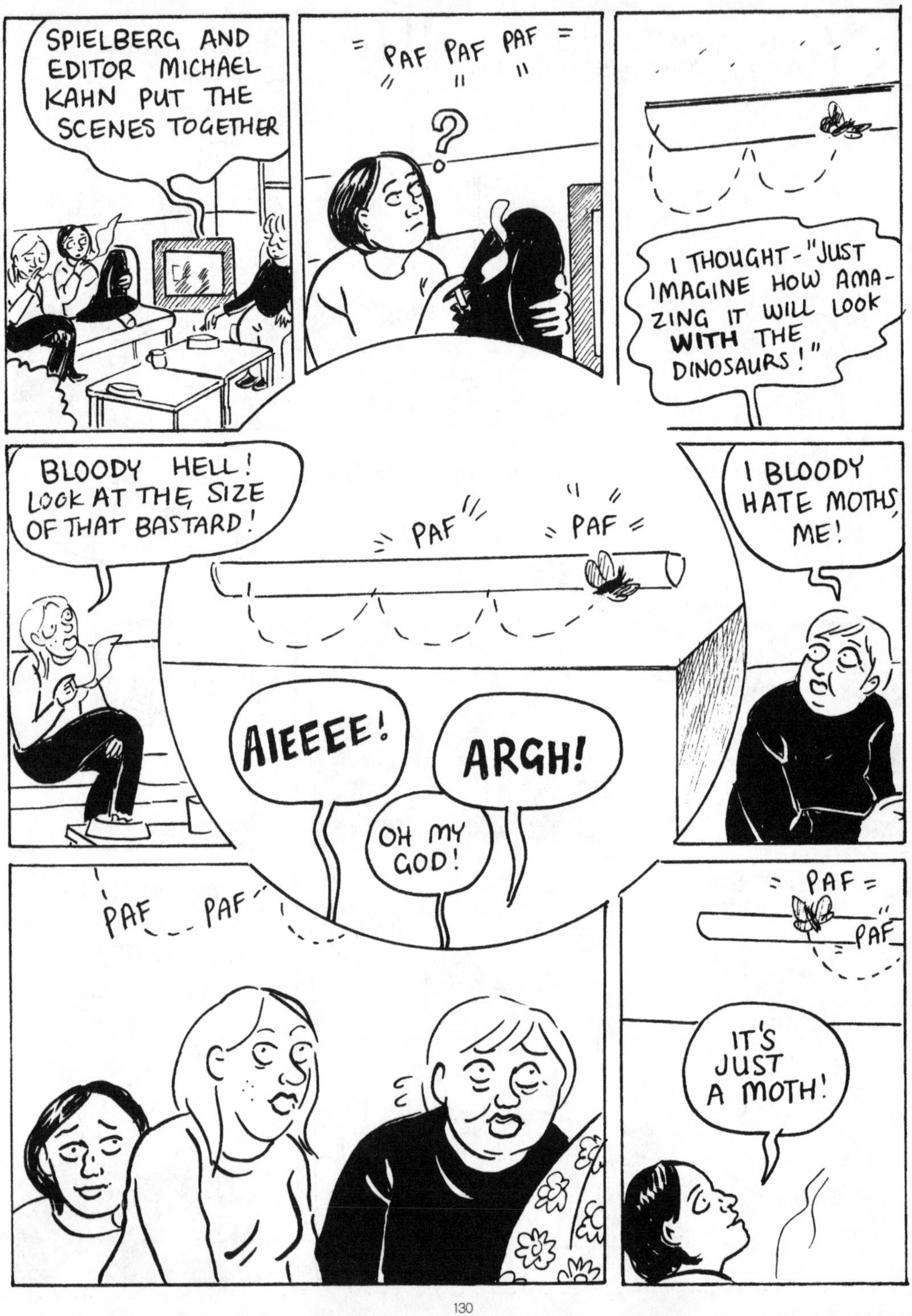
SPIELBERG AND EDITOR MICHAEL KAHN PUT THE SCENES TOGETHER
PAF PAF PAF
?
I THOUGHT - "JUST IMAGINE HOW AMAZING IT WILL LOOK **WITH** THE DINOSAURS!"
BLOODY HELL! LOOK AT THE SIZE OF THAT BASTARD!
PAF
PAF
I BLOODY HATE MOTHS ME!
AIEEEE!
ARGH!
OH MY GOD!
PAF
PAF
PAF
PAF
IT'S JUST A MOTH!

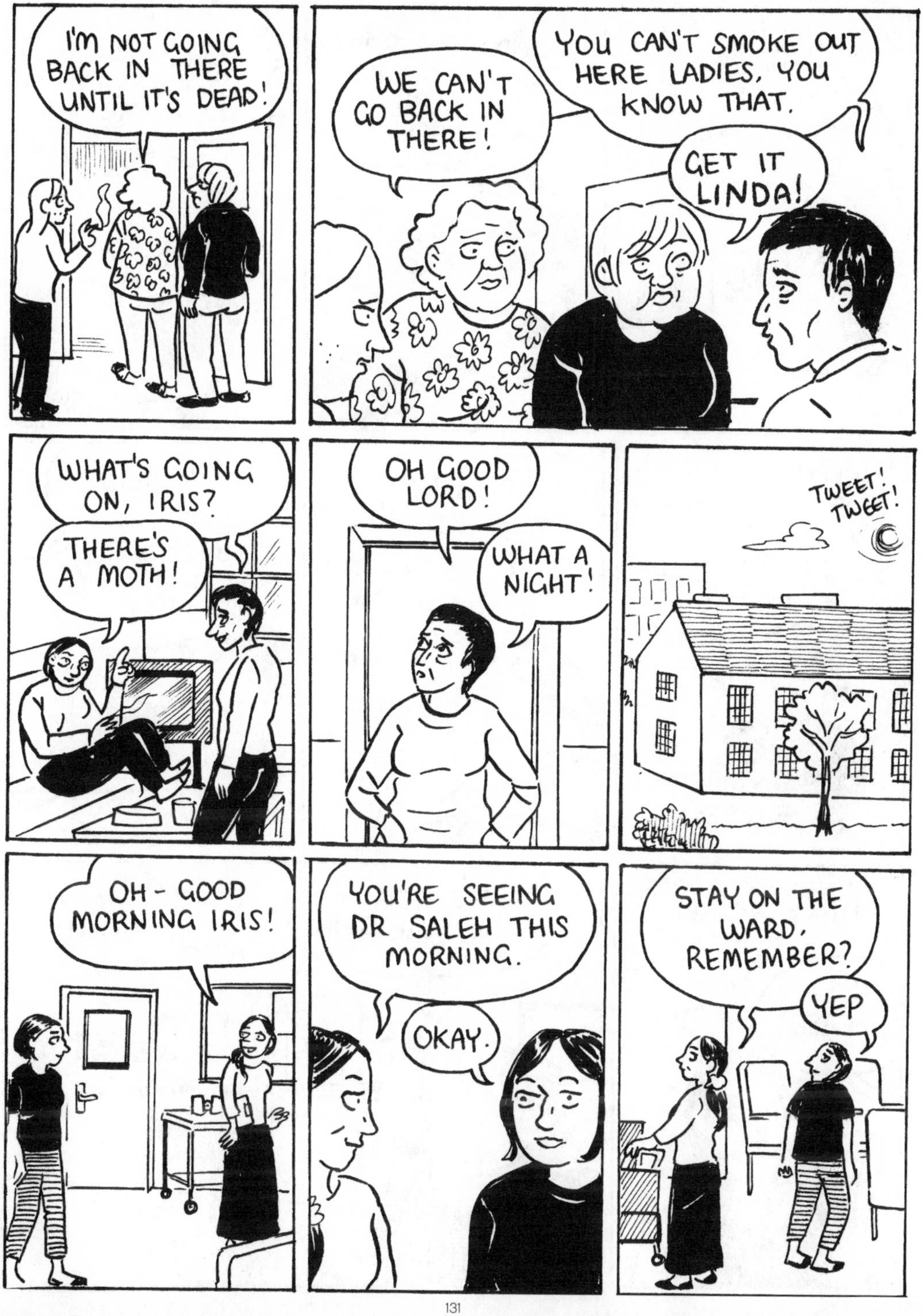
I'M NOT GOING BACK IN THERE UNTIL IT'S DEAD!
WE CAN'T GO BACK IN THERE!
YOU CAN'T SMOKE OUT HERE LADIES, YOU KNOW THAT.
GET IT LINDA!
WHAT'S GOING ON, IRIS?
THERE'S A MOTH!
OH GOOD LORD!
WHAT A NIGHT!
TWEET! TWEET!
OH - GOOD MORNING IRIS!
YOU'RE SEEING DR SALEH THIS MORNING.
OKAY.
STAY ON THE WARD, REMEMBER?
YEP

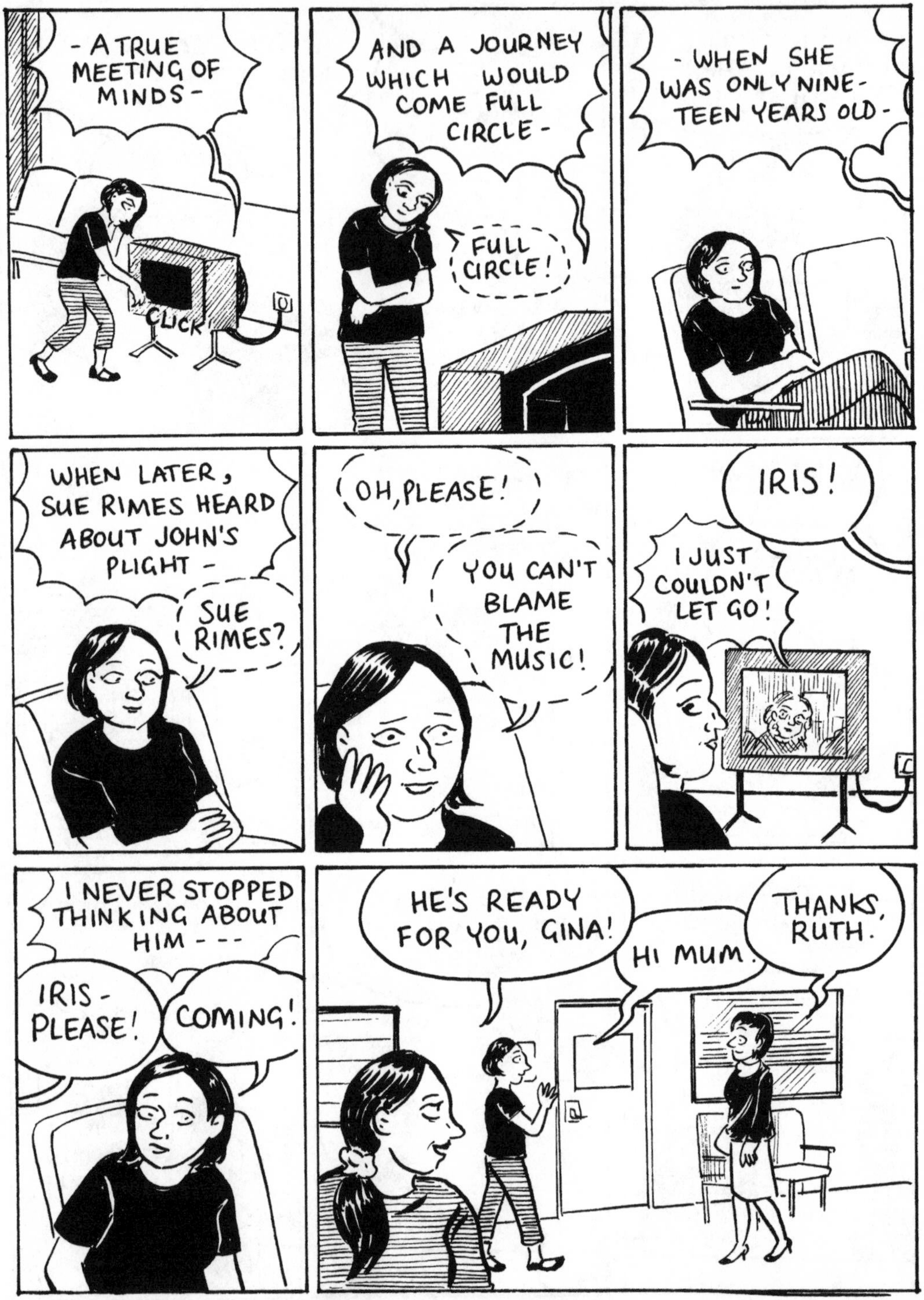

- A TRUE MEETING OF MINDS -
CLICK
AND A JOURNEY WHICH WOULD COME FULL CIRCLE -
FULL CIRCLE!
- WHEN SHE WAS ONLY NINE-TEEN YEARS OLD -
WHEN LATER, SUE RIMES HEARD ABOUT JOHN'S PLIGHT -
SUE RIMES?
OH, PLEASE!
YOU CAN'T BLAME THE MUSIC!
IRIS!
I JUST COULDN'T LET GO!
I NEVER STOPPED THINKING ABOUT HIM ---
IRIS - PLEASE!
COMING!
HE'S READY FOR YOU, GINA!
HI MUM.
THANKS, RUTH.

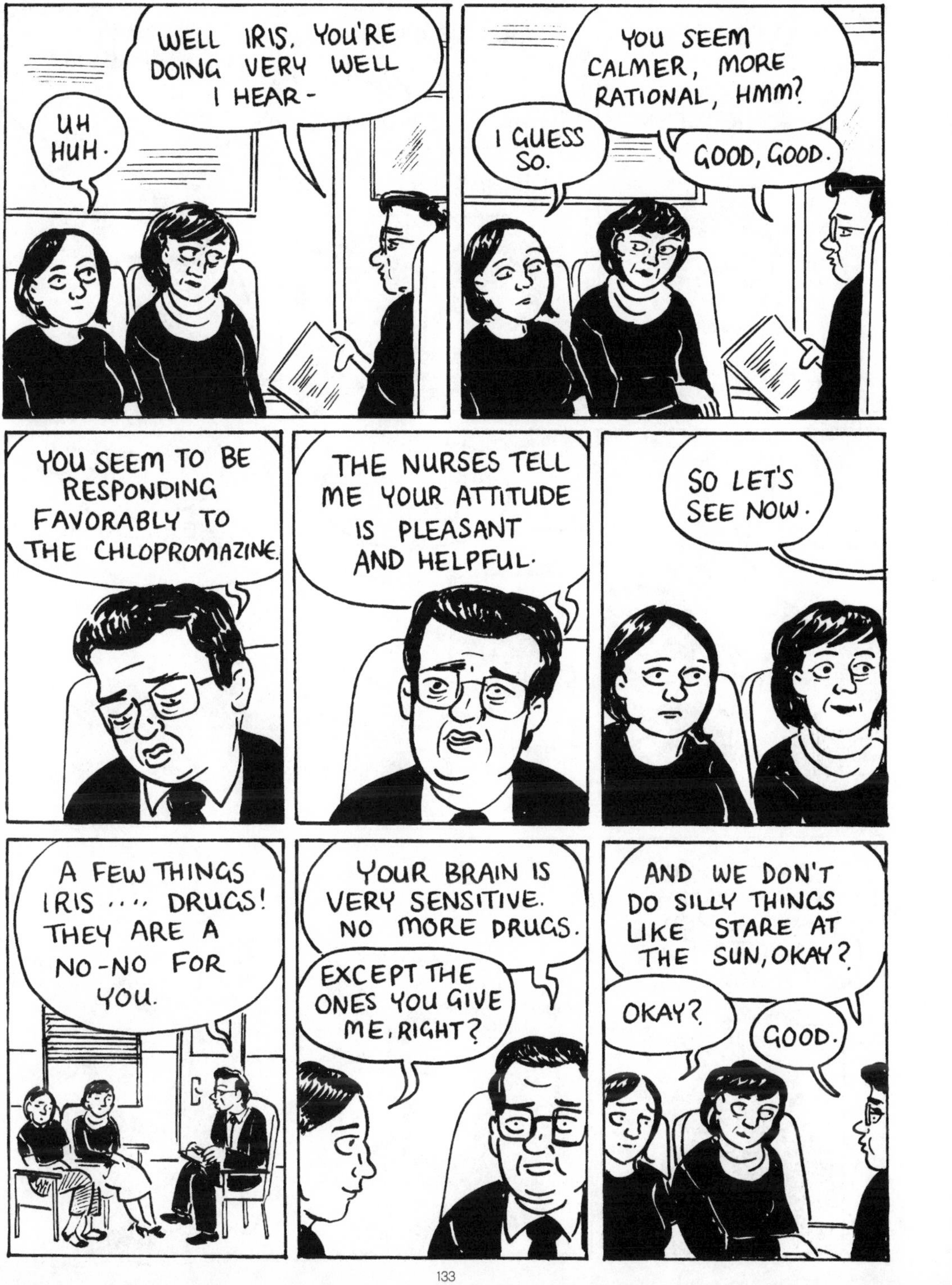
UH HUH.
WELL IRIS, YOU'RE DOING VERY WELL I HEAR-
YOU SEEM CALMER, MORE RATIONAL, HMM?
I GUESS SO.
GOOD, GOOD.
YOU SEEM TO BE RESPONDING FAVORABLY TO THE CHLOPROMAZINE.
THE NURSES TELL ME YOUR ATTITUDE IS PLEASANT AND HELPFUL.
SO LET'S SEE NOW.
A FEW THINGS IRIS .... DRUGS! THEY ARE A NO-NO FOR YOU.
YOUR BRAIN IS VERY SENSITIVE. NO MORE DRUGS.
EXCEPT THE ONES YOU GIVE ME, RIGHT?
AND WE DON'T DO SILLY THINGS LIKE STARE AT THE SUN, OKAY?
OKAY?
GOOD.

SO LET'S SEE— WE CAN HAVE YOU BACK HERE IN FOUR WEEKS.

MRS. NEUFIELD, IF YOU MAKE AN APPOINTMENT WITH OUT-PATIENTS.

OUT-PATIENTS?

YES, I'M RECOMMENDING A FULL DISCHARGE TODAY.

MUM!

WELL, VERY GOOD!

GOODBYE IRIS.

GOODBYE!

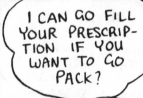

I CAN GO FILL YOUR PRESCRIP- TION IF YOU WANT TO GO PACK?

OKAY.

YES!

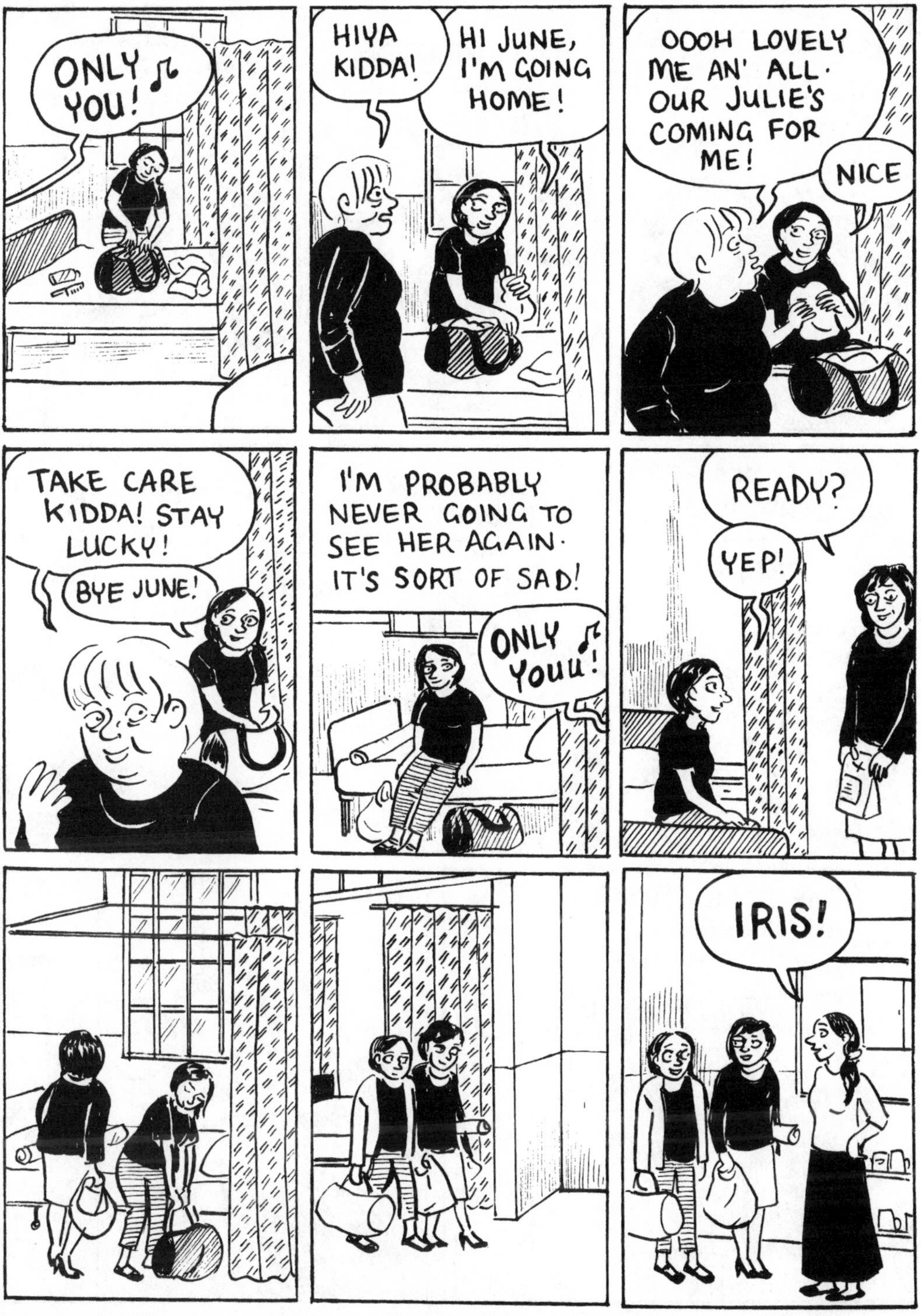
ONLY YOU! ♫
HIYA KIDDA!
HI JUNE, I'M GOING HOME!
OOOH LOVELY ME AN' ALL. OUR JULIE'S COMING FOR ME!
NICE
TAKE CARE KIDDA! STAY LUCKY!
BYE JUNE!
I'M PROBABLY NEVER GOING TO SEE HER AGAIN. IT'S SORT OF SAD!
ONLY YOUU! ♫
READY?
YEP!
IRIS!

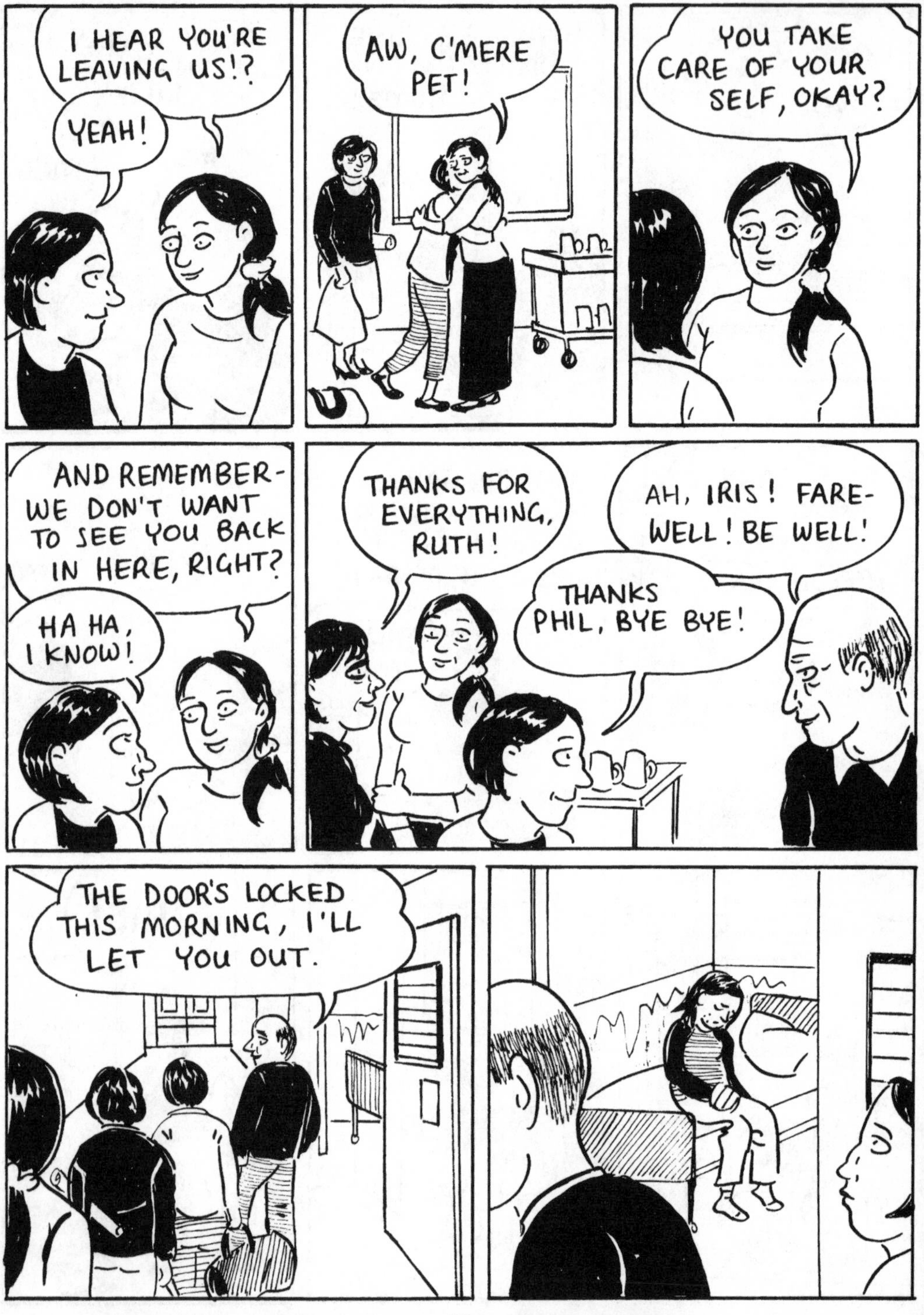

I HEAR YOU'RE LEAVING US!?
YEAH!
AW, C'MERE PET!
YOU TAKE CARE OF YOUR SELF, OKAY?
AND REMEMBER-WE DON'T WANT TO SEE YOU BACK IN HERE, RIGHT?
HA HA, I KNOW!
THANKS FOR EVERYTHING, RUTH!
AH, IRIS! FARE-WELL! BE WELL!
THANKS PHIL, BYE BYE!
THE DOOR'S LOCKED THIS MORNING, I'LL LET YOU OUT.

WELL, HERE WE ARE!

I'M GOING TO TAKE MY BAG UPSTAIRS-

OKAY, I'LL PUT THE KETTLE ON!

WHEN WE GOT OUT OF THE TAXI THERE WAS A WHITE FEATHER ON THE GROUND. I SAW IT.

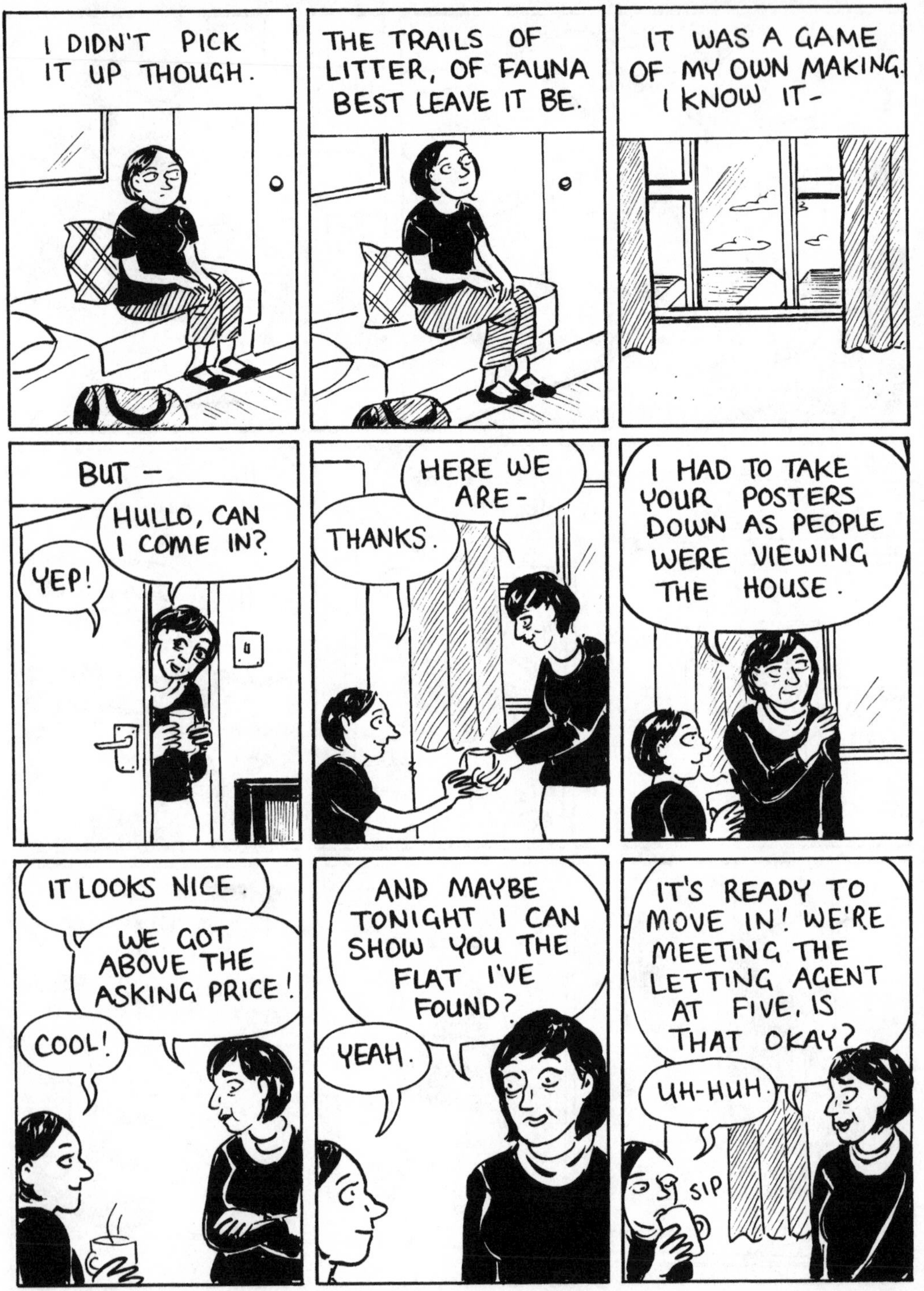
I DIDN'T PICK IT UP THOUGH.
THE TRAILS OF LITTER, OF FAUNA BEST LEAVE IT BE.
IT WAS A GAME OF MY OWN MAKING. I KNOW IT-
BUT -
HULLO, CAN I COME IN?
YEP!
HERE WE ARE-
THANKS.
I HAD TO TAKE YOUR POSTERS DOWN AS PEOPLE WERE VIEWING THE HOUSE.
IT LOOKS NICE.
WE GOT ABOVE THE ASKING PRICE!
COOL!
AND MAYBE TONIGHT I CAN SHOW YOU THE FLAT I'VE FOUND?
YEAH.
IT'S READY TO MOVE IN! WE'RE MEETING THE LETTING AGENT AT FIVE, IS THAT OKAY?
UH-HUH.
SIP

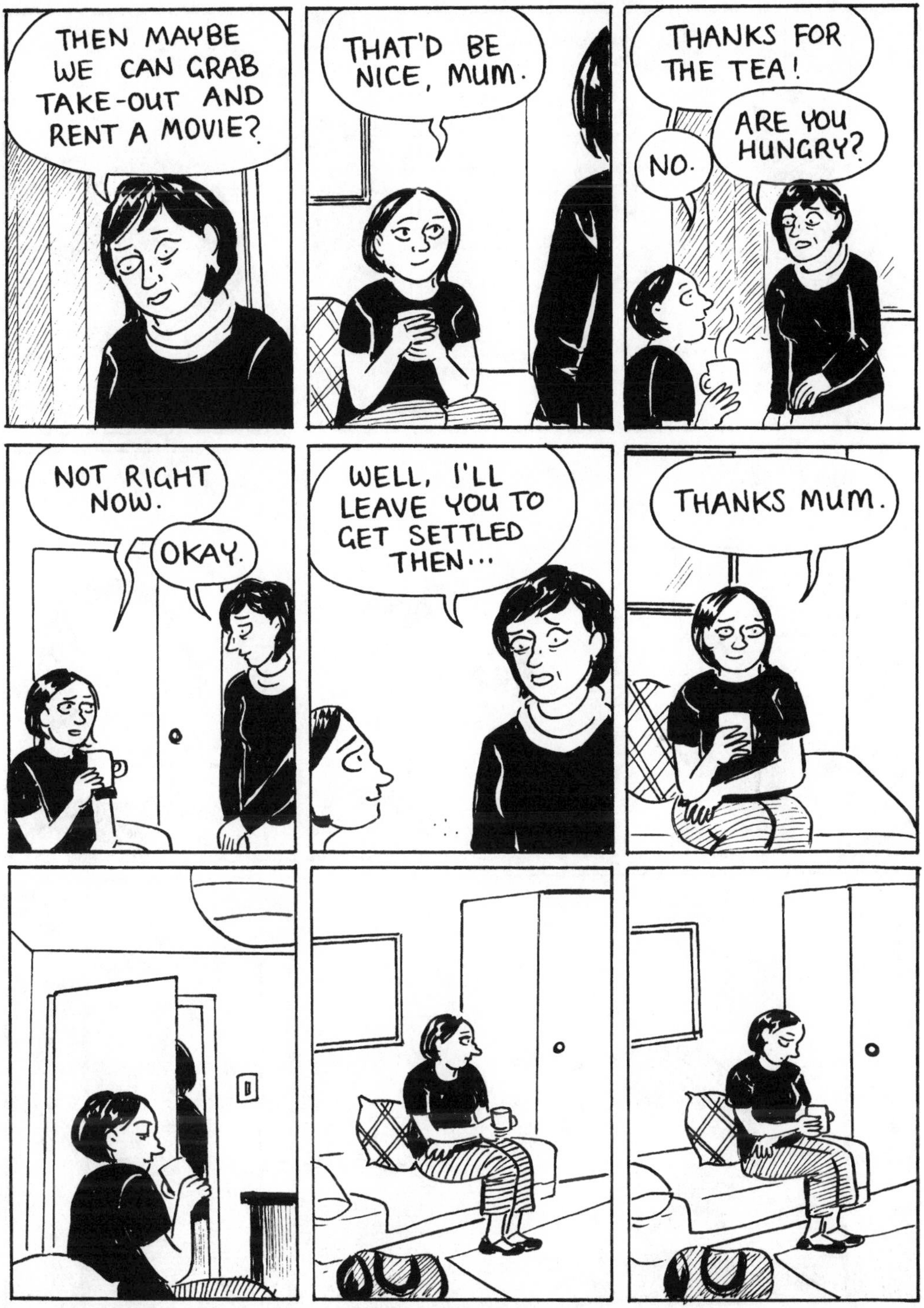
THEN MAYBE WE CAN GRAB TAKE-OUT AND RENT A MOVIE?
THAT'D BE NICE, MUM.
THANKS FOR THE TEA!
ARE YOU HUNGRY?
NO.
NOT RIGHT NOW.
OKAY.
WELL, I'LL LEAVE YOU TO GET SETTLED THEN...
THANKS MUM.

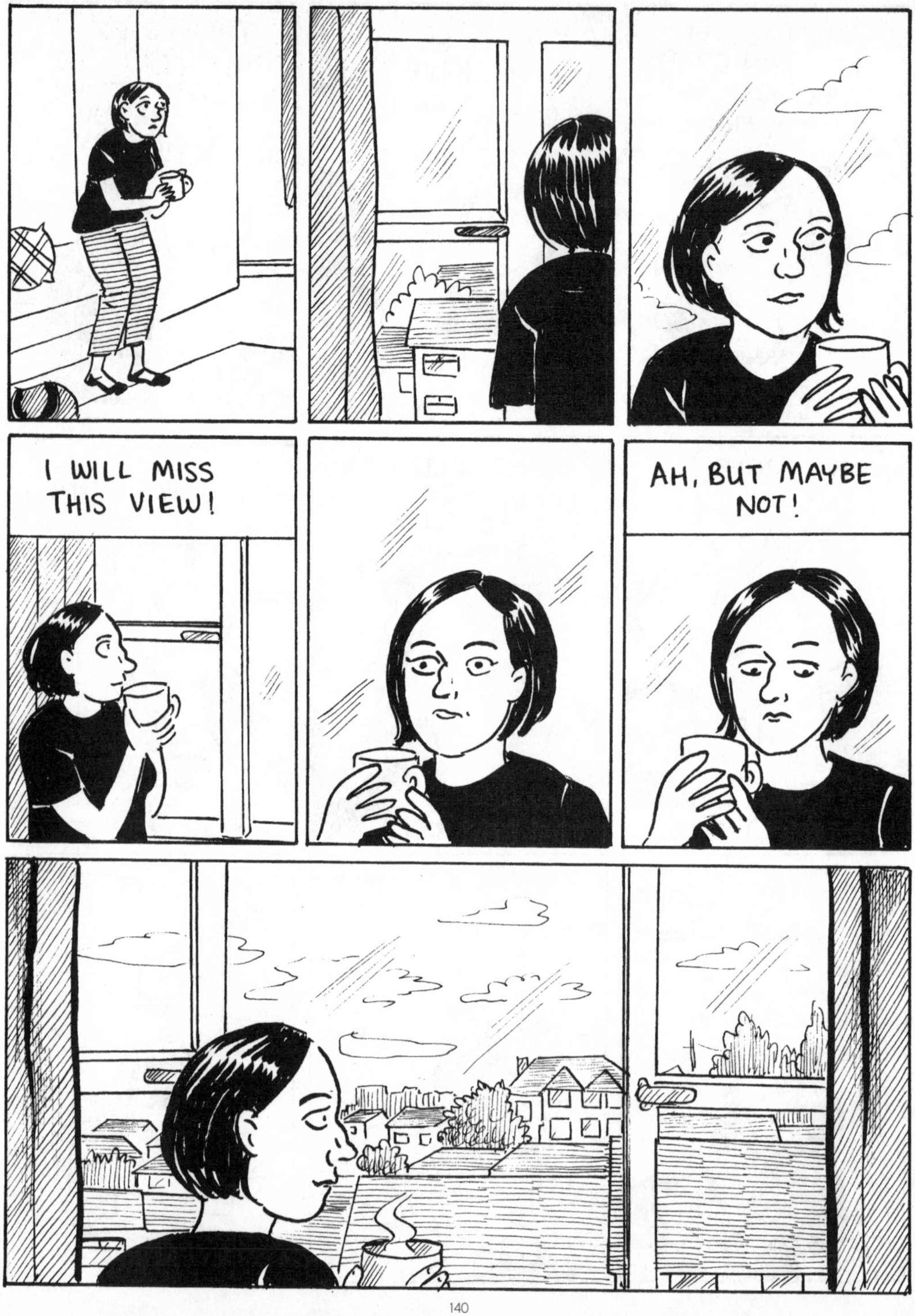
I WILL MISS THIS VIEW!
AH, BUT MAYBE NOT!

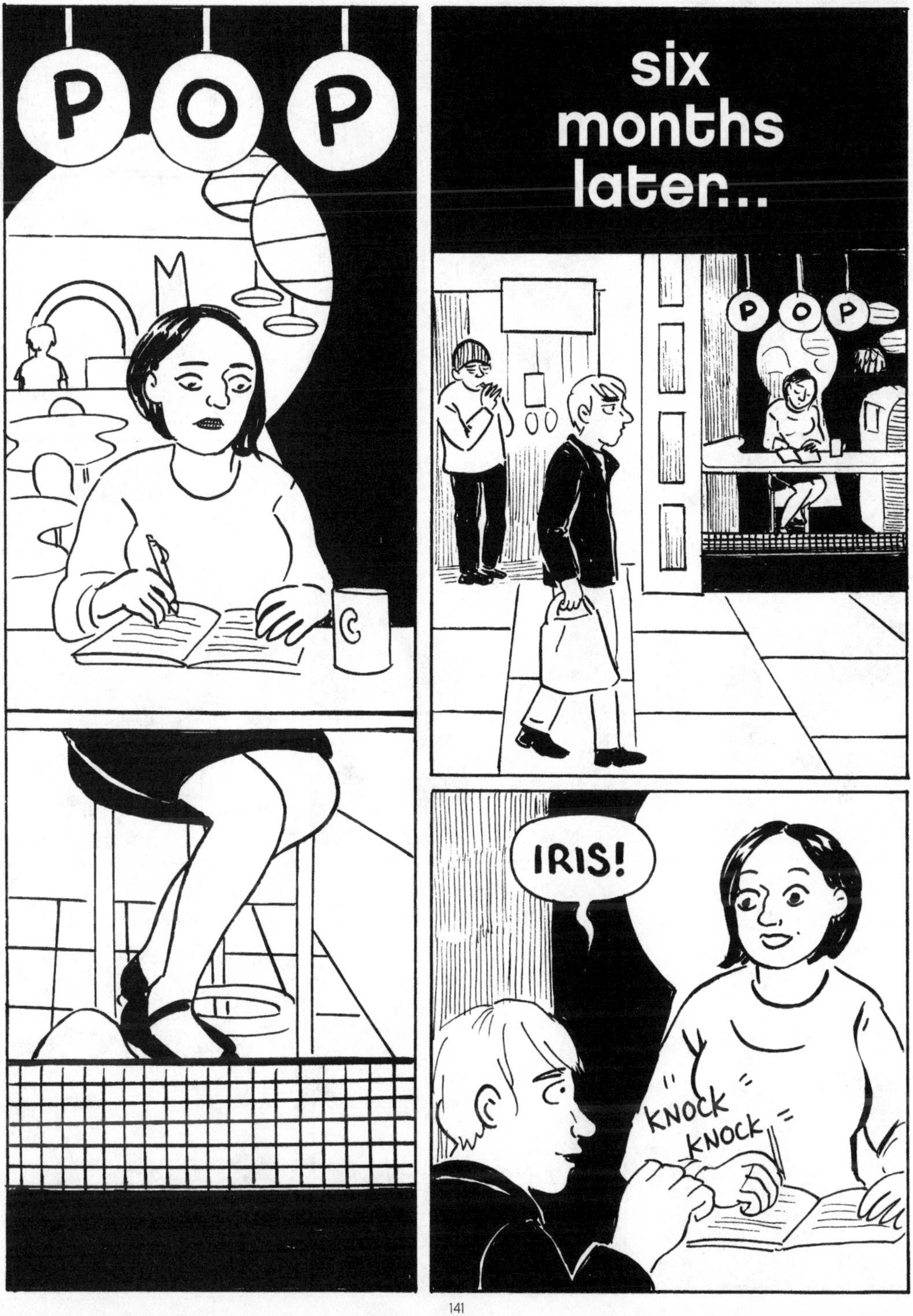
POP
six months later...
POP
IRIS!
KNOCK KNOCK

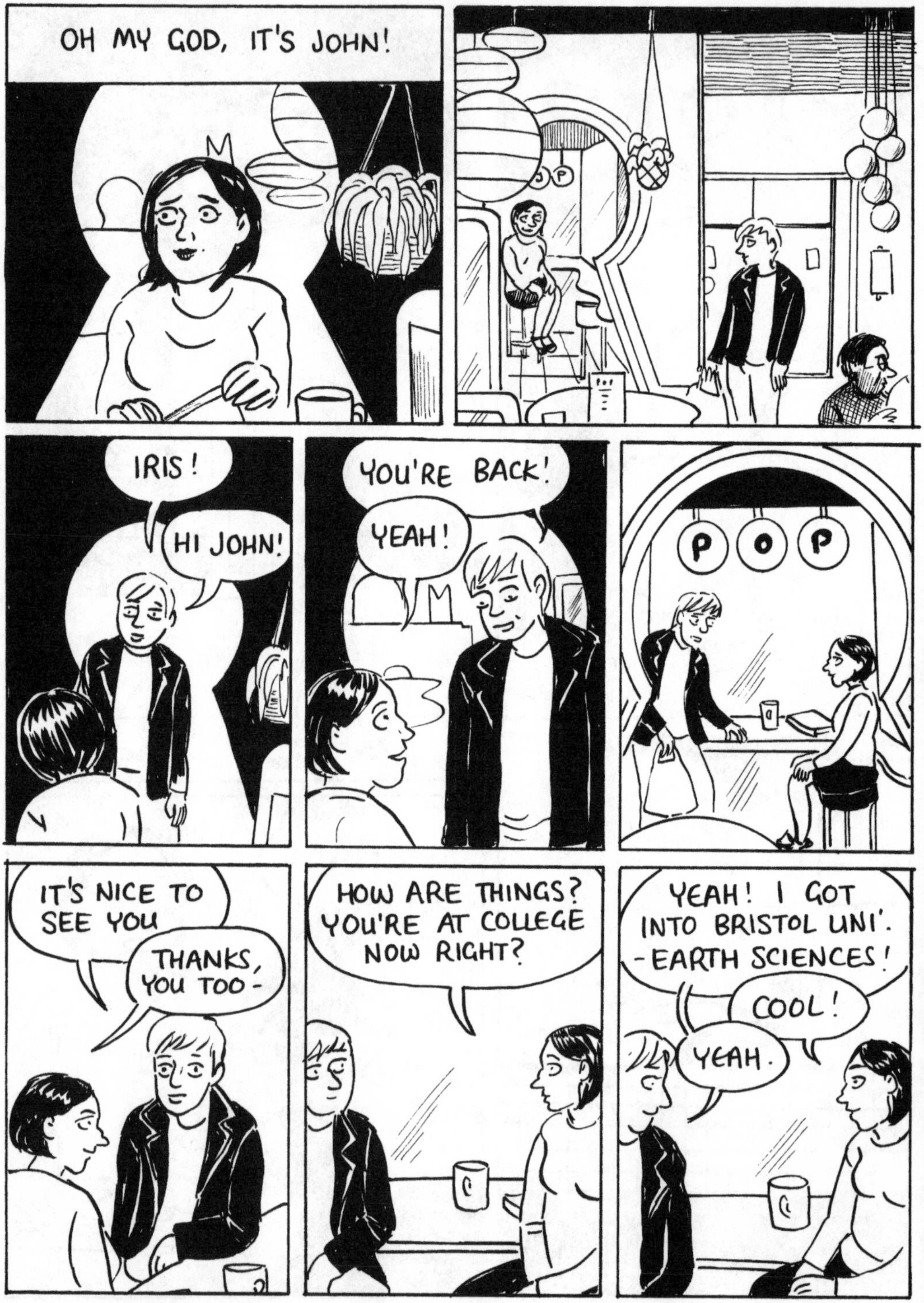
OH MY GOD, IT'S JOHN!
POP
IRIS!
HI JOHN!
YOU'RE BACK!
YEAH!
POP
IT'S NICE TO SEE YOU
THANKS, YOU TOO-
HOW ARE THINGS? YOU'RE AT COLLEGE NOW RIGHT?
YEAH! I GOT INTO BRISTOL UNI'. -EARTH SCIENCES!
COOL!
YEAH.

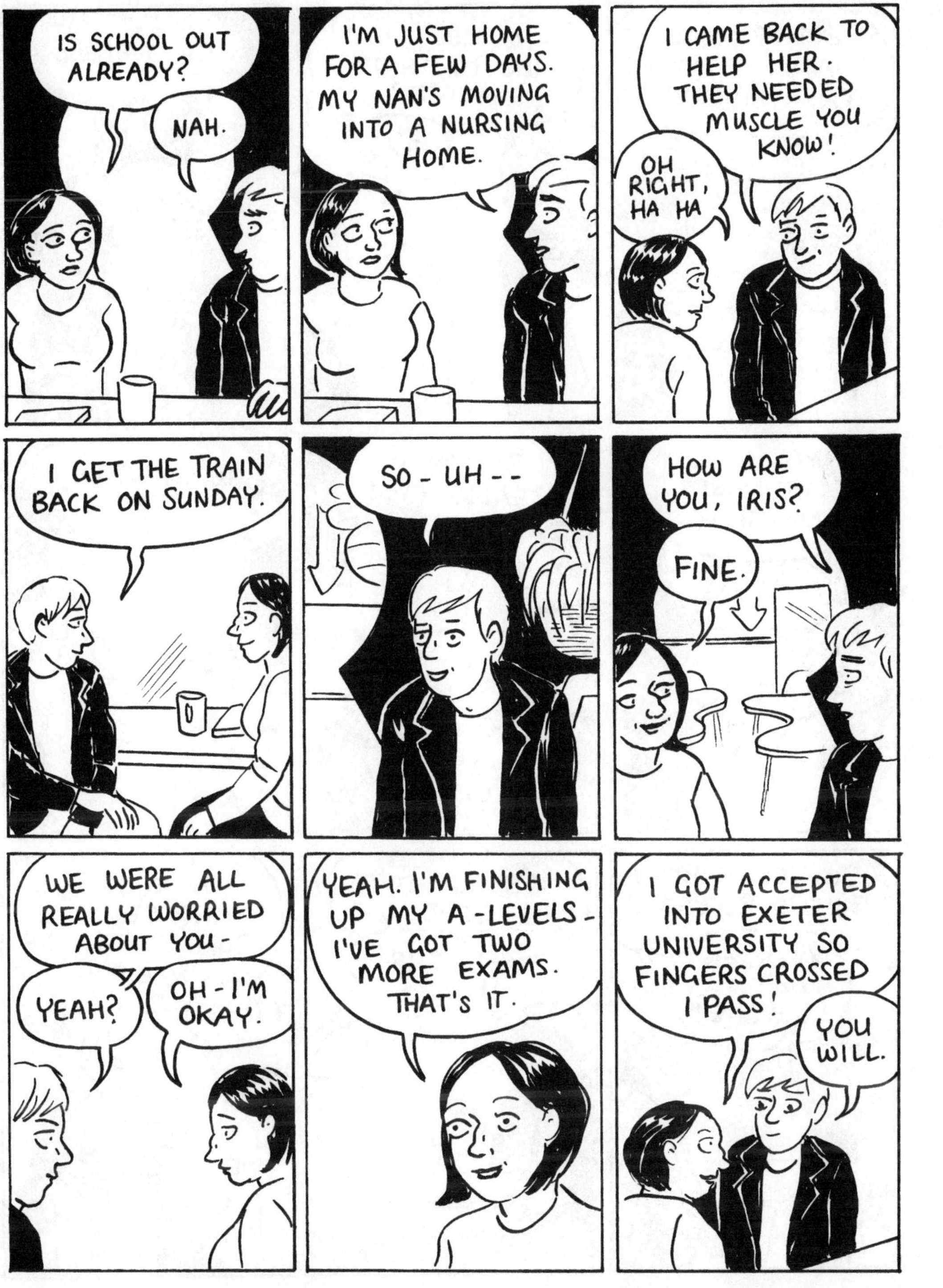
IS SCHOOL OUT ALREADY?
NAH.
I'M JUST HOME FOR A FEW DAYS. MY NAN'S MOVING INTO A NURSING HOME.
I CAME BACK TO HELP HER. THEY NEEDED MUSCLE YOU KNOW!
OH RIGHT, HA HA
I GET THE TRAIN BACK ON SUNDAY.
SO - UH - -
HOW ARE YOU, IRIS?
FINE.
WE WERE ALL REALLY WORRIED ABOUT YOU -
YEAH?
OH - I'M OKAY.
YEAH. I'M FINISHING UP MY A-LEVELS - I'VE GOT TWO MORE EXAMS. THAT'S IT.
I GOT ACCEPTED INTO EXETER UNIVERSITY SO FINGERS CROSSED I PASS!
YOU WILL.

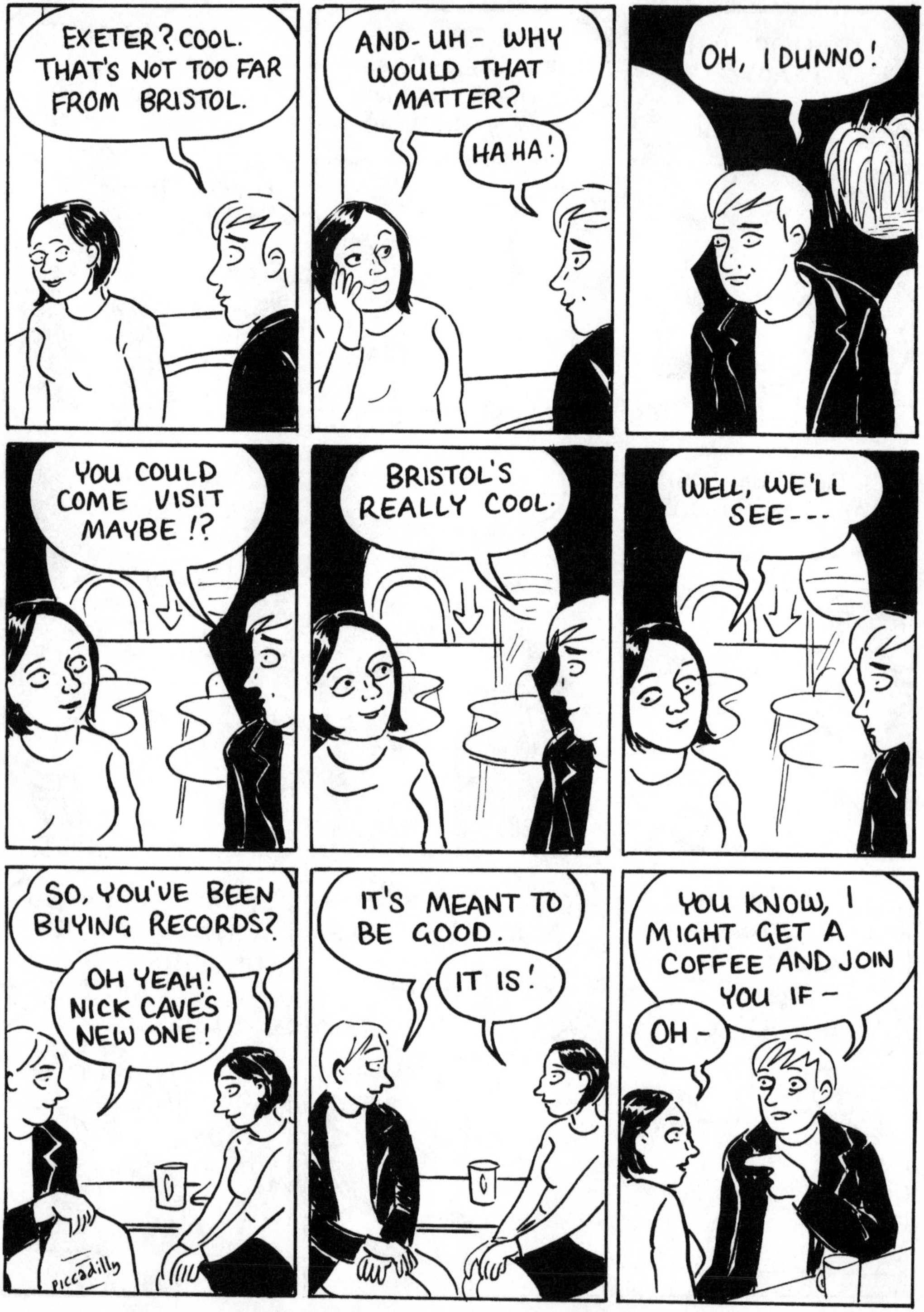
EXETER? COOL. THAT'S NOT TOO FAR FROM BRISTOL.
AND- UH- WHY WOULD THAT MATTER?
HA HA!
OH, I DUNNO!
YOU COULD COME VISIT MAYBE !?
BRISTOL'S REALLY COOL.
WELL, WE'LL SEE---
SO, YOU'VE BEEN BUYING RECORDS?
OH YEAH! NICK CAVE'S NEW ONE!
Piccadilly
IT'S MEANT TO BE GOOD.
IT IS!
YOU KNOW, I MIGHT GET A COFFEE AND JOIN YOU IF -
OH -

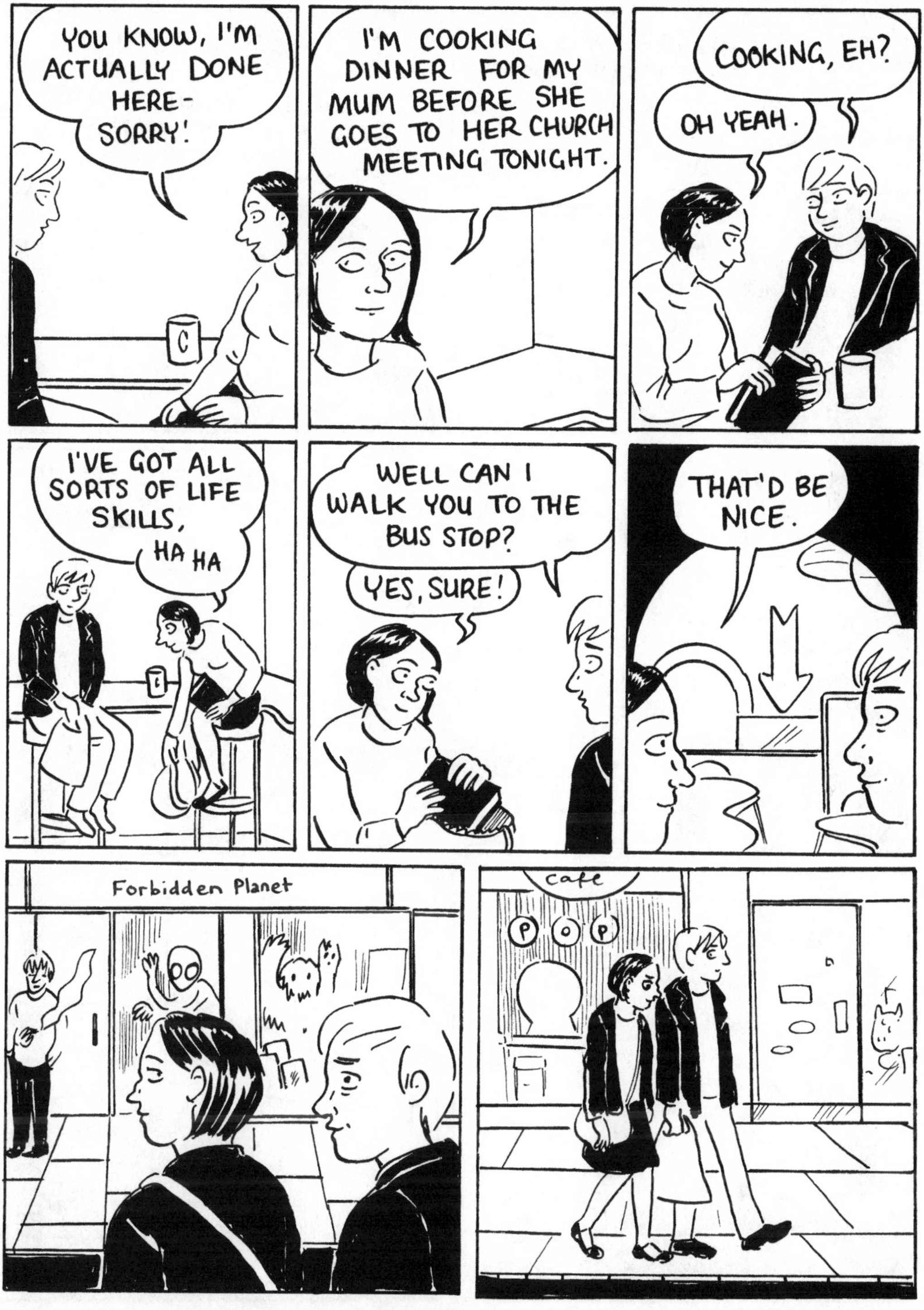
YOU KNOW, I'M ACTUALLY DONE HERE- SORRY!
I'M COOKING DINNER FOR MY MUM BEFORE SHE GOES TO HER CHURCH MEETING TONIGHT.
COOKING, EH?
OH YEAH.
I'VE GOT ALL SORTS OF LIFE SKILLS,
HA HA
WELL CAN I WALK YOU TO THE BUS STOP?
YES, SURE!
THAT'D BE NICE.
Forbidden Planet
cafe
POP

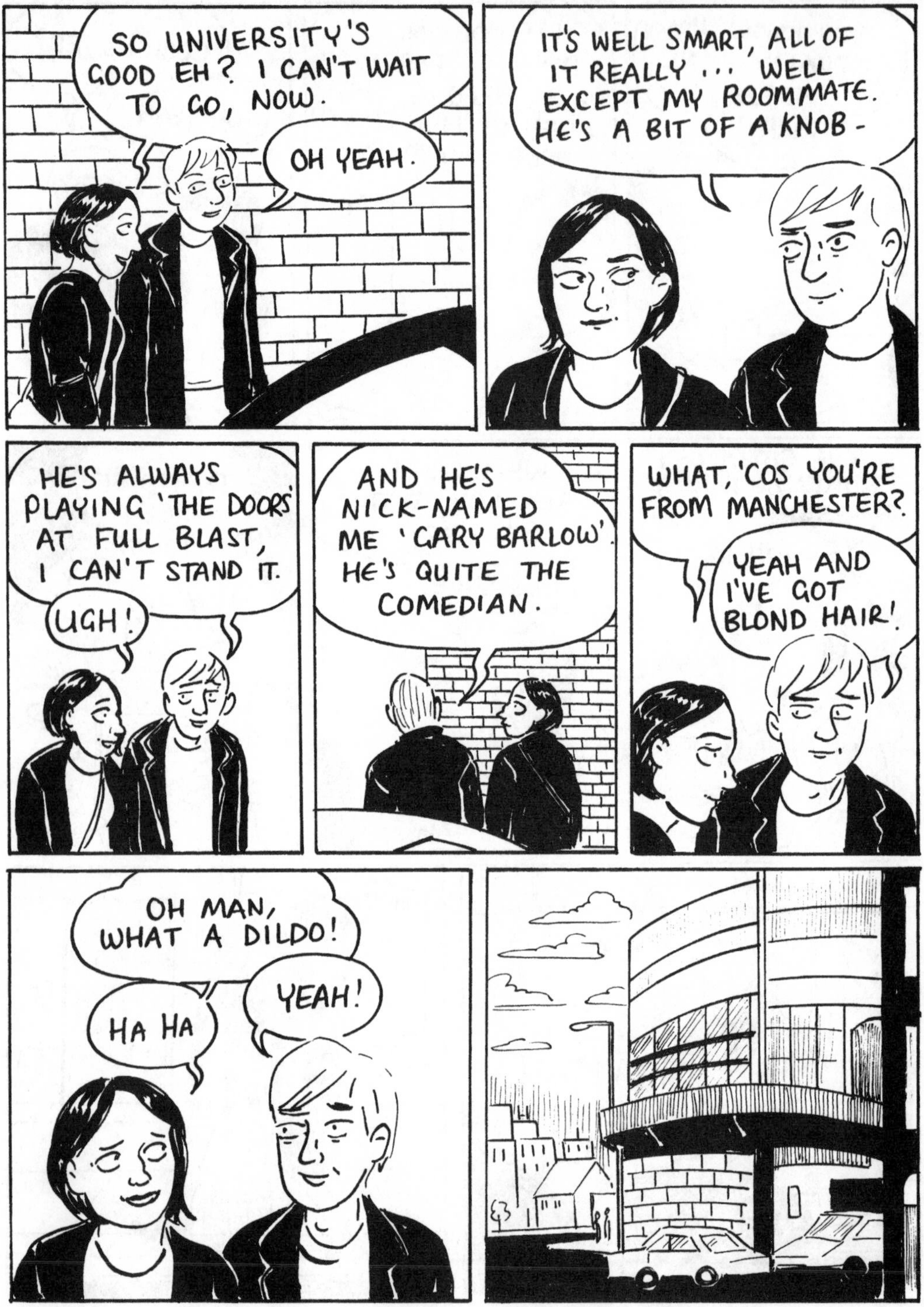
SO UNIVERSITY'S GOOD EH? I CAN'T WAIT TO GO, NOW.
OH YEAH.
IT'S WELL SMART, ALL OF IT REALLY ... WELL EXCEPT MY ROOMMATE. HE'S A BIT OF A KNOB -
HE'S ALWAYS PLAYING 'THE DOORS' AT FULL BLAST, I CAN'T STAND IT.
UGH!
AND HE'S NICK-NAMED ME 'GARY BARLOW'. HE'S QUITE THE COMEDIAN.
WHAT, 'COS YOU'RE FROM MANCHESTER?
YEAH AND I'VE GOT BLOND HAIR!
OH MAN, WHAT A DILDO!
HA HA
YEAH!

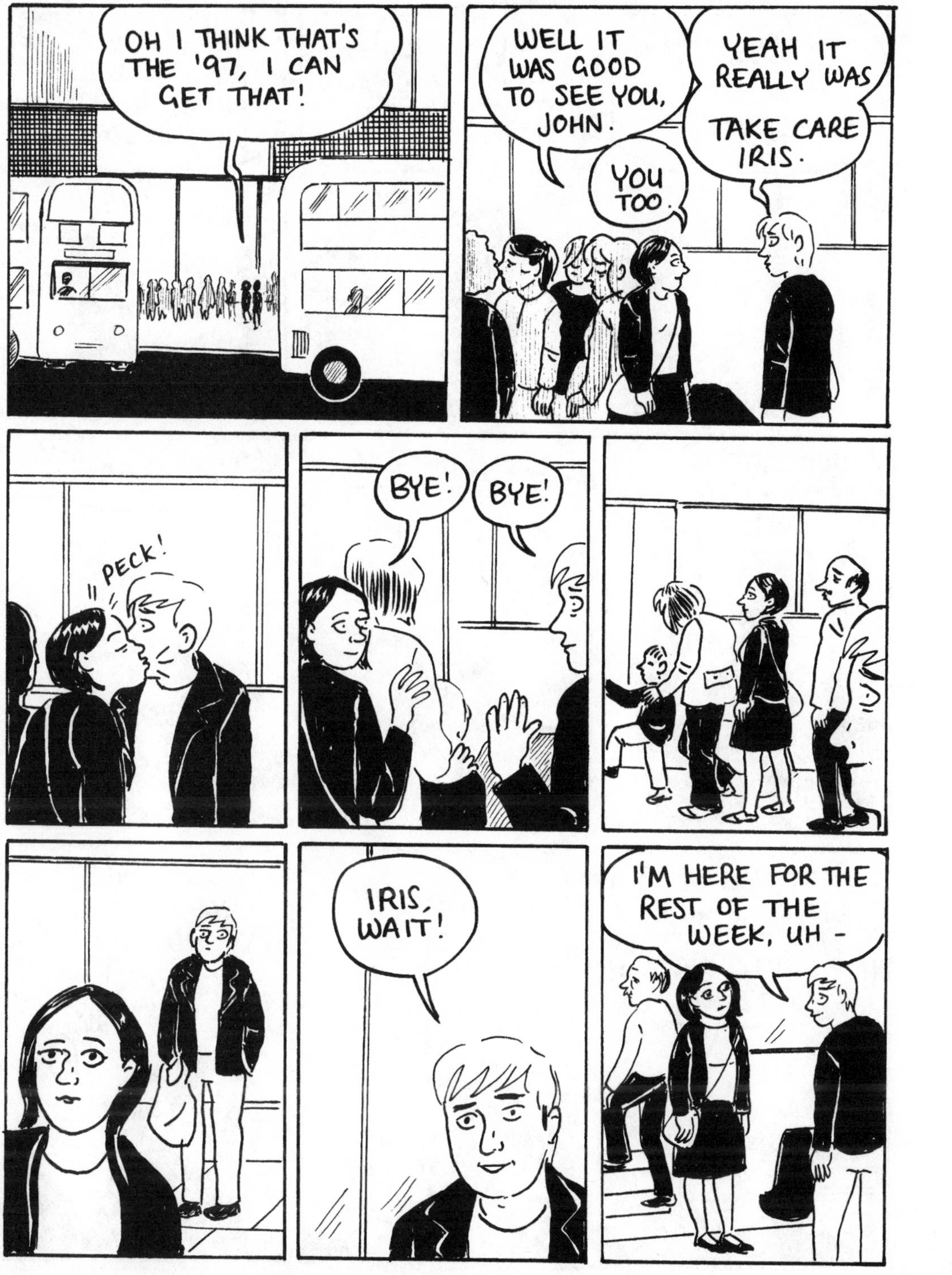
OH I THINK THAT'S THE '97, I CAN GET THAT!
WELL IT WAS GOOD TO SEE YOU, JOHN.
YOU TOO.
YEAH IT REALLY WAS
TAKE CARE IRIS.
PECK!
BYE!
BYE!
IRIS, WAIT!
I'M HERE FOR THE REST OF THE WEEK, UH -

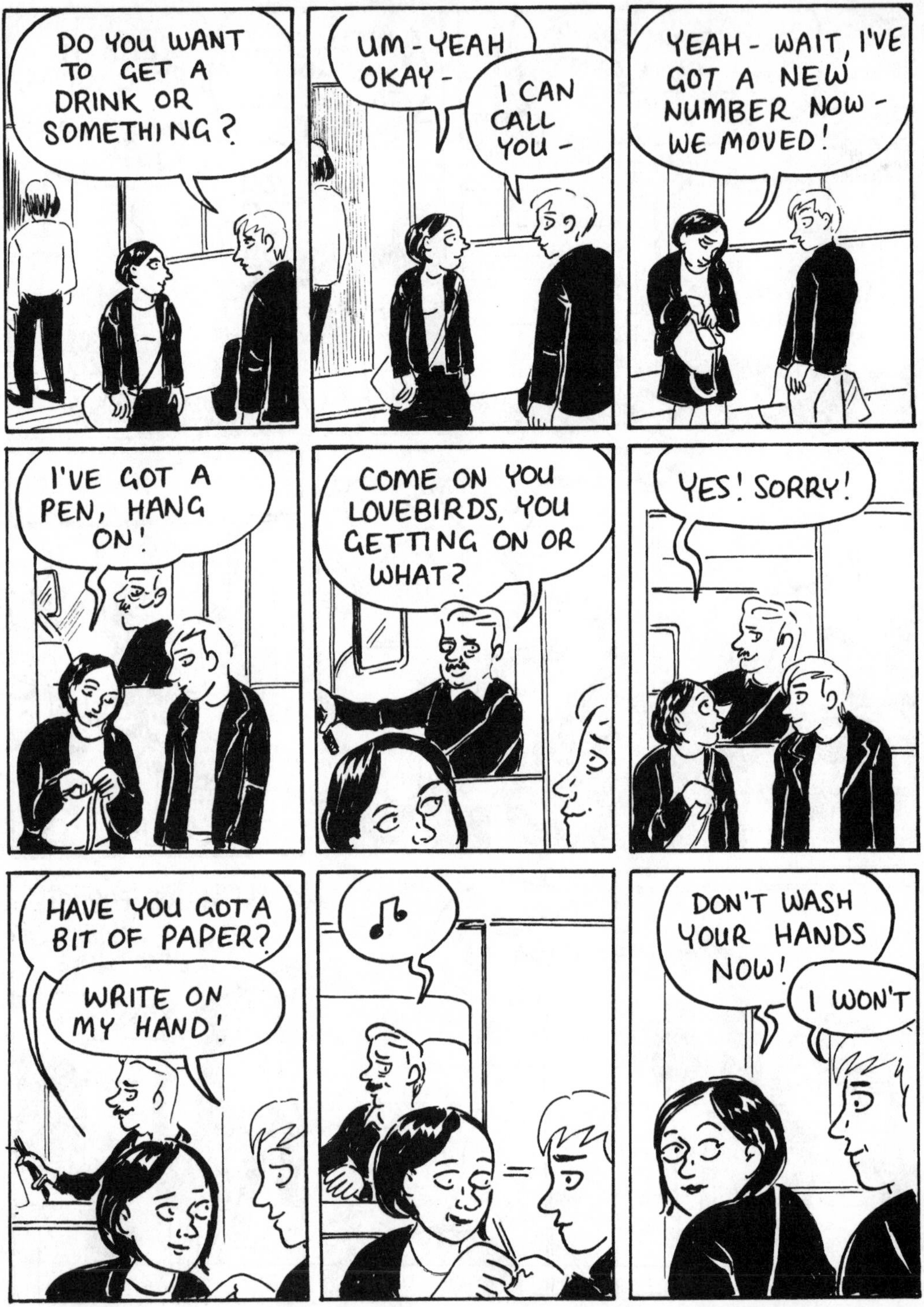
DO YOU WANT TO GET A DRINK OR SOMETHING?
UM-YEAH OKAY-
I CAN CALL YOU-
YEAH- WAIT, I'VE GOT A NEW NUMBER NOW- WE MOVED!
I'VE GOT A PEN, HANG ON!
COME ON YOU LOVEBIRDS, YOU GETTING ON OR WHAT?
YES! SORRY!
HAVE YOU GOT A BIT OF PAPER?
WRITE ON MY HAND!
DON'T WASH YOUR HANDS NOW!
I WON'T

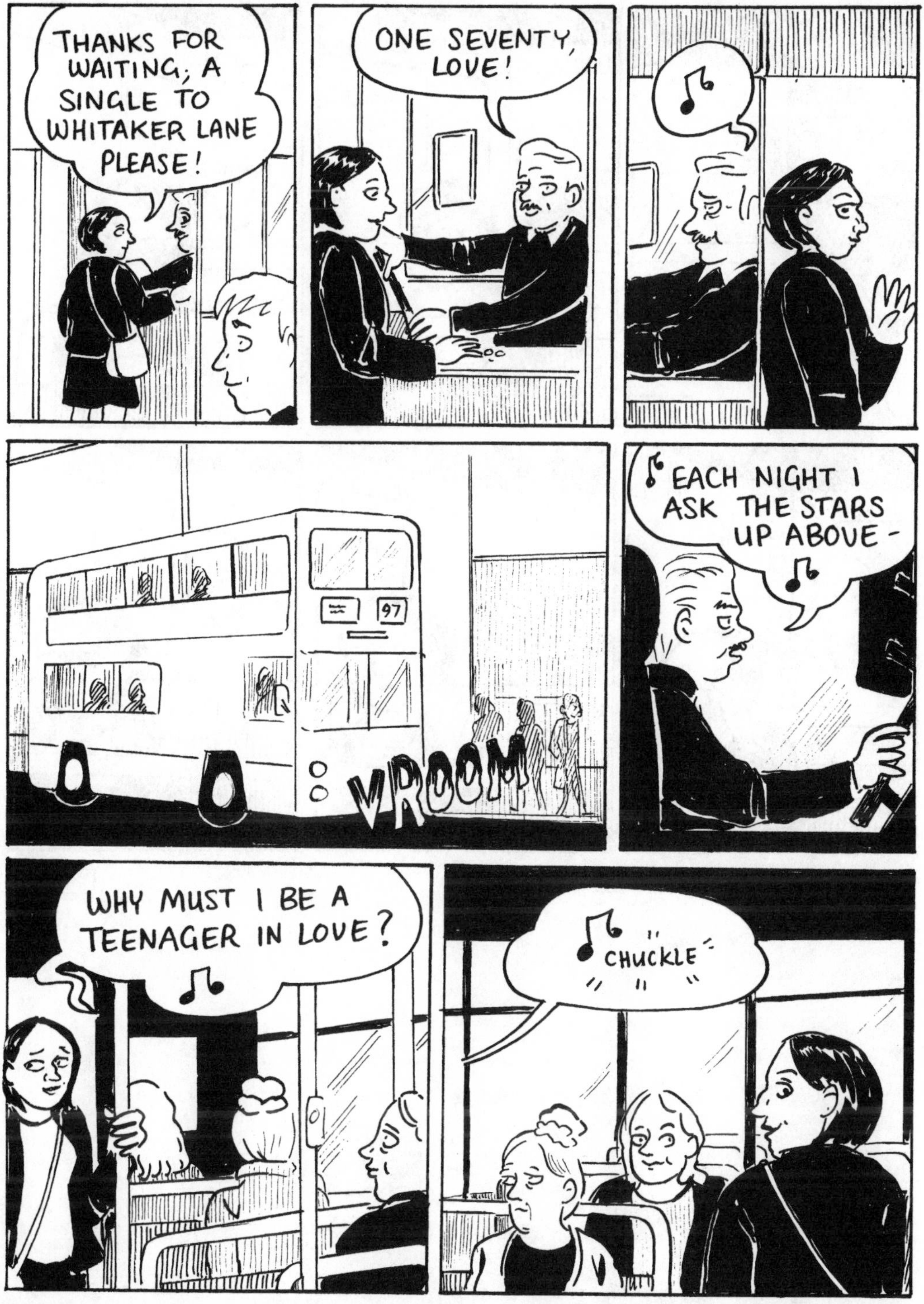
THANKS FOR WAITING; A SINGLE TO WHITAKER LANE PLEASE!
ONE SEVENTY, LOVE!
EACH NIGHT I ASK THE STARS UP ABOVE -
WHY MUST I BE A TEENAGER IN LOVE?
CHUCKLE

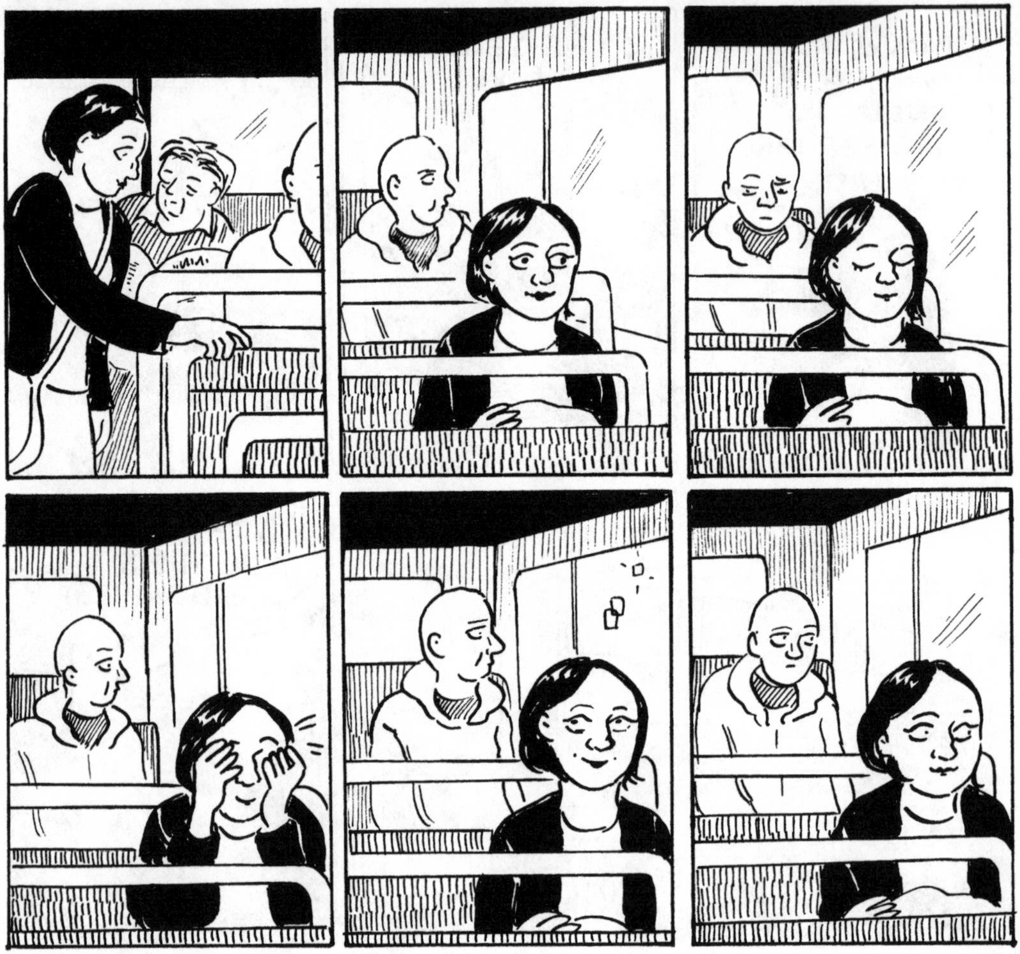

END

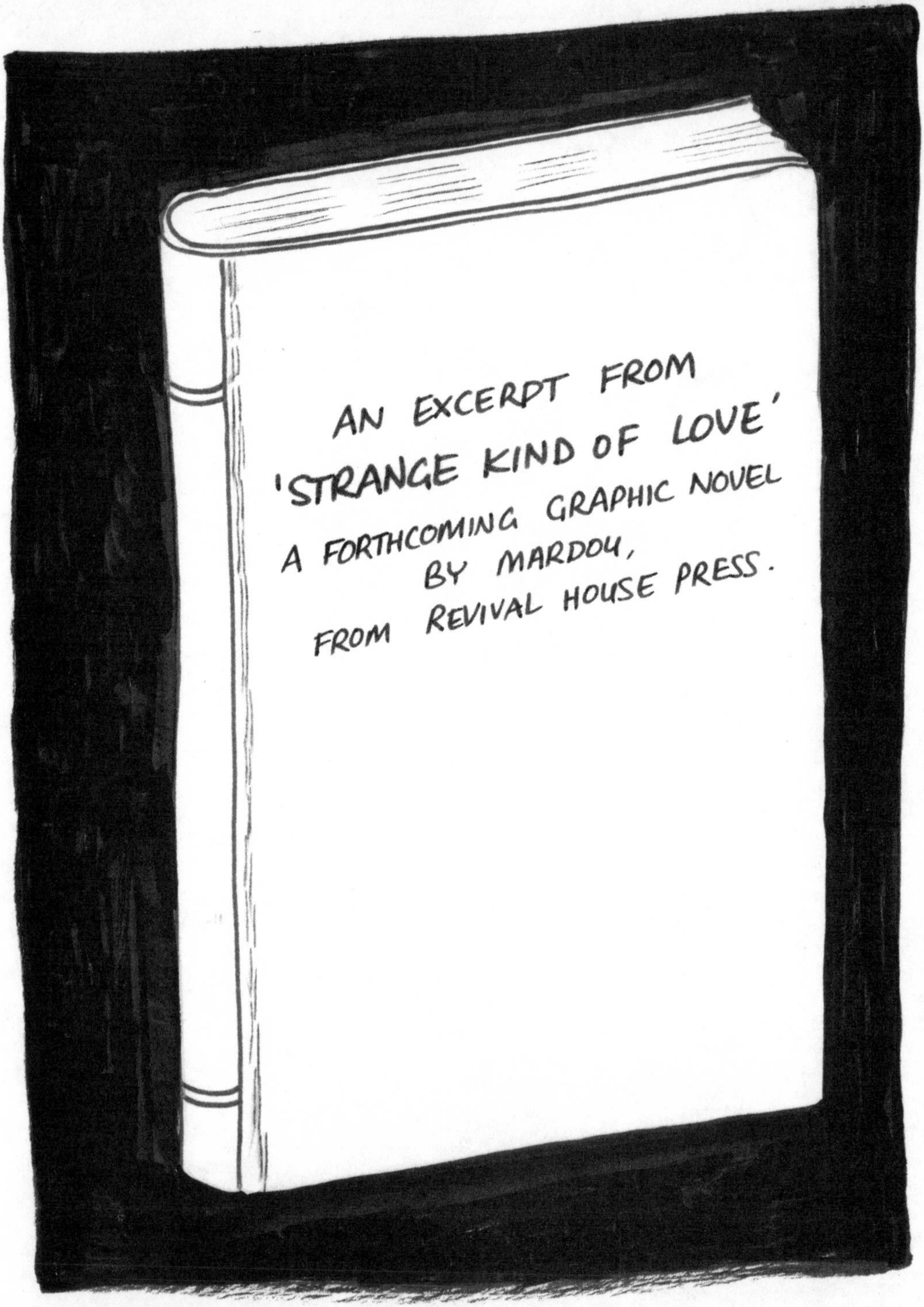
AN EXCERPT FROM
'STRANGE KIND OF LOVE'
A FORTHCOMING GRAPHIC NOVEL
BY MARDOU,
FROM REVIVAL HOUSE PRESS.

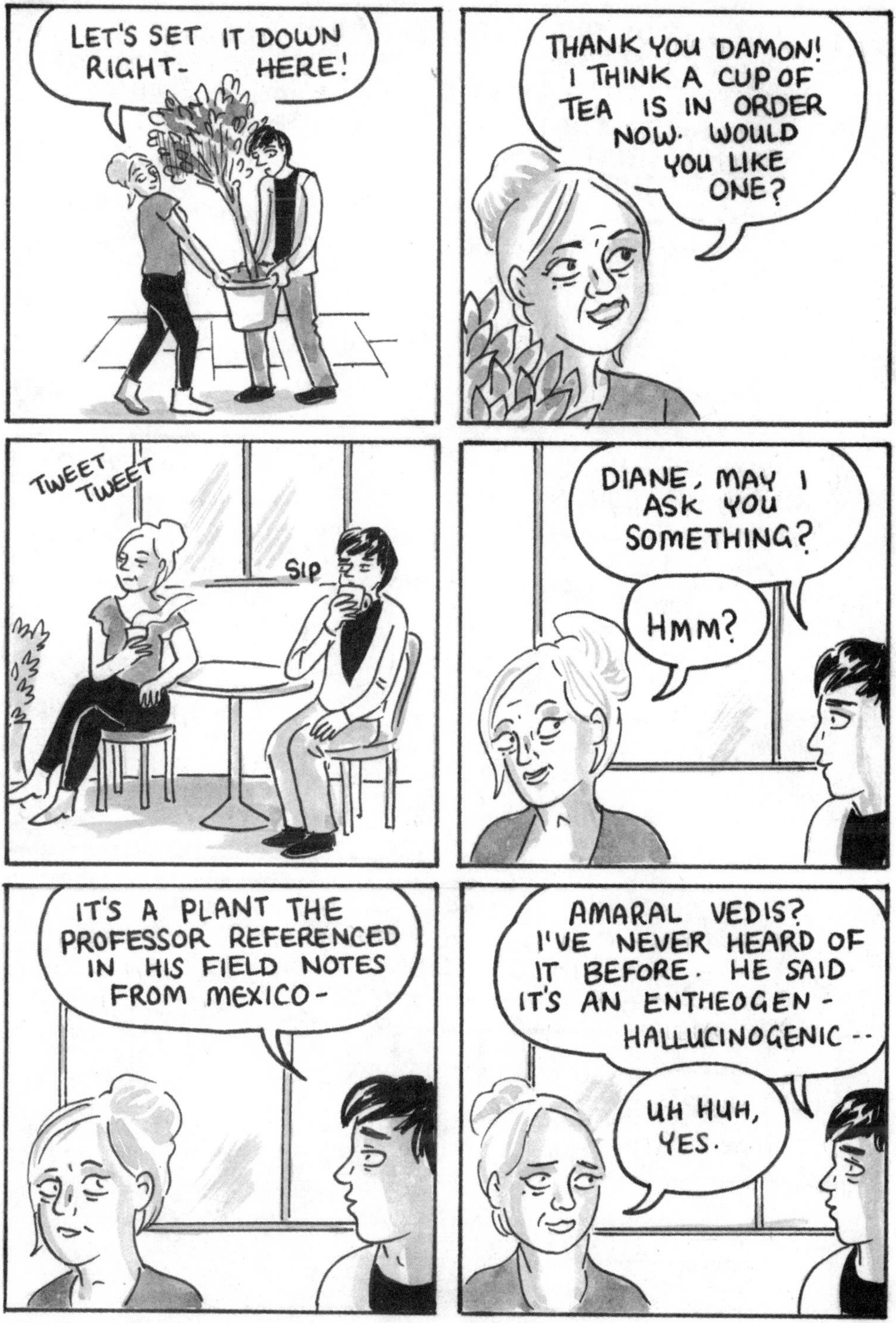
LET'S SET IT DOWN RIGHT- HERE!
THANK YOU DAMON! I THINK A CUP OF TEA IS IN ORDER NOW. WOULD YOU LIKE ONE?
TWEET TWEET
SIP
DIANE, MAY I ASK YOU SOMETHING?
HMM?
IT'S A PLANT THE PROFESSOR REFERENCED IN HIS FIELD NOTES FROM MEXICO-
AMARAL VEDIS? I'VE NEVER HEARD OF IT BEFORE. HE SAID IT'S AN ENTHEOGEN - HALLUCINOGENIC --
UH HUH, YES.

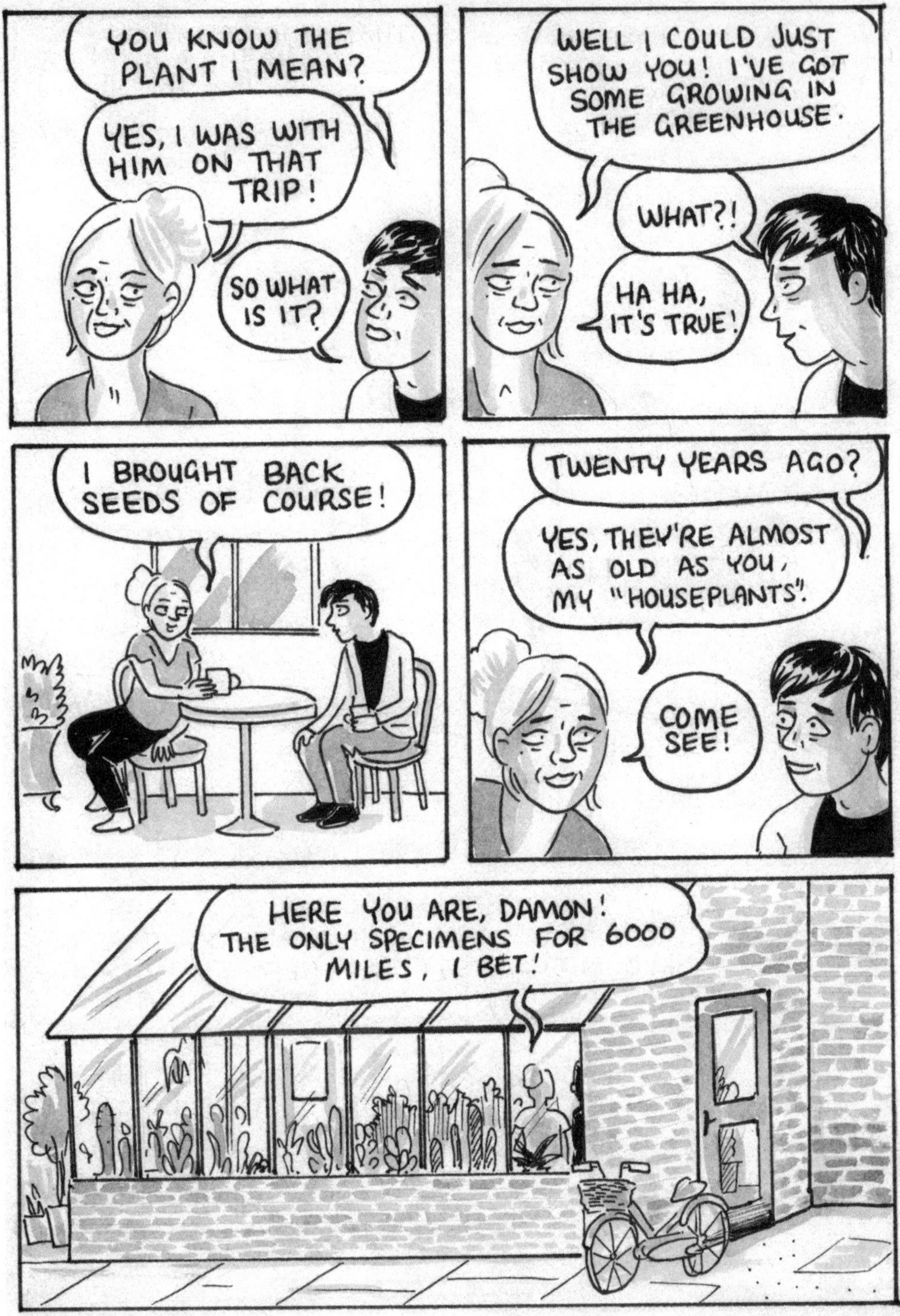
YOU KNOW THE PLANT I MEAN?
YES, I WAS WITH HIM ON THAT TRIP!
SO WHAT IS IT?
WELL I COULD JUST SHOW YOU! I'VE GOT SOME GROWING IN THE GREENHOUSE.
WHAT?!
HA HA, IT'S TRUE!
I BROUGHT BACK SEEDS OF COURSE!
TWENTY YEARS AGO?
YES, THEY'RE ALMOST AS OLD AS YOU, MY "HOUSEPLANTS".
COME SEE!
HERE YOU ARE, DAMON! THE ONLY SPECIMENS FOR 6000 MILES, I BET!

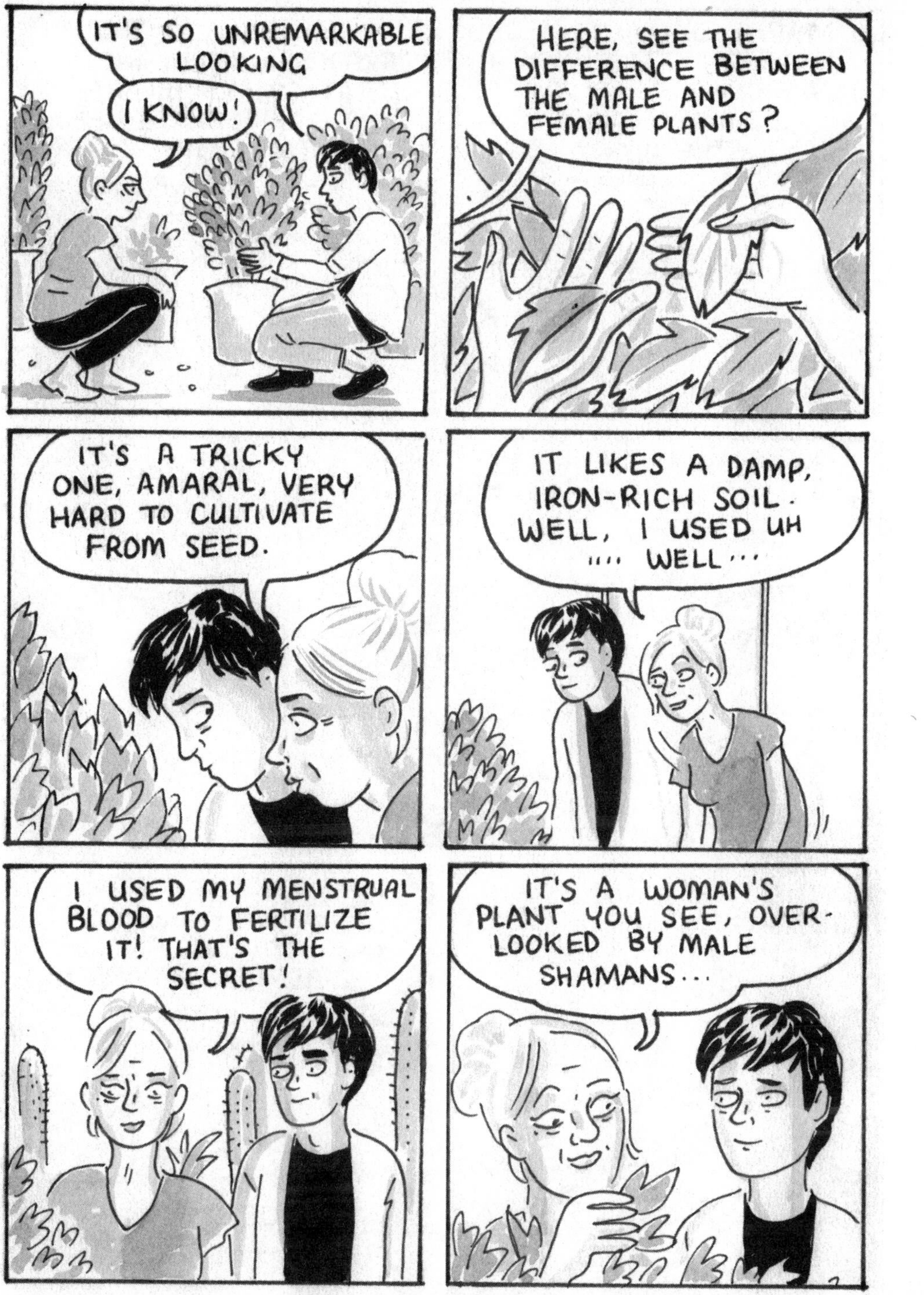
IT'S SO UNREMARKABLE LOOKING
I KNOW!
HERE, SEE THE DIFFERENCE BETWEEN THE MALE AND FEMALE PLANTS?
IT'S A TRICKY ONE, AMARAL, VERY HARD TO CULTIVATE FROM SEED.
IT LIKES A DAMP, IRON-RICH SOIL. WELL, I USED UH .... WELL...
I USED MY MENSTRUAL BLOOD TO FERTILIZE IT! THAT'S THE SECRET!
IT'S A WOMAN'S PLANT YOU SEE, OVER-LOOKED BY MALE SHAMANS...

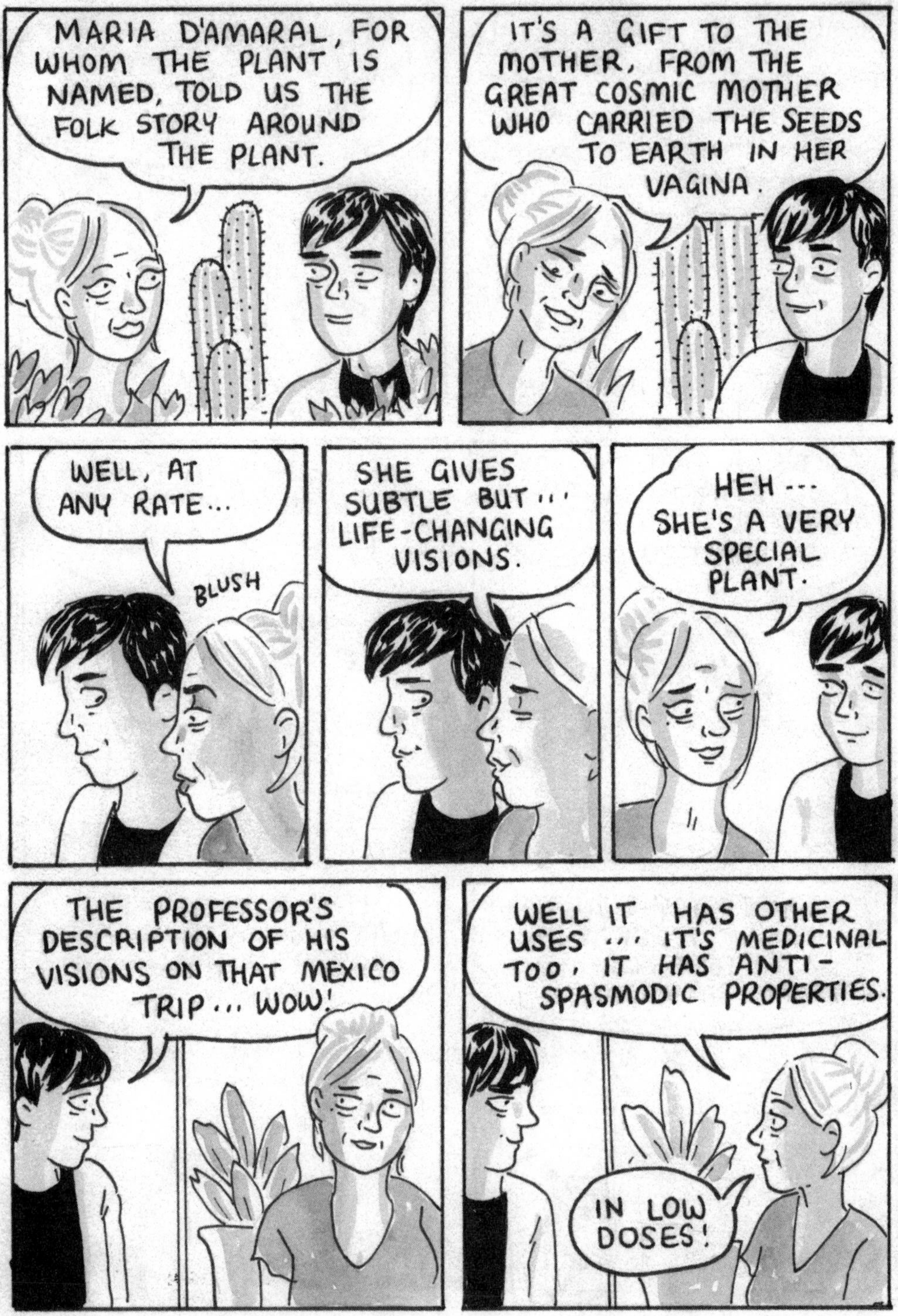
MARIA D'AMARAL, FOR WHOM THE PLANT IS NAMED, TOLD US THE FOLK STORY AROUND THE PLANT.
IT'S A GIFT TO THE MOTHER, FROM THE GREAT COSMIC MOTHER WHO CARRIED THE SEEDS TO EARTH IN HER VAGINA.
WELL, AT ANY RATE...
BLUSH
SHE GIVES SUBTLE BUT... LIFE-CHANGING VISIONS.
HEH ... SHE'S A VERY SPECIAL PLANT.
THE PROFESSOR'S DESCRIPTION OF HIS VISIONS ON THAT MEXICO TRIP... WOW!
WELL IT HAS OTHER USES ... IT'S MEDICINAL TOO, IT HAS ANTI-SPASMODIC PROPERTIES.
IN LOW DOSES!

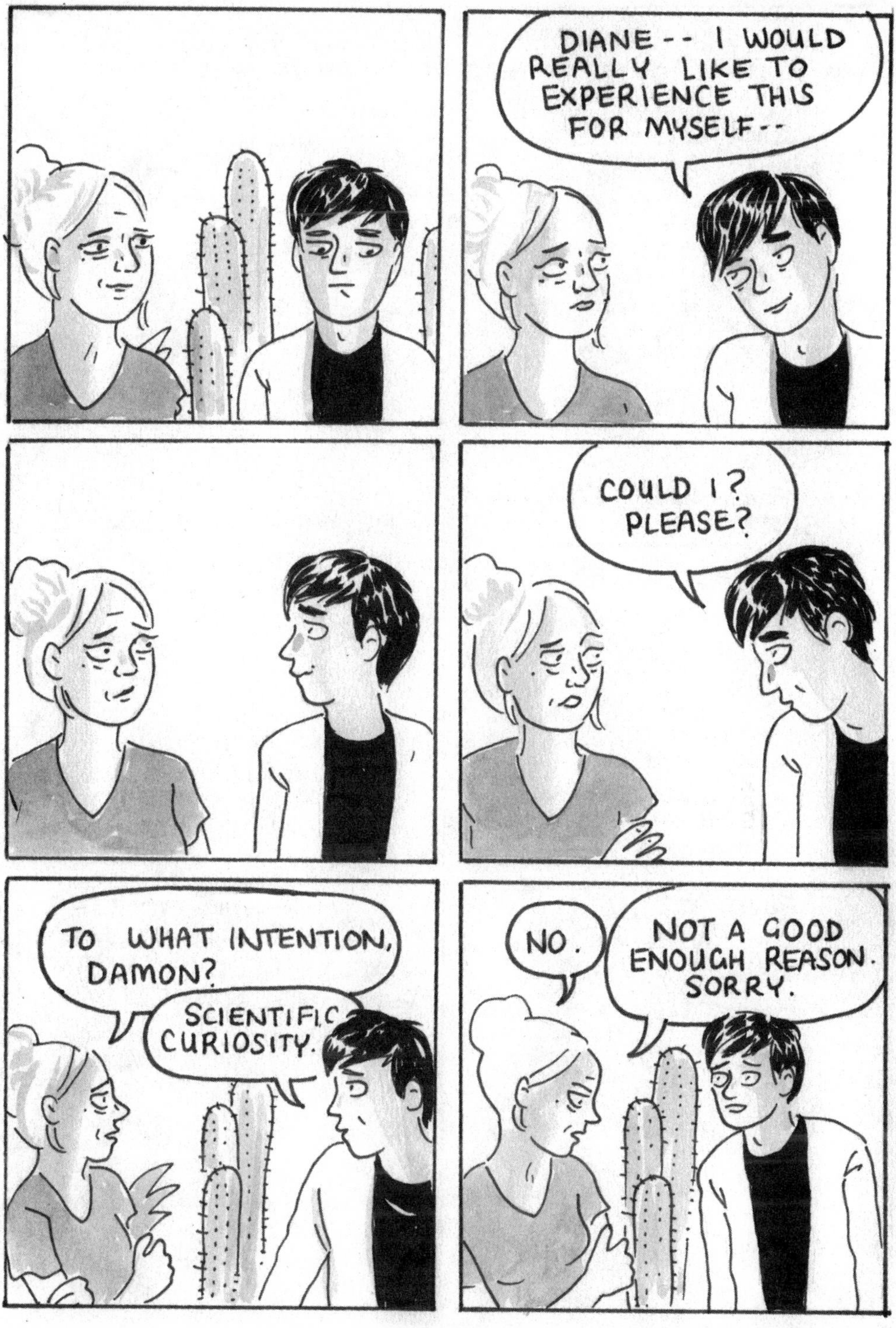
DIANE -- I WOULD REALLY LIKE TO EXPERIENCE THIS FOR MYSELF --
COULD I? PLEASE?
TO WHAT INTENTION, DAMON?
SCIENTIFIC CURIOSITY.
NO.
NOT A GOOD ENOUGH REASON. SORRY.

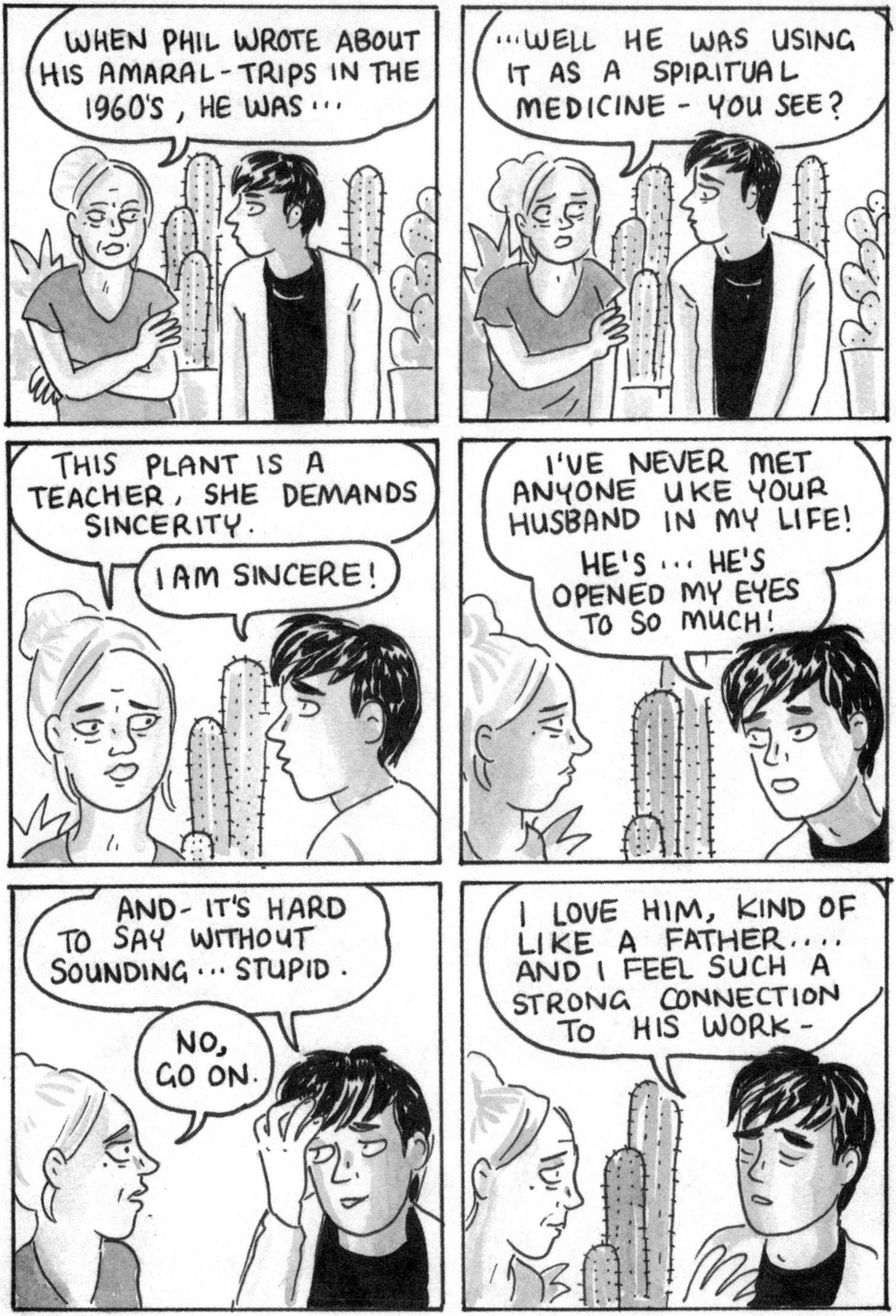
WHEN PHIL WROTE ABOUT HIS AMARAL-TRIPS IN THE 1960'S, HE WAS...
...WELL HE WAS USING IT AS A SPIRITUAL MEDICINE - YOU SEE?
THIS PLANT IS A TEACHER, SHE DEMANDS SINCERITY.
I AM SINCERE!
I'VE NEVER MET ANYONE LIKE YOUR HUSBAND IN MY LIFE!
HE'S... HE'S OPENED MY EYES TO SO MUCH!
AND- IT'S HARD TO SAY WITHOUT SOUNDING... STUPID.
NO, GO ON.
I LOVE HIM, KIND OF LIKE A FATHER.... AND I FEEL SUCH A STRONG CONNECTION TO HIS WORK-

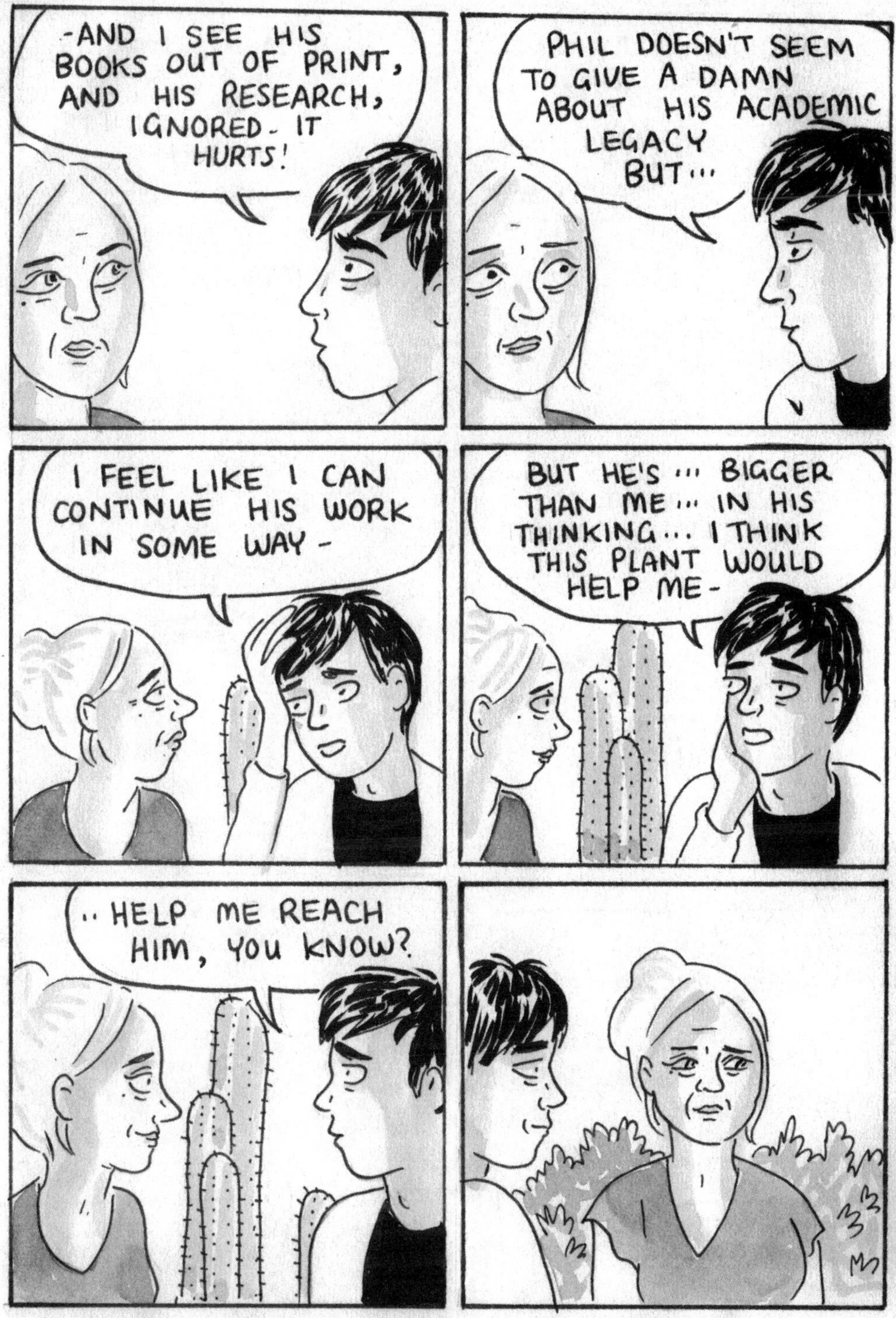
-AND I SEE HIS BOOKS OUT OF PRINT, AND HIS RESEARCH, IGNORED- IT HURTS!
PHIL DOESN'T SEEM TO GIVE A DAMN ABOUT HIS ACADEMIC LEGACY BUT...
I FEEL LIKE I CAN CONTINUE HIS WORK IN SOME WAY-
BUT HE'S ... BIGGER THAN ME ... IN HIS THINKING ... I THINK THIS PLANT WOULD HELP ME-
.. HELP ME REACH HIM, YOU KNOW?

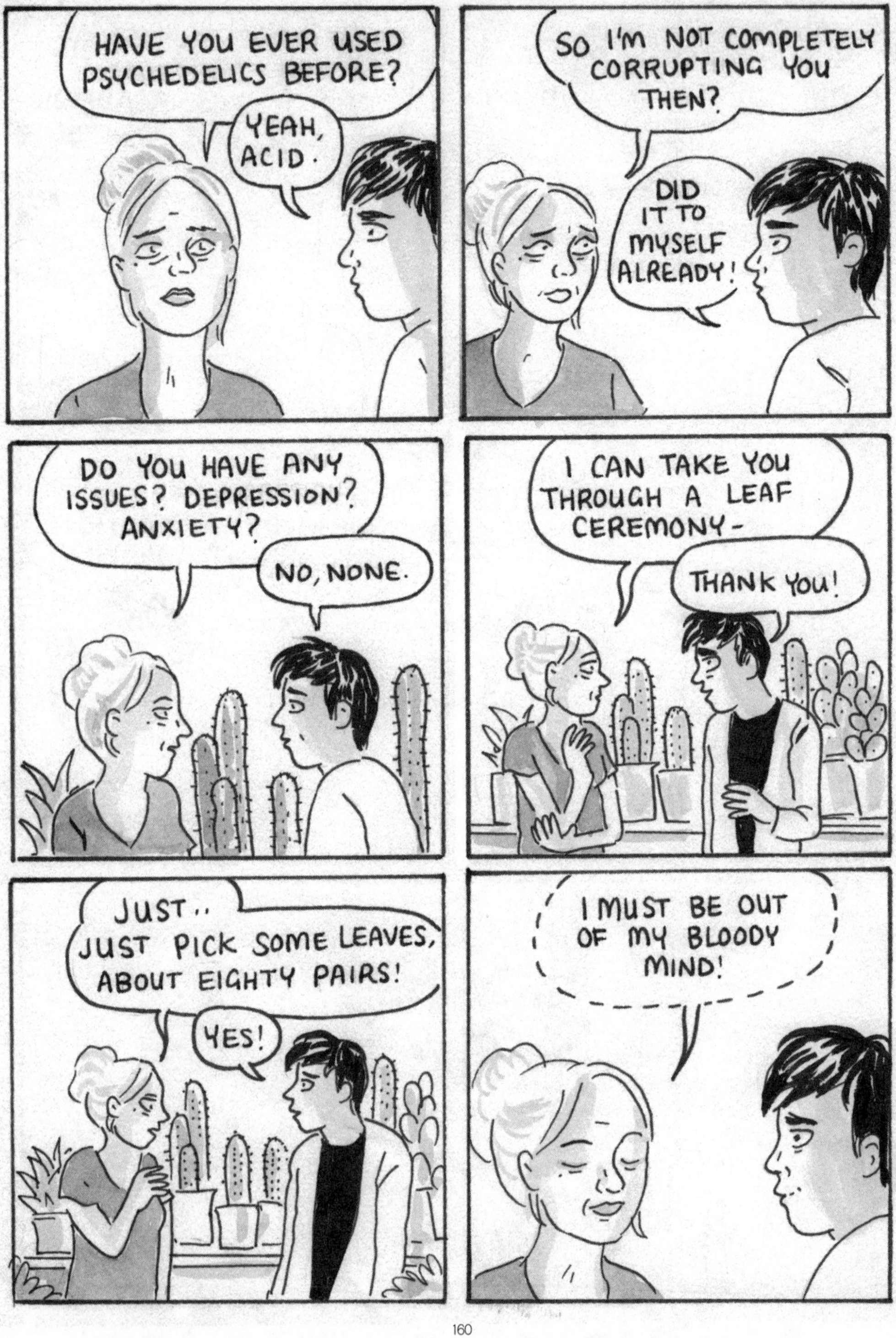
HAVE YOU EVER USED PSYCHEDELICS BEFORE?
YEAH, ACID.
SO I'M NOT COMPLETELY CORRUPTING YOU THEN?
DID IT TO MYSELF ALREADY!
DO YOU HAVE ANY ISSUES? DEPRESSION? ANXIETY?
NO, NONE.
I CAN TAKE YOU THROUGH A LEAF CEREMONY-
THANK YOU!
JUST..
JUST PICK SOME LEAVES, ABOUT EIGHTY PAIRS!
YES!
I MUST BE OUT OF MY BLOODY MIND!

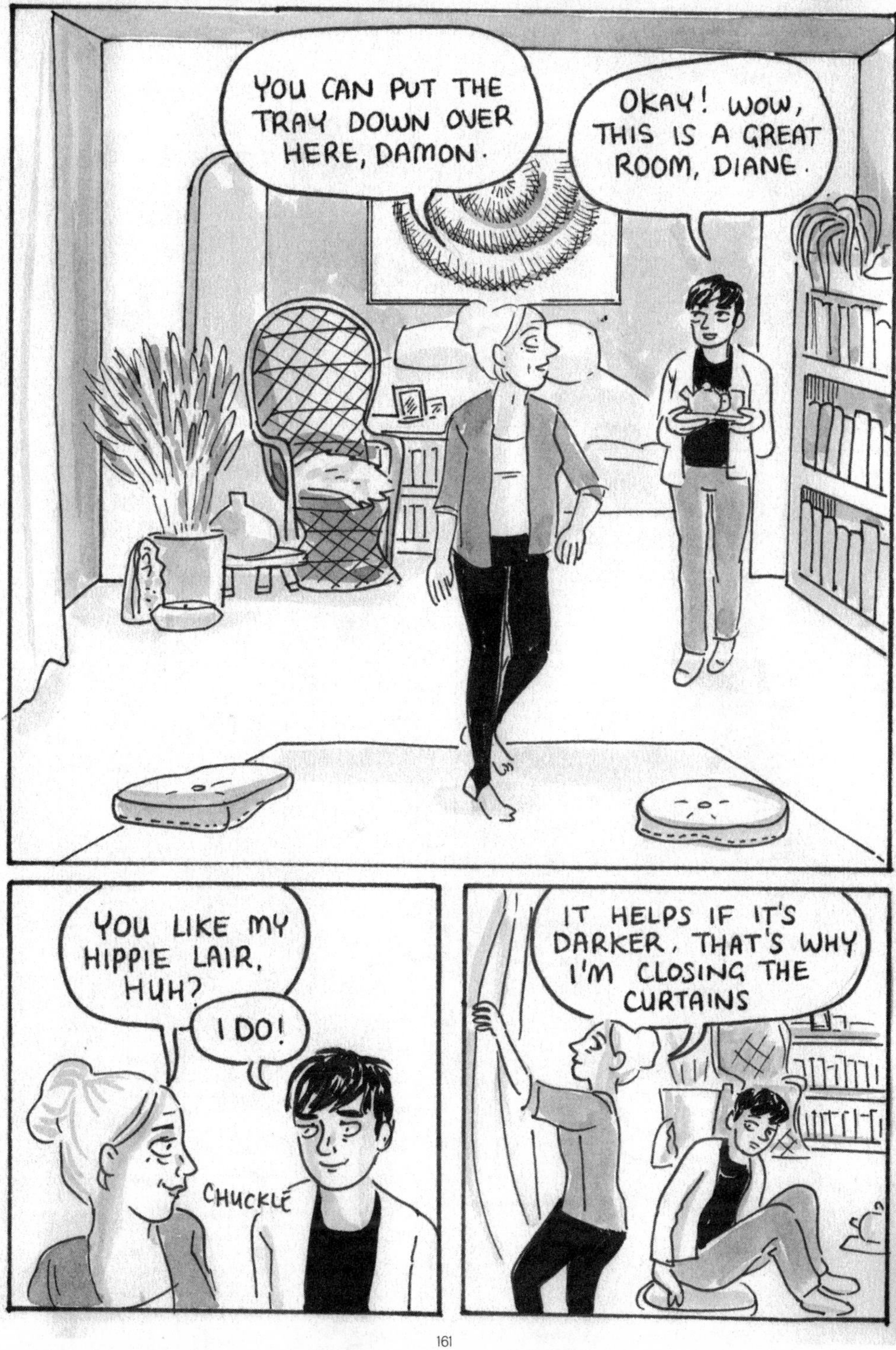
YOU CAN PUT THE TRAY DOWN OVER HERE, DAMON.
OKAY! WOW, THIS IS A GREAT ROOM, DIANE.
YOU LIKE MY HIPPIE LAIR, HUH?
I DO!
CHUCKLE
IT HELPS IF IT'S DARKER, THAT'S WHY I'M CLOSING THE CURTAINS

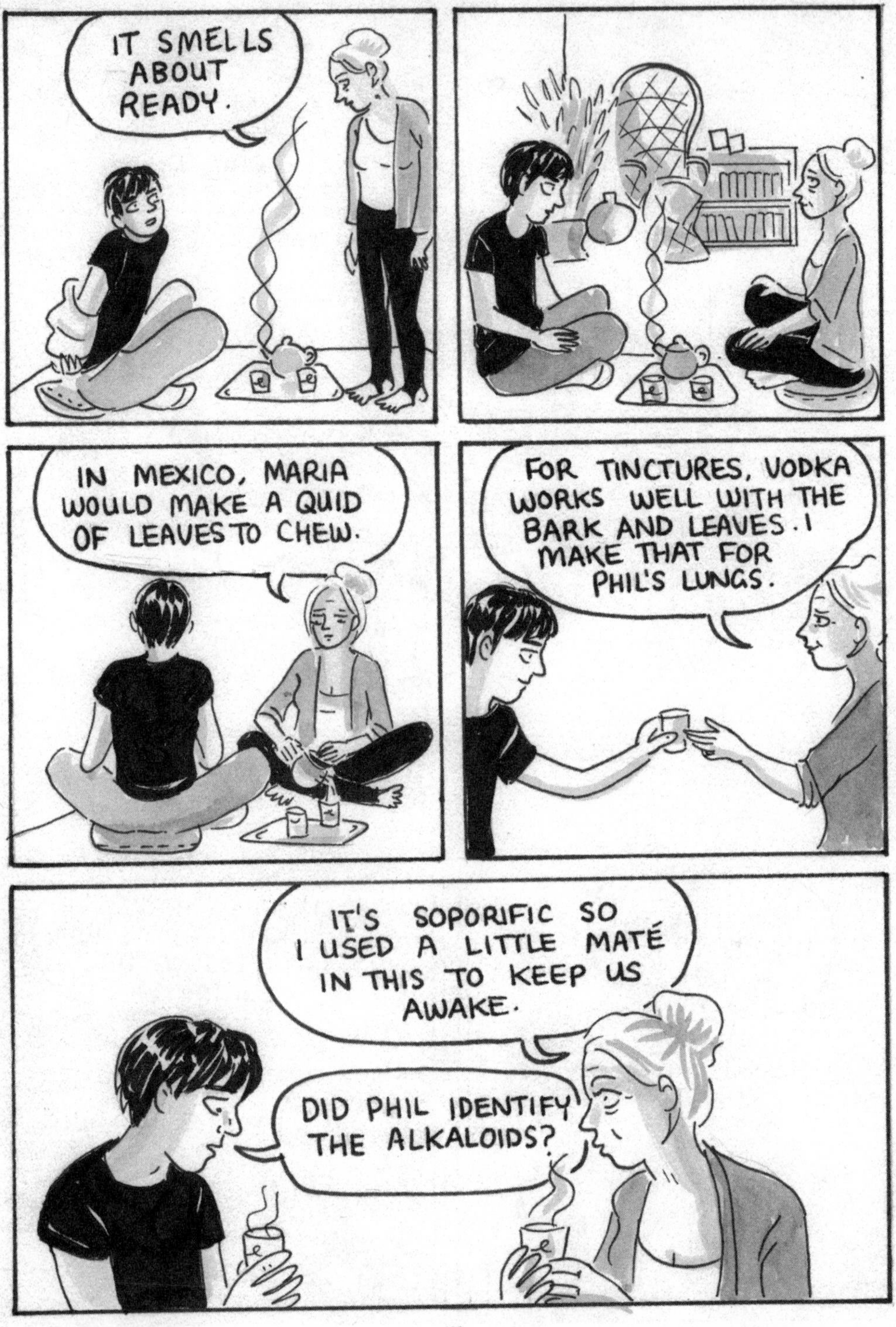
IT SMELLS ABOUT READY.
IN MEXICO, MARIA WOULD MAKE A QUID OF LEAVES TO CHEW.
FOR TINCTURES, VODKA WORKS WELL WITH THE BARK AND LEAVES. I MAKE THAT FOR PHIL'S LUNGS.
IT'S SOPORIFIC SO I USED A LITTLE MATÉ IN THIS TO KEEP US AWAKE.
DID PHIL IDENTIFY THE ALKALOIDS?

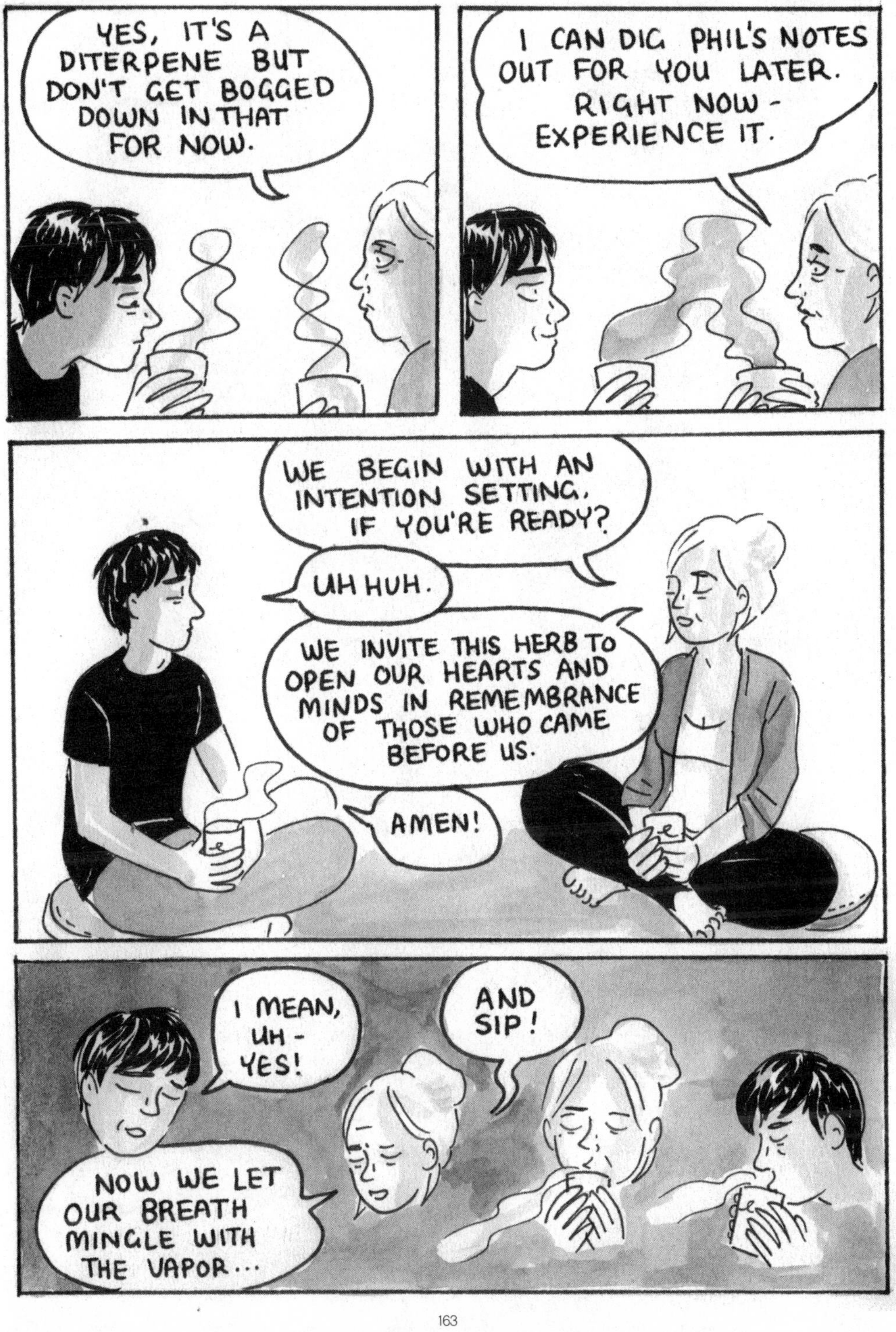
YES, IT'S A DITERPENE BUT DON'T GET BOGGED DOWN IN THAT FOR NOW.
I CAN DIG PHIL'S NOTES OUT FOR YOU LATER. RIGHT NOW - EXPERIENCE IT.
WE BEGIN WITH AN INTENTION SETTING, IF YOU'RE READY?
UH HUH.
WE INVITE THIS HERB TO OPEN OUR HEARTS AND MINDS IN REMEMBRANCE OF THOSE WHO CAME BEFORE US.
AMEN!
I MEAN, UH - YES!
NOW WE LET OUR BREATH MINGLE WITH THE VAPOR...
AND SIP!

OKAY, LET'S GET INTO THIS!
SOON:
I DON'T SEE ANYTHING...
IS ANYTHING MEANT TO BE HAPPENING?
IS IT WORKING FOR HER?
OH, YEAH, IT'S WORKING!
POP!

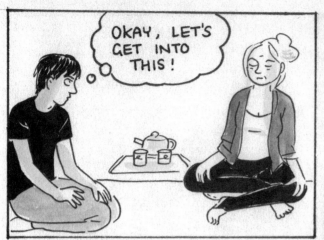

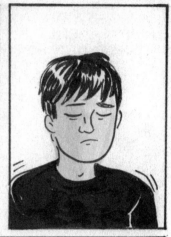

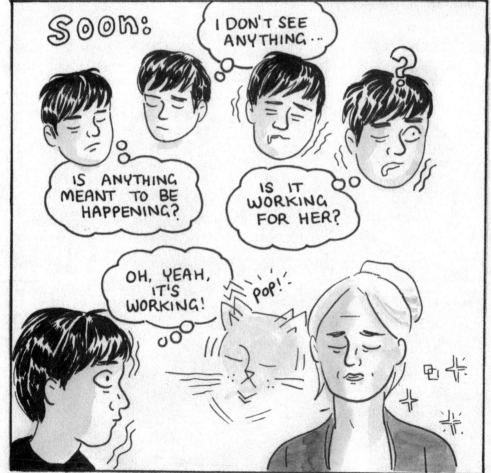

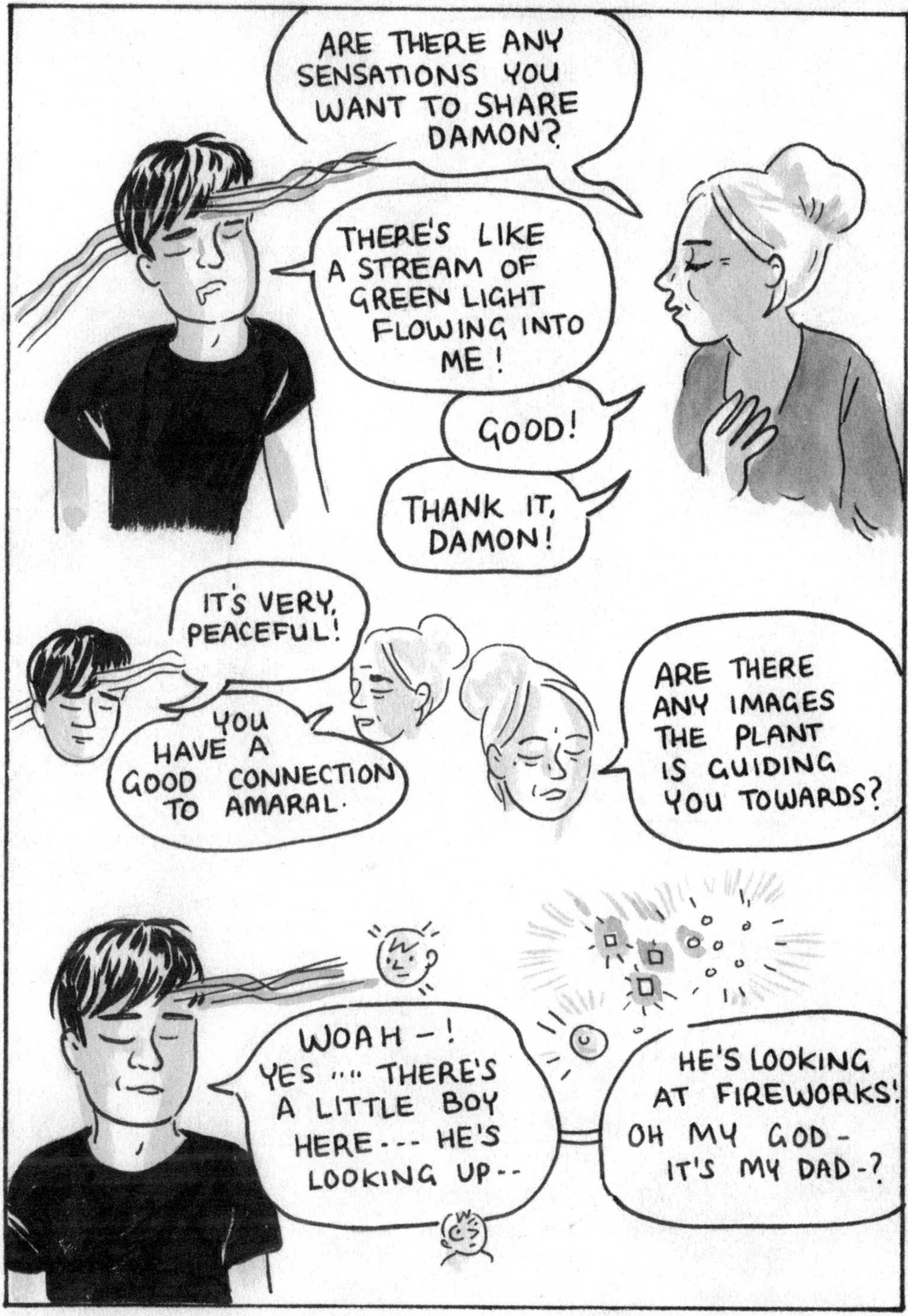
ARE THERE ANY SENSATIONS YOU WANT TO SHARE DAMON?
THERE'S LIKE A STREAM OF GREEN LIGHT FLOWING INTO ME!
GOOD!
THANK IT, DAMON!
IT'S VERY, PEACEFUL!
YOU HAVE A GOOD CONNECTION TO AMARAL.
ARE THERE ANY IMAGES THE PLANT IS GUIDING YOU TOWARDS?
WOAH-! YES .... THERE'S A LITTLE BOY HERE--- HE'S LOOKING UP--
HE'S LOOKING AT FIREWORKS! OH MY GOD- IT'S MY DAD-?

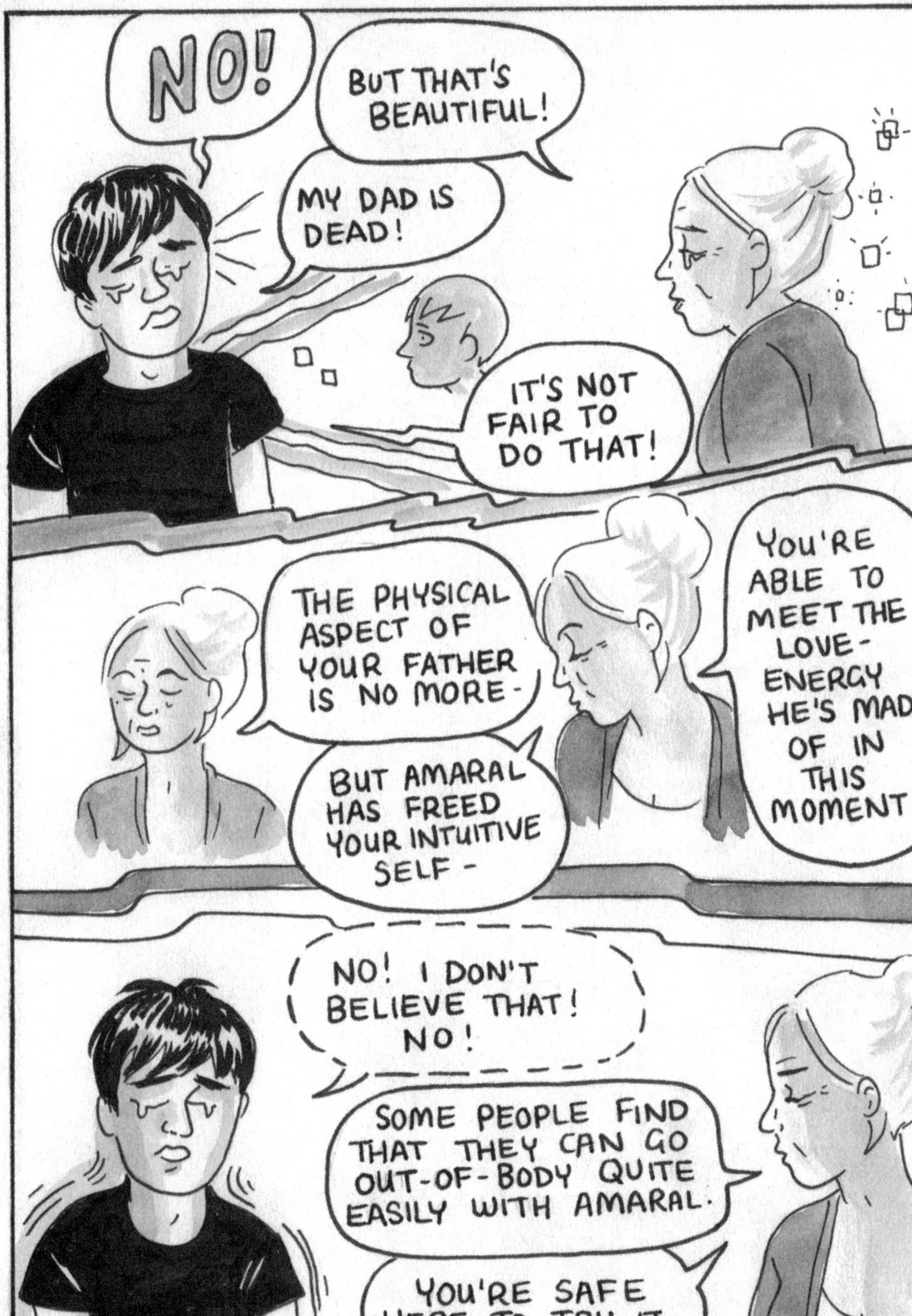

NO!
BUT THAT'S BEAUTIFUL!
MY DAD IS DEAD!
IT'S NOT FAIR TO DO THAT!
THE PHYSICAL ASPECT OF YOUR FATHER IS NO MORE-
BUT AMARAL HAS FREED YOUR INTUITIVE SELF -
YOU'RE ABLE TO MEET THE LOVE-ENERGY HE'S MADE OF IN THIS MOMENT!
NO! I DON'T BELIEVE THAT! NO!
SOME PEOPLE FIND THAT THEY CAN GO OUT-OF-BODY QUITE EASILY WITH AMARAL.
YOU'RE SAFE HERE TO TRY IT DAMON!

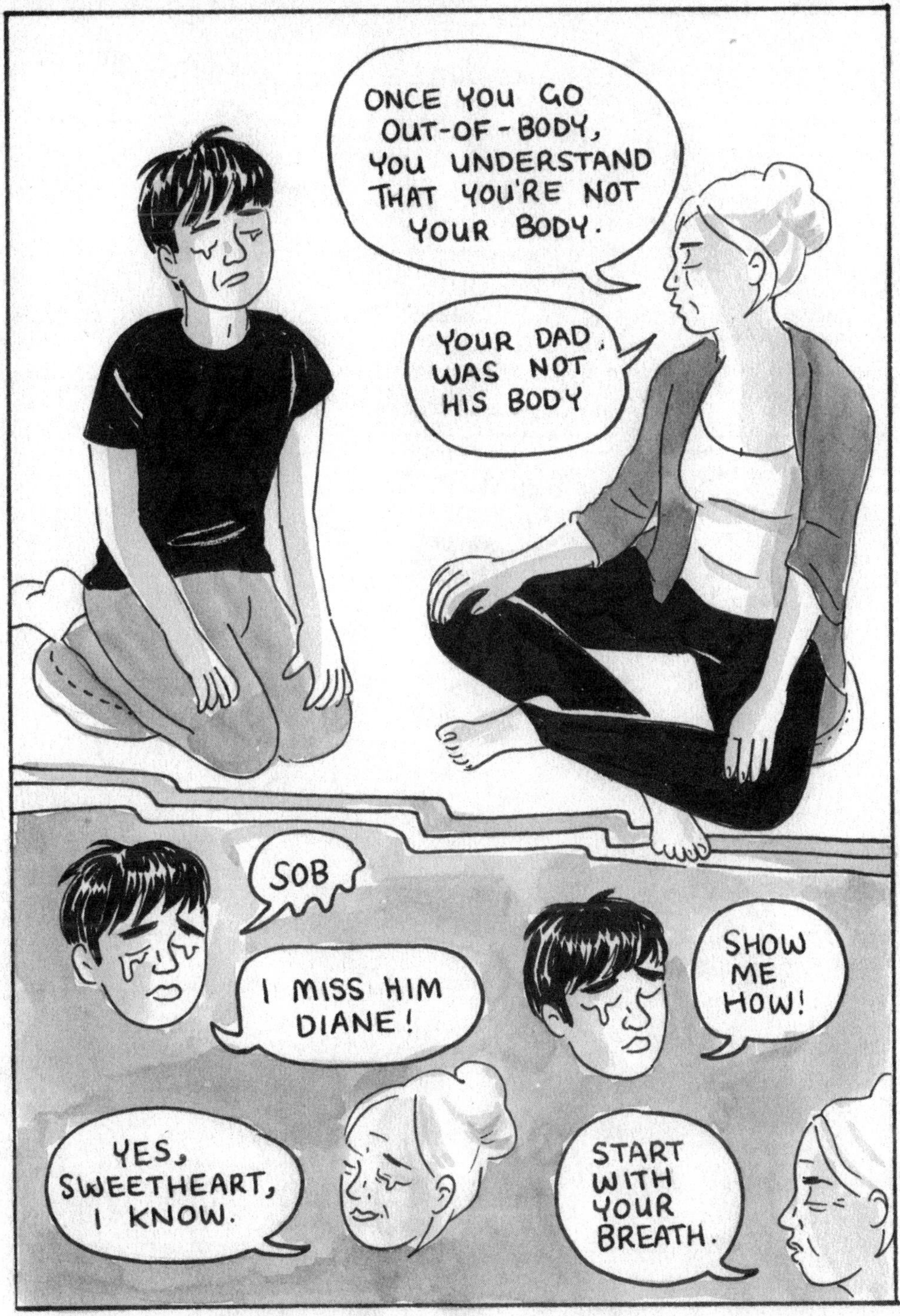
ONCE YOU GO OUT-OF-BODY, YOU UNDERSTAND THAT YOU'RE NOT YOUR BODY.
YOUR DAD WAS NOT HIS BODY
SOB
I MISS HIM DIANE!
SHOW ME HOW!
YES, SWEETHEART, I KNOW.
START WITH YOUR BREATH.

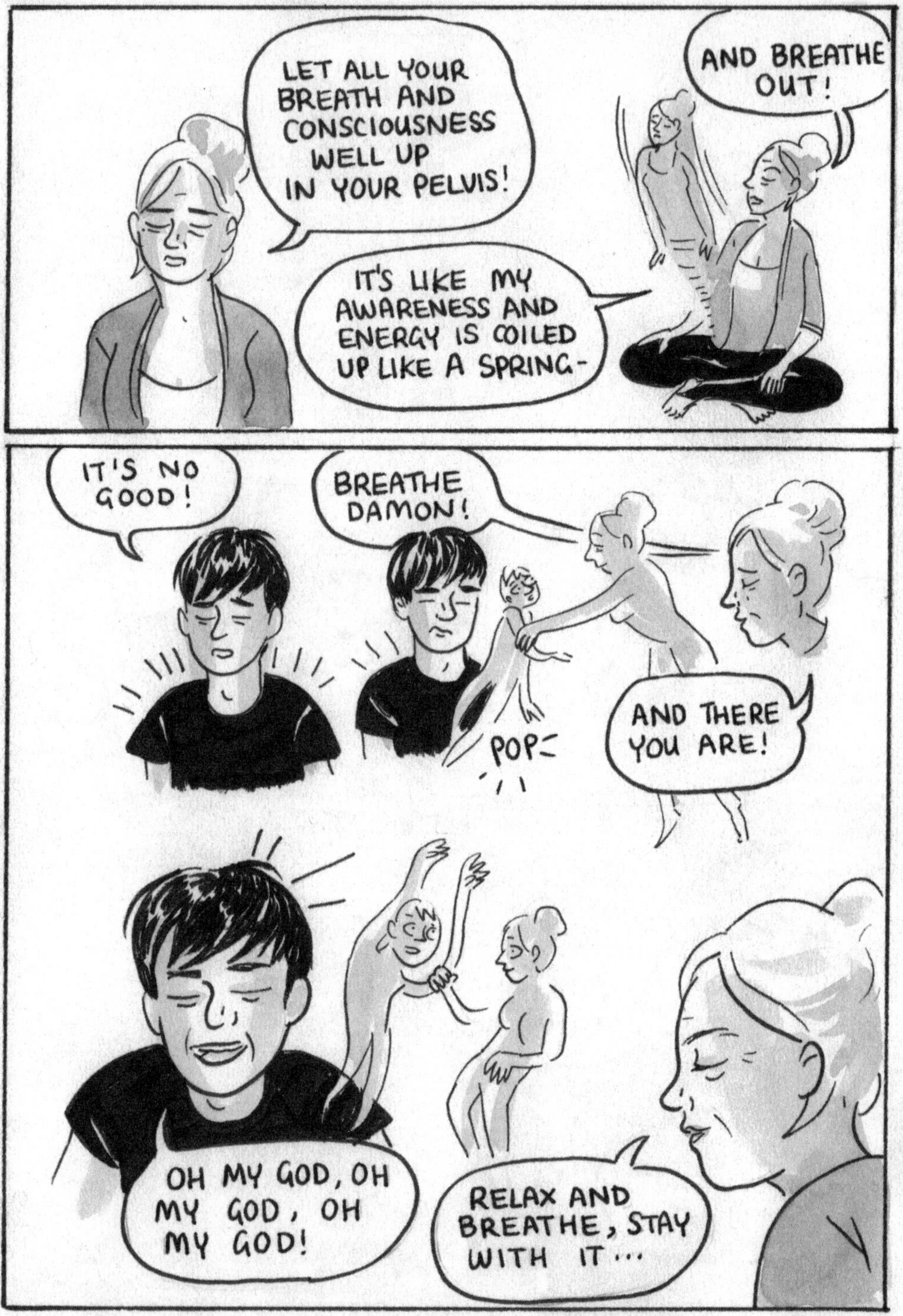
LET ALL YOUR BREATH AND CONSCIOUSNESS WELL UP IN YOUR PELVIS!
AND BREATHE OUT!
IT'S LIKE MY AWARENESS AND ENERGY IS COILED UP LIKE A SPRING-
IT'S NO GOOD!
BREATHE DAMON!
POP
AND THERE YOU ARE!
OH MY GOD, OH MY GOD, OH MY GOD!
RELAX AND BREATHE, STAY WITH IT...

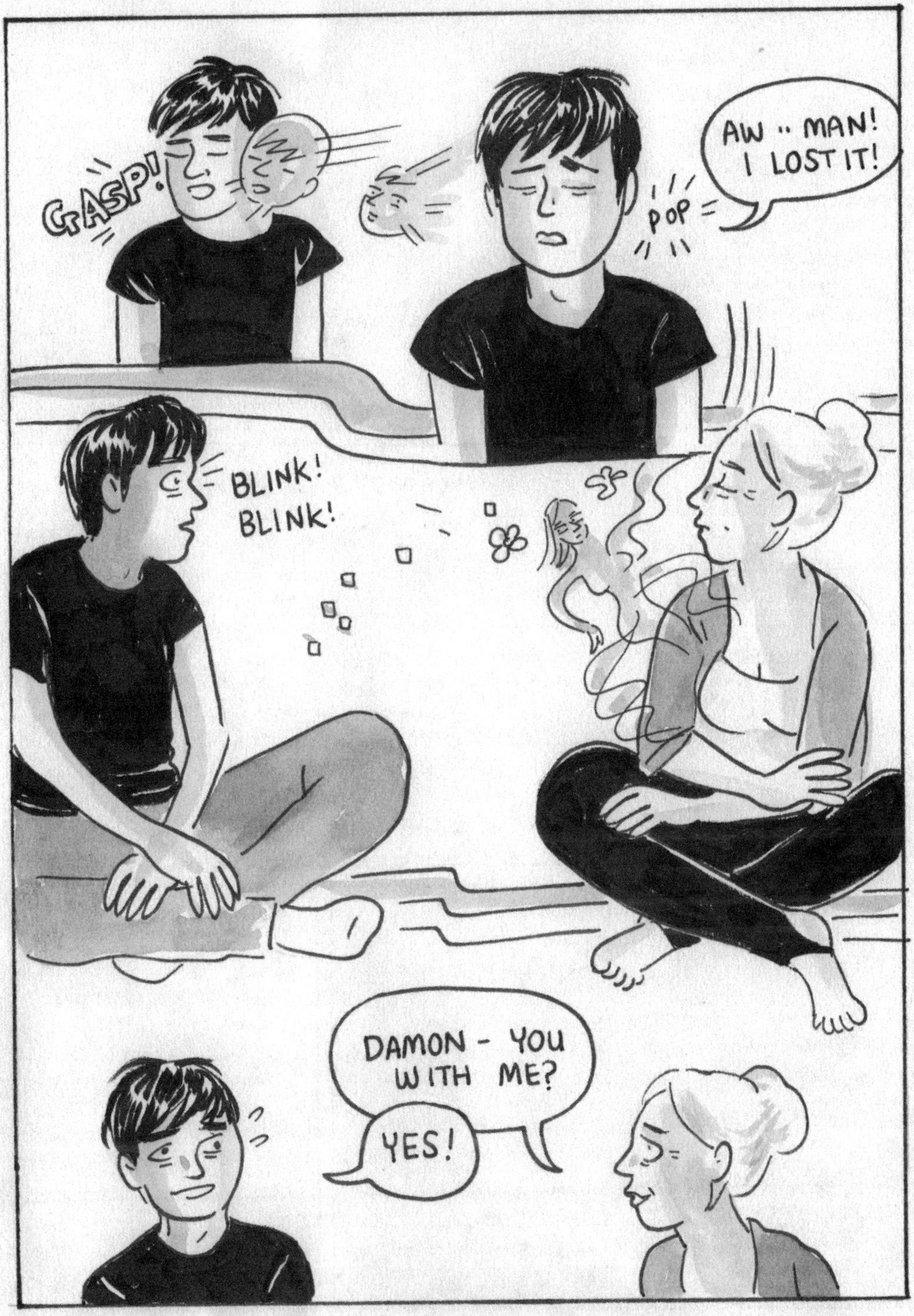
GASP!
AW .. MAN! I LOST IT!
POP
BLINK! BLINK!
DAMON - YOU WITH ME?
YES!

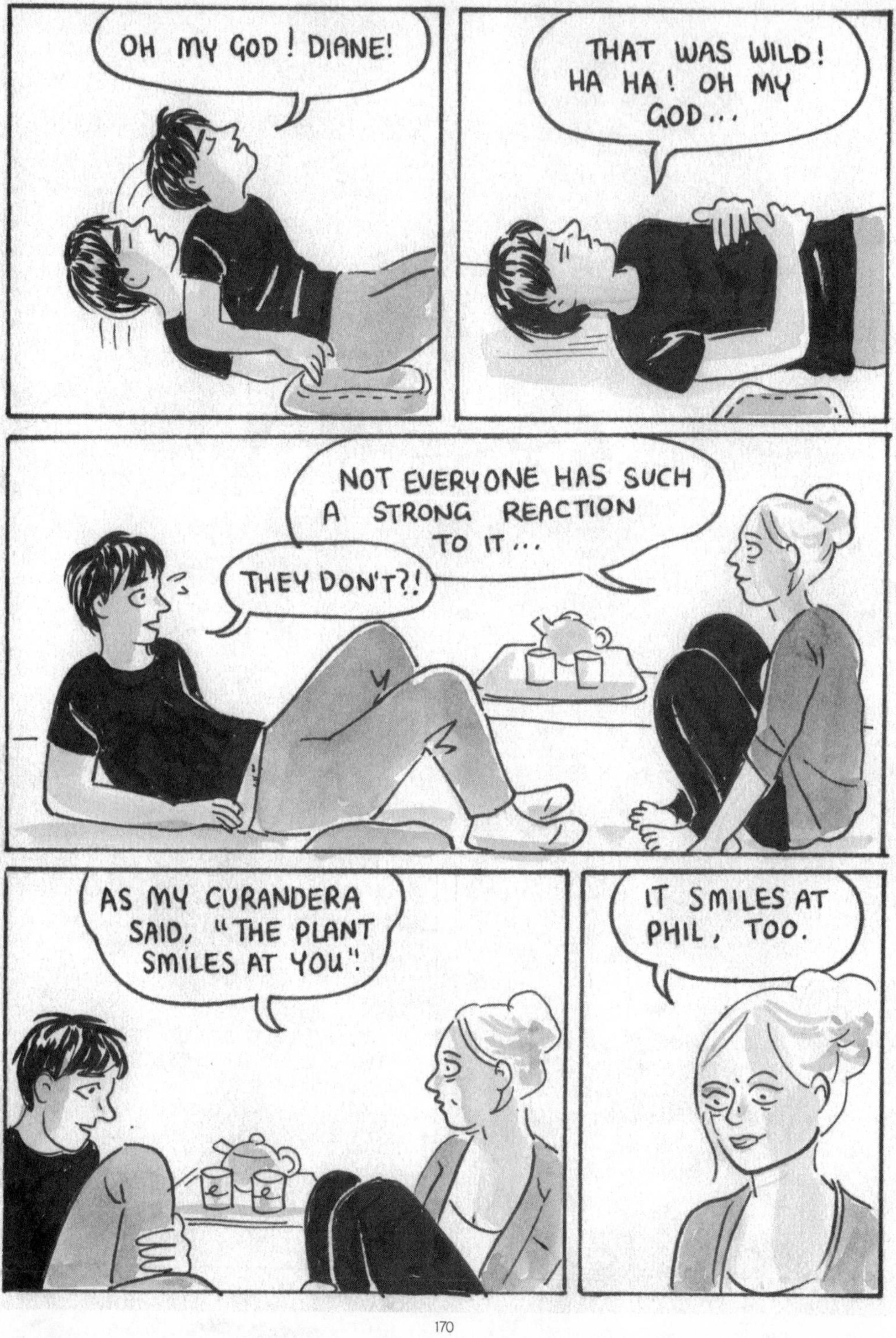
OH MY GOD! DIANE!
THAT WAS WILD! HA HA! OH MY GOD...
NOT EVERYONE HAS SUCH A STRONG REACTION TO IT...
THEY DON'T?!
AS MY CURANDERA SAID, "THE PLANT SMILES AT YOU".
IT SMILES AT PHIL, TOO.

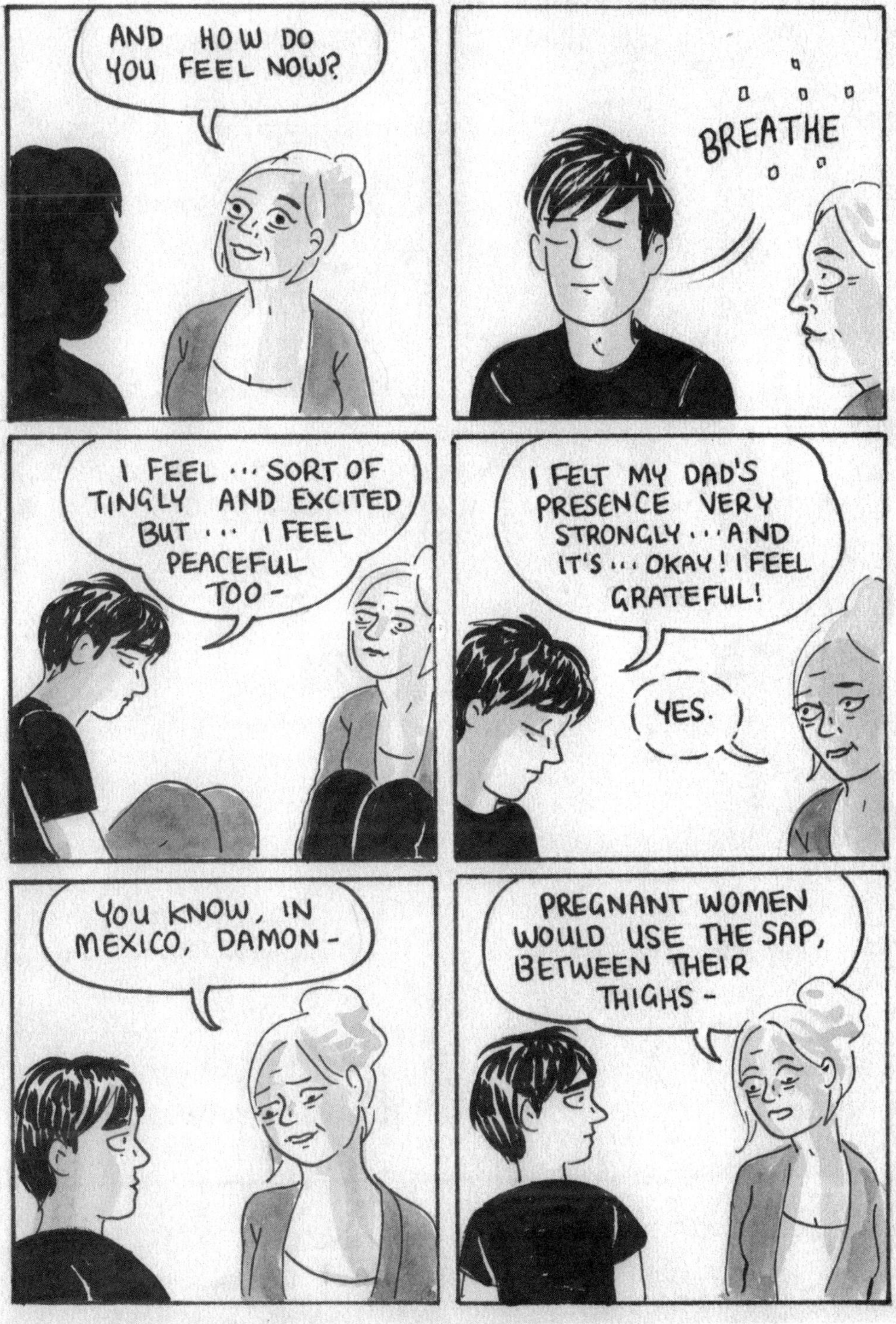
AND HOW DO YOU FEEL NOW?
BREATHE
I FEEL ... SORT OF TINGLY AND EXCITED BUT ... I FEEL PEACEFUL TOO -
I FELT MY DAD'S PRESENCE VERY STRONGLY ... AND IT'S ... OKAY! I FEEL GRATEFUL!
YES.
YOU KNOW, IN MEXICO, DAMON -
PREGNANT WOMEN WOULD USE THE SAP, BETWEEN THEIR THIGHS -

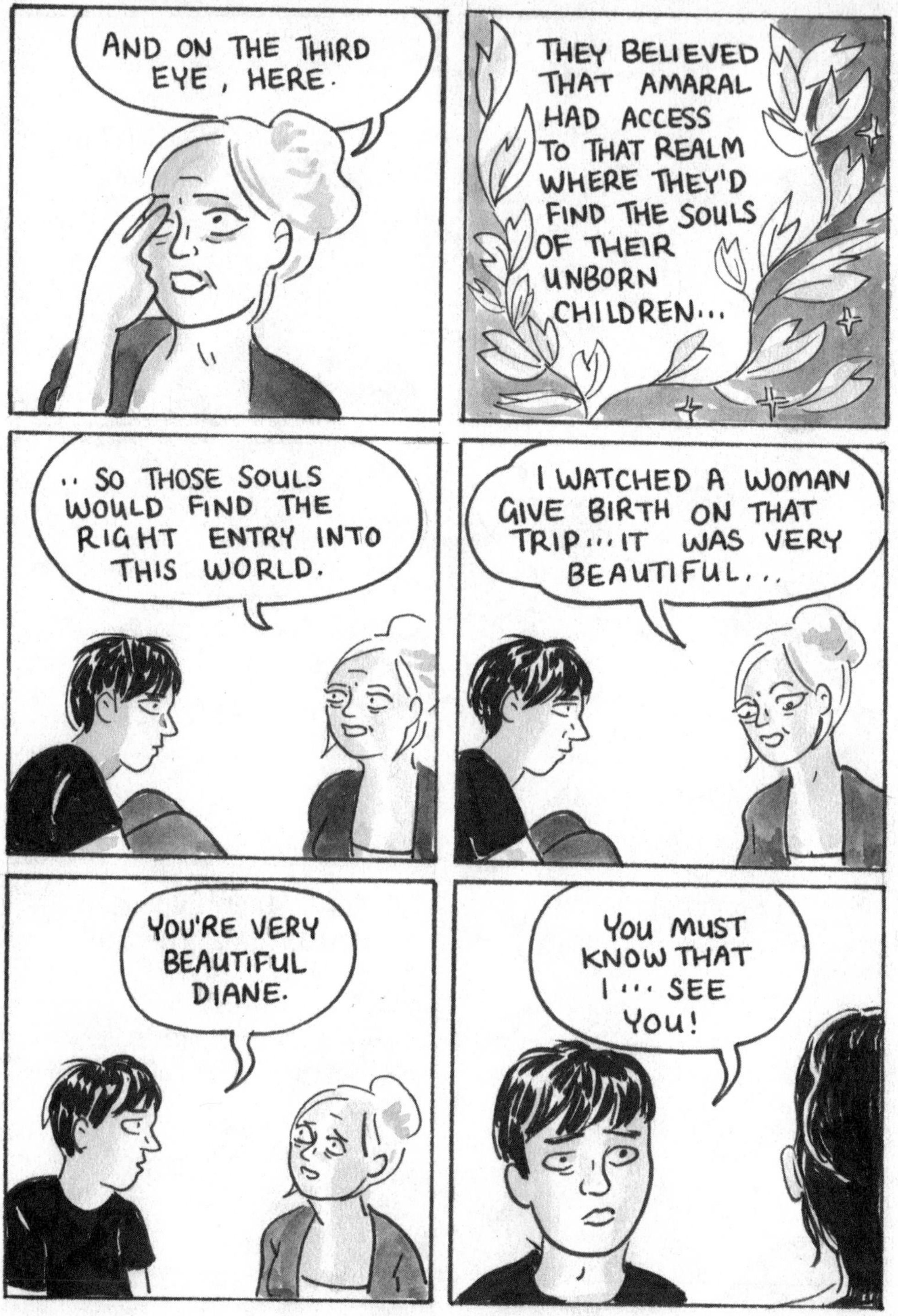
AND ON THE THIRD EYE, HERE.
THEY BELIEVED THAT AMARAL HAD ACCESS TO THAT REALM WHERE THEY'D FIND THE SOULS OF THEIR UNBORN CHILDREN...
.. SO THOSE SOULS WOULD FIND THE RIGHT ENTRY INTO THIS WORLD.
I WATCHED A WOMAN GIVE BIRTH ON THAT TRIP... IT WAS VERY BEAUTIFUL...
YOU'RE VERY BEAUTIFUL DIANE.
YOU MUST KNOW THAT I... SEE YOU!

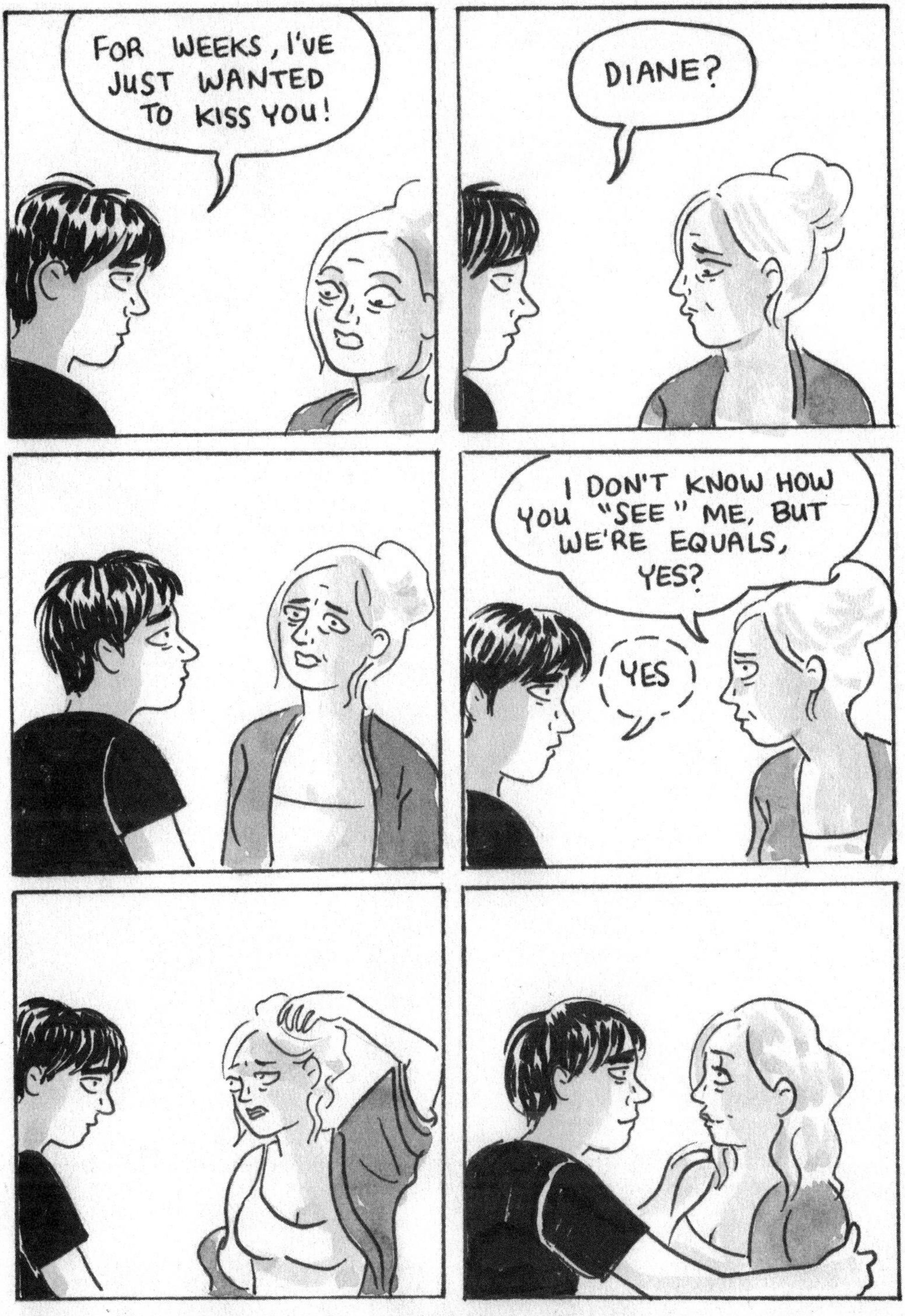
FOR WEEKS, I'VE JUST WANTED TO KISS YOU!
DIANE?
I DON'T KNOW HOW YOU "SEE" ME, BUT WE'RE EQUALS, YES?
YES

Mardou was born in Manchester, England and now makes a home in St. Louis, Missouri with her family. She's been making mini-comics since 2001, and has more recently made comics for web, print and film. Her next graphic novel, *Strange Kind of Love*, a story about the perils of encountering dream lovers on the astral plane, will be published by Revival House Press in 2021.

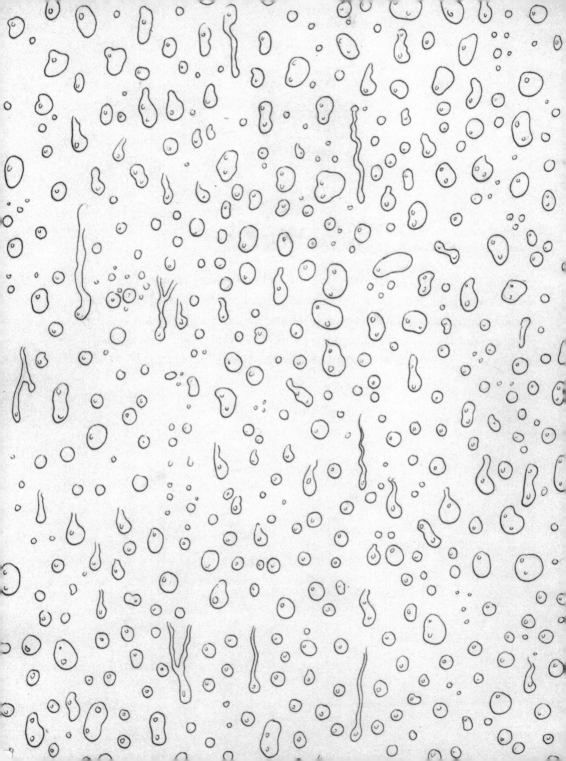